I went home to visit my parents for the first time in a long while. The clouds I saw out the airplane window were very pleasant and made me remember that I like clouds.

—*Masashi Kishimoto, 2008*

Author/artist Masashi Kishimoto was born in 1974 in rural Okayama Prefecture, Japan. After spending time in art college, he won the Hop Step Award for new manga artists with his manga **Karakuri** (Mechanism). Kishimoto decided to base his next story on traditional Japanese culture. His first version of **Naruto**, drawn in 1997, was a one-shot story about fox spirits; his final version, which debuted in **Weekly Shonen Jump** in 1999, quickly became the most popular ninja manga in Japan.

NARUTO VOL. 44
The SHONEN JUMP Manga Edition

STORY AND ART BY MASASHI KISHIMOTO

Translation/Mari Morimoto
English Adaptation/Deric A. Hughes
Touch-up Art & Lettering/Mark McMurray
Design/Gerry Serrano
Series Editor/Joel Enos
Editor/Megan Bates

Editor in Chief, Books/Alvin Lu
Editor in Chief, Magazines/Marc Weidenbaum
VP, Publishing Licensing/Rika Inouye
VP, Sales & Product Marketing/Gonzalo Ferreyra
VP, Creative/Linda Espinosa
Publisher/Hyoe Narita

Printed in the U.S.A.

Published by VIZ Media, LLC
P.O. Box 77010
San Francisco, CA 94107

SHONEN JUMP Manga Edition
10 9 8 7 6 5 4 3 2 1
First printing, April 2009

SH[redacted]DITION

NARUTO

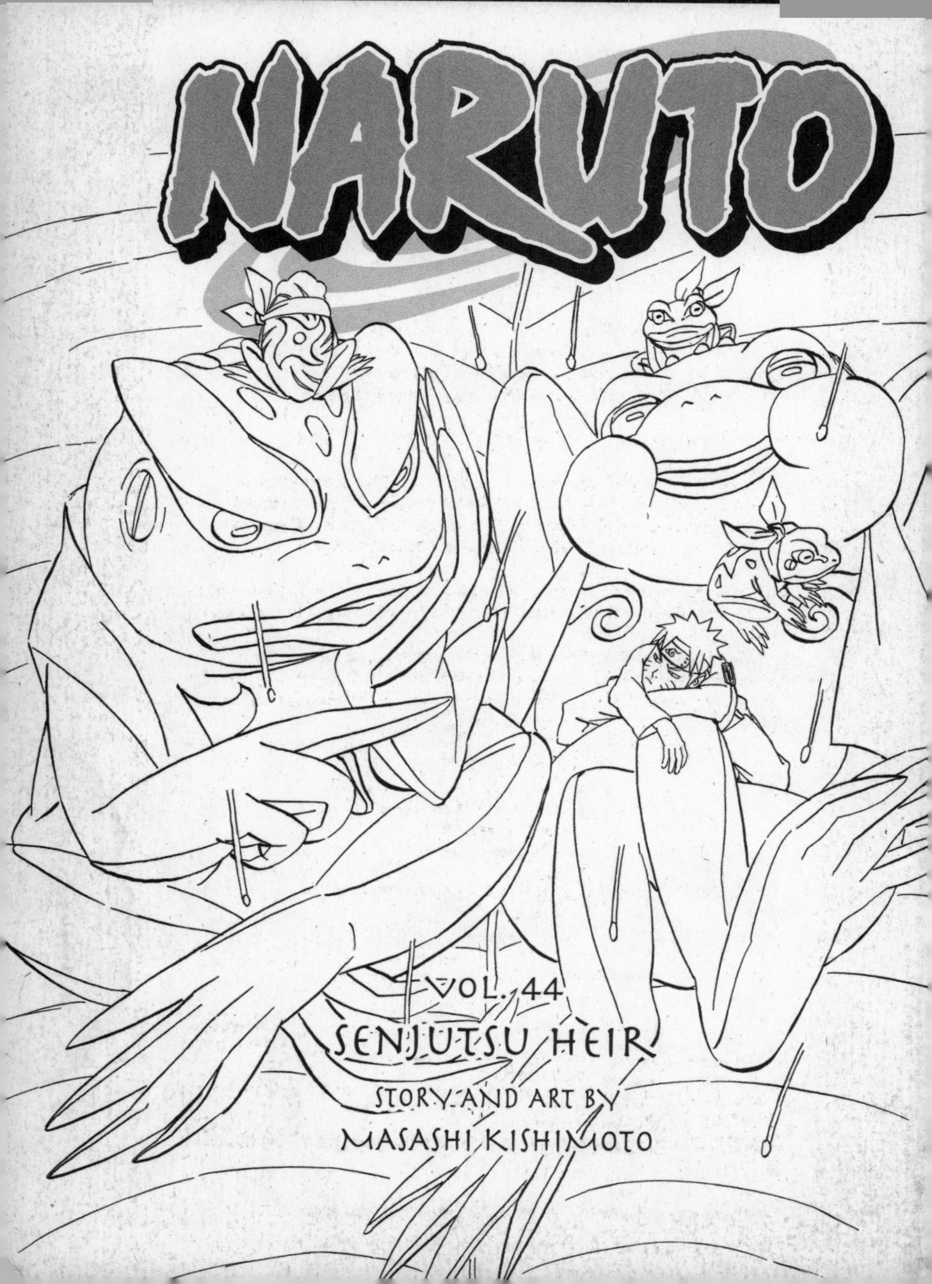

VOL. 44

SENJUTSU HEIR

STORY AND ART BY

MASASHI KISHIMOTO

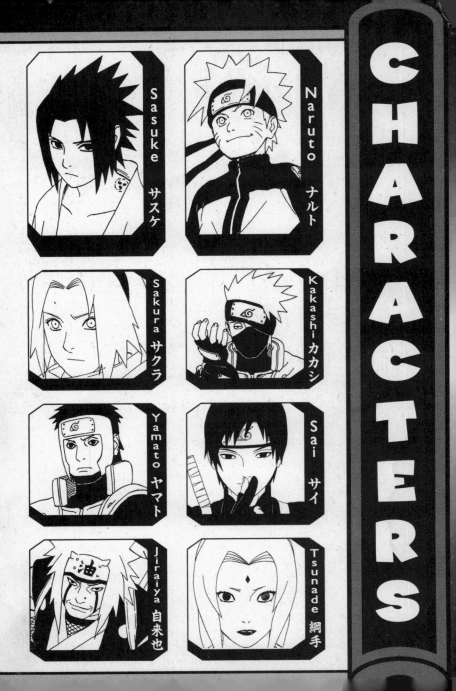

Sasuke　サスケ

Naruto　ナルト

Sakura　サクラ

Kakashi　カカシ

Yamato　ヤマト

Sai　サイ

Jiraiya　自来也

Tsunade　綱手

CHARACTERS

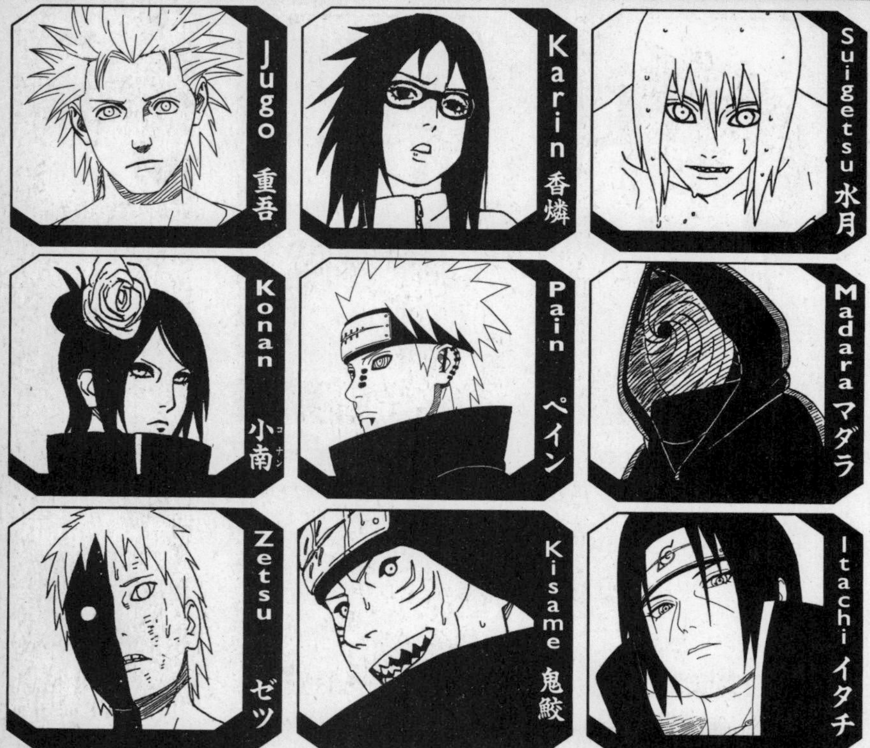
Suigetsu 水月
Karin 香燐
Jugo 重吾
Madara マダラ
Pain ペイン
Konan 小南
Itachi イタチ
Kisame 鬼鮫
Zetsu ゼツ

THE STORY SO FAR...

Naruto, the biggest troublemaker at the Ninja Academy in the Village of Konohagakure, finally becomes a ninja along with his classmates Sasuke and Sakura. They grow and mature through countless trials and battles. However, Sasuke, unable to give up his quest for vengeance, leaves Konohagakure to seek Orochimaru and his power...

Two years pass. Naruto and his comrades grow up and head out once more. As their fierce battles against the Tailed Beast-targeting Akatsuki rage on, Sasuke rebels against Orochimaru and takes everything from him. Sasuke then gathers new companions and chases after Itachi. The heroic sibling battle eventually concludes with Itachi's grim death. Sasuke may have fulfilled his lifelong goal, but Madara then tells him the tragic truth about his older brother, Itachi–how he achieved revenge against the Uchiha clan by allowing Sasuke to defeat him and become Konaha's hero. After discovering Itachi's true motivations, Sasuke renames his team Taka, claiming to exist for one sole reason: to *destroy Konoha*!!

NARUTO

VOL. 44
SENJUTSU HEIR

CONTENTS

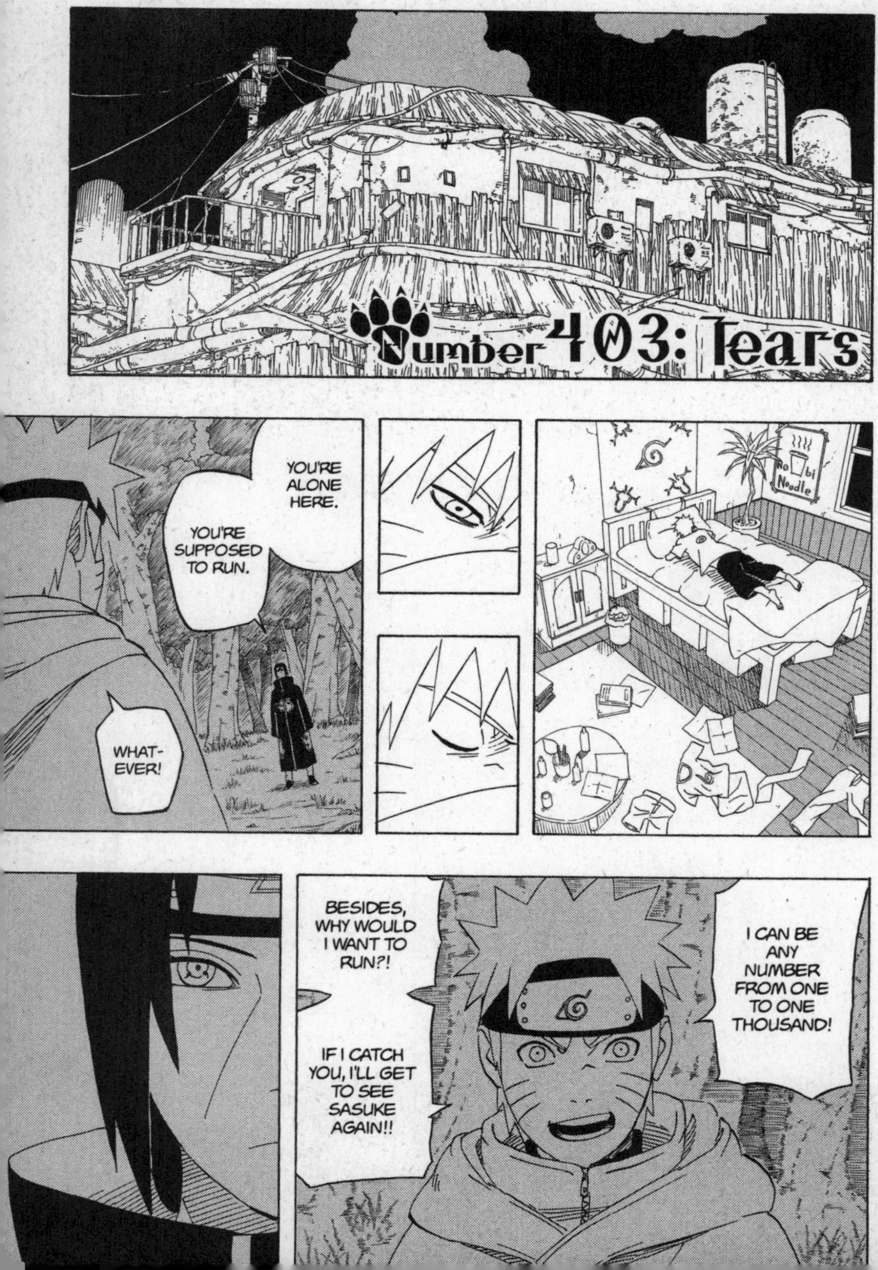
Number 403: Tears
No bi Noodle
YOU'RE ALONE HERE.
YOU'RE SUPPOSED TO RUN.
WHAT-EVER!
I CAN BE ANY NUMBER FROM ONE TO ONE THOUSAND!
BESIDES, WHY WOULD I WANT TO RUN?!
IF I CATCH YOU, I'LL GET TO SEE SASUKE AGAIN!!

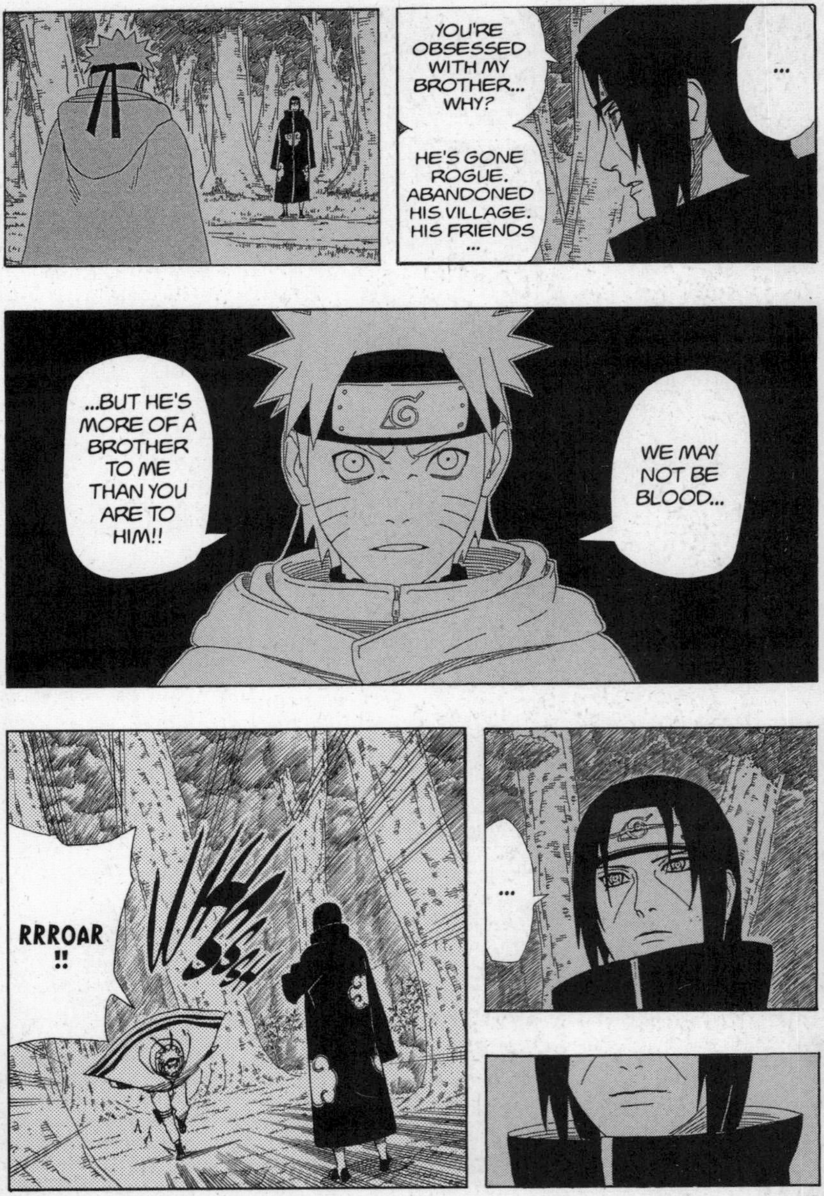
...
YOU'RE OBSESSED WITH MY BROTHER... WHY?
HE'S GONE ROGUE. ABANDONED HIS VILLAGE. HIS FRIENDS ...
WE MAY NOT BE BLOOD...
...BUT HE'S MORE OF A BROTHER TO ME THAN YOU ARE TO HIM!!
...
RRROAR !!

READ THIS WAY

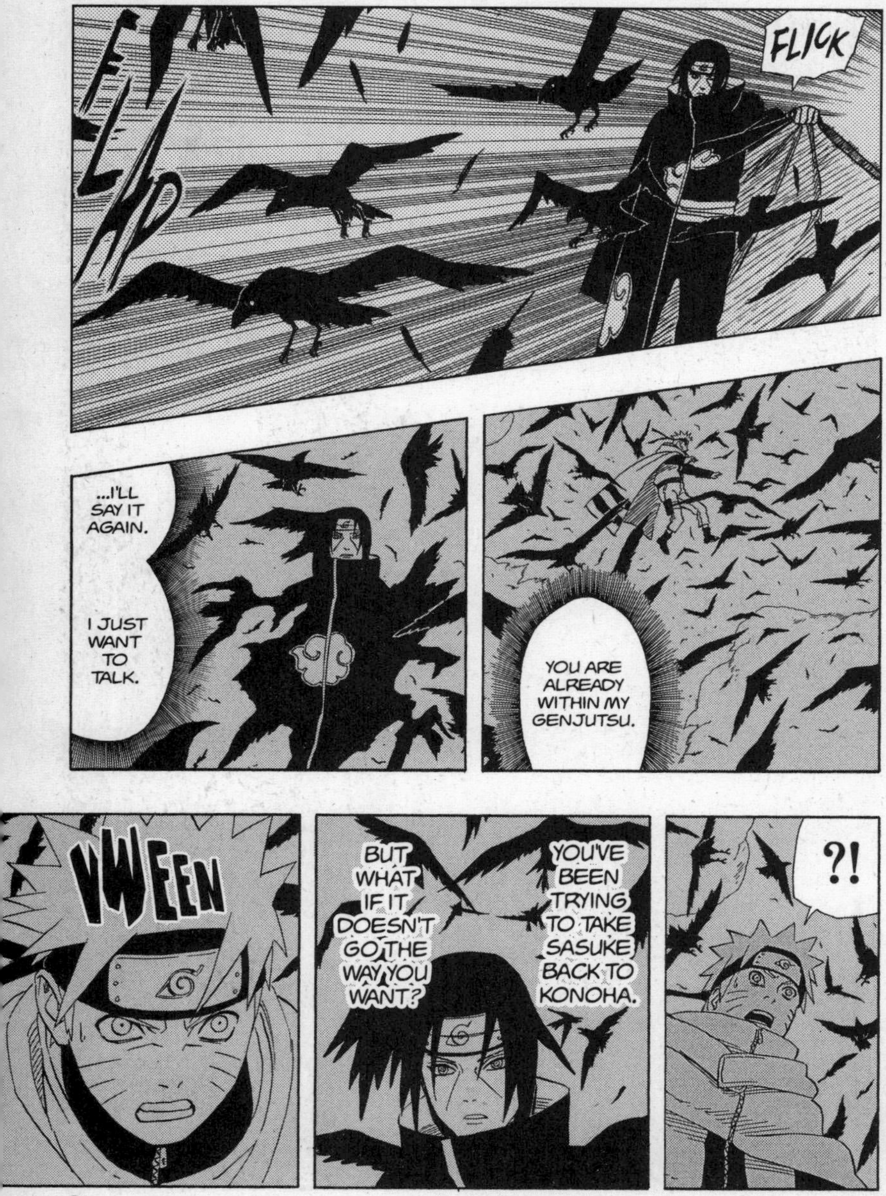
FLICK
FLAP
YOU ARE ALREADY WITHIN MY GENJUTSU.
...I'LL SAY IT AGAIN.
I JUST WANT TO TALK.
?!
YOU'VE BEEN TRYING TO TAKE SASUKE BACK TO KONOHA.
BUT WHAT IF IT DOESN'T GO THE WAY YOU WANT?
VWEEN

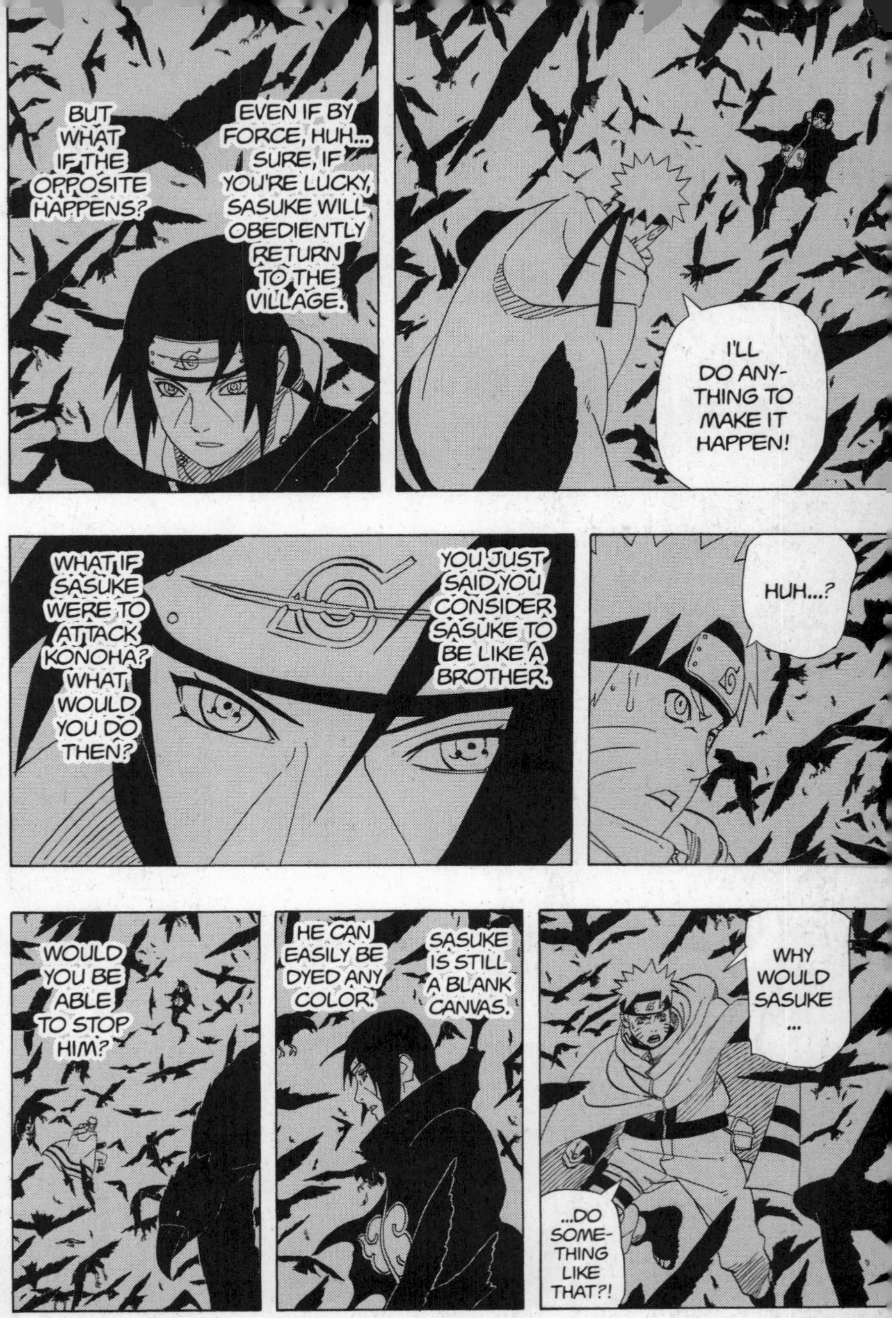
I'LL DO ANY-THING TO MAKE IT HAPPEN!
EVEN IF BY FORCE, HUH... SURE, IF YOU'RE LUCKY, SASUKE WILL OBEDIENTLY RETURN TO THE VILLAGE.
BUT WHAT IF THE OPPOSITE HAPPENS?
HUH...?
YOU JUST SAID YOU CONSIDER SASUKE TO BE LIKE A BROTHER.
WHAT IF SASUKE WERE TO ATTACK KONOHA? WHAT WOULD YOU DO THEN?
WHY WOULD SASUKE ...
...DO SOME-THING LIKE THAT?!
SASUKE IS STILL A BLANK CANVAS.
HE CAN EASILY BE DYED ANY COLOR.
WOULD YOU BE ABLE TO STOP HIM?

READ THIS WAY

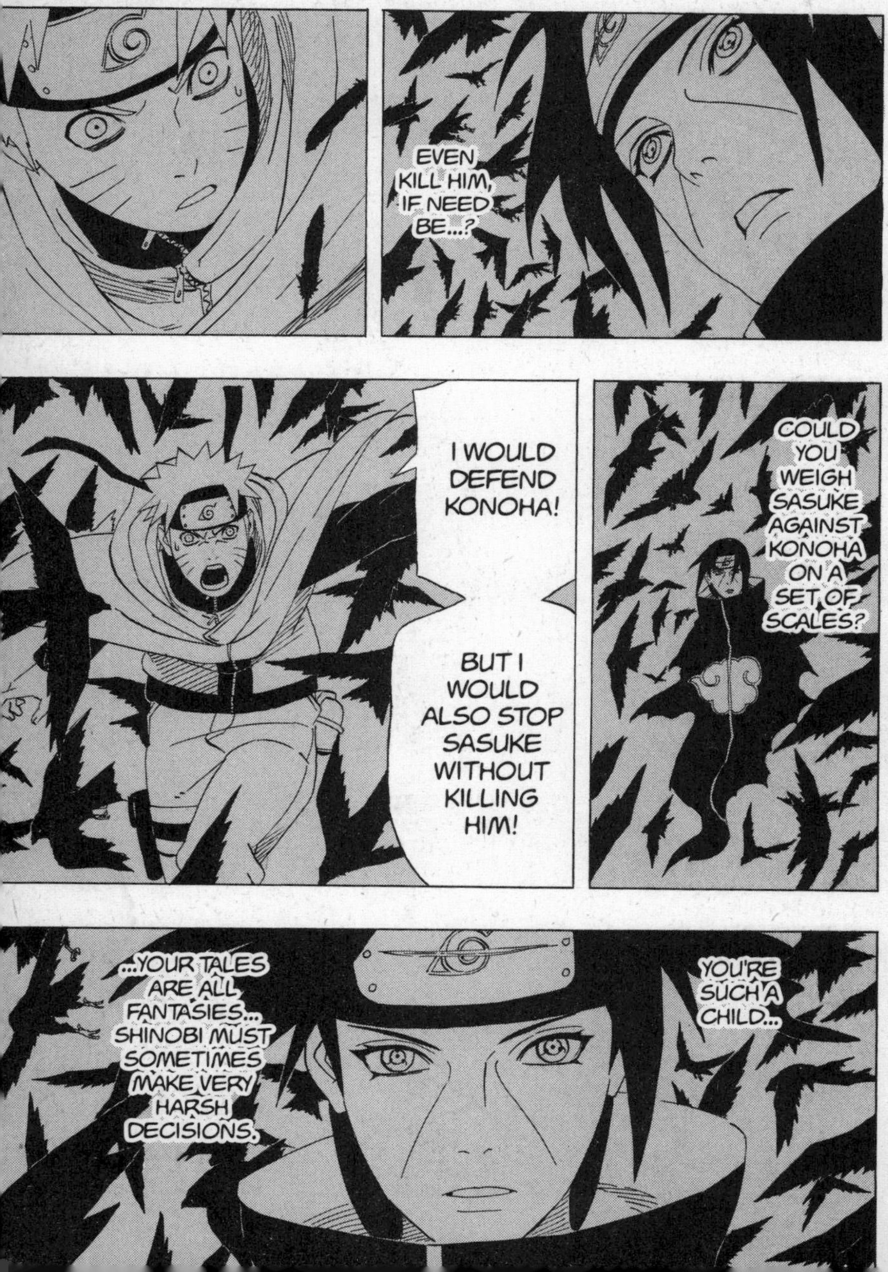
EVEN KILL HIM, IF NEED BE...?
COULD YOU WEIGH SASUKE AGAINST KONOHA ON A SET OF SCALES?
I WOULD DEFEND KONOHA!
BUT I WOULD ALSO STOP SASUKE WITHOUT KILLING HIM!
YOU'RE SUCH A CHILD...
...YOUR TALES ARE ALL FANTASIES... SHINOBI MUST SOMETIMES MAKE VERY HARSH DECISIONS.

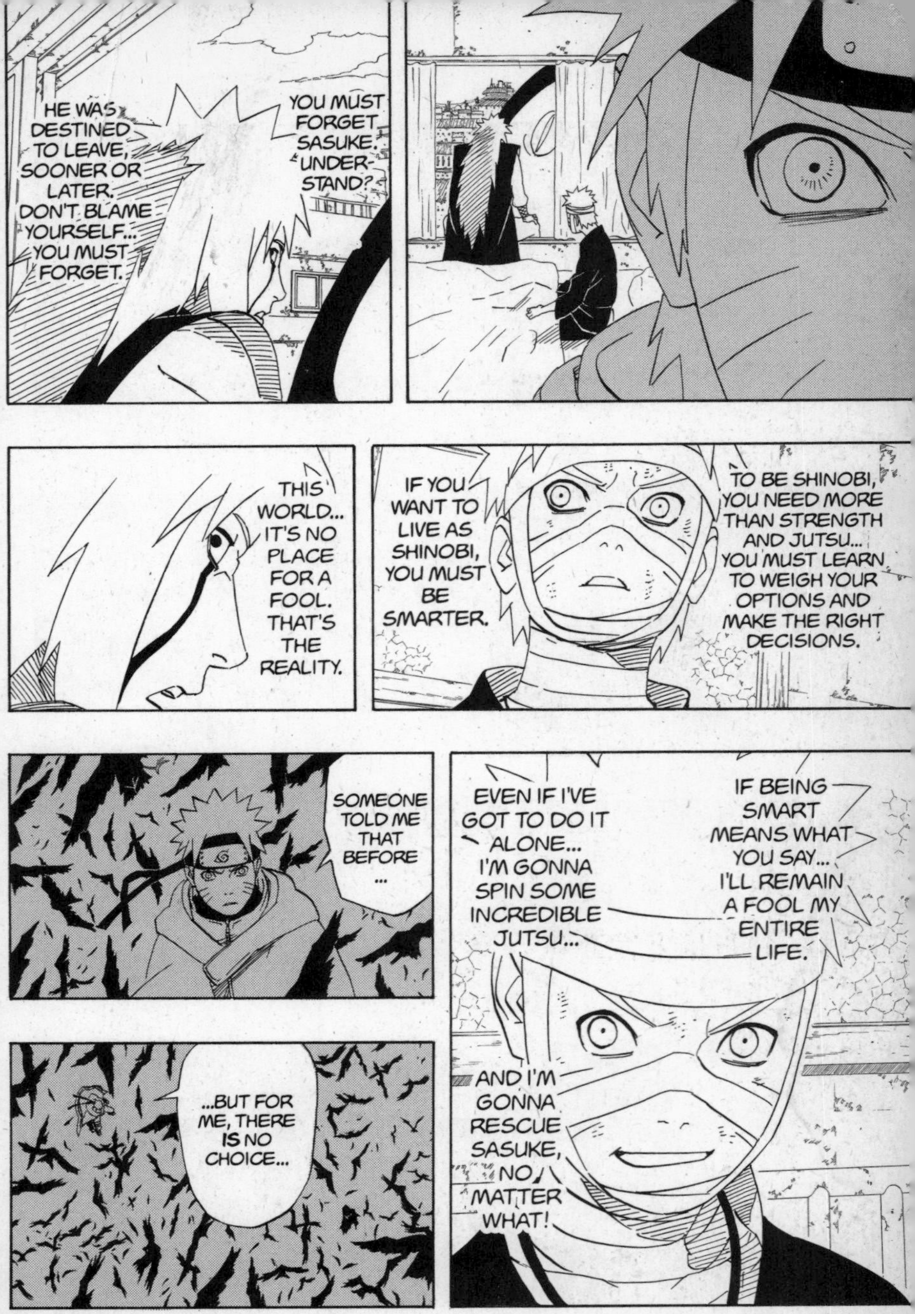

YOU MUST FORGET SASUKE. UNDERSTAND?
HE WAS DESTINED TO LEAVE, SOONER OR LATER. DON'T BLAME YOURSELF... YOU MUST FORGET.
TO BE SHINOBI, YOU NEED MORE THAN STRENGTH AND JUTSU... YOU MUST LEARN TO WEIGH YOUR OPTIONS AND MAKE THE RIGHT DECISIONS.
IF YOU WANT TO LIVE AS SHINOBI, YOU MUST BE SMARTER.
THIS WORLD... IT'S NO PLACE FOR A FOOL. THAT'S THE REALITY.
IF BEING SMART MEANS WHAT YOU SAY... I'LL REMAIN A FOOL MY ENTIRE LIFE.
EVEN IF I'VE GOT TO DO IT ALONE... I'M GONNA SPIN SOME INCREDIBLE JUTSU...
AND I'M GONNA RESCUE SASUKE, NO MATTER WHAT!
SOMEONE TOLD ME THAT BEFORE ...
...BUT FOR ME, THERE **IS** NO CHOICE...

READ THIS WAY

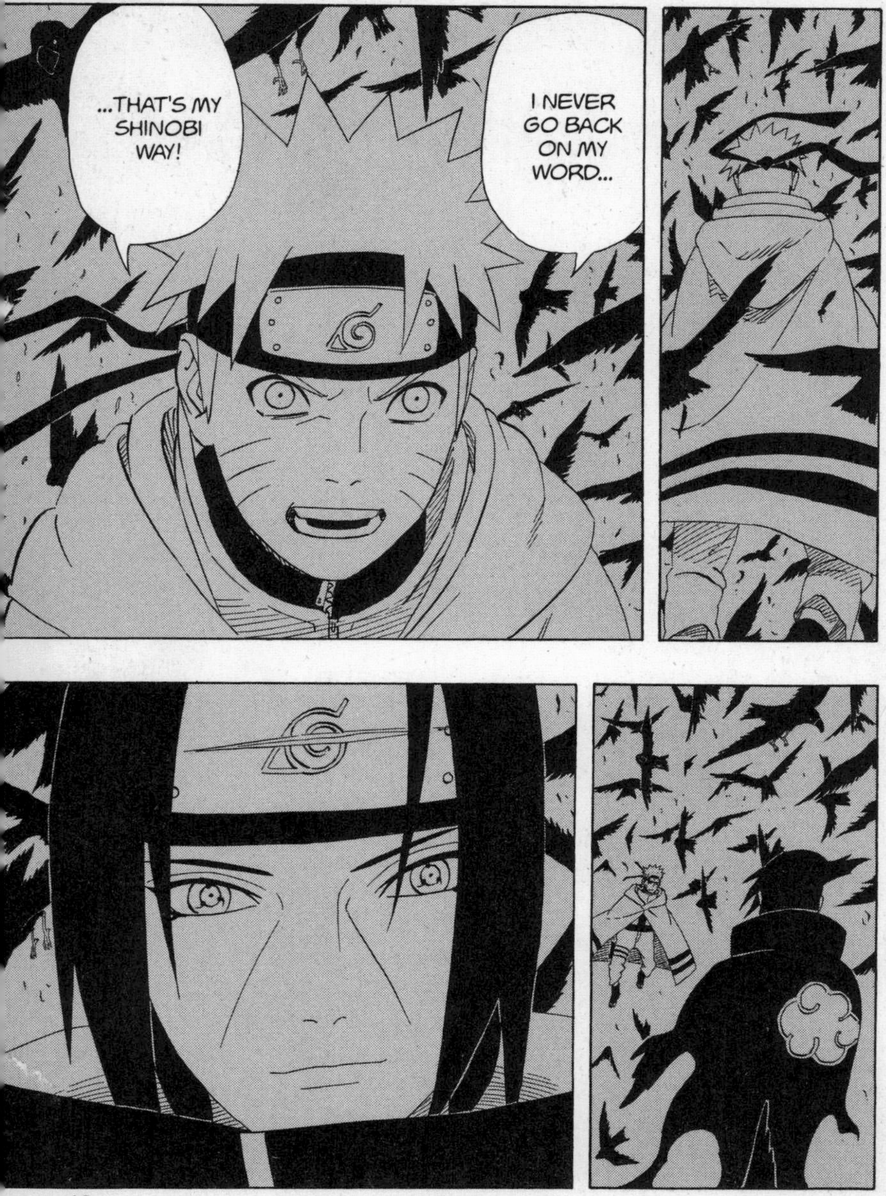
I NEVER GO BACK ON MY WORD...
...THAT'S MY SHINOBI WAY!

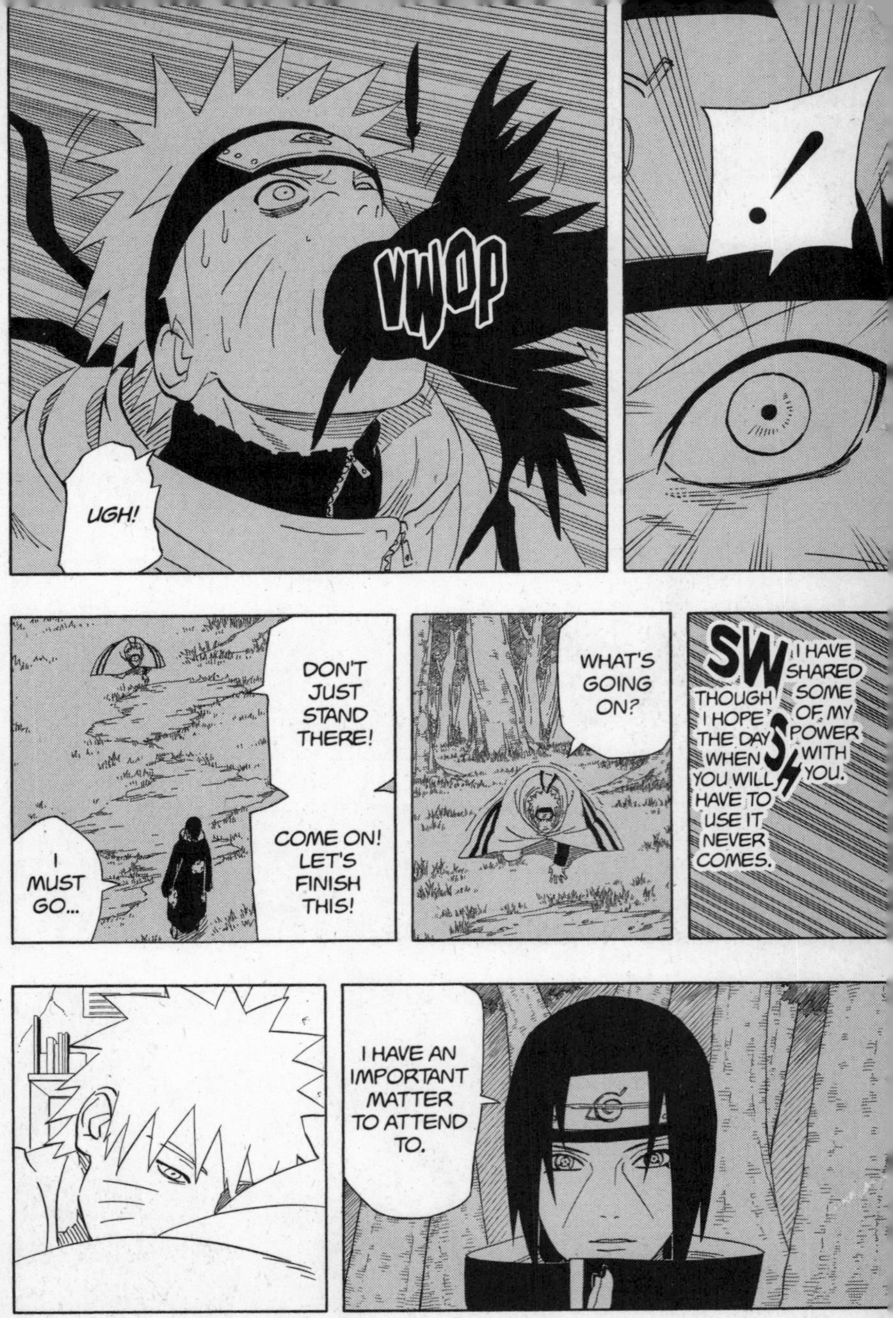
!
!
VWOP
UGH!
SWSH
I HAVE SHARED SOME OF MY POWER WITH YOU.
THOUGH I HOPE THE DAY WHEN YOU WILL HAVE TO USE IT NEVER COMES.
WHAT'S GOING ON?
DON'T JUST STAND THERE!
COME ON! LET'S FINISH THIS!
I MUST GO...
I HAVE AN IMPORTANT MATTER TO ATTEND TO.

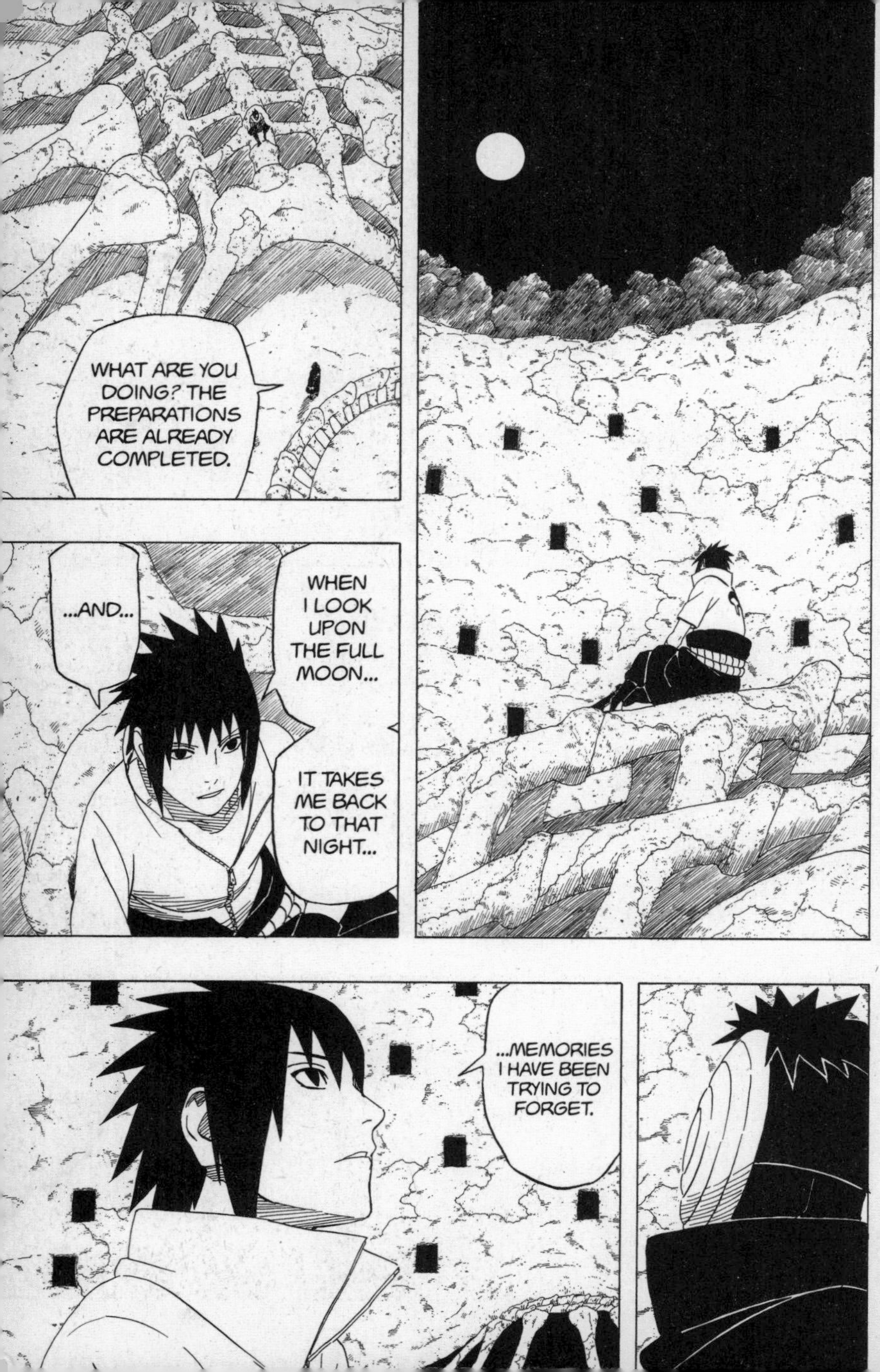
WHAT ARE YOU DOING? THE PREPARATIONS ARE ALREADY COMPLETED.
WHEN I LOOK UPON THE FULL MOON...
IT TAKES ME BACK TO THAT NIGHT...
...AND...
...MEMORIES I HAVE BEEN TRYING TO FORGET.

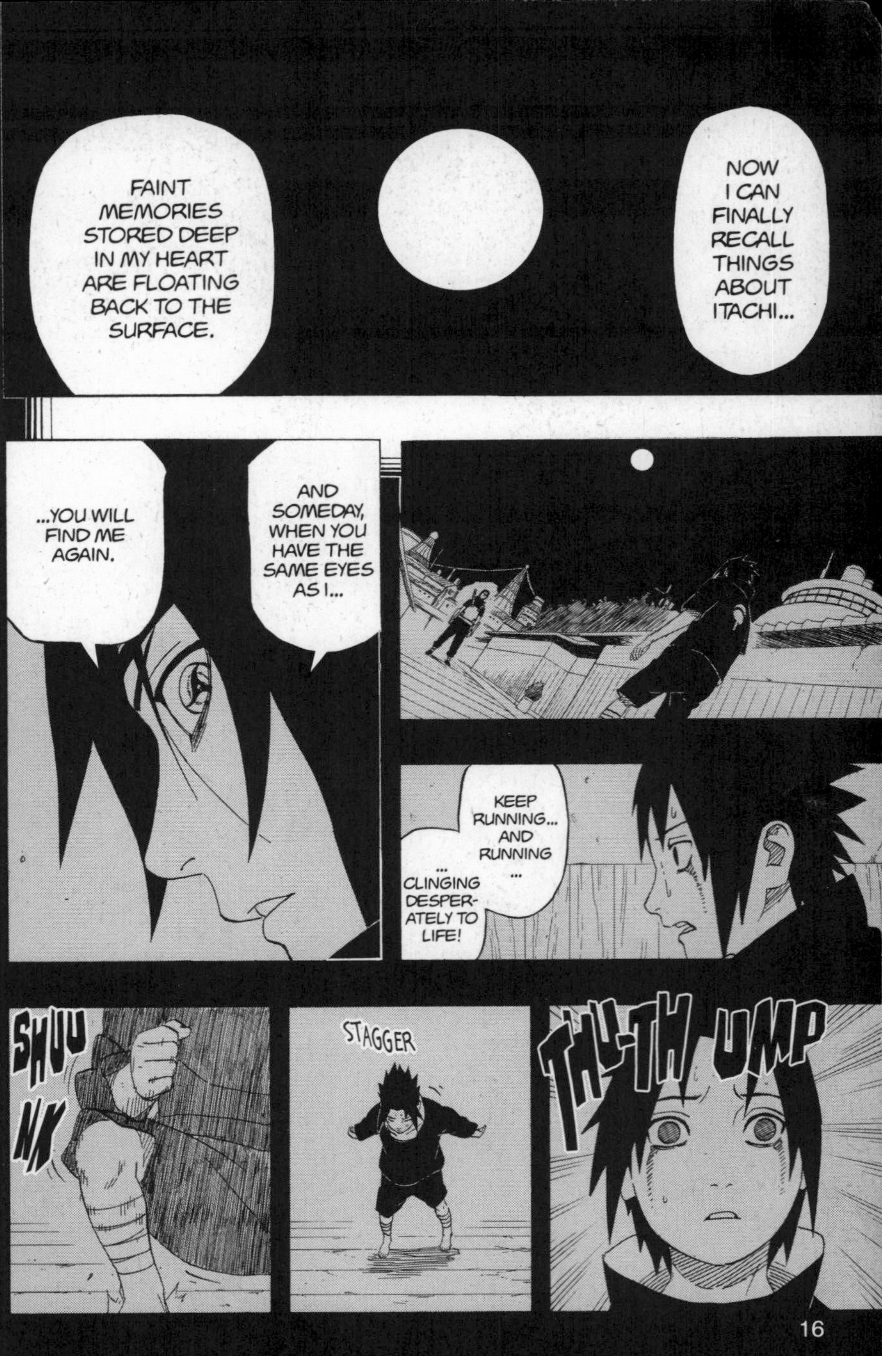
NOW I CAN FINALLY RECALL THINGS ABOUT ITACHI...
FAINT MEMORIES STORED DEEP IN MY HEART ARE FLOATING BACK TO THE SURFACE.
KEEP RUNNING... AND RUNNING ...
... CLINGING DESPER-ATELY TO LIFE!
AND SOMEDAY, WHEN YOU HAVE THE SAME EYES AS I...
...YOU WILL FIND ME AGAIN.
THU-THUMP
STAGGER
SHUUNK

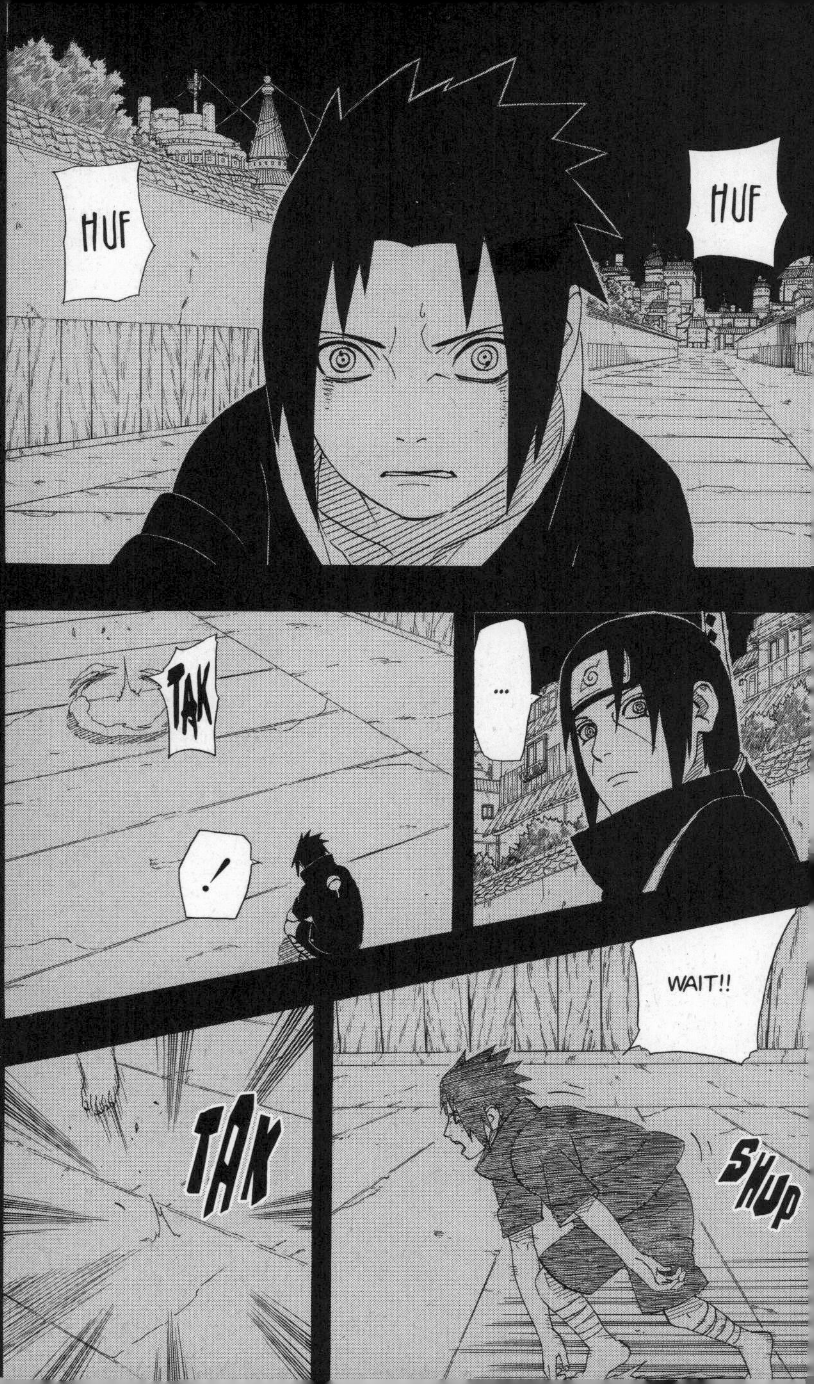
HUF
HUF
...
TAK
!
WAIT!!
SHUP
TAK

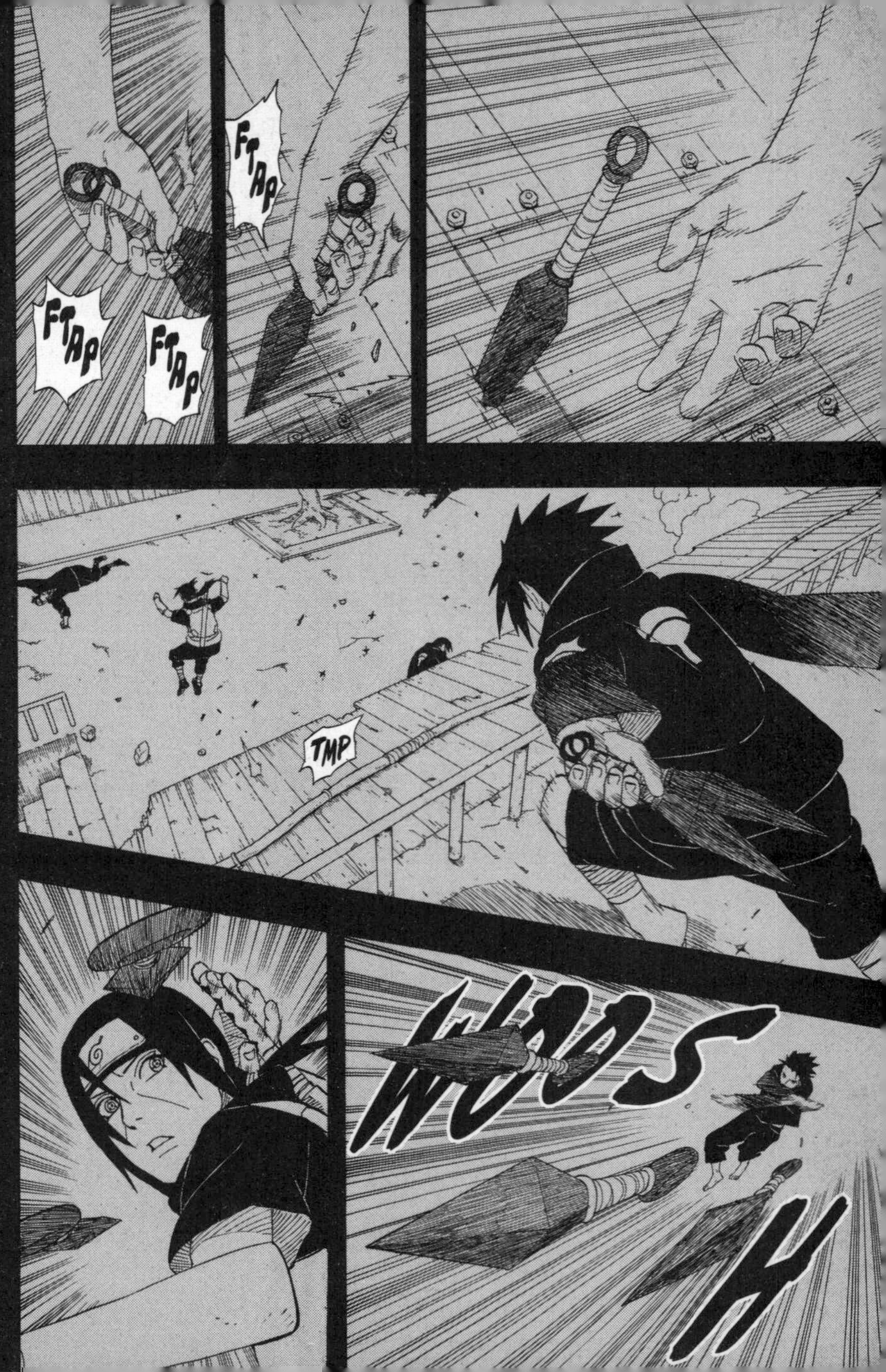
FTAP
FTAP
FTAP
TMP
WHOOSH

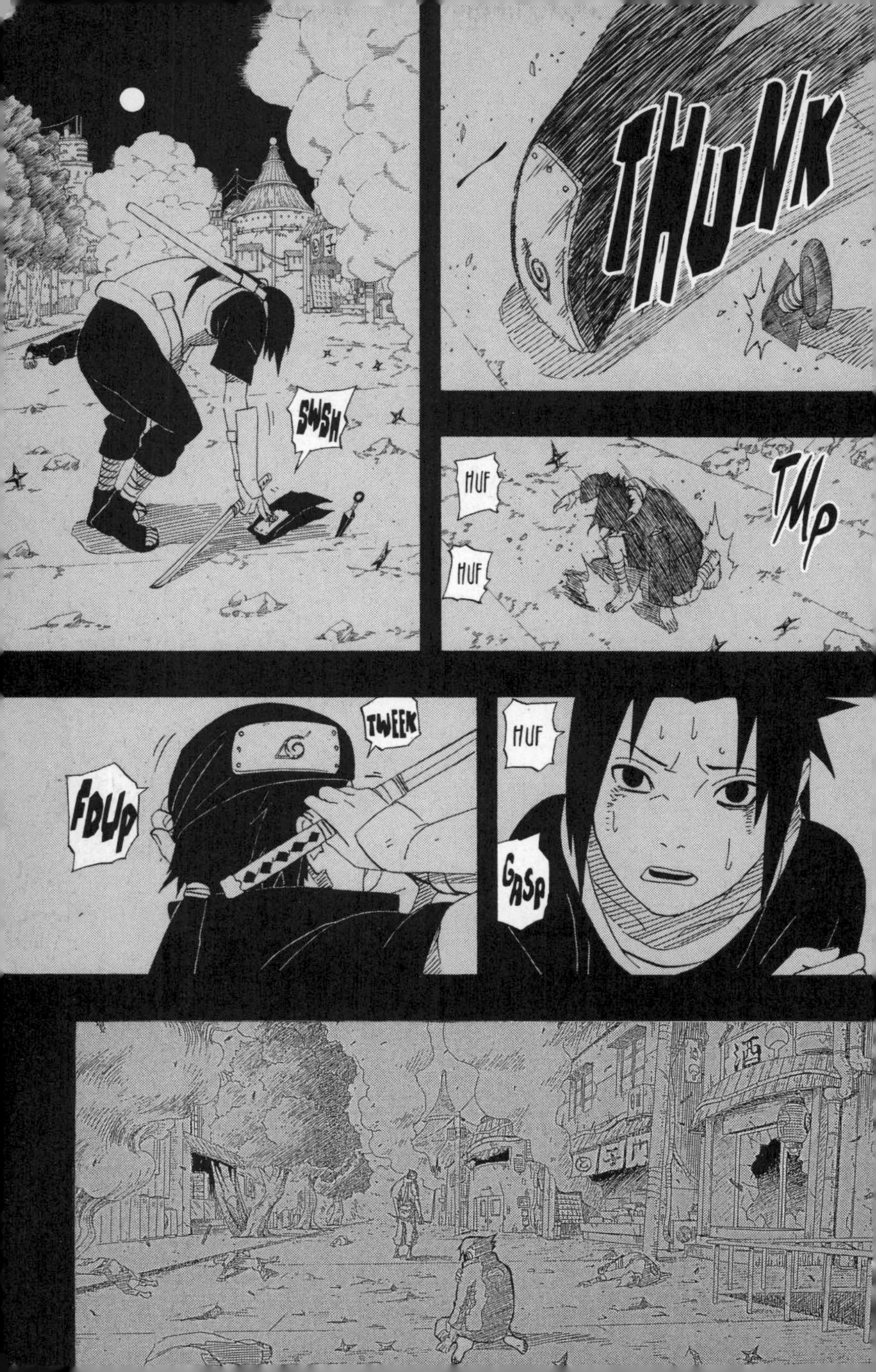
THUNK
HUF
HUF
TMP
SWSH
HUF
GASP
TWEEK
FDUP

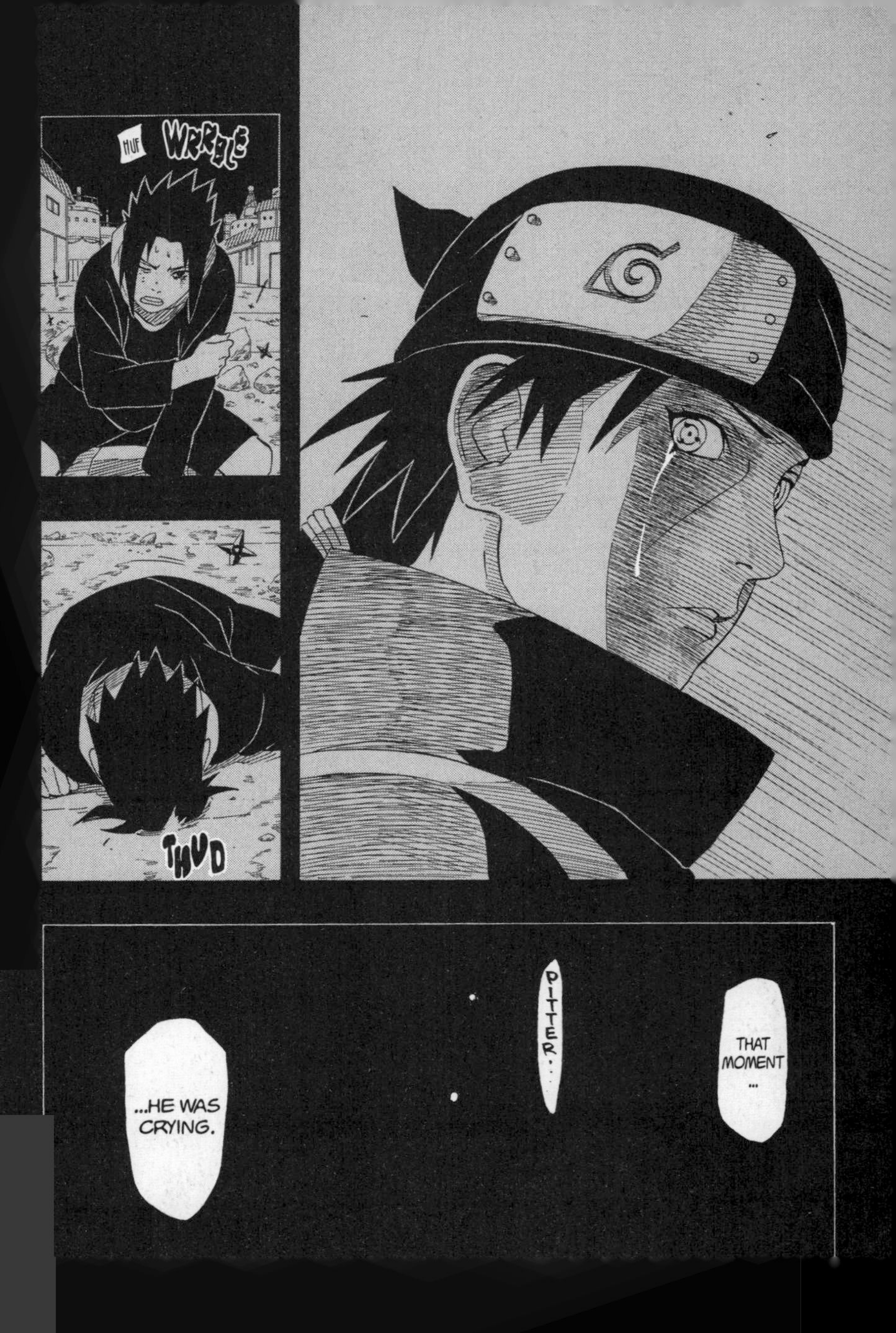
HUF
WRRBLE
THUD
THAT MOMENT...
PITTER...
...HE WAS CRYING.

READ THIS WAY

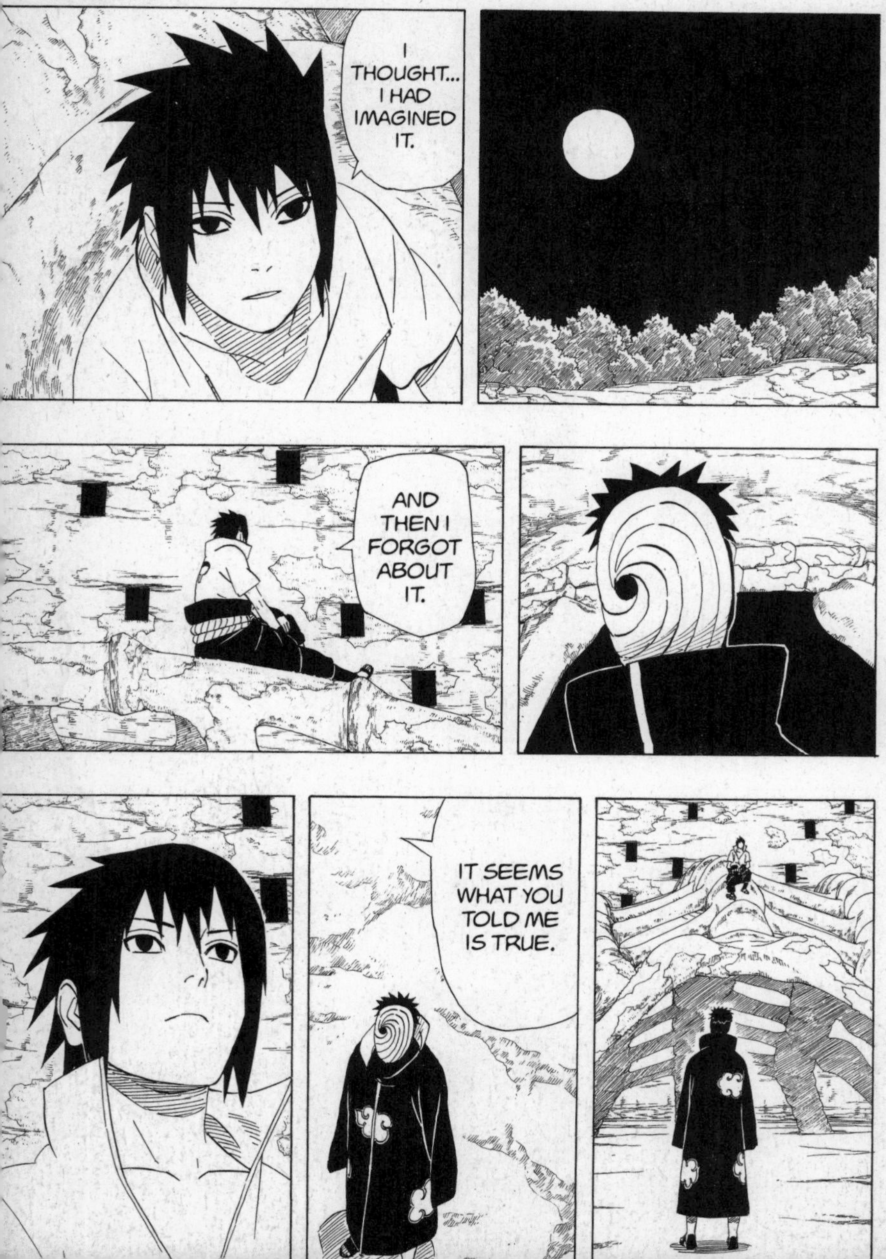
I THOUGHT... I HAD IMAGINED IT.
AND THEN I FORGOT ABOUT IT.
IT SEEMS WHAT YOU TOLD ME IS TRUE.

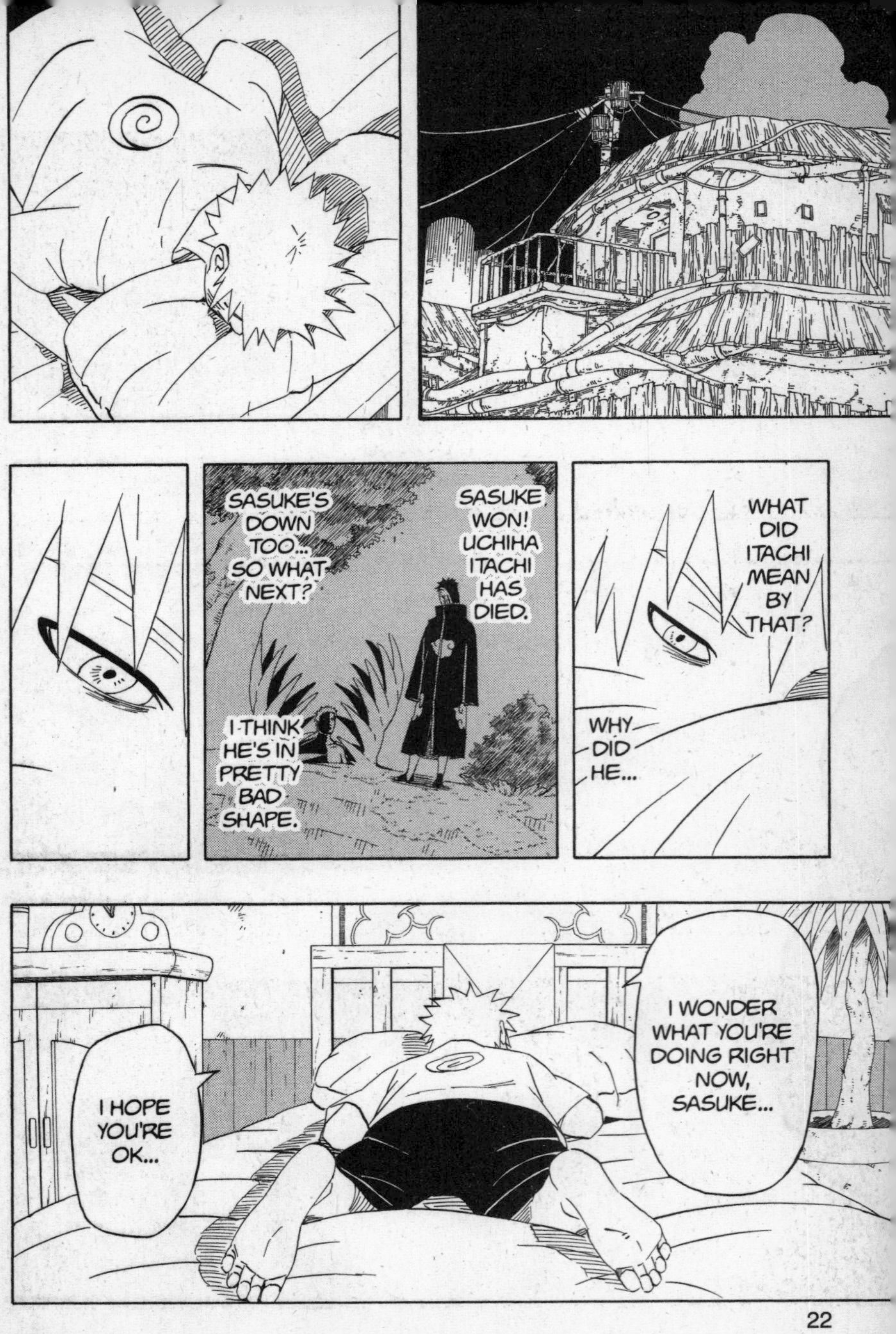
WHAT DID ITACHI MEAN BY THAT?
WHY DID HE...
SASUKE WON! UCHIHA ITACHI HAS DIED.
SASUKE'S DOWN TOO... SO WHAT NEXT?
I THINK HE'S IN PRETTY BAD SHAPE.
I WONDER WHAT YOU'RE DOING RIGHT NOW, SASUKE...
I HOPE YOU'RE OK...

READ THIS WAY

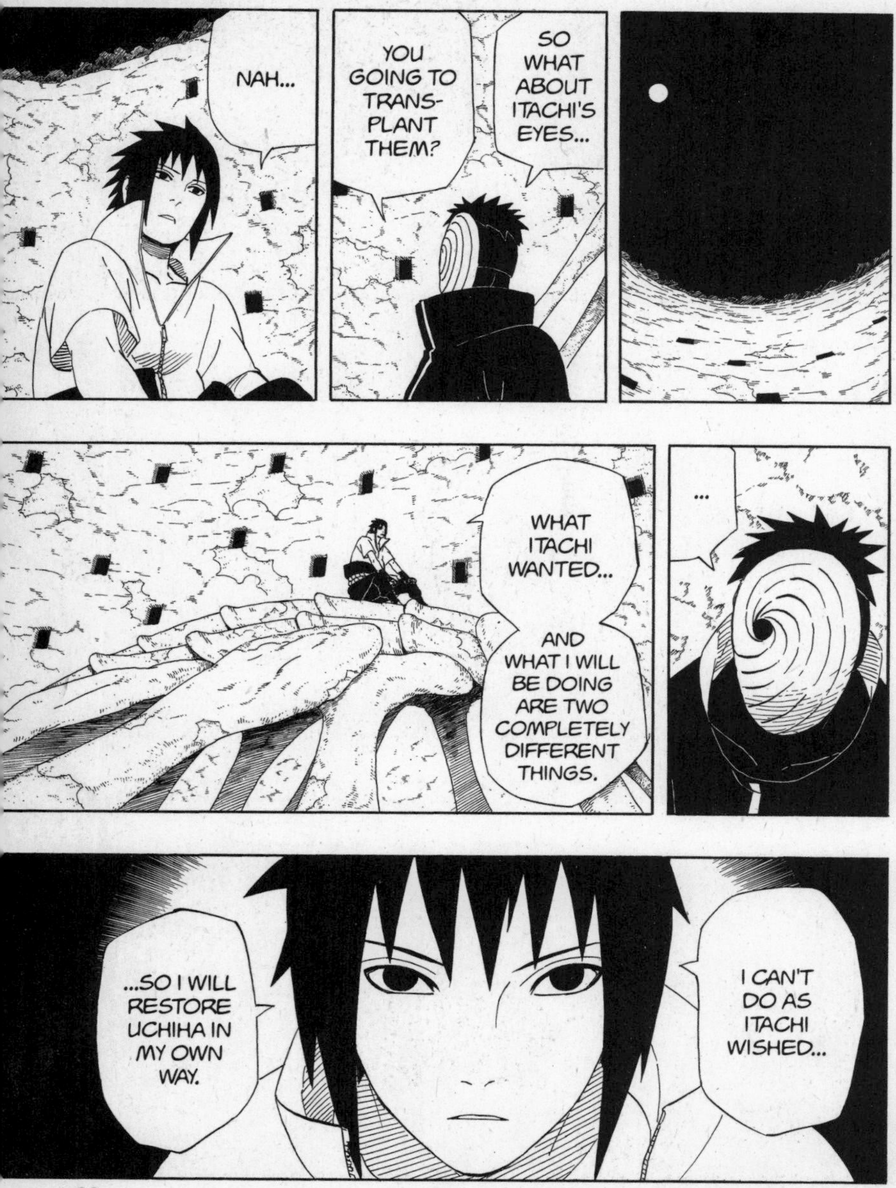
SO WHAT ABOUT ITACHI'S EYES...
YOU GOING TO TRANS-PLANT THEM?
NAH...
...
WHAT ITACHI WANTED...
AND WHAT I WILL BE DOING ARE TWO COMPLETELY DIFFERENT THINGS.
I CAN'T DO AS ITACHI WISHED...
...SO I WILL RESTORE UCHIHA IN MY OWN WAY.

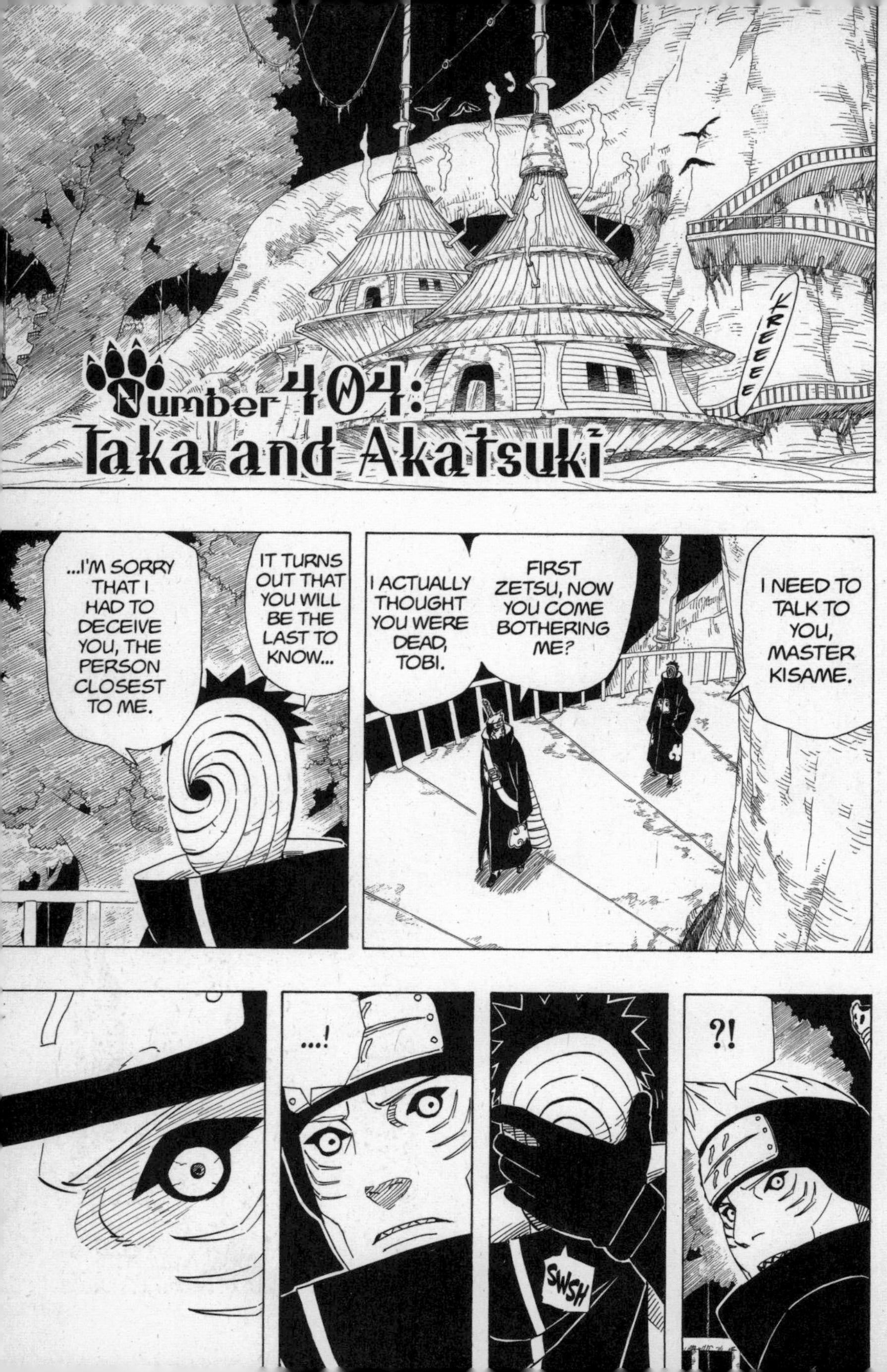
Number 404:
Taka and Akatsuki
KREEEE
I NEED TO TALK TO YOU, MASTER KISAME.
FIRST ZETSU, NOW YOU COME BOTHERING ME?
I ACTUALLY THOUGHT YOU WERE DEAD, TOBI.
IT TURNS OUT THAT YOU WILL BE THE LAST TO KNOW...
...I'M SORRY THAT I HAD TO DECEIVE YOU, THE PERSON CLOSEST TO ME.
?!
SWSH
...!

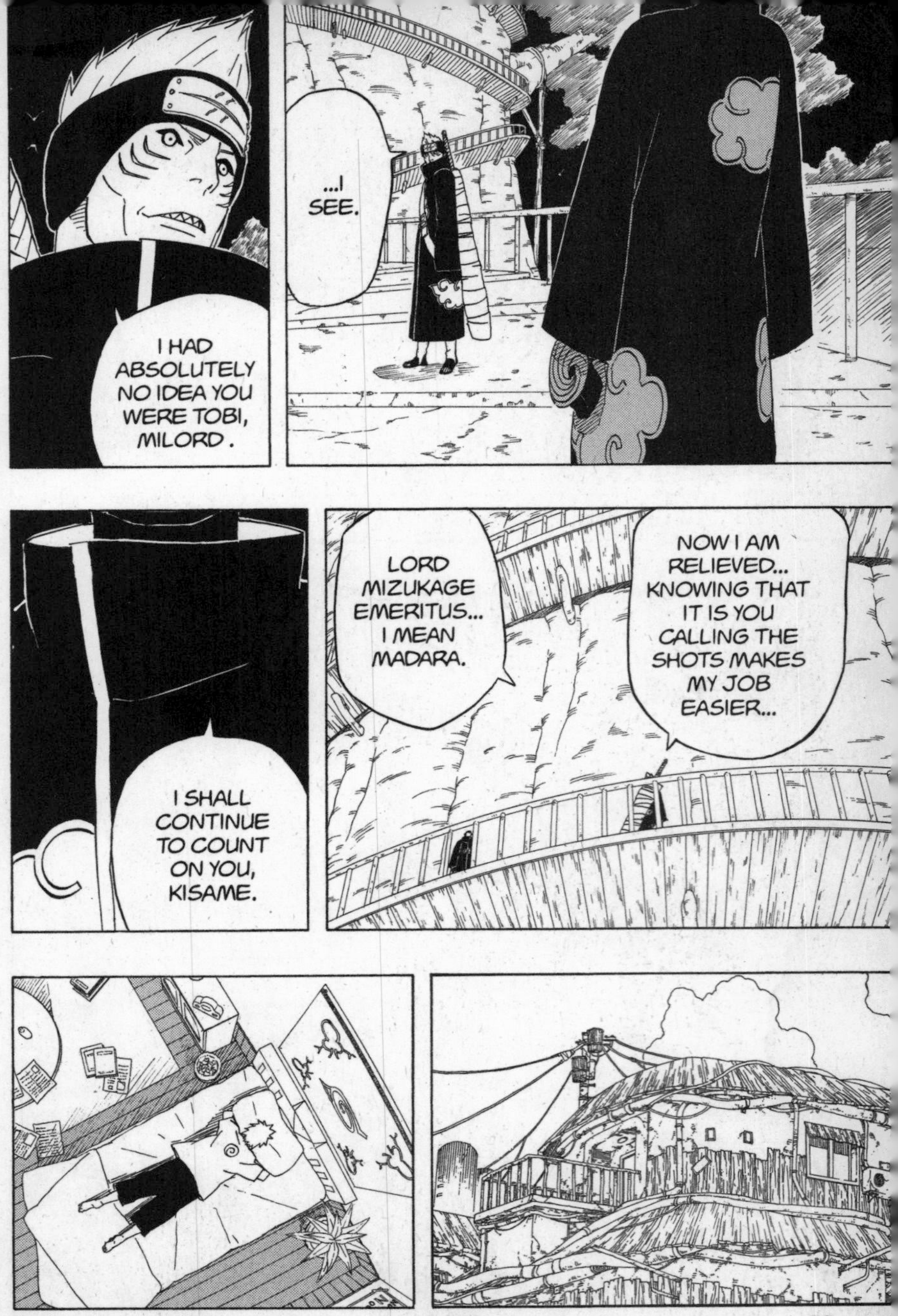
...I SEE.
I HAD ABSOLUTELY NO IDEA YOU WERE TOBI, MILORD.
NOW I AM RELIEVED... KNOWING THAT IT IS YOU CALLING THE SHOTS MAKES MY JOB EASIER...
LORD MIZUKAGE EMERITUS... I MEAN MADARA.
I SHALL CONTINUE TO COUNT ON YOU, KISAME.

READ THIS WAY

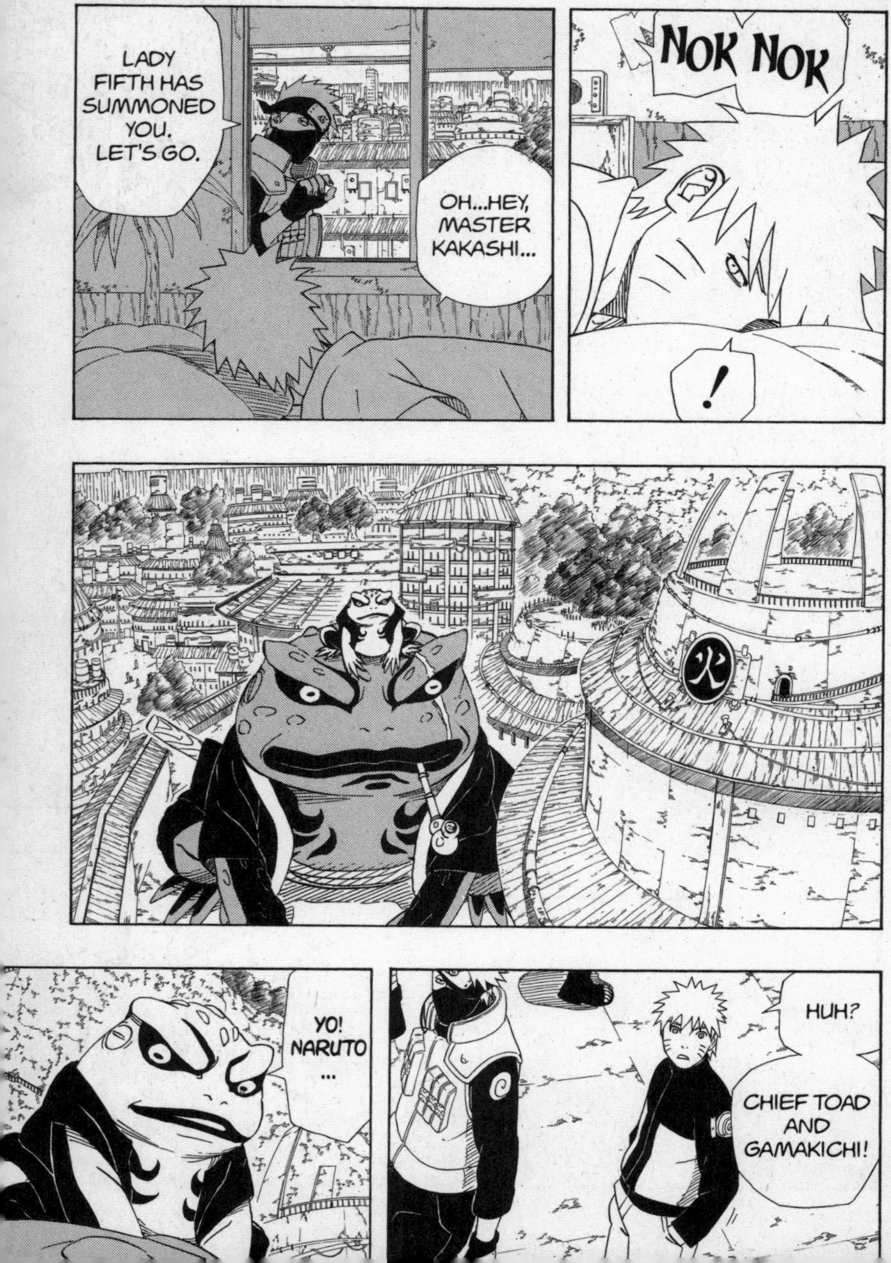
NOK NOK
!
OH...HEY, MASTER KAKASHI...
LADY FIFTH HAS SUMMONED YOU. LET'S GO.
HUH?
CHIEF TOAD AND GAMAKICHI!
YO! NARUTO ...

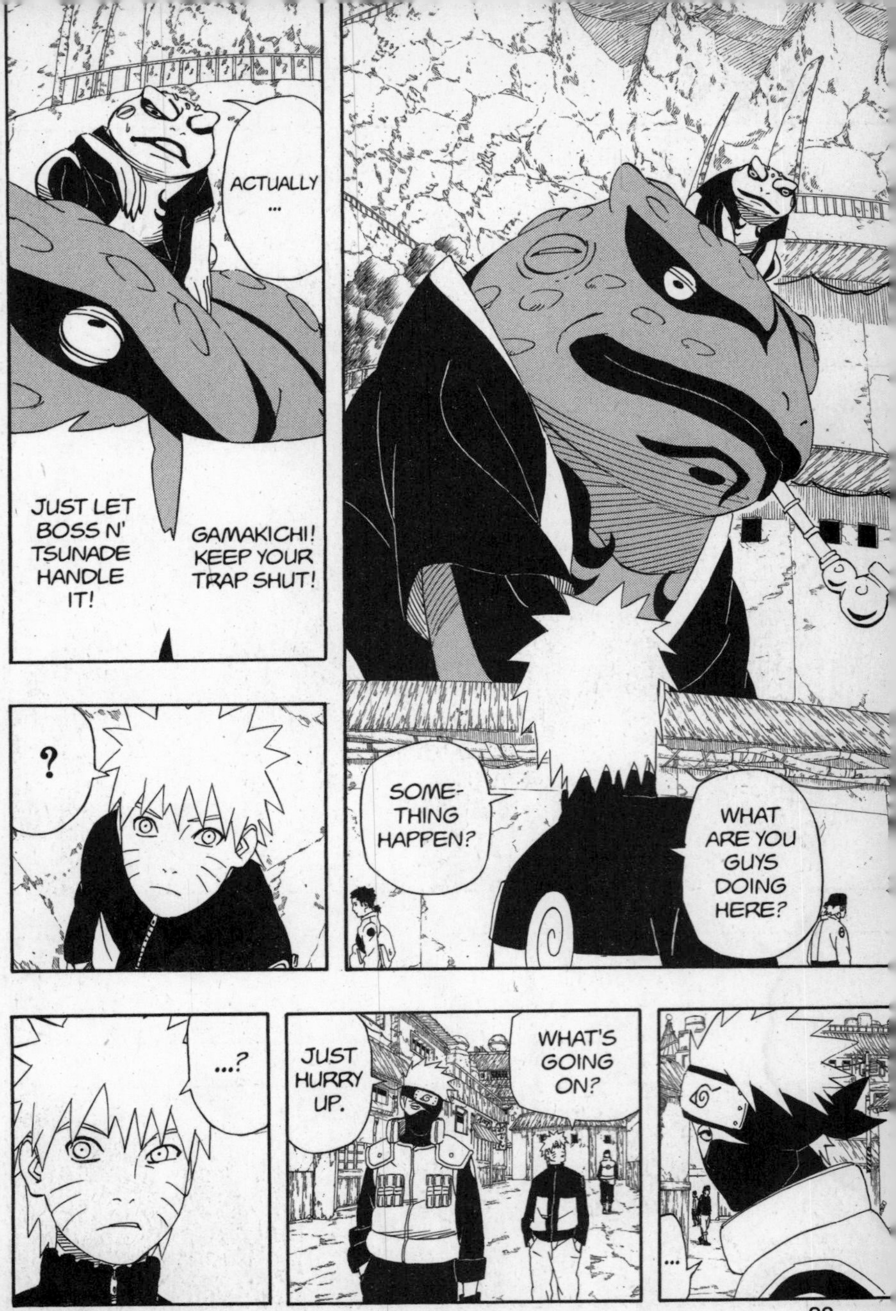
WHAT ARE YOU GUYS DOING HERE?
SOME-THING HAPPEN?
ACTUALLY ...
GAMAKICHI! KEEP YOUR TRAP SHUT!
JUST LET BOSS N' TSUNADE HANDLE IT!
?
...
WHAT'S GOING ON?
JUST HURRY UP.
...?

READ THIS WAY

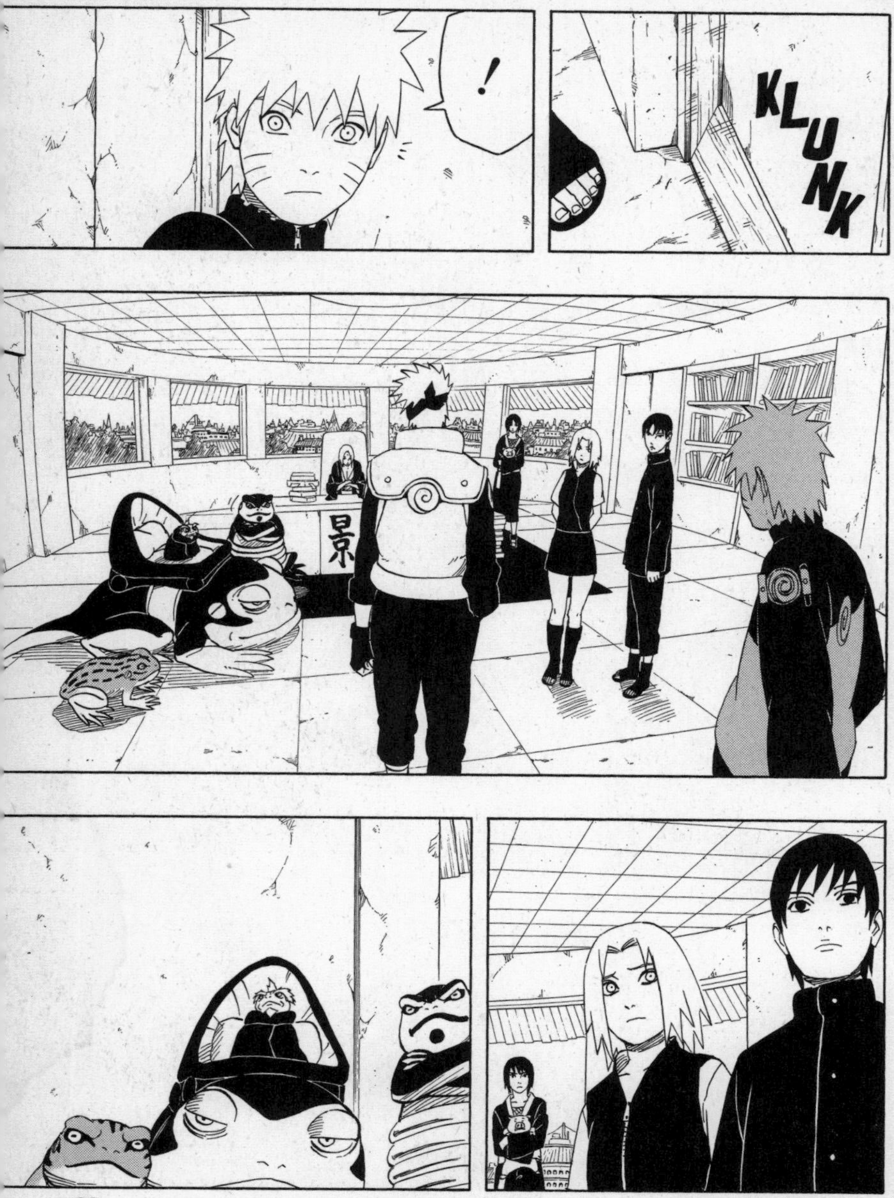
KLUNK
!
景

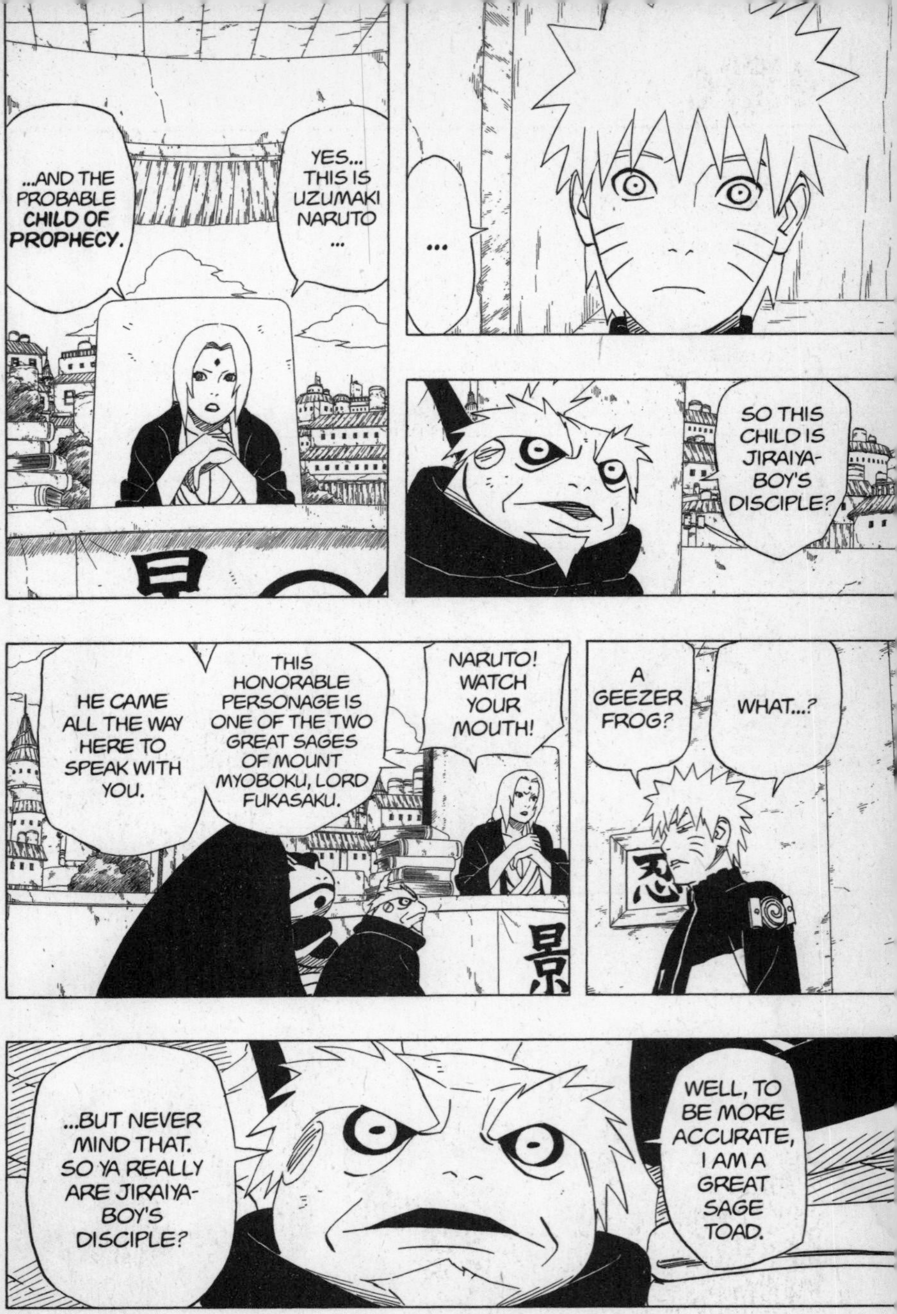
...
SO THIS CHILD IS JIRAIYA-BOY'S DISCIPLE?
YES... THIS IS UZUMAKI NARUTO ...
...AND THE PROBABLE CHILD OF PROPHECY.
WHAT...?
A GEEZER FROG?
NARUTO! WATCH YOUR MOUTH!
THIS HONORABLE PERSONAGE IS ONE OF THE TWO GREAT SAGES OF MOUNT MYOBOKU, LORD FUKASAKU.
HE CAME ALL THE WAY HERE TO SPEAK WITH YOU.
WELL, TO BE MORE ACCURATE, I AM A GREAT SAGE TOAD.
...BUT NEVER MIND THAT. SO YA REALLY ARE JIRAIYA-BOY'S DISCIPLE?

READ THIS WAY

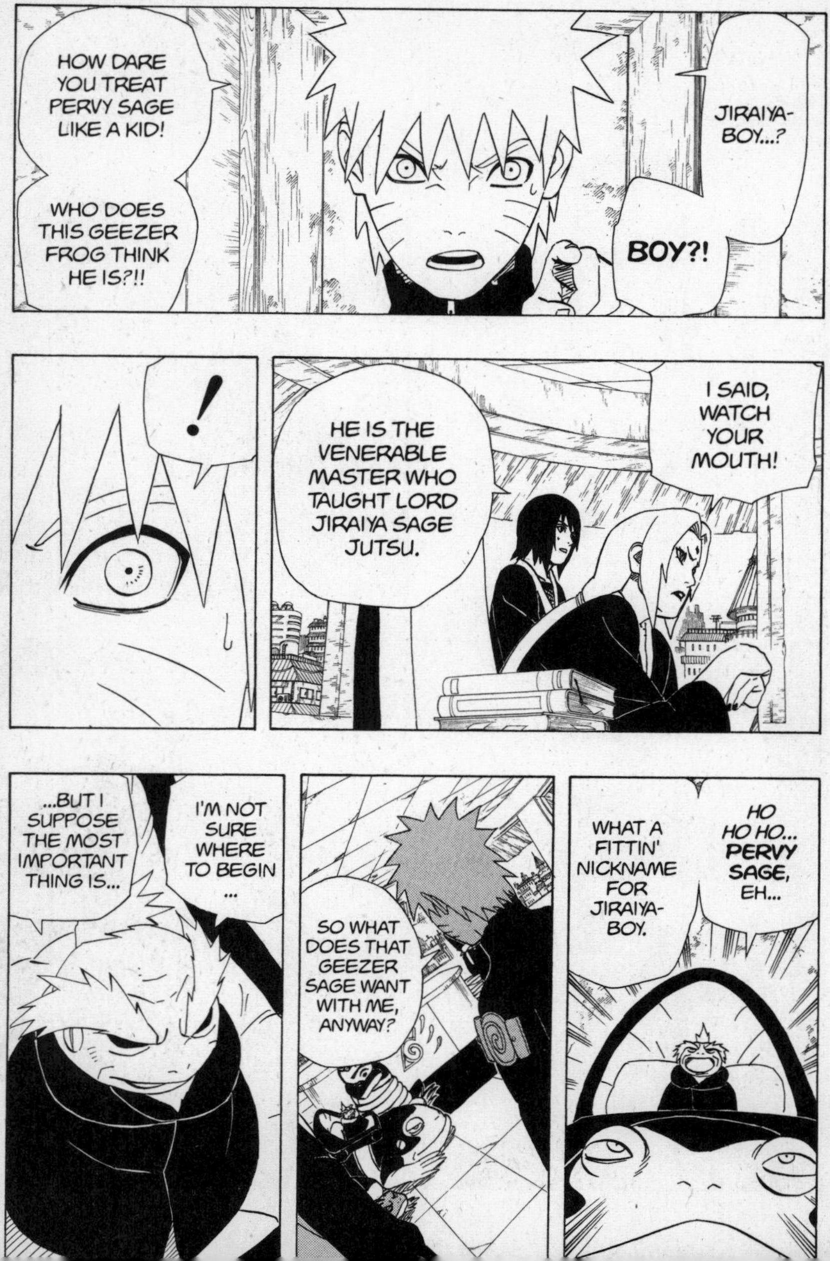

JIRAIYA-BOY...?
BOY?!
HOW DARE YOU TREAT PERVY SAGE LIKE A KID!
WHO DOES THIS GEEZER FROG THINK HE IS?!!
I SAID, WATCH YOUR MOUTH!
HE IS THE VENERABLE MASTER WHO TAUGHT LORD JIRAIYA SAGE JUTSU.
!
HO HO HO... PERVY SAGE, EH...
WHAT A FITTIN' NICKNAME FOR JIRAIYA-BOY.
SO WHAT DOES THAT GEEZER SAGE WANT WITH ME, ANYWAY?
I'M NOT SURE WHERE TO BEGIN...
...BUT I SUPPOSE THE MOST IMPORTANT THING IS...

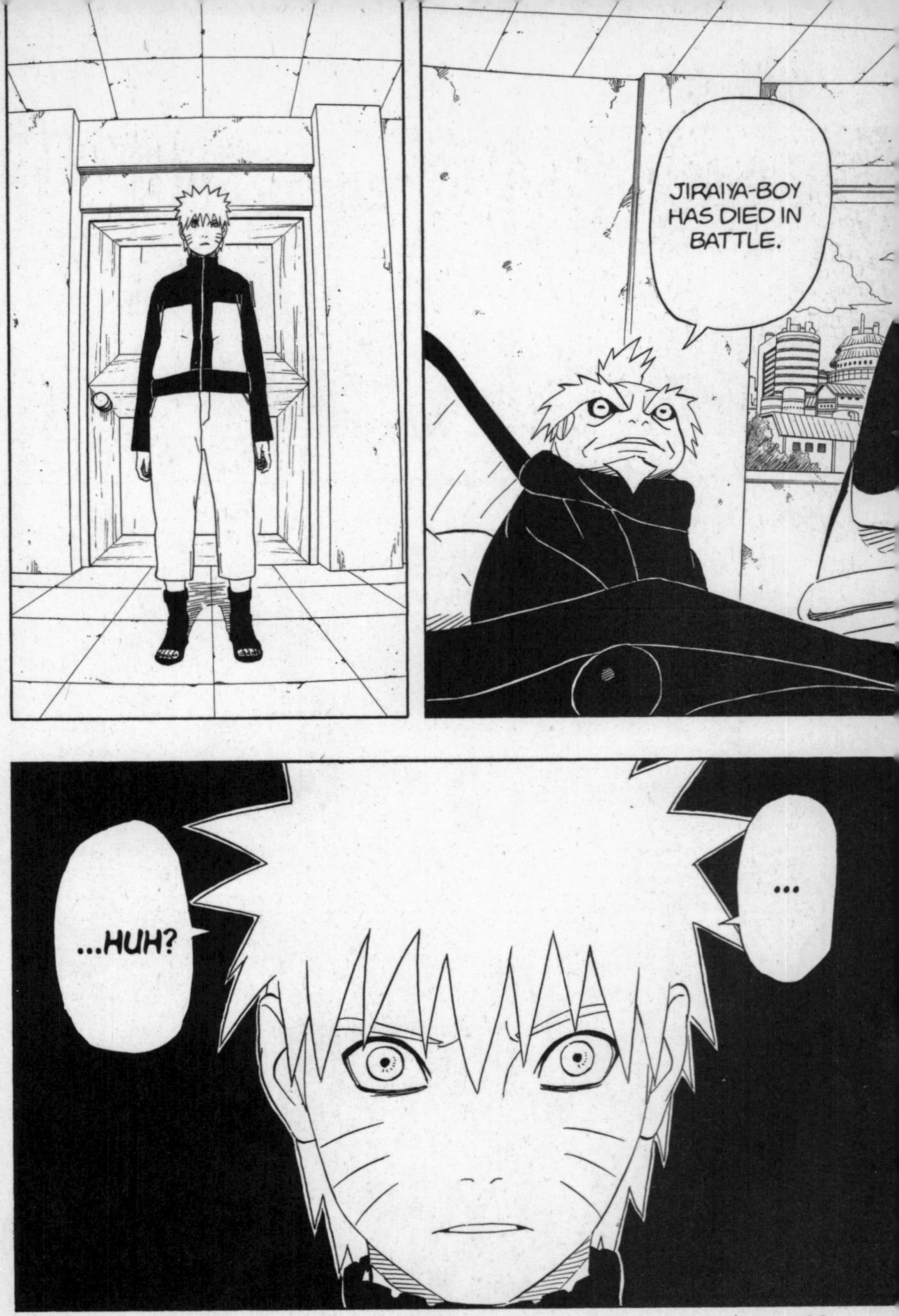
JIRAIYA-BOY HAS DIED IN BATTLE.
...
...HUH?

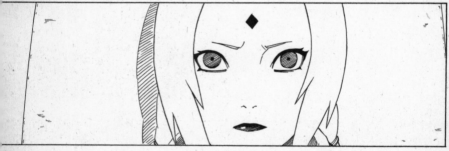

WHA-
WHAT ARE
YOU
TALKING
ABOUT...

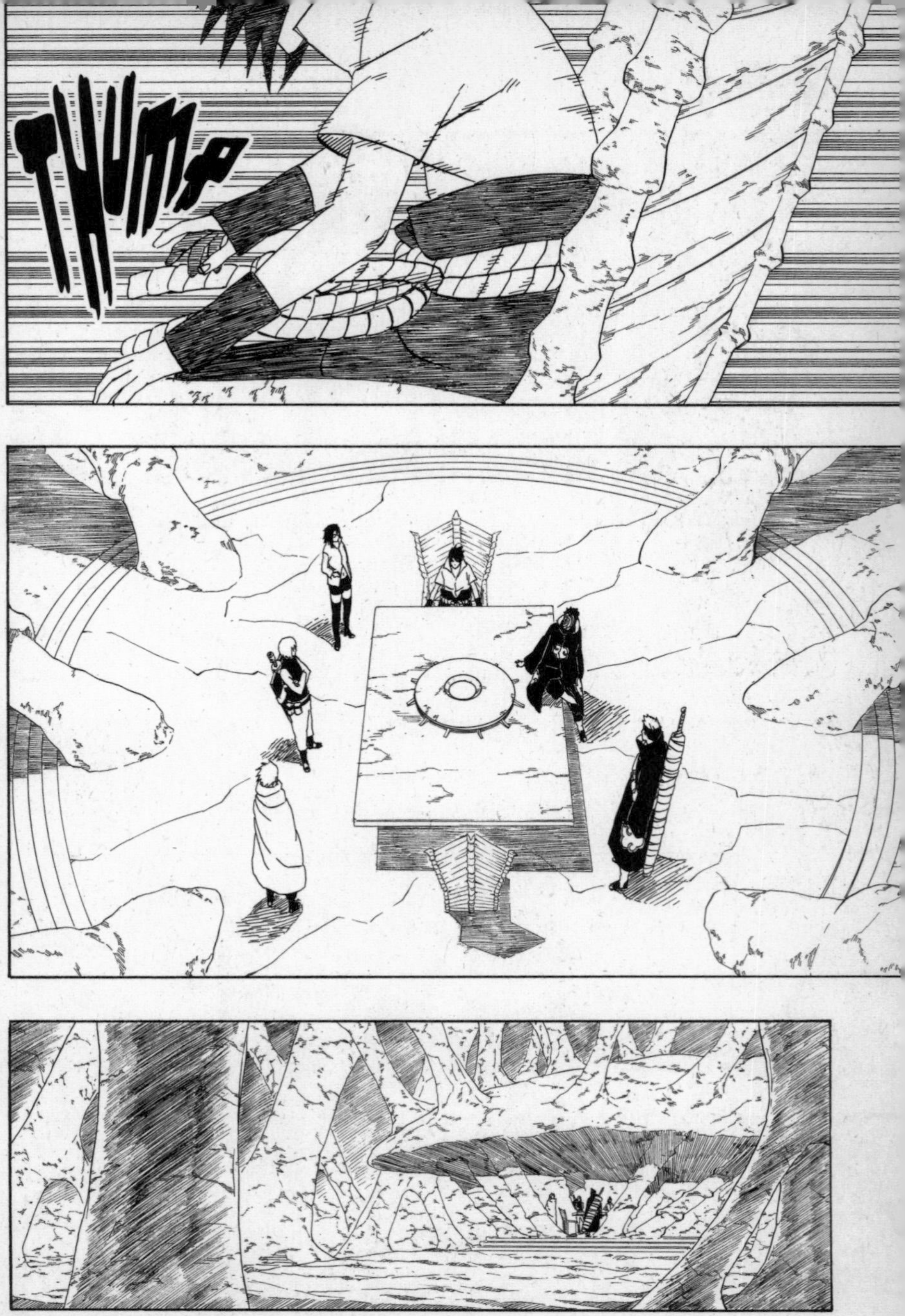
THUMP

READ THIS WAY

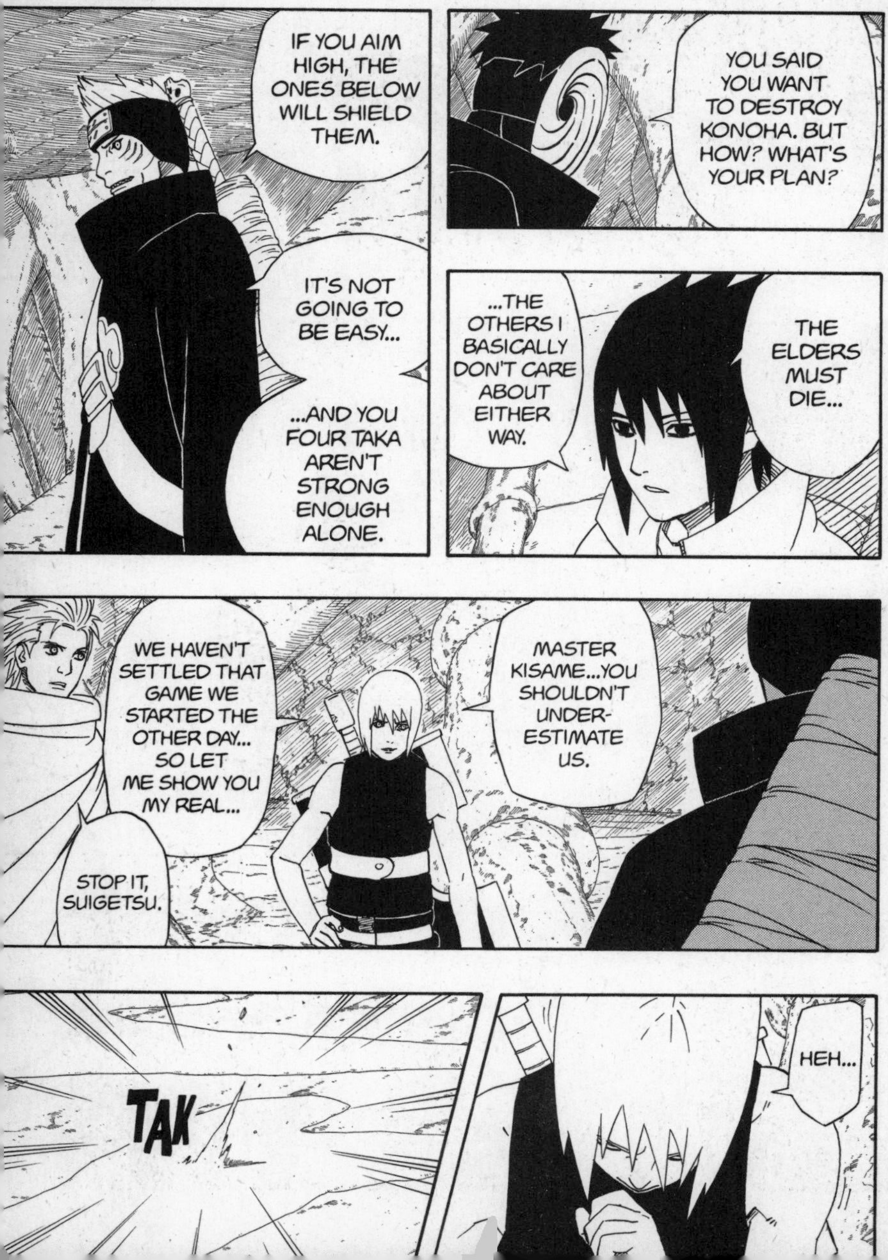

YOU SAID YOU WANT TO DESTROY KONOHA. BUT HOW? WHAT'S YOUR PLAN?
THE ELDERS MUST DIE...
...THE OTHERS I BASICALLY DON'T CARE ABOUT EITHER WAY.
IF YOU AIM HIGH, THE ONES BELOW WILL SHIELD THEM.
IT'S NOT GOING TO BE EASY...
...AND YOU FOUR TAKA AREN'T STRONG ENOUGH ALONE.
MASTER KISAME...YOU SHOULDN'T UNDER-ESTIMATE US.
WE HAVEN'T SETTLED THAT GAME WE STARTED THE OTHER DAY... SO LET ME SHOW YOU MY REAL...
STOP IT, SUIGETSU.
HEH...
TAK

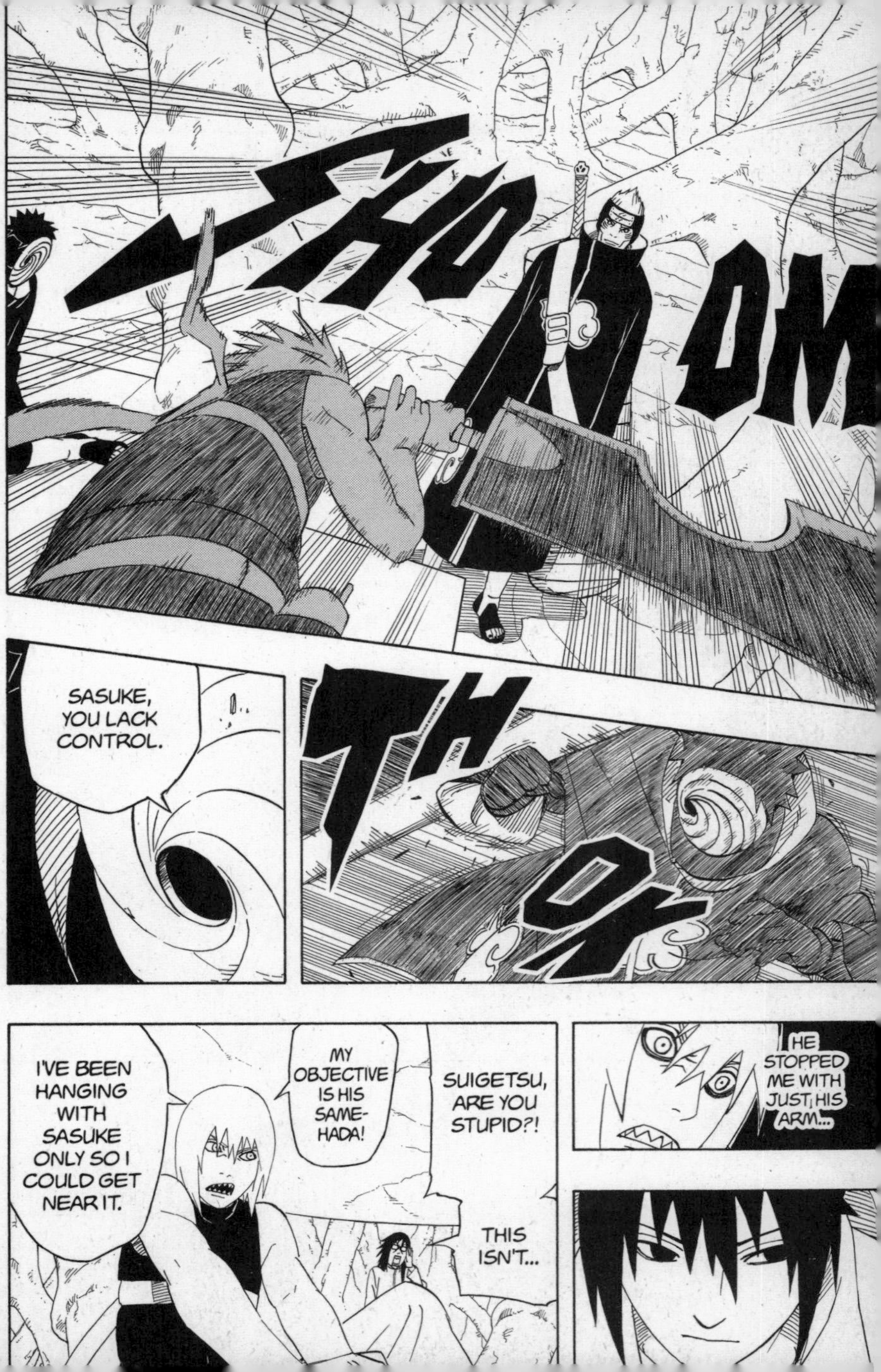
ZHO
OM
TH
OK
SASUKE, YOU LACK CONTROL.
HE STOPPED ME WITH JUST HIS ARM...
SUIGETSU, ARE YOU STUPID?!
MY OBJECTIVE IS HIS SAME-HADA!
I'VE BEEN HANGING WITH SASUKE ONLY SO I COULD GET NEAR IT.
THIS ISN'T...

READ THIS WAY

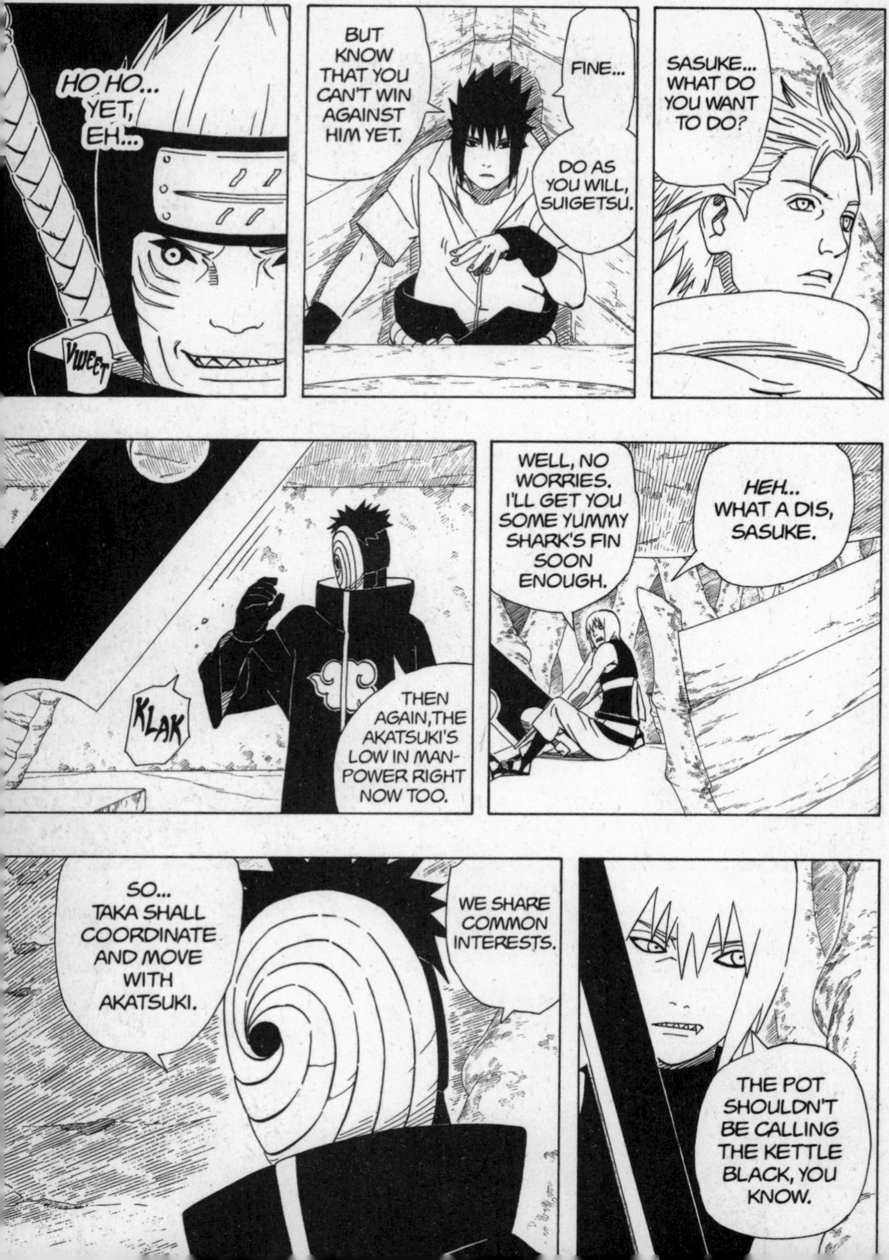
SASUKE... WHAT DO YOU WANT TO DO?
FINE...
DO AS YOU WILL, SUIGETSU.
BUT KNOW THAT YOU CAN'T WIN AGAINST HIM YET.
HO HO... YET, EH...
VWEET
HEH... WHAT A DIS, SASUKE.
WELL, NO WORRIES. I'LL GET YOU SOME YUMMY SHARK'S FIN SOON ENOUGH.
THEN AGAIN, THE AKATSUKI'S LOW IN MAN-POWER RIGHT NOW TOO.
KLAK
THE POT SHOULDN'T BE CALLING THE KETTLE BLACK, YOU KNOW.
WE SHARE COMMON INTERESTS.
SO... TAKA SHALL COORDINATE AND MOVE WITH AKATSUKI.

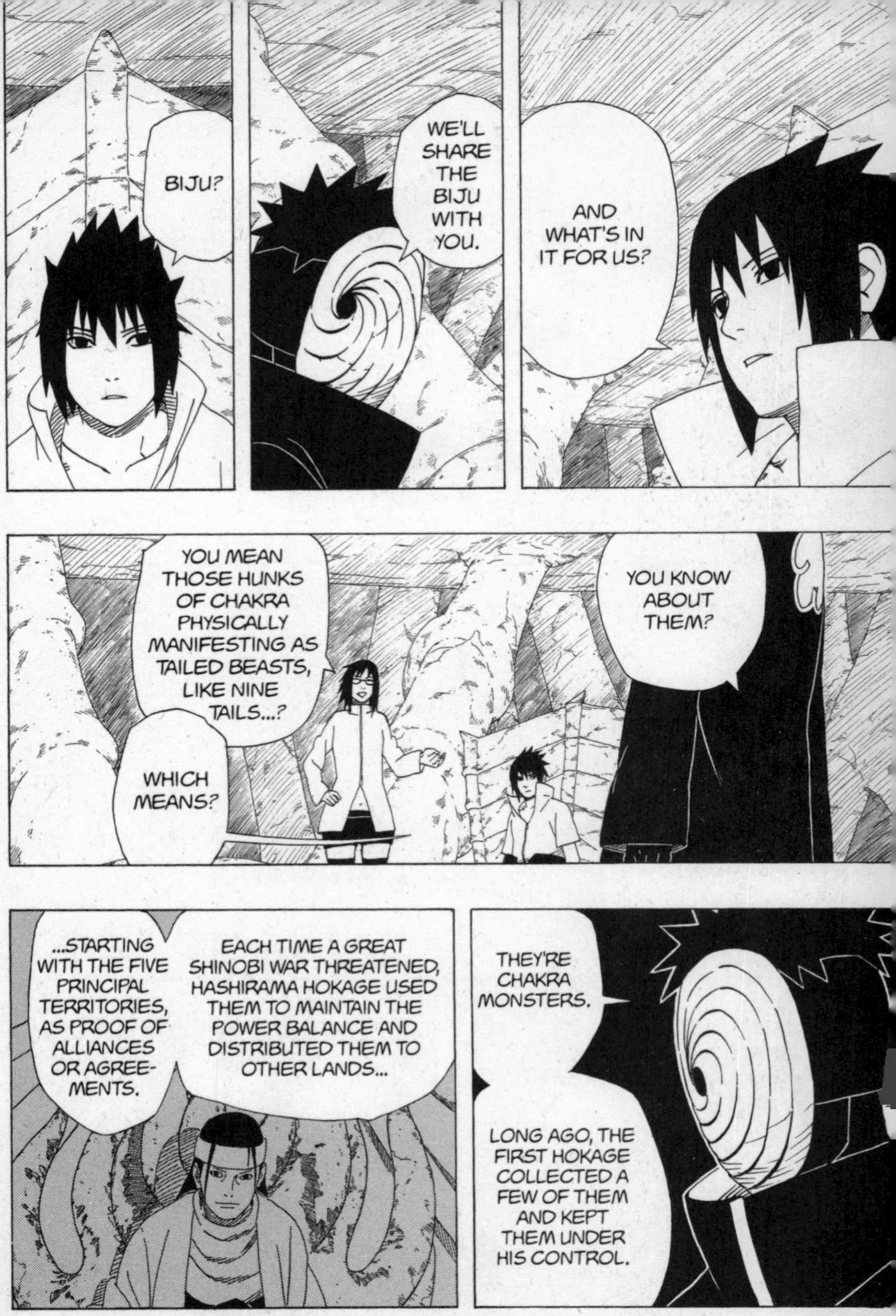
AND WHAT'S IN IT FOR US?
WE'LL SHARE THE BIJU WITH YOU.
BIJU?
YOU MEAN THOSE HUNKS OF CHAKRA PHYSICALLY MANIFESTING AS TAILED BEASTS, LIKE NINE TAILS...?
YOU KNOW ABOUT THEM?
WHICH MEANS?
THEY'RE CHAKRA MONSTERS.
LONG AGO, THE FIRST HOKAGE COLLECTED A FEW OF THEM AND KEPT THEM UNDER HIS CONTROL.
EACH TIME A GREAT SHINOBI WAR THREATENED, HASHIRAMA HOKAGE USED THEM TO MAINTAIN THE POWER BALANCE AND DISTRIBUTED THEM TO OTHER LANDS...
...STARTING WITH THE FIVE PRINCIPAL TERRITORIES, AS PROOF OF ALLIANCES OR AGREE-MENTS.

READ THIS WAY

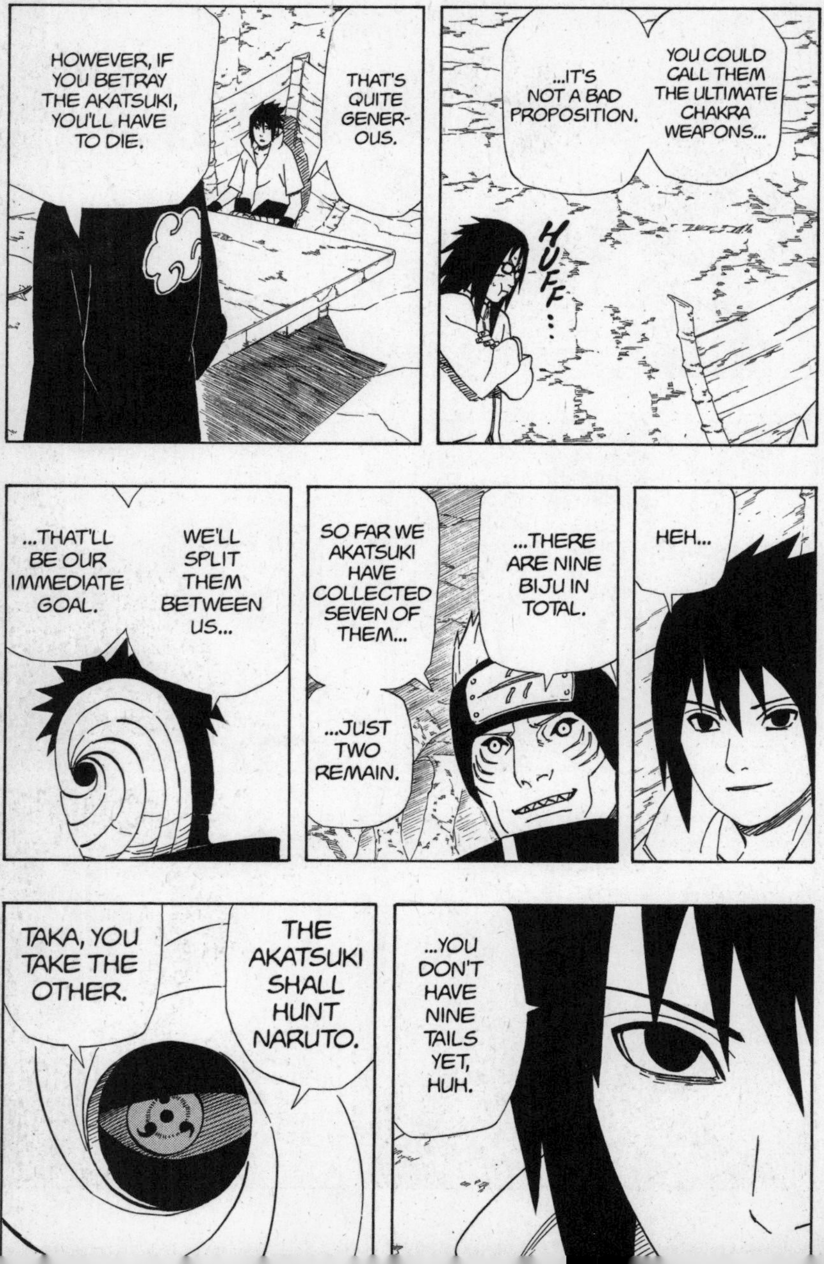
YOU COULD CALL THEM THE ULTIMATE CHAKRA WEAPONS...
...IT'S NOT A BAD PROPOSITION.
HUFF...
THAT'S QUITE GENER-OUS.
HOWEVER, IF YOU BETRAY THE AKATSUKI, YOU'LL HAVE TO DIE.
HEH...
...THERE ARE NINE BIJU IN TOTAL.
SO FAR WE AKATSUKI HAVE COLLECTED SEVEN OF THEM...
...JUST TWO REMAIN.
WE'LL SPLIT THEM BETWEEN US...
...THAT'LL BE OUR IMMEDIATE GOAL.
...YOU DON'T HAVE NINE TAILS YET, HUH.
THE AKATSUKI SHALL HUNT NARUTO.
TAKA, YOU TAKE THE OTHER.

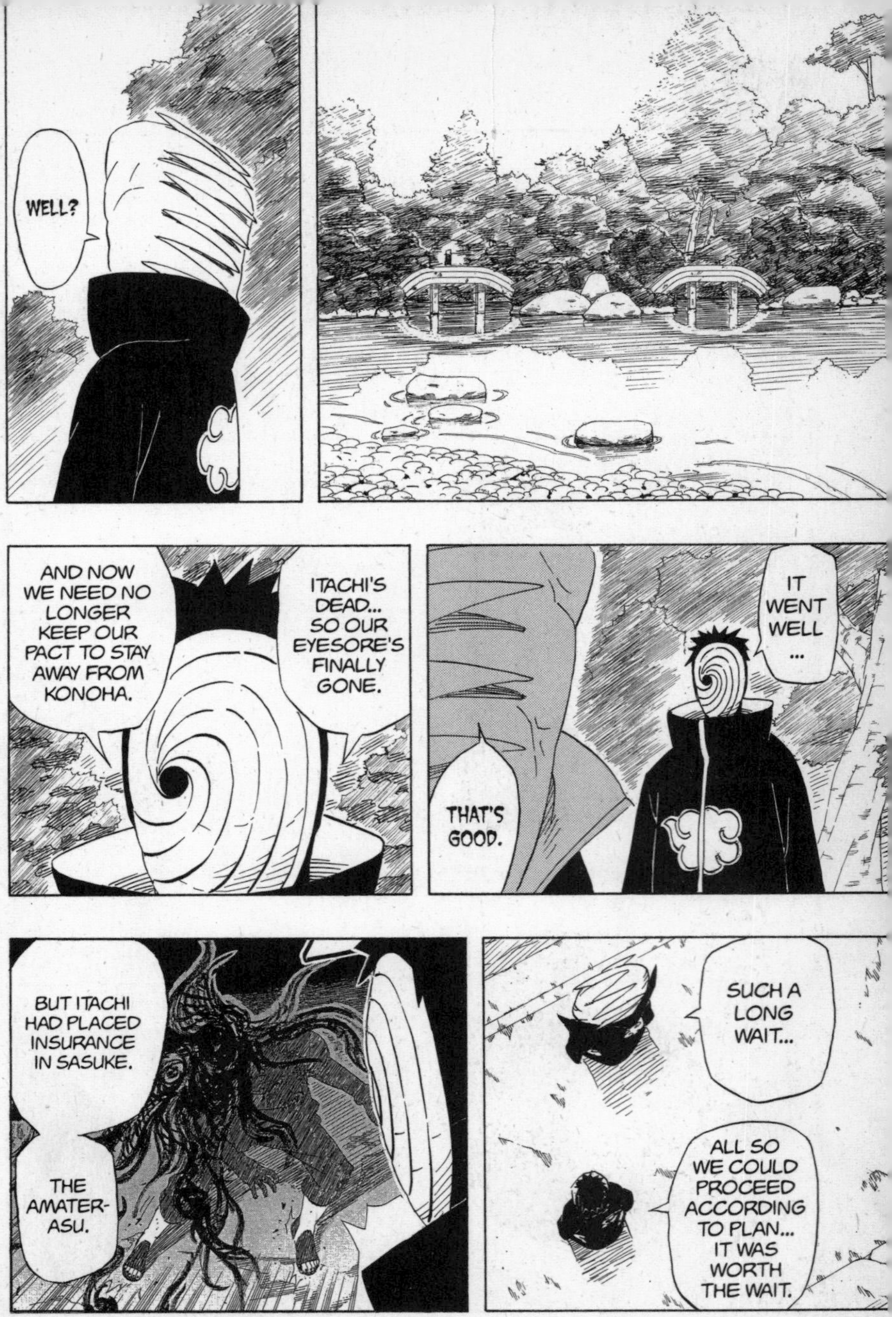
WELL?
IT WENT WELL ...
THAT'S GOOD.
ITACHI'S DEAD... SO OUR EYESORE'S FINALLY GONE.
AND NOW WE NEED NO LONGER KEEP OUR PACT TO STAY AWAY FROM KONOHA.
SUCH A LONG WAIT...
ALL SO WE COULD PROCEED ACCORDING TO PLAN... IT WAS WORTH THE WAIT.
BUT ITACHI HAD PLACED INSURANCE IN SASUKE.
THE AMATER-ASU.

READ THIS WAY

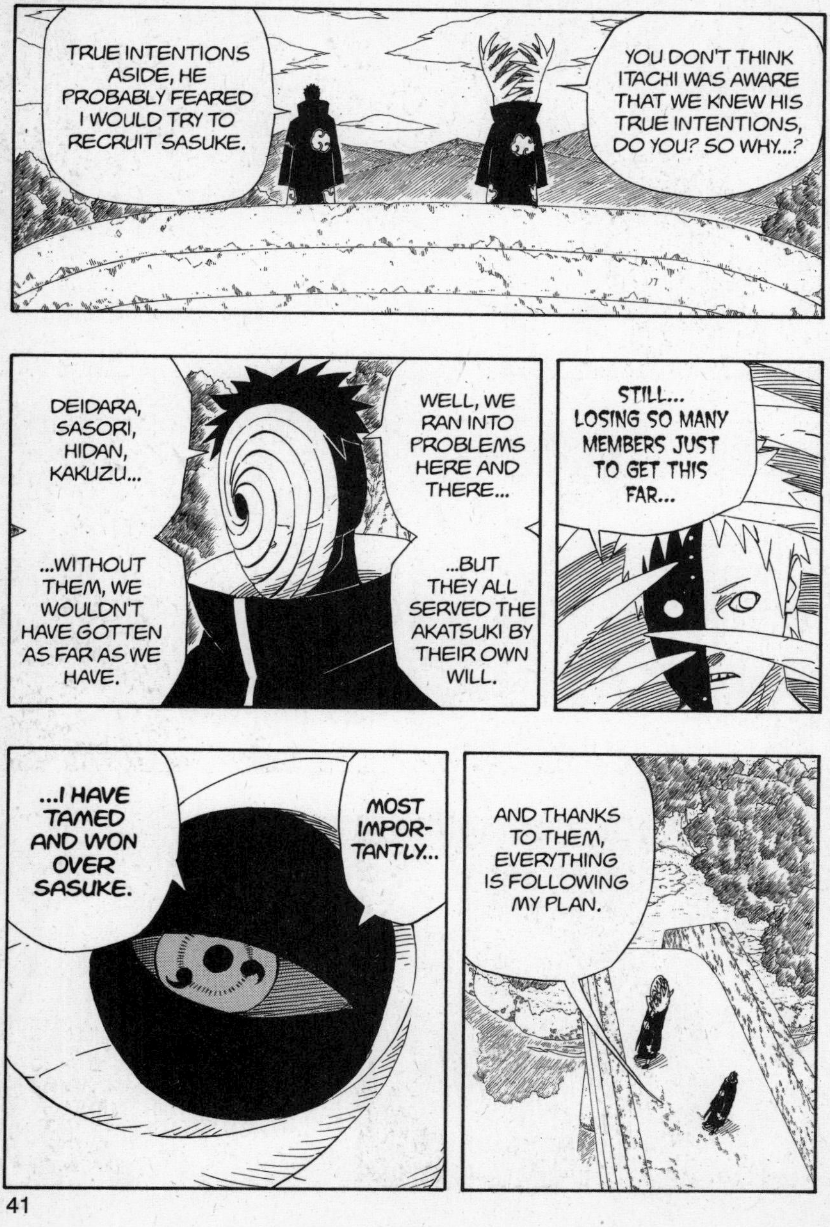

YOU DON'T THINK ITACHI WAS AWARE THAT WE KNEW HIS TRUE INTENTIONS, DO YOU? SO WHY...?
TRUE INTENTIONS ASIDE, HE PROBABLY FEARED I WOULD TRY TO RECRUIT SASUKE.
STILL... LOSING SO MANY MEMBERS JUST TO GET THIS FAR...
WELL, WE RAN INTO PROBLEMS HERE AND THERE...
...BUT THEY ALL SERVED THE AKATSUKI BY THEIR OWN WILL.
DEIDARA, SASORI, HIDAN, KAKUZU...
...WITHOUT THEM, WE WOULDN'T HAVE GOTTEN AS FAR AS WE HAVE.
AND THANKS TO THEM, EVERYTHING IS FOLLOWING MY PLAN.
MOST IMPORTANTLY...
...I HAVE TAMED AND WON OVER SASUKE.

NARUTO

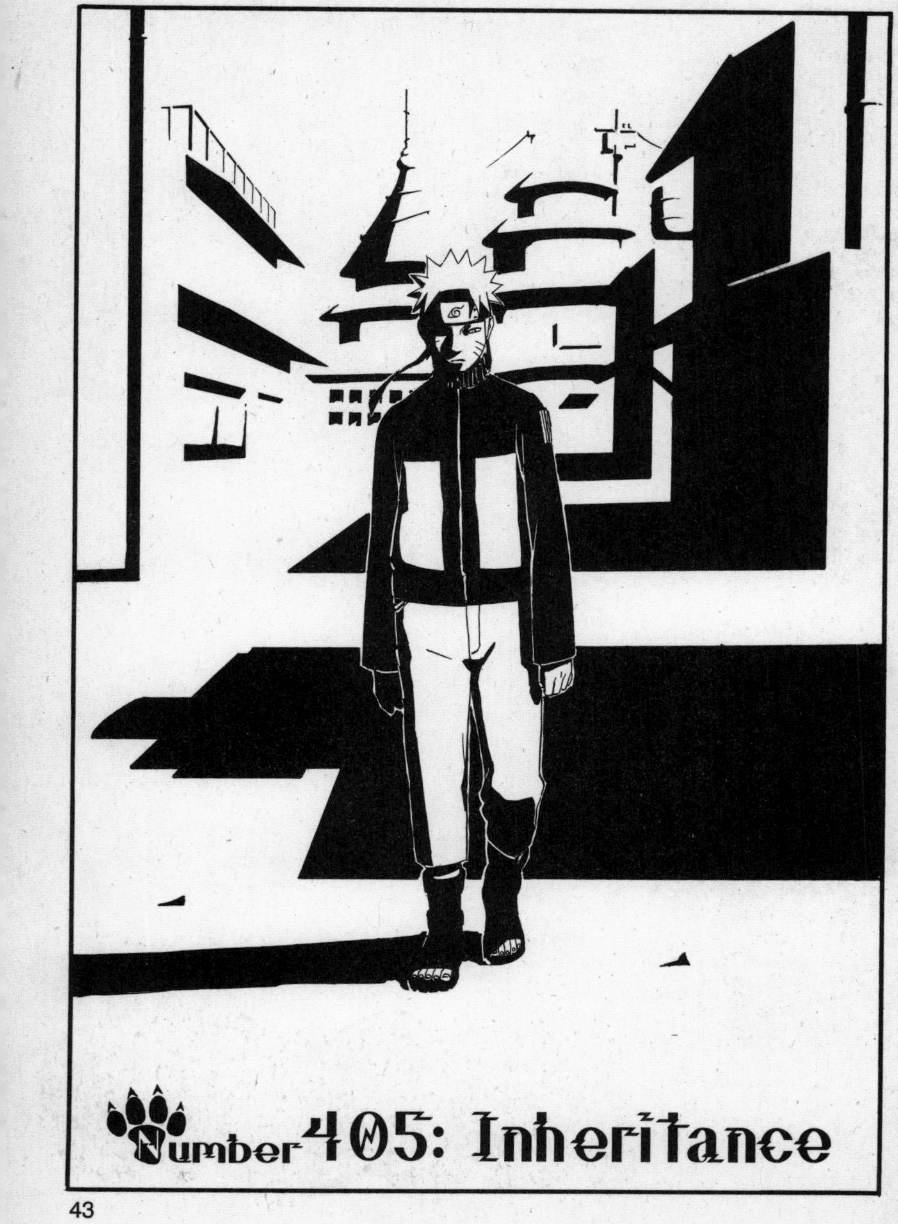

Number 405: Inheritance

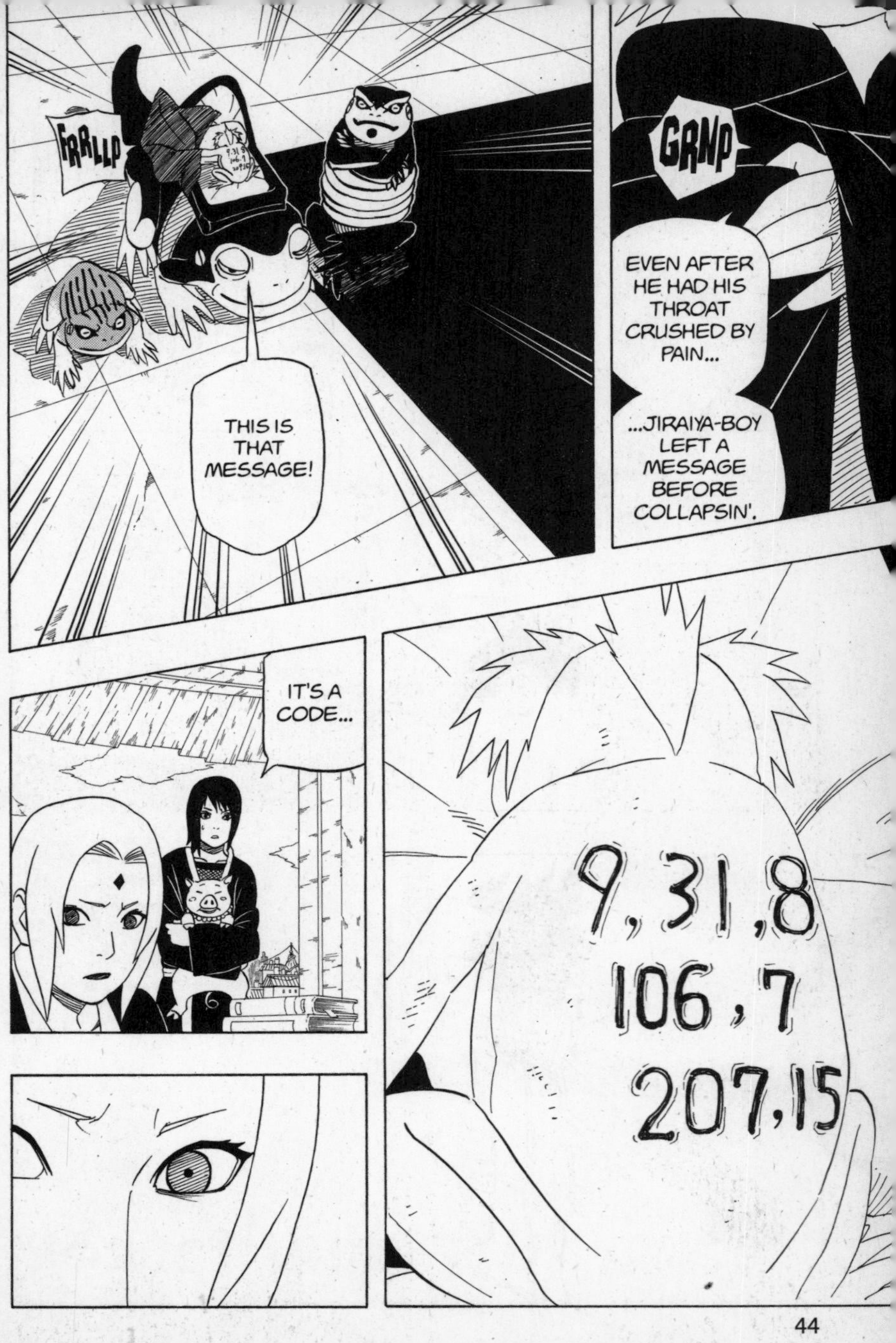
GRNP
EVEN AFTER HE HAD HIS THROAT CRUSHED BY PAIN...
...JIRAIYA-BOY LEFT A MESSAGE BEFORE COLLAPSIN'.
FRRLLP
THIS IS THAT MESSAGE!
9,31,8
106,7
207,15
IT'S A CODE...

READ THIS WAY

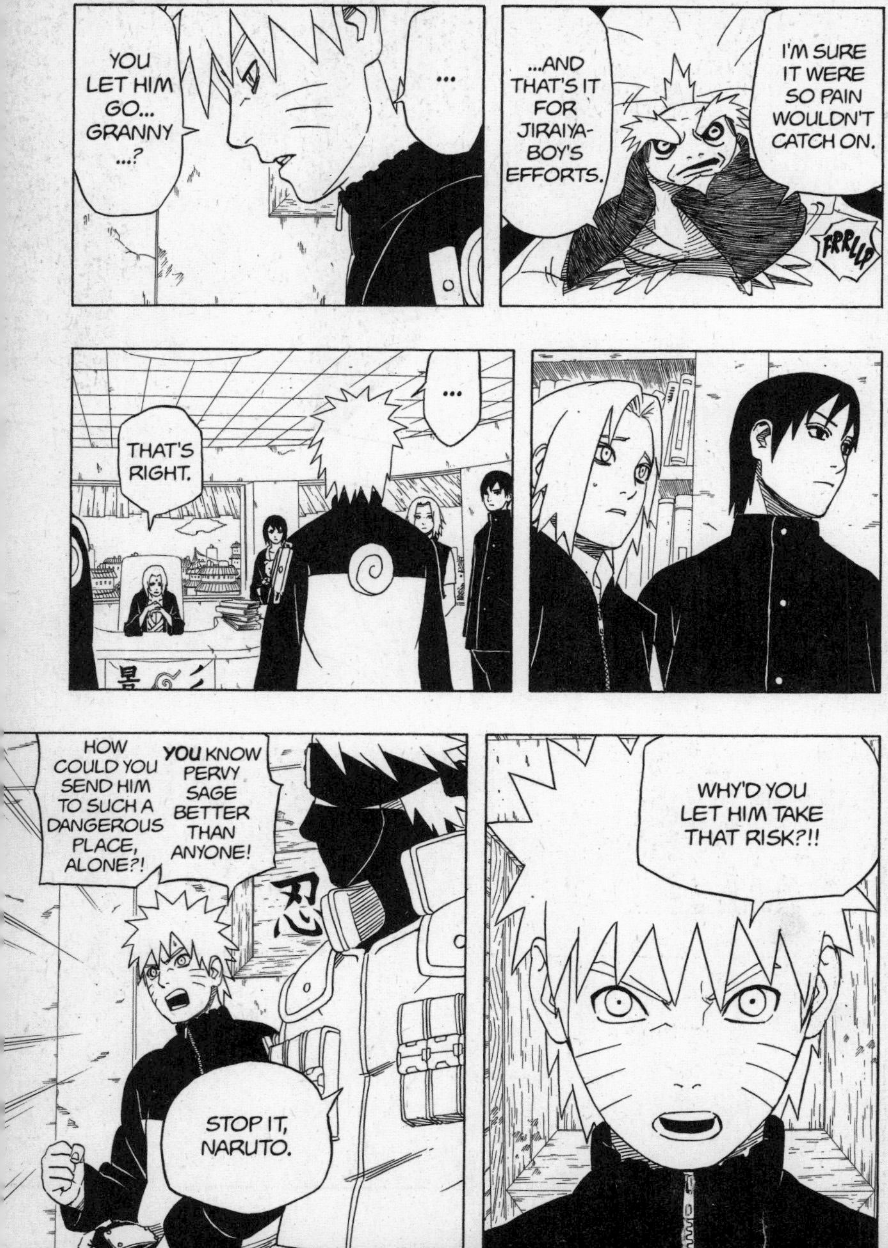
I'M SURE IT WERE SO PAIN WOULDN'T CATCH ON.
...AND THAT'S IT FOR JIRAIYA-BOY'S EFFORTS.
FRRLLP
...
YOU LET HIM GO... GRANNY ...?
...
THAT'S RIGHT.
WHY'D YOU LET HIM TAKE THAT RISK?!!
YOU KNOW PERVY SAGE BETTER THAN ANYONE!
HOW COULD YOU SEND HIM TO SUCH A DANGEROUS PLACE, ALONE?!
STOP IT, NARUTO.

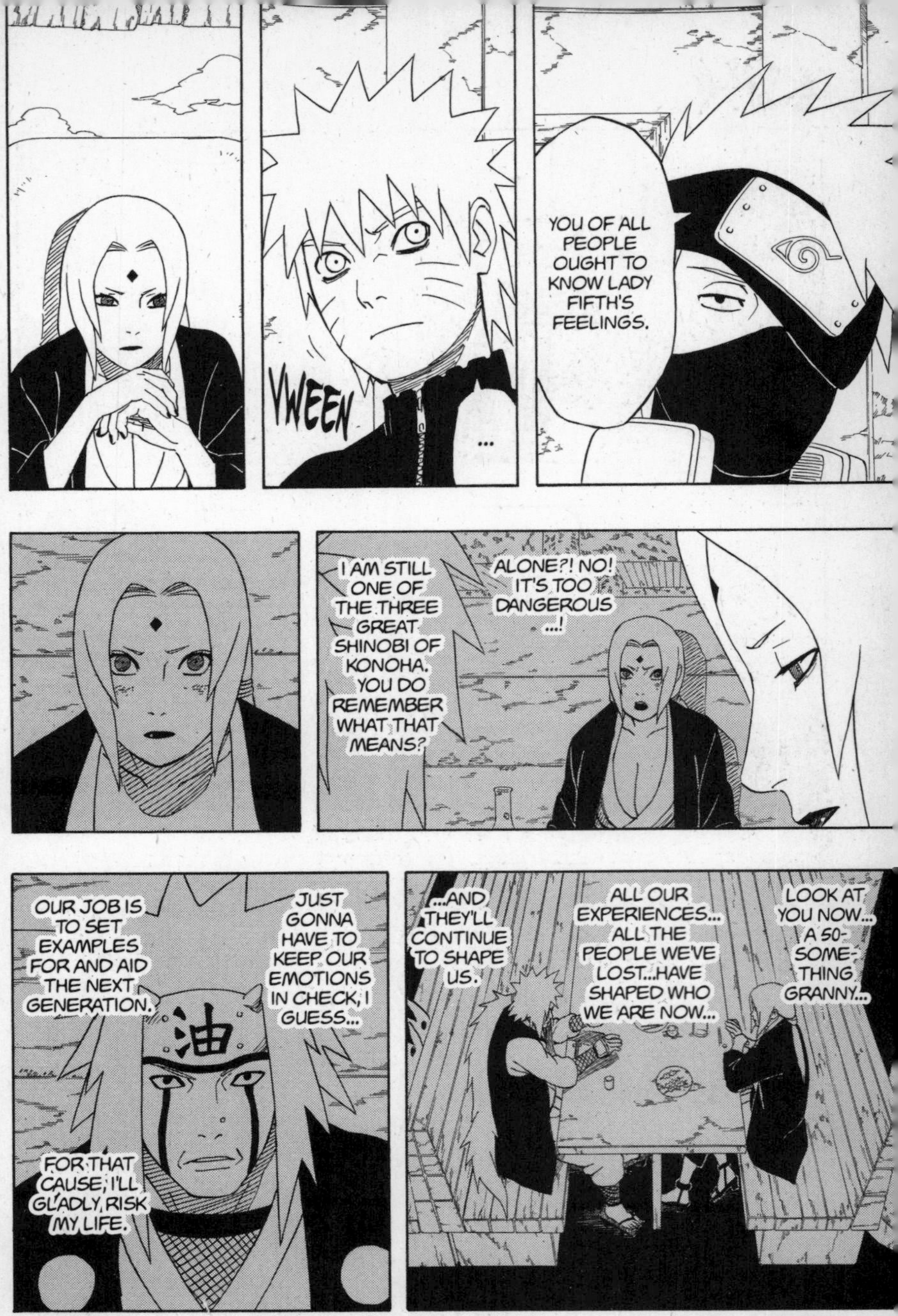
YOU OF ALL PEOPLE OUGHT TO KNOW LADY FIFTH'S FEELINGS.
VWEEN
...
ALONE?! NO! IT'S TOO DANGEROUS ...!
I AM STILL ONE OF THE THREE GREAT SHINOBI OF KONOHA. YOU DO REMEMBER WHAT THAT MEANS?
LOOK AT YOU NOW... A 50-SOMETHING GRANNY...
ALL OUR EXPERIENCES... ALL THE PEOPLE WE'VE LOST...HAVE SHAPED WHO WE ARE NOW...
...AND THEY'LL CONTINUE TO SHAPE US.
JUST GONNA HAVE TO KEEP OUR EMOTIONS IN CHECK, I GUESS...
OUR JOB IS TO SET EXAMPLES FOR AND AID THE NEXT GENERATION.
FOR THAT CAUSE, I'LL GLADLY RISK MY LIFE.

READ THIS WAY

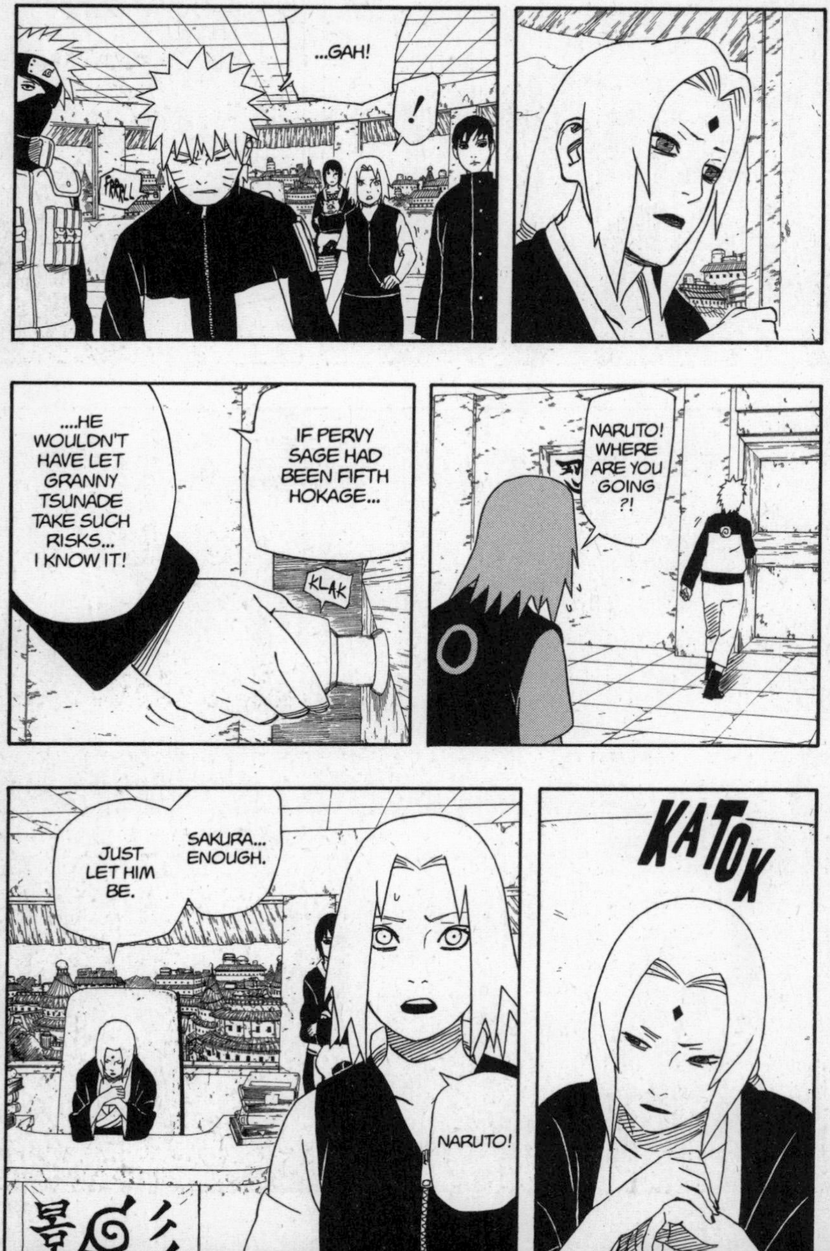
...GAH!
!
FRRRLL
NARUTO! WHERE ARE YOU GOING ?!
IF PERVY SAGE HAD BEEN FIFTH HOKAGE...
....HE WOULDN'T HAVE LET GRANNY TSUNADE TAKE SUCH RISKS... I KNOW IT!
KLAK
KATOK
SAKURA... ENOUGH.
JUST LET HIM BE.
NARUTO!

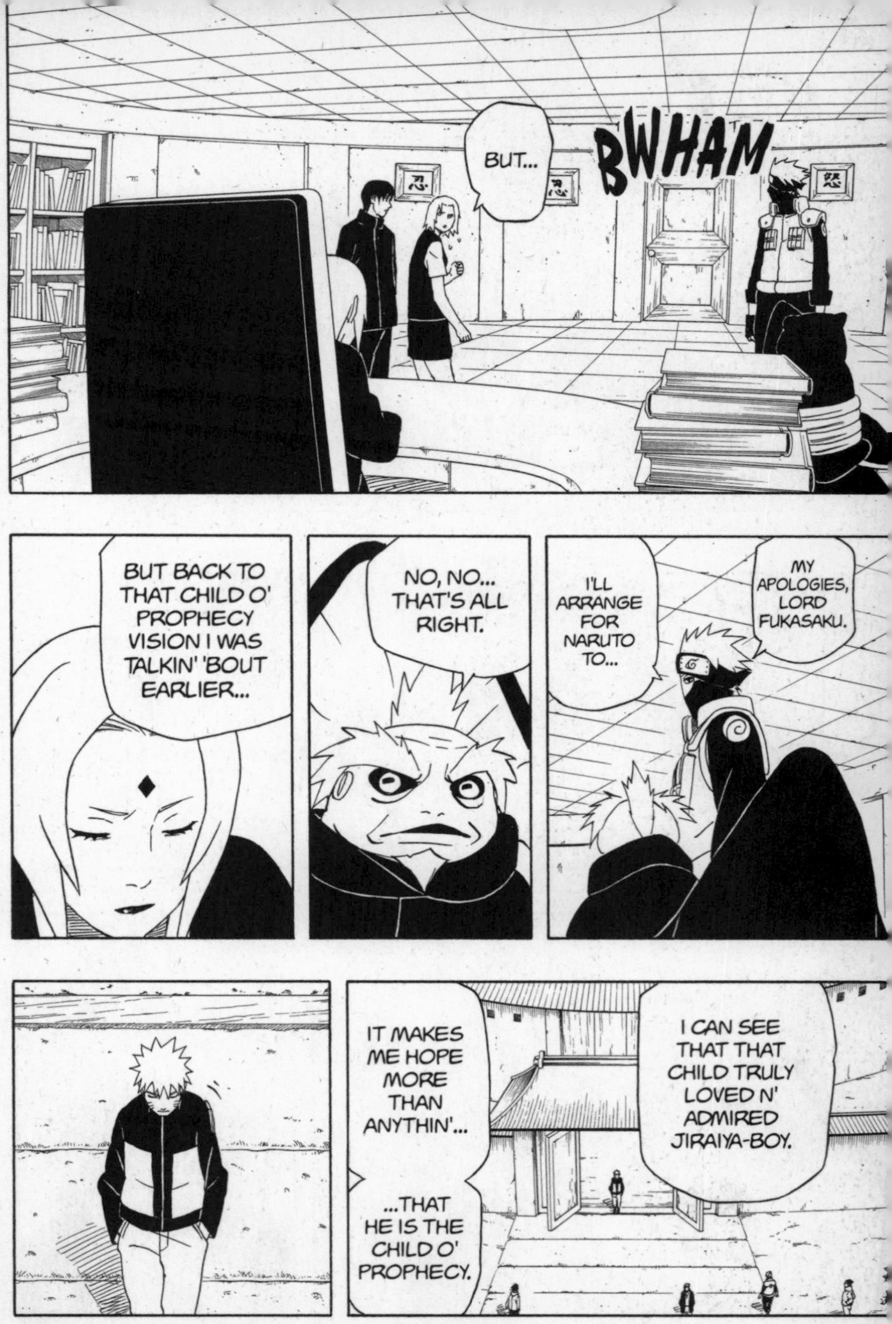
BWHAM
BUT...
MY APOLOGIES, LORD FUKASAKU.
I'LL ARRANGE FOR NARUTO TO...
NO, NO... THAT'S ALL RIGHT.
BUT BACK TO THAT CHILD O' PROPHECY VISION I WAS TALKIN' 'BOUT EARLIER...
I CAN SEE THAT THAT CHILD TRULY LOVED N' ADMIRED JIRAIYA-BOY.
IT MAKES ME HOPE MORE THAN ANYTHIN'...
...THAT HE IS THE CHILD O' PROPHECY.

READ THIS WAY

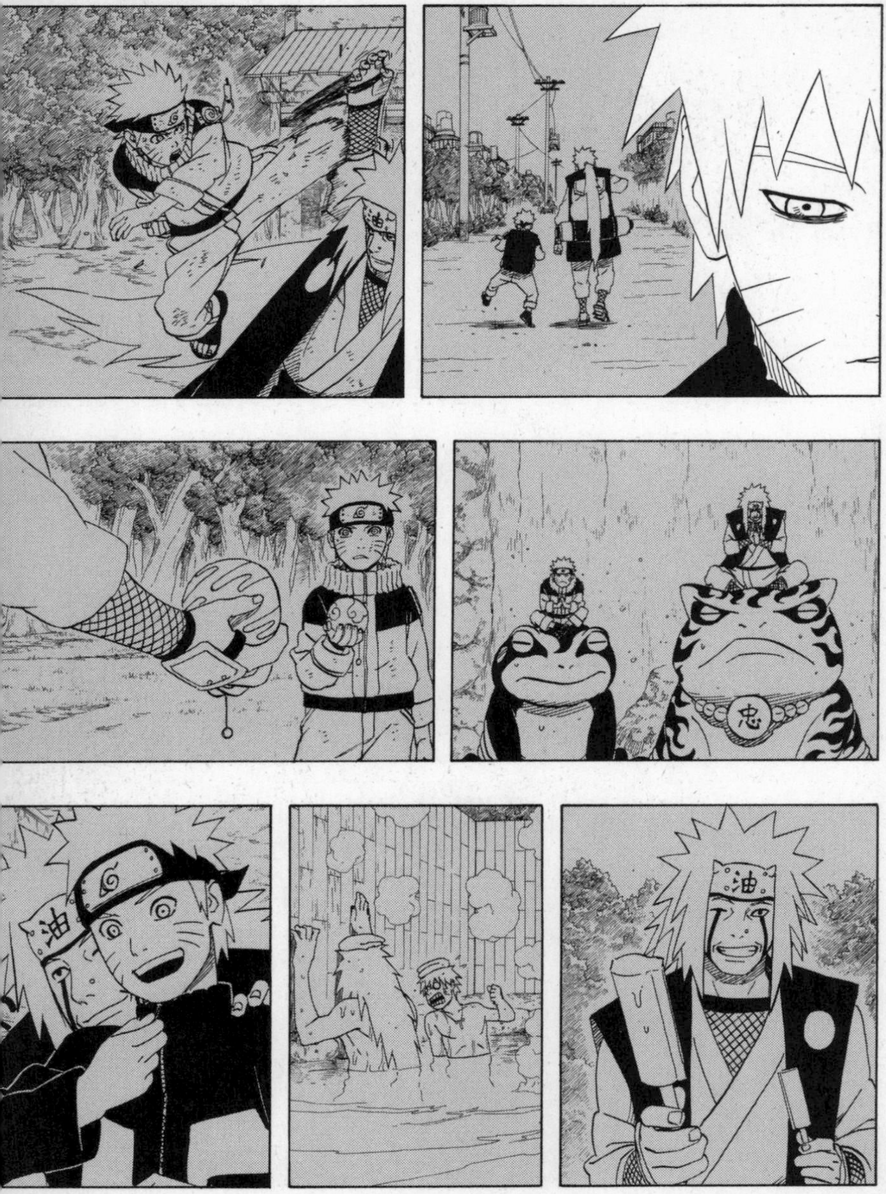
忠
油
油

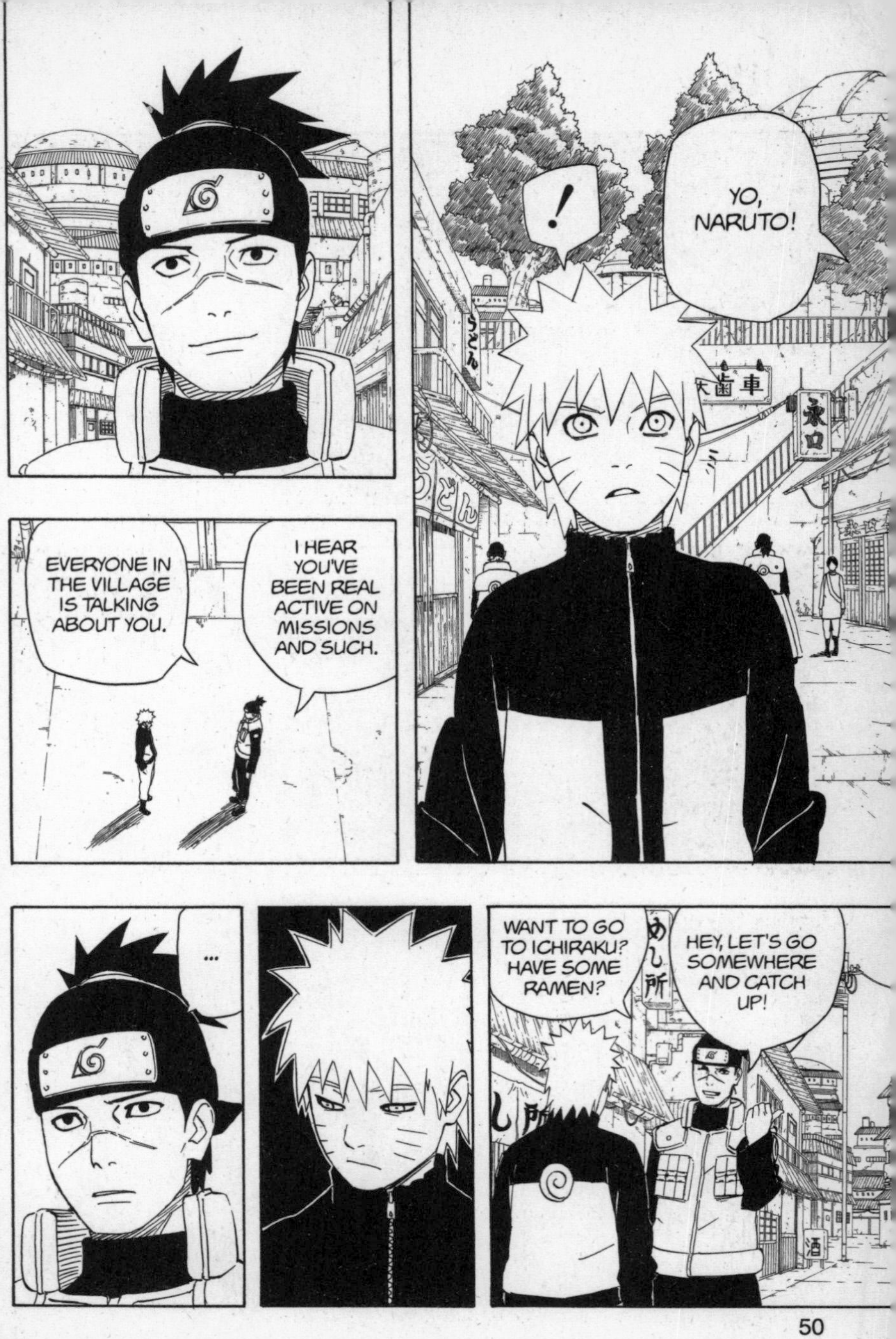
YO, NARUTO!
!
I HEAR YOU'VE BEEN REAL ACTIVE ON MISSIONS AND SUCH.
EVERYONE IN THE VILLAGE IS TALKING ABOUT YOU.
HEY, LET'S GO SOMEWHERE AND CATCH UP!
WANT TO GO TO ICHIRAKU? HAVE SOME RAMEN?
...

READ THIS WAY

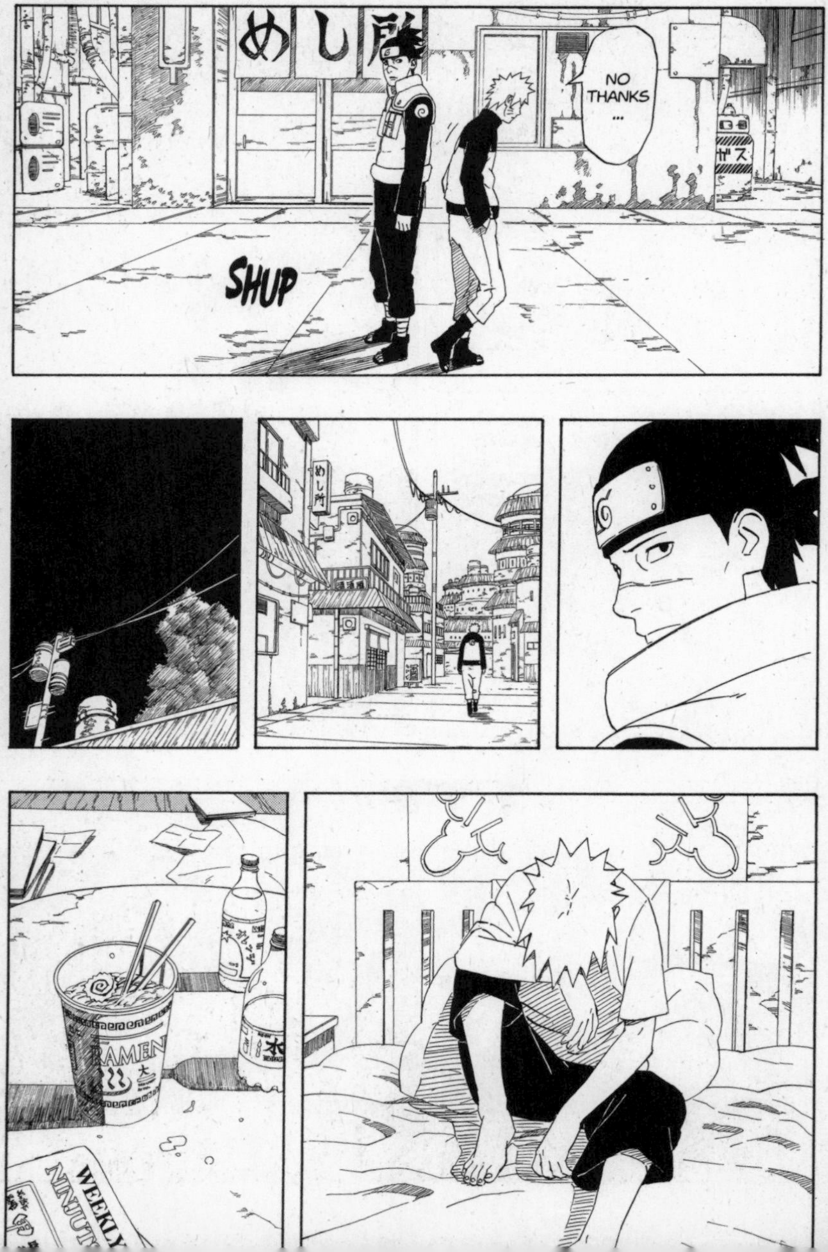
めし所
NO THANKS ...
SHUP
RAMEN
WEEKLY

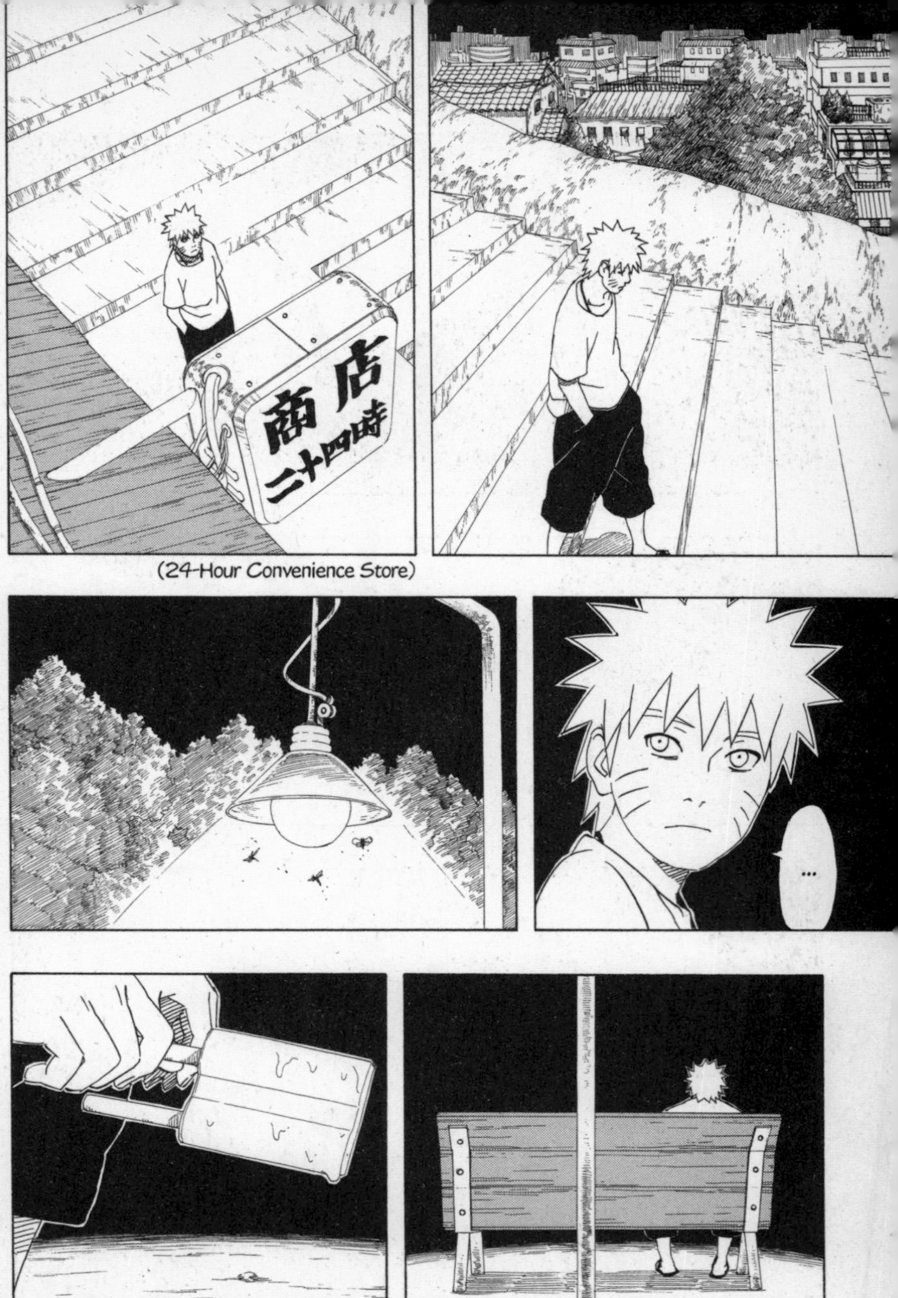
商店
二十四時
(24-Hour Convenience Store)
...

READ THIS WAY

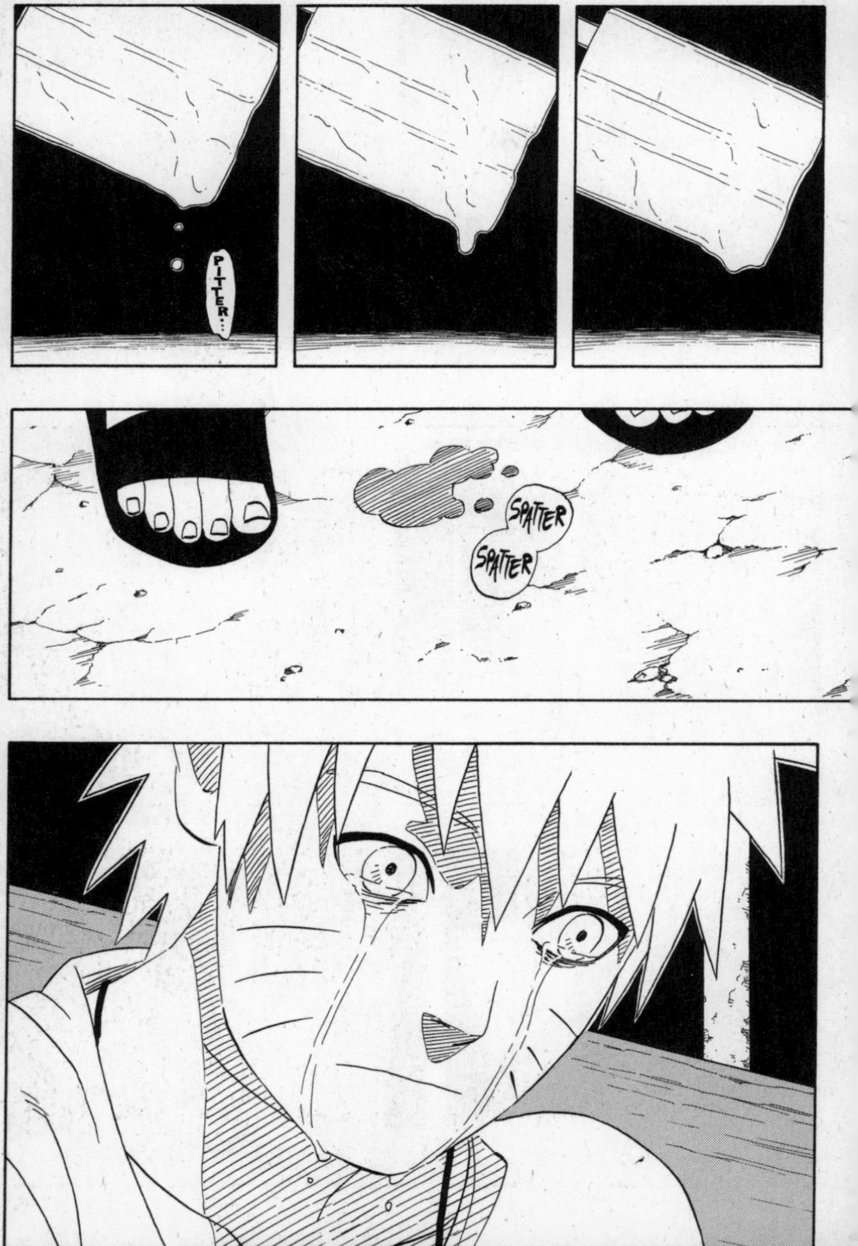
PITTER...
SPATTER
SPATTER

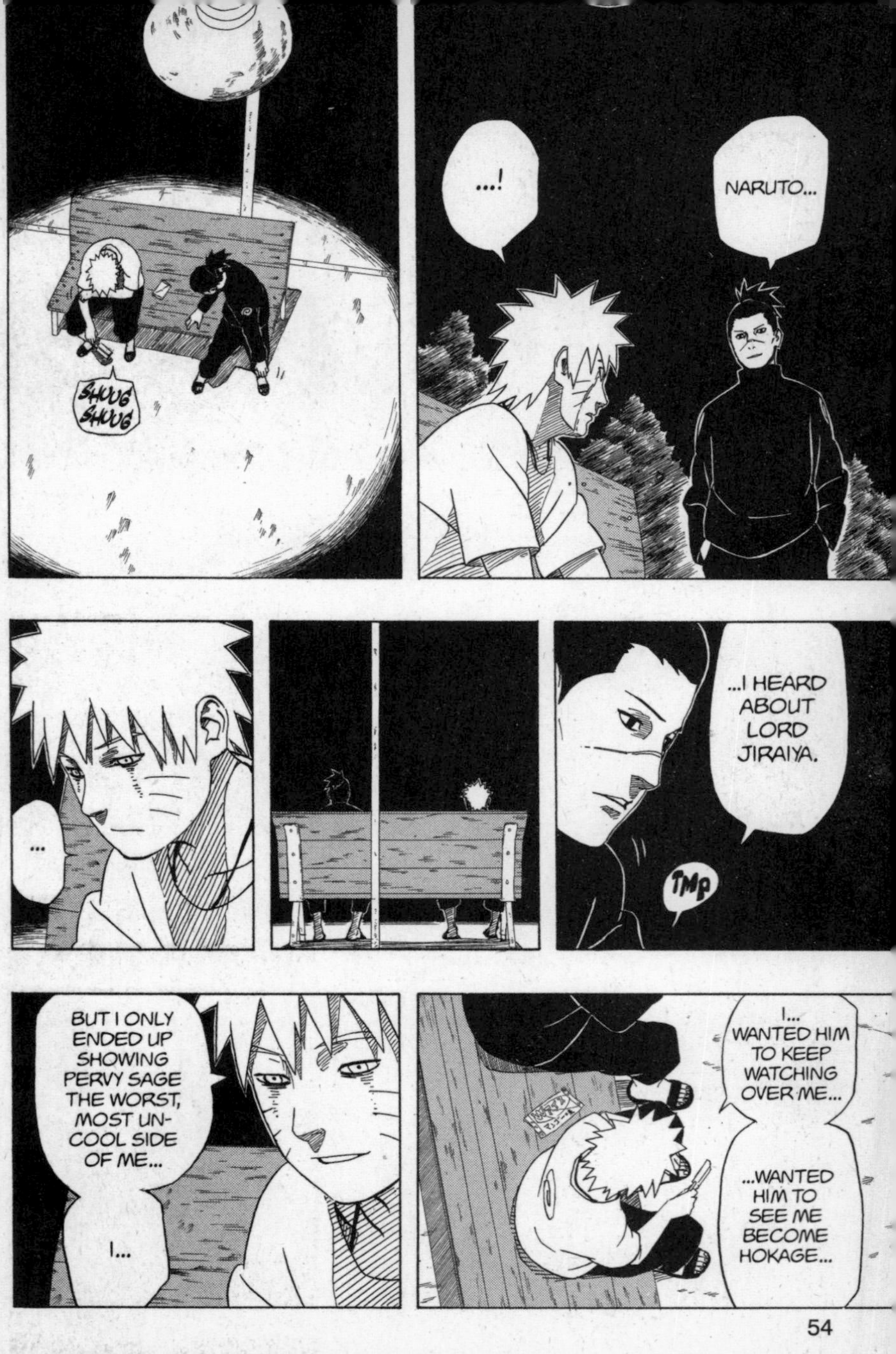
NARUTO...
...!
SHUUG SHUUG
...I HEARD ABOUT LORD JIRAIYA.
TMP
...
I... WANTED HIM TO KEEP WATCHING OVER ME...
...WANTED HIM TO SEE ME BECOME HOKAGE...
BUT I ONLY ENDED UP SHOWING PERVY SAGE THE WORST, MOST UN-COOL SIDE OF ME...
I...

READ THIS WAY

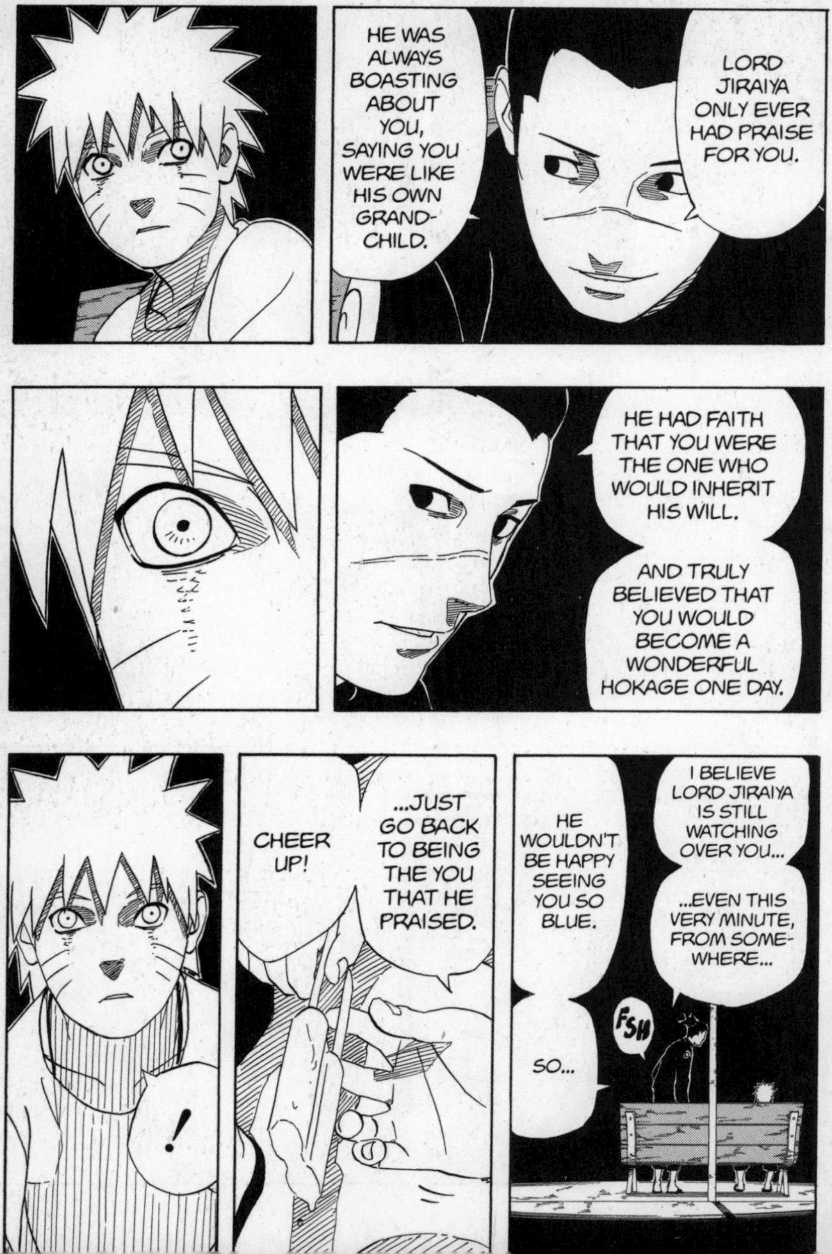

LORD JIRAIYA ONLY EVER HAD PRAISE FOR YOU.
HE WAS ALWAYS BOASTING ABOUT YOU, SAYING YOU WERE LIKE HIS OWN GRAND-CHILD.
HE HAD FAITH THAT YOU WERE THE ONE WHO WOULD INHERIT HIS WILL.
AND TRULY BELIEVED THAT YOU WOULD BECOME A WONDERFUL HOKAGE ONE DAY.
I BELIEVE LORD JIRAIYA IS STILL WATCHING OVER YOU...
...EVEN THIS VERY MINUTE, FROM SOME-WHERE...
HE WOULDN'T BE HAPPY SEEING YOU SO BLUE.
SO...
FSH
...JUST GO BACK TO BEING THE YOU THAT HE PRAISED.
CHEER UP!
!

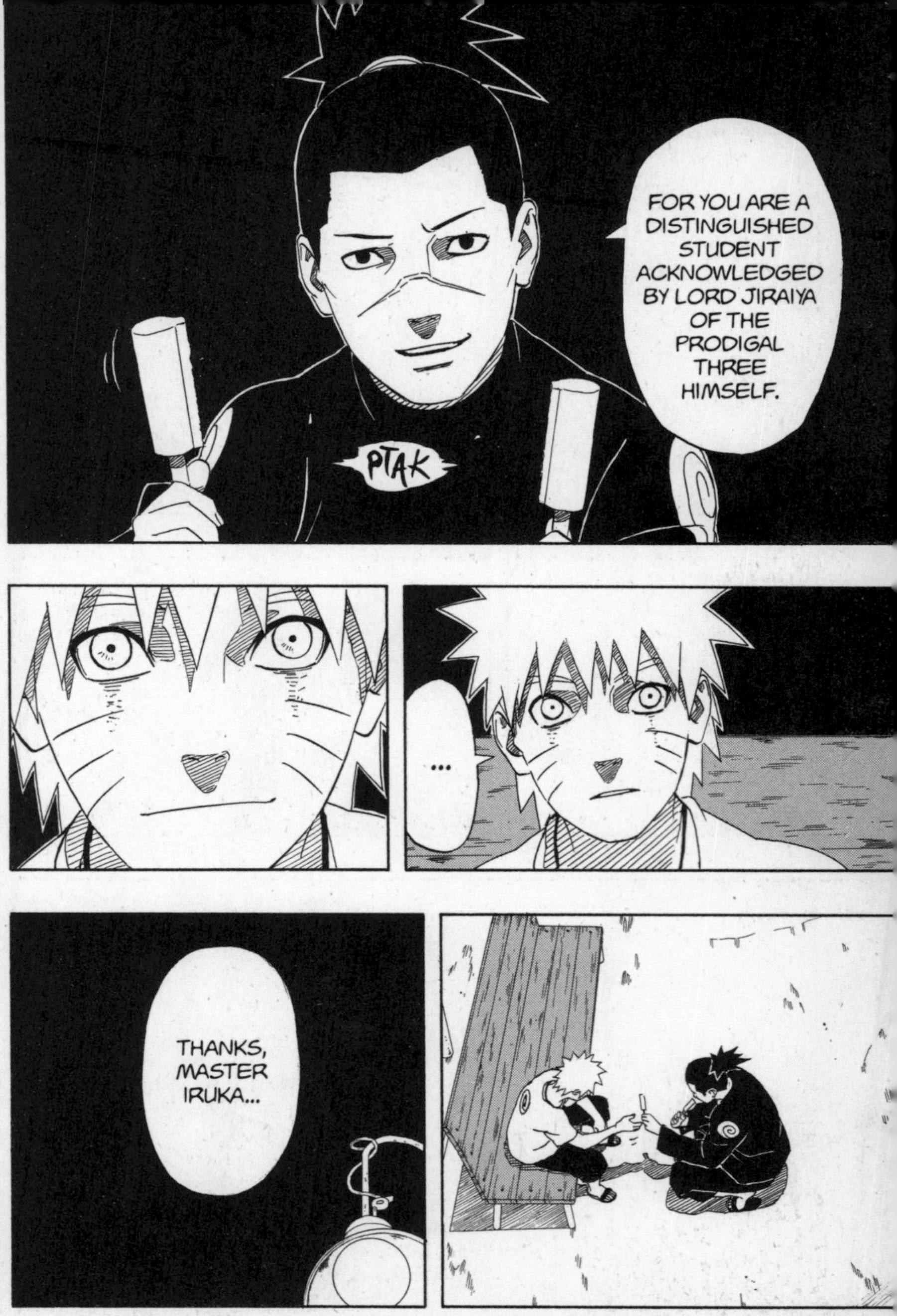
FOR YOU ARE A DISTINGUISHED STUDENT ACKNOWLEDGED BY LORD JIRAIYA OF THE PRODIGAL THREE HIMSELF.
PTAK
...
THANKS, MASTER IRUKA...

READ THIS WAY

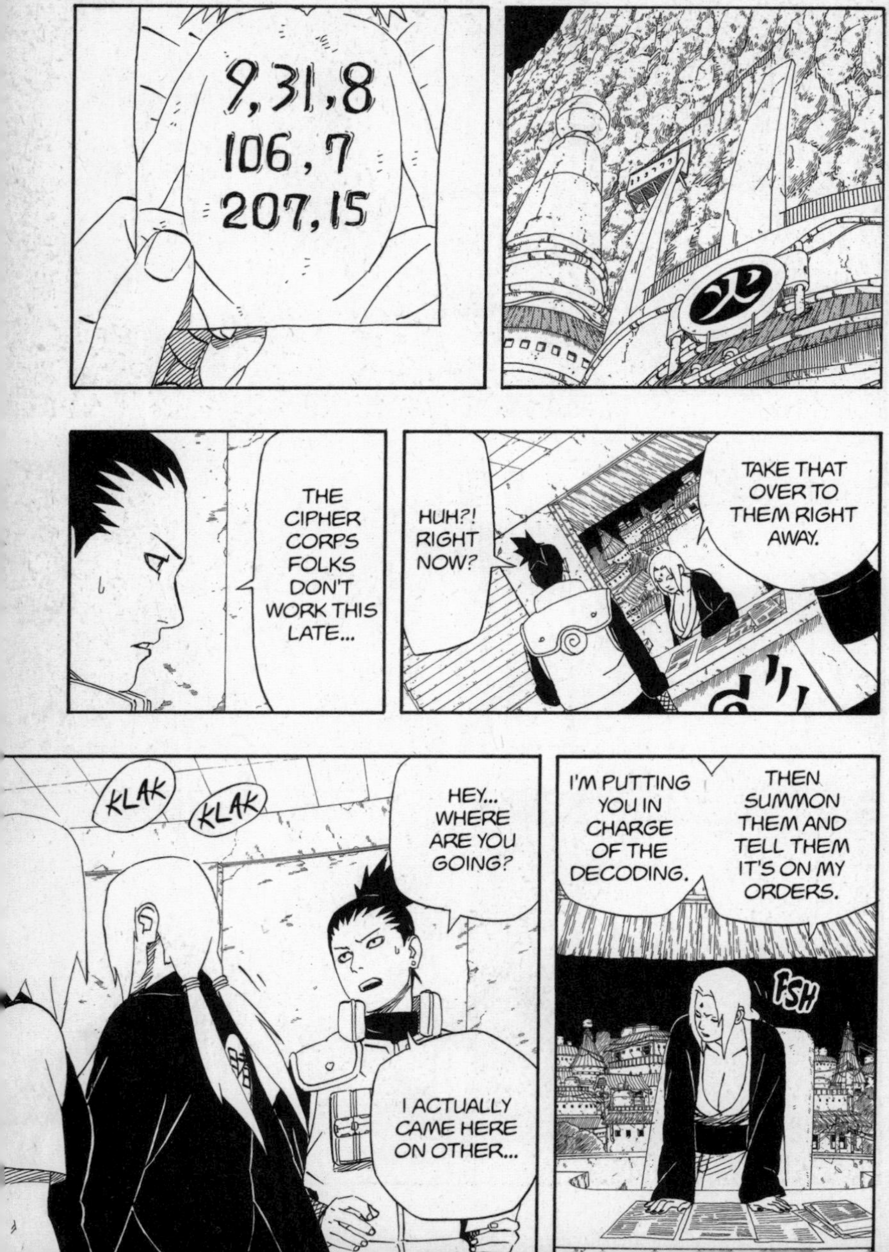
9,31,8
106,7
207,15
TAKE THAT OVER TO THEM RIGHT AWAY.
HUH?! RIGHT NOW?
THE CIPHER CORPS FOLKS DON'T WORK THIS LATE...
THEN SUMMON THEM AND TELL THEM IT'S ON MY ORDERS.
I'M PUTTING YOU IN CHARGE OF THE DECODING.
FSH
HEY... WHERE ARE YOU GOING?
KLAK
KLAK
I ACTUALLY CAME HERE ON OTHER...

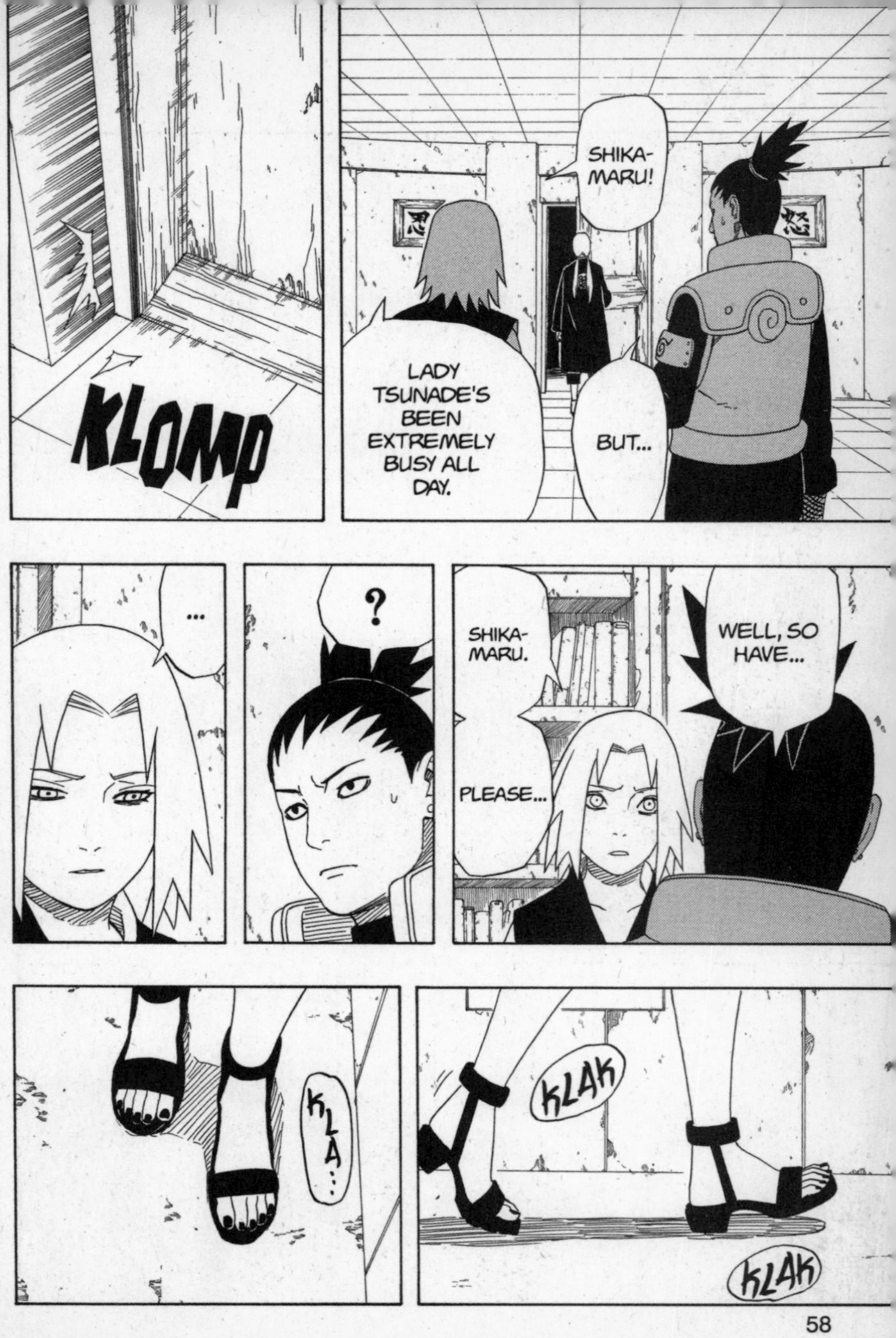

SHIKA-MARU!
LADY TSUNADE'S BEEN EXTREMELY BUSY ALL DAY.
BUT...
KLOMP
WELL, SO HAVE...
SHIKA-MARU.
PLEASE...
?
...
KLAK
KLAK
KLA...

READ THIS WAY

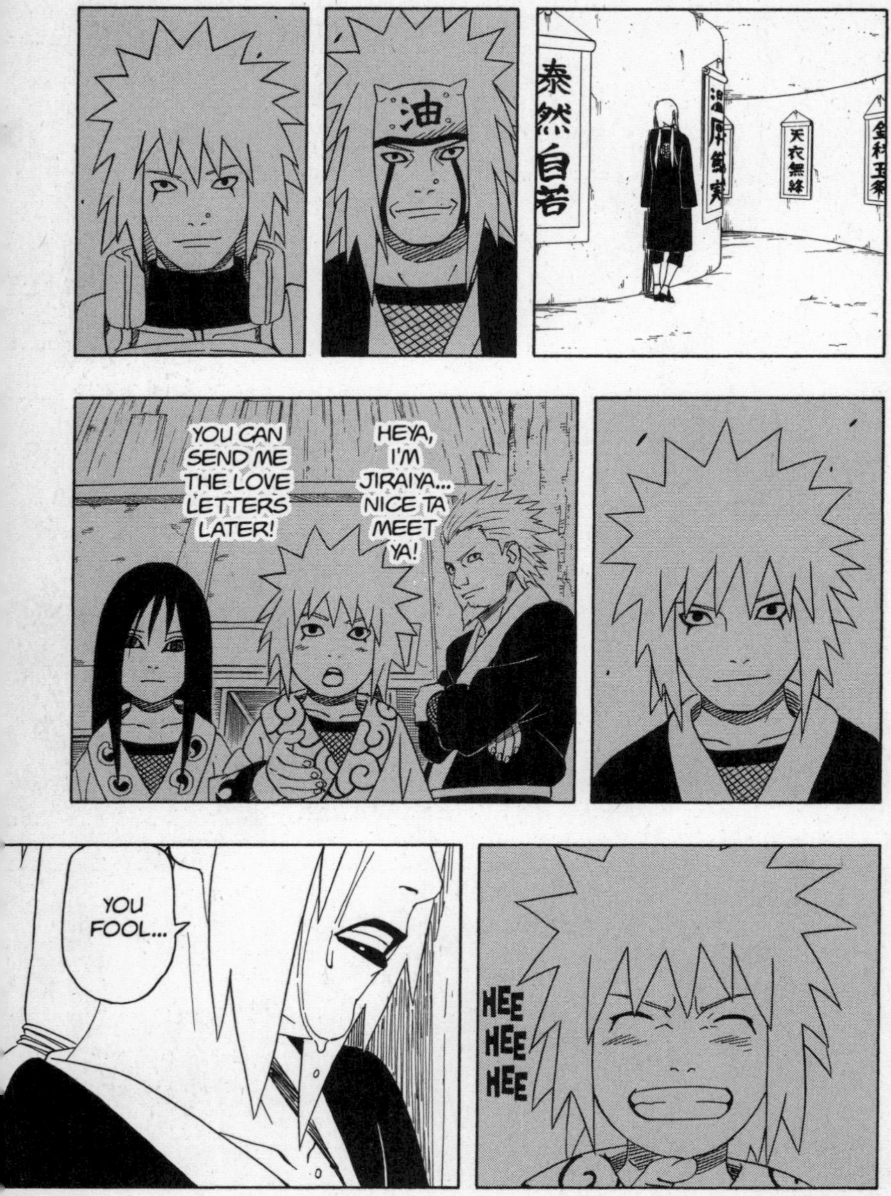
泰然自若
天衣無縫
油
HEYA, I'M JIRAIYA... NICE TA MEET YA!
YOU CAN SEND ME THE LOVE LETTERS LATER!
HEE HEE HEE
YOU FOOL...

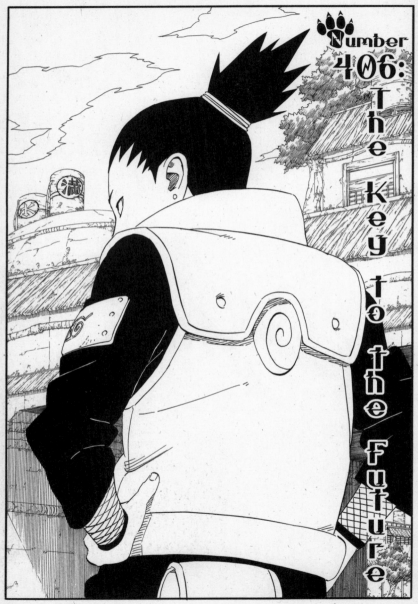

Number 406: The Key to the Future

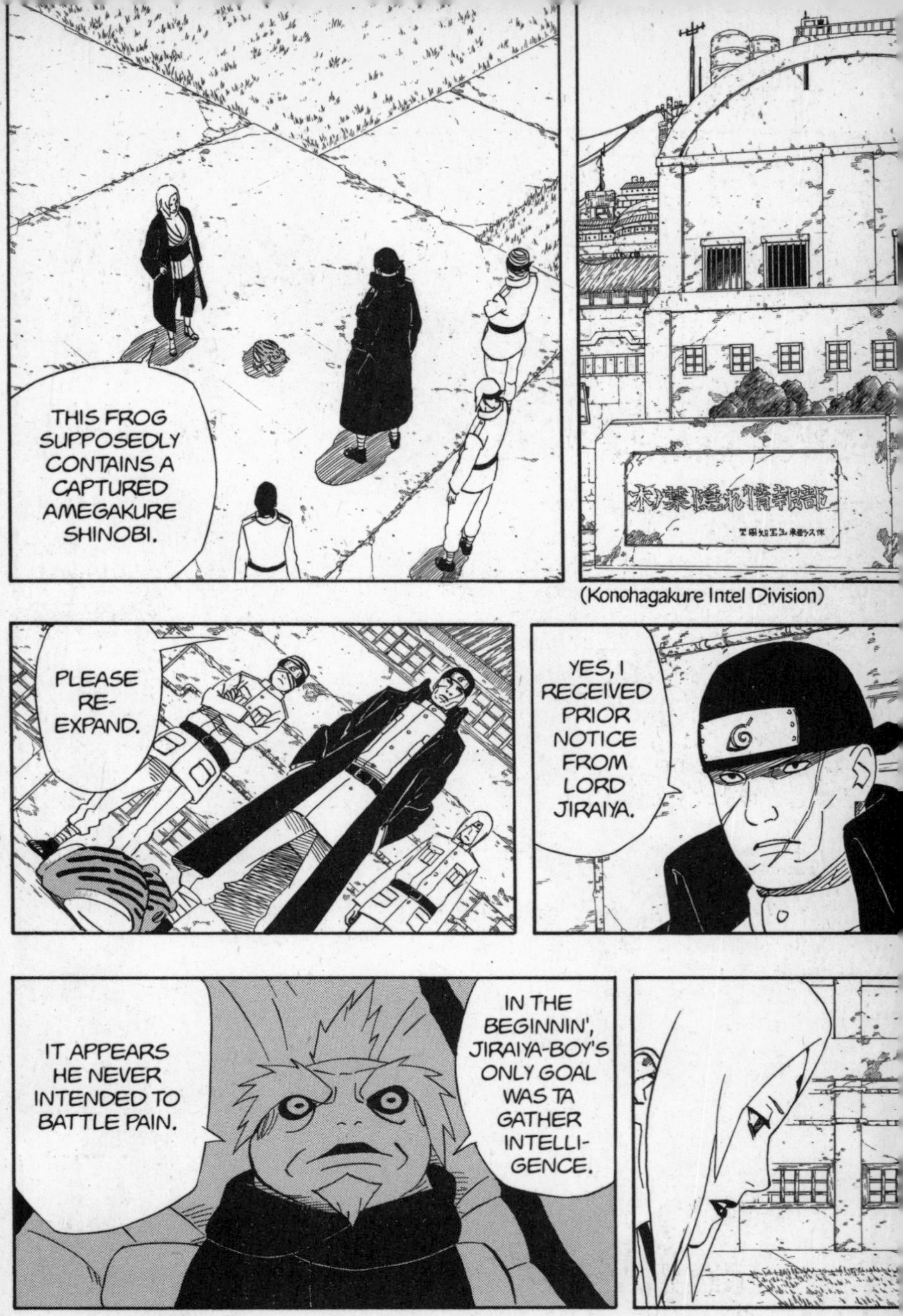
(Konohagakure Intel Division)
THIS FROG SUPPOSEDLY CONTAINS A CAPTURED AMEGAKURE SHINOBI.
YES, I RECEIVED PRIOR NOTICE FROM LORD JIRAIYA.
PLEASE RE-EXPAND.
IN THE BEGINNIN', JIRAIYA-BOY'S ONLY GOAL WAS TA GATHER INTELLI-GENCE.
IT APPEARS HE NEVER INTENDED TO BATTLE PAIN.

READ THIS WAY

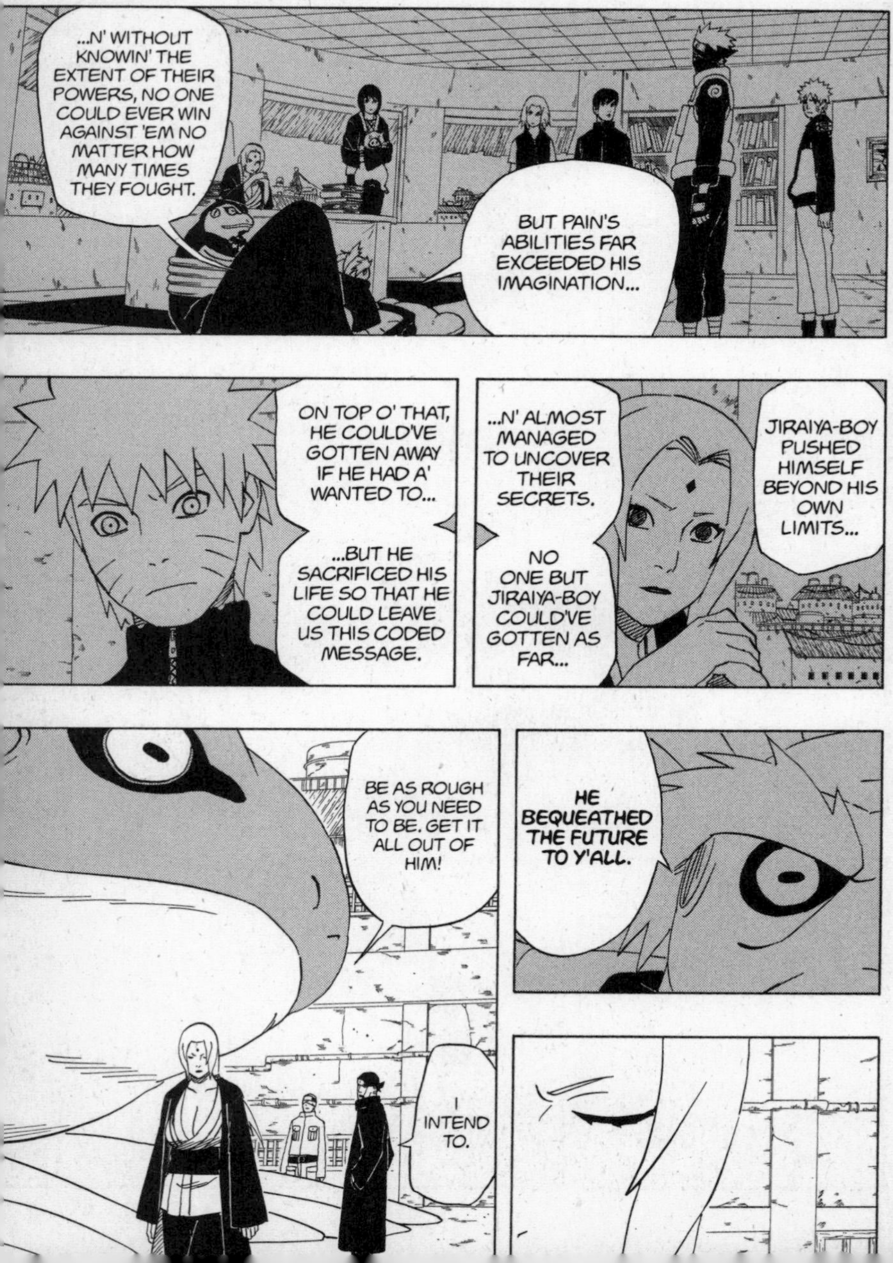
...N' WITHOUT KNOWIN' THE EXTENT OF THEIR POWERS, NO ONE COULD EVER WIN AGAINST 'EM NO MATTER HOW MANY TIMES THEY FOUGHT.
BUT PAIN'S ABILITIES FAR EXCEEDED HIS IMAGINATION...
JIRAIYA-BOY PUSHED HIMSELF BEYOND HIS OWN LIMITS...
...N' ALMOST MANAGED TO UNCOVER THEIR SECRETS.
NO ONE BUT JIRAIYA-BOY COULD'VE GOTTEN AS FAR...
ON TOP O' THAT, HE COULD'VE GOTTEN AWAY IF HE HAD A' WANTED TO...
...BUT HE SACRIFICED HIS LIFE SO THAT HE COULD LEAVE US THIS CODED MESSAGE.
HE BEQUEATHED THE FUTURE TO Y'ALL.
BE AS ROUGH AS YOU NEED TO BE. GET IT ALL OUT OF HIM!
I INTEND TO.

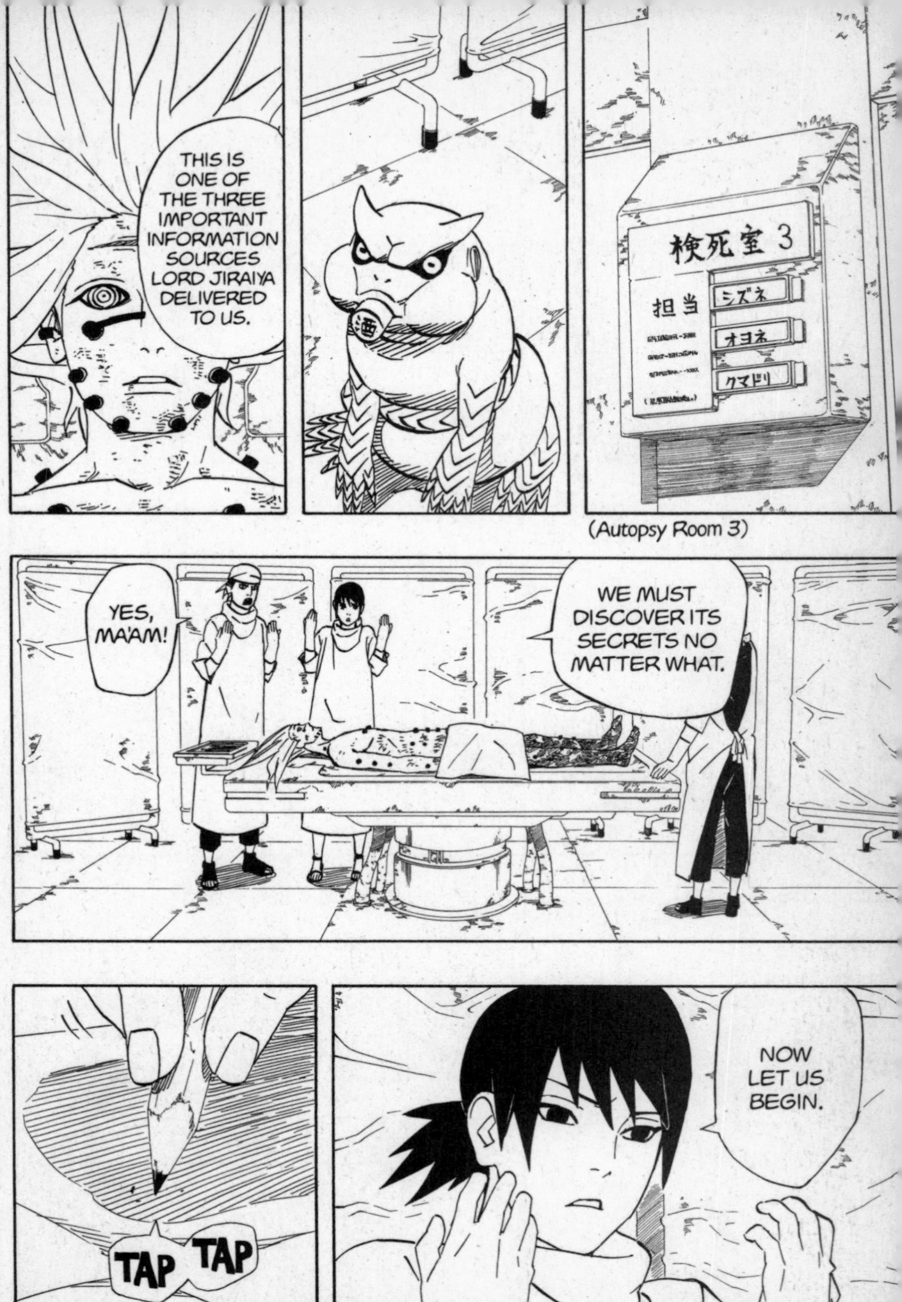
検死室 3
担当
シズネ
オヨネ
クマドリ
(Autopsy Room 3)
酒
THIS IS ONE OF THE THREE IMPORTANT INFORMATION SOURCES LORD JIRAIYA DELIVERED TO US.
WE MUST DISCOVER ITS SECRETS NO MATTER WHAT.
YES, MA'AM!
NOW LET US BEGIN.
TAP TAP

READ THIS WAY

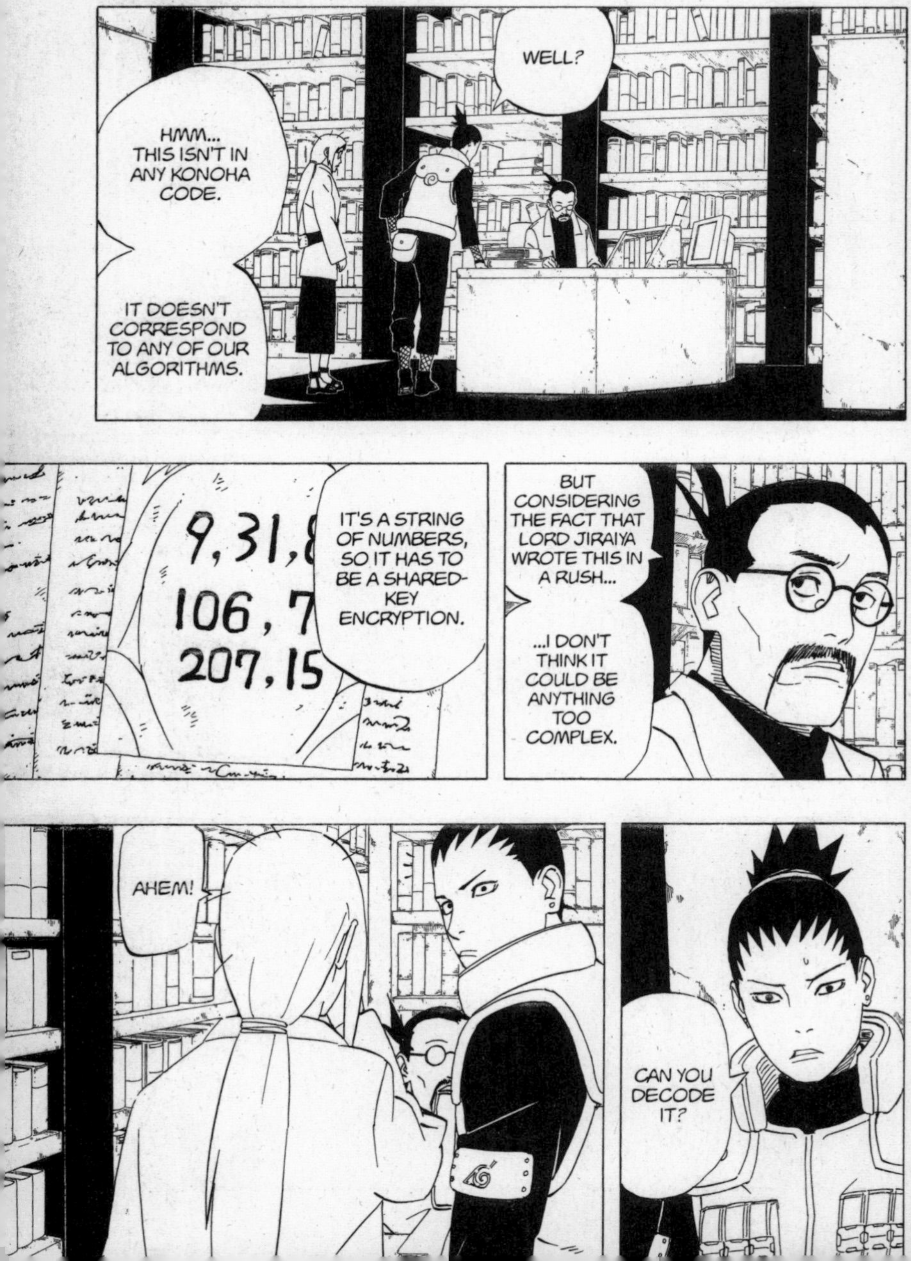
WELL?
HMM... THIS ISN'T IN ANY KONOHA CODE.
IT DOESN'T CORRESPOND TO ANY OF OUR ALGORITHMS.
BUT CONSIDERING THE FACT THAT LORD JIRAIYA WROTE THIS IN A RUSH...
...I DON'T THINK IT COULD BE ANYTHING TOO COMPLEX.
IT'S A STRING OF NUMBERS, SO IT HAS TO BE A SHARED-KEY ENCRYPTION.
9, 31, 8
106, 7
207, 15
CAN YOU DECODE IT?
AHEM!

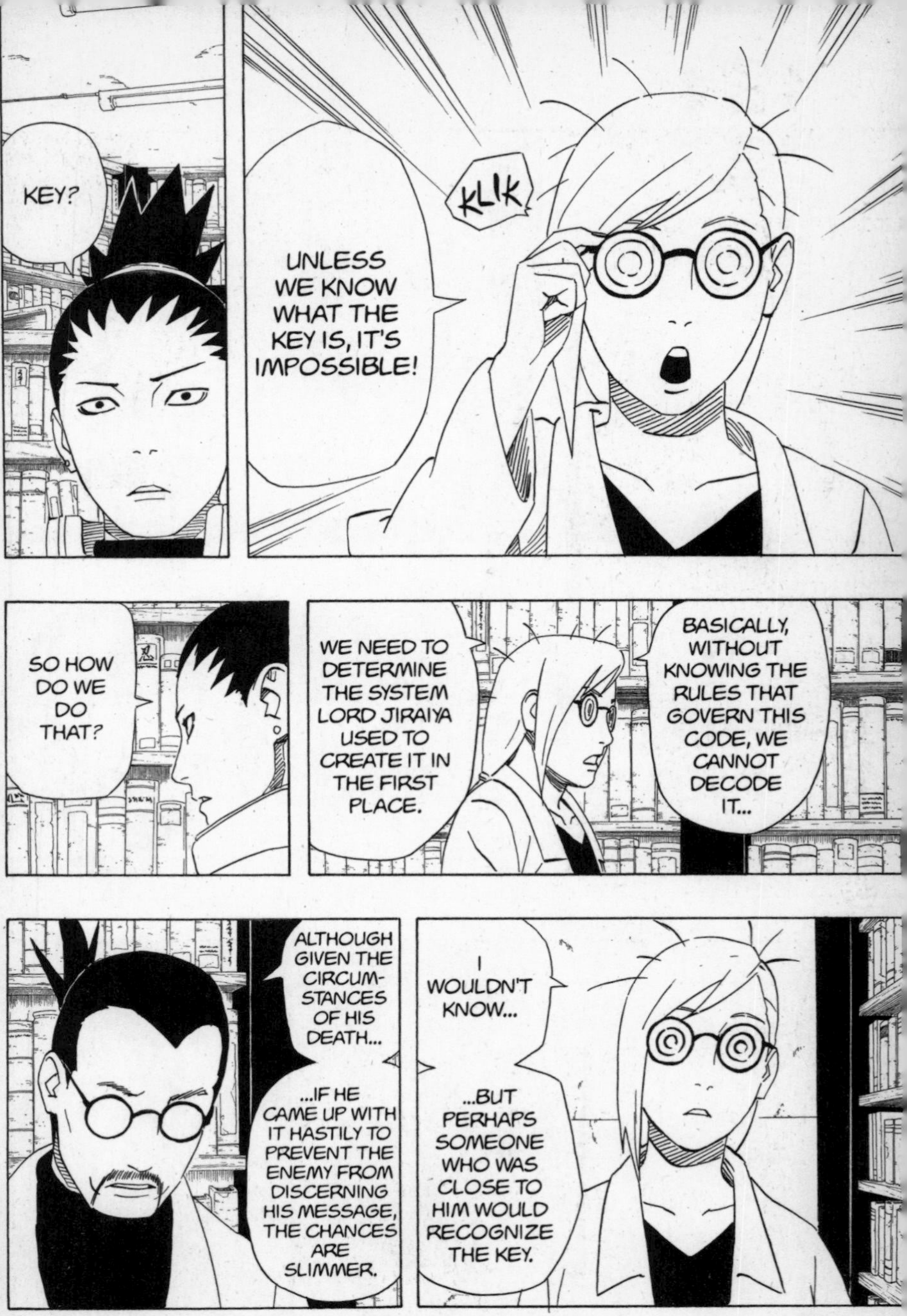
KLIK
UNLESS WE KNOW WHAT THE KEY IS, IT'S IMPOSSIBLE!
KEY?
BASICALLY, WITHOUT KNOWING THE RULES THAT GOVERN THIS CODE, WE CANNOT DECODE IT...
WE NEED TO DETERMINE THE SYSTEM LORD JIRAIYA USED TO CREATE IT IN THE FIRST PLACE.
SO HOW DO WE DO THAT?
I WOULDN'T KNOW...
...BUT PERHAPS SOMEONE WHO WAS CLOSE TO HIM WOULD RECOGNIZE THE KEY.
ALTHOUGH GIVEN THE CIRCUM-STANCES OF HIS DEATH...
...IF HE CAME UP WITH IT HASTILY TO PREVENT THE ENEMY FROM DISCERNING HIS MESSAGE, THE CHANCES ARE SLIMMER.

READ THIS WAY

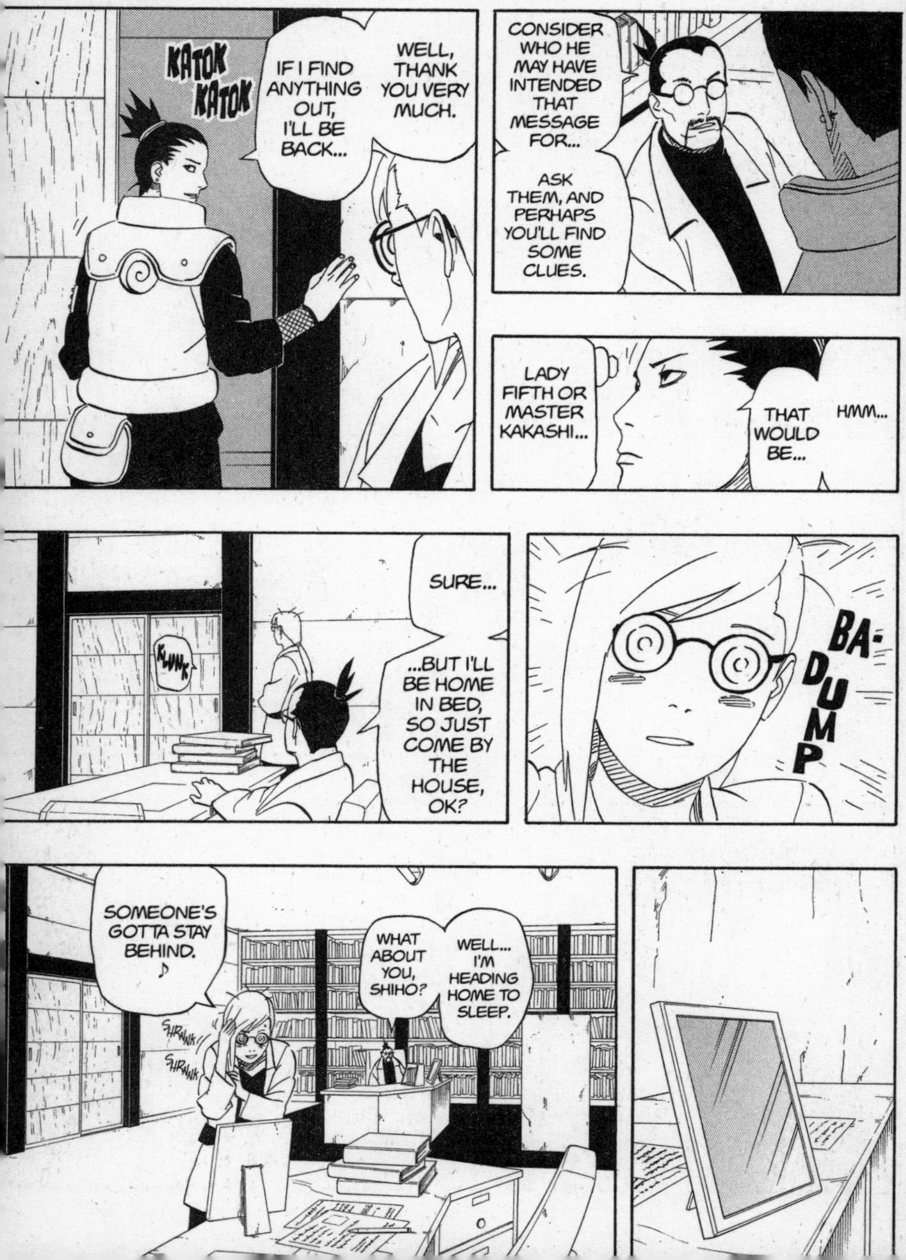
CONSIDER WHO HE MAY HAVE INTENDED THAT MESSAGE FOR...
ASK THEM, AND PERHAPS YOU'LL FIND SOME CLUES.
HMM...
THAT WOULD BE...
LADY FIFTH OR MASTER KAKASHI...
WELL, THANK YOU VERY MUCH.
IF I FIND ANYTHING OUT, I'LL BE BACK...
KATOK KATOK
BA-DUMP
SURE...
...BUT I'LL BE HOME IN BED, SO JUST COME BY THE HOUSE, OK?
KLUNK
WELL... I'M HEADING HOME TO SLEEP.
WHAT ABOUT YOU, SHIHO?
SOMEONE'S GOTTA STAY BEHIND. ♪
SHRNK
SHRNK

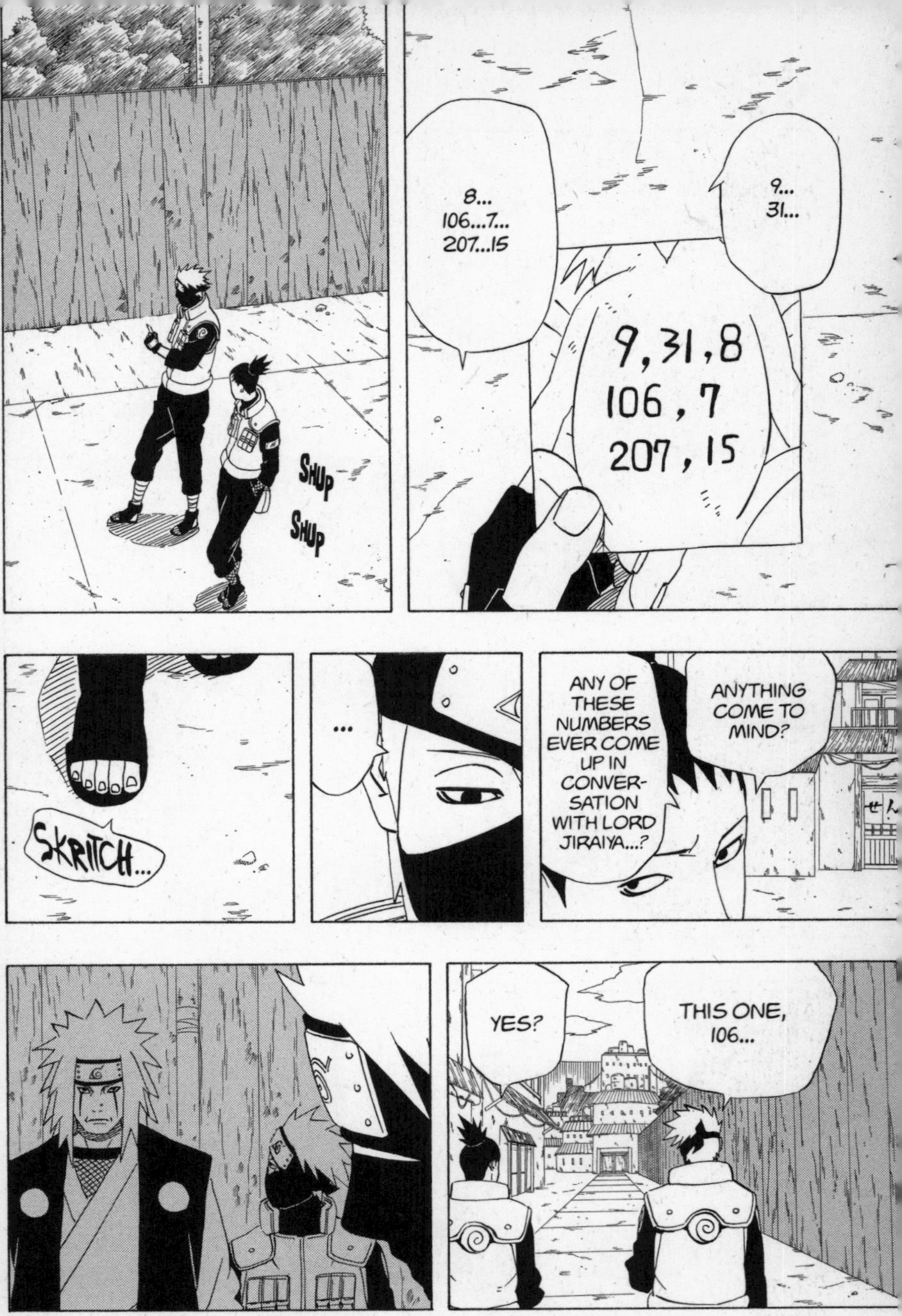
9... 31...
8... 106...7... 207...15
9,31,8 106,7 207,15
SHUP
SHUP
ANYTHING COME TO MIND?
ANY OF THESE NUMBERS EVER COME UP IN CONVERSATION WITH LORD JIRAIYA...?
...
SKRITCH...
THIS ONE, 106...
YES?

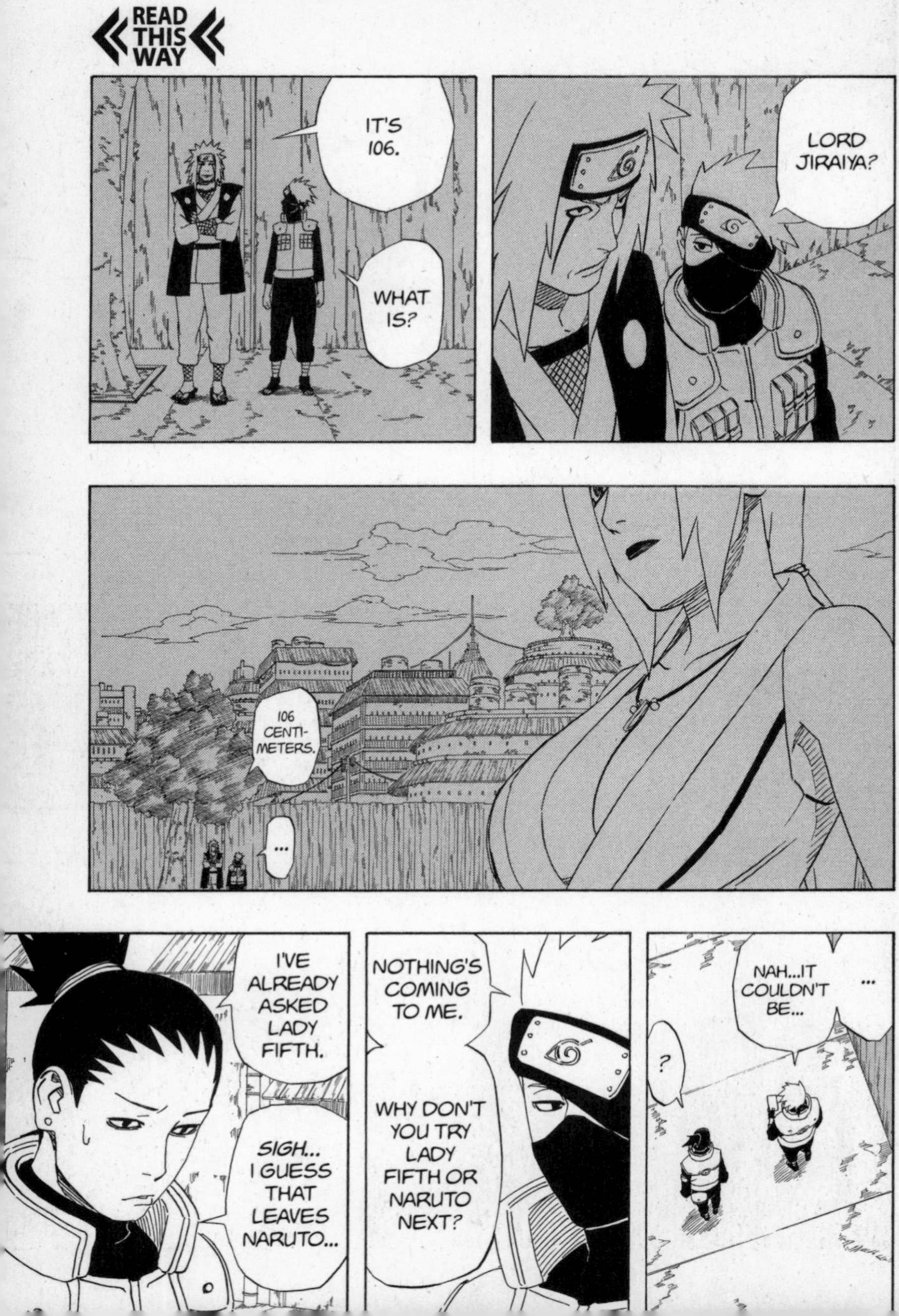
READ THIS WAY
LORD JIRAIYA?
IT'S 106.
WHAT IS?
106 CENTIMETERS.
...
...
NAH...IT COULDN'T BE...
?
NOTHING'S COMING TO ME.
WHY DON'T YOU TRY LADY FIFTH OR NARUTO NEXT?
I'VE ALREADY ASKED LADY FIFTH.
SIGH... I GUESS THAT LEAVES NARUTO...

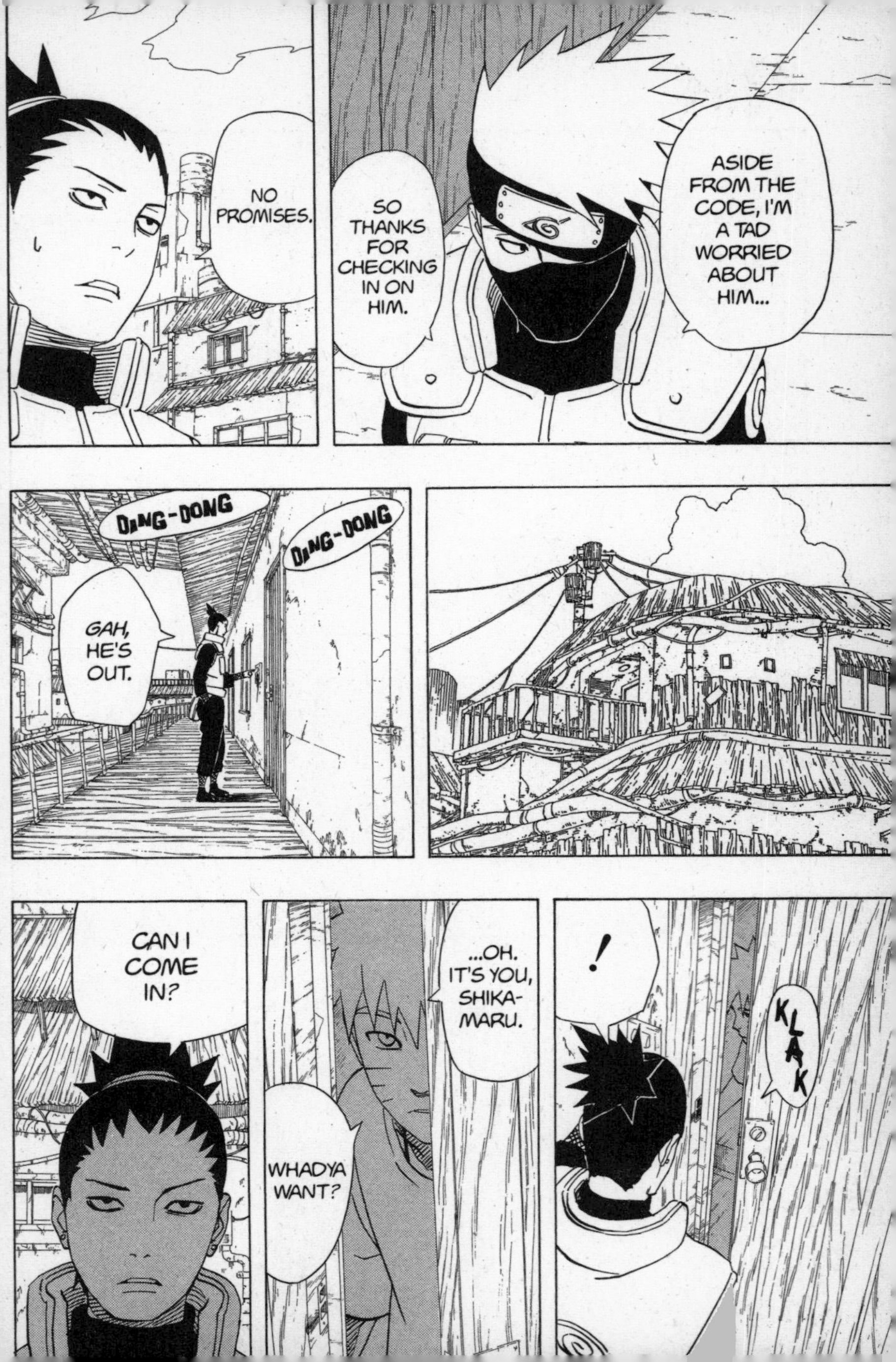
ASIDE FROM THE CODE, I'M A TAD WORRIED ABOUT HIM...
SO THANKS FOR CHECKING IN ON HIM.
NO PROMISES.
DING-DONG
DING-DONG
GAH, HE'S OUT.
KLAK
!
...OH. IT'S YOU, SHIKA-MARU.
WHADYA WANT?
CAN I COME IN?

READ THIS WAY

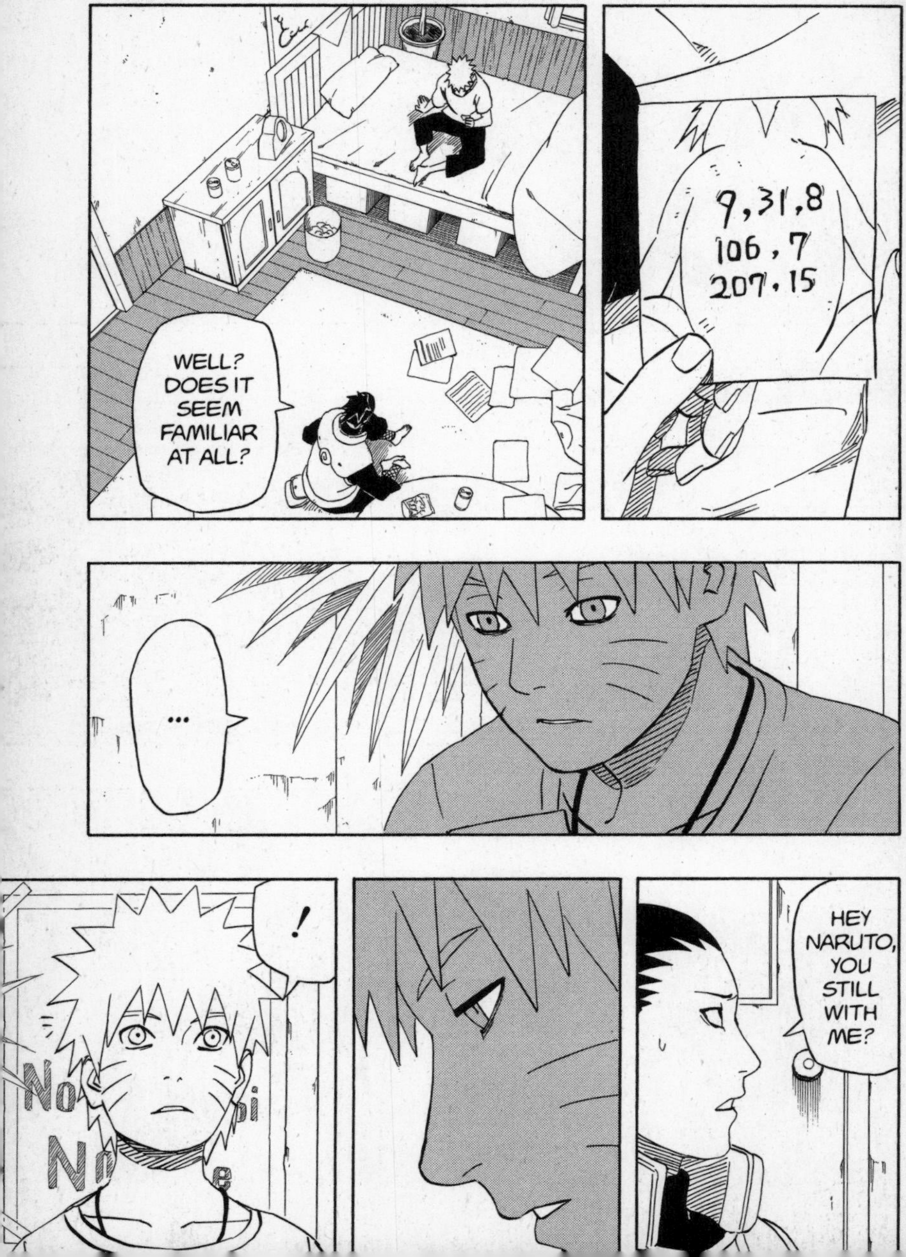
9, 31, 8
106, 7
207, 15
WELL? DOES IT SEEM FAMILIAR AT ALL?
...
HEY NARUTO, YOU STILL WITH ME?
!

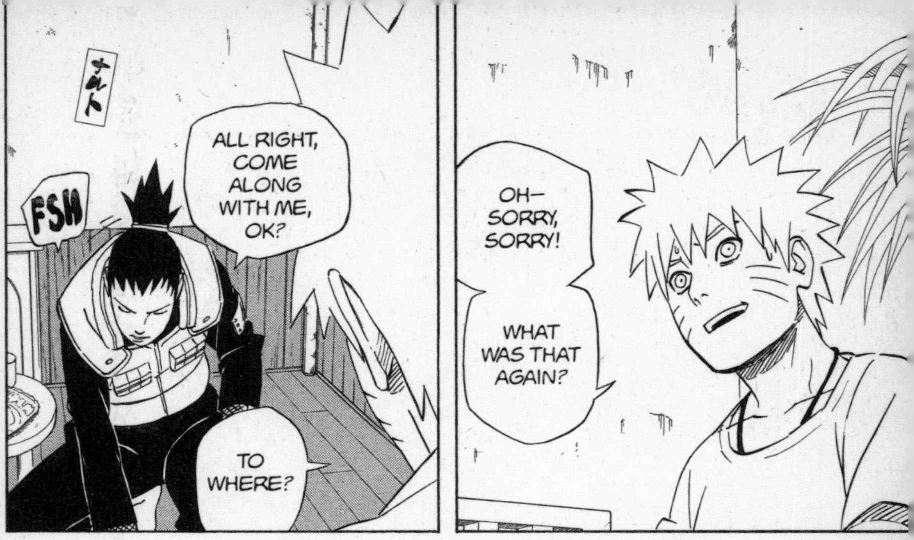
OH— SORRY, SORRY!
WHAT WAS THAT AGAIN?
ALL RIGHT, COME ALONG WITH ME, OK?
ナルト
FSH
TO WHERE?

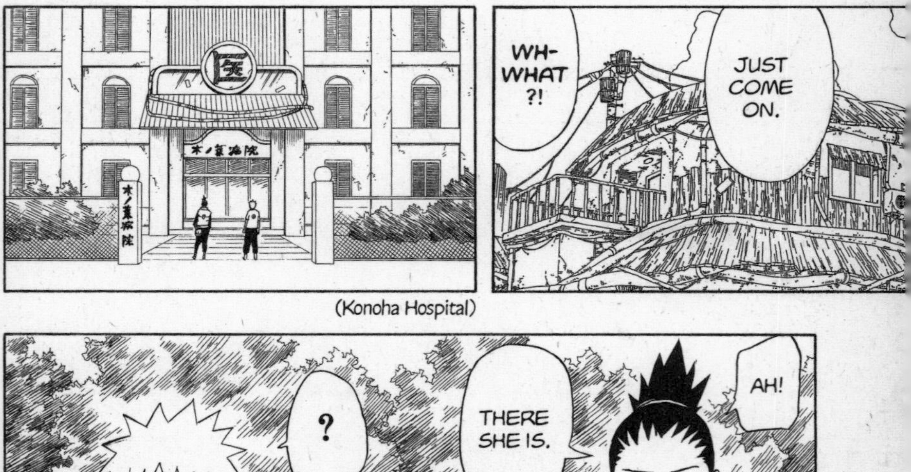
JUST COME ON.
WH- WHAT ?!

(Konoha Hospital)

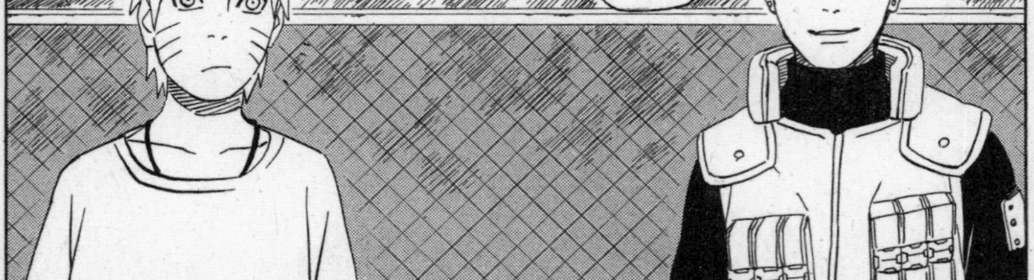
AH!
THERE SHE IS.
?

READ THIS WAY

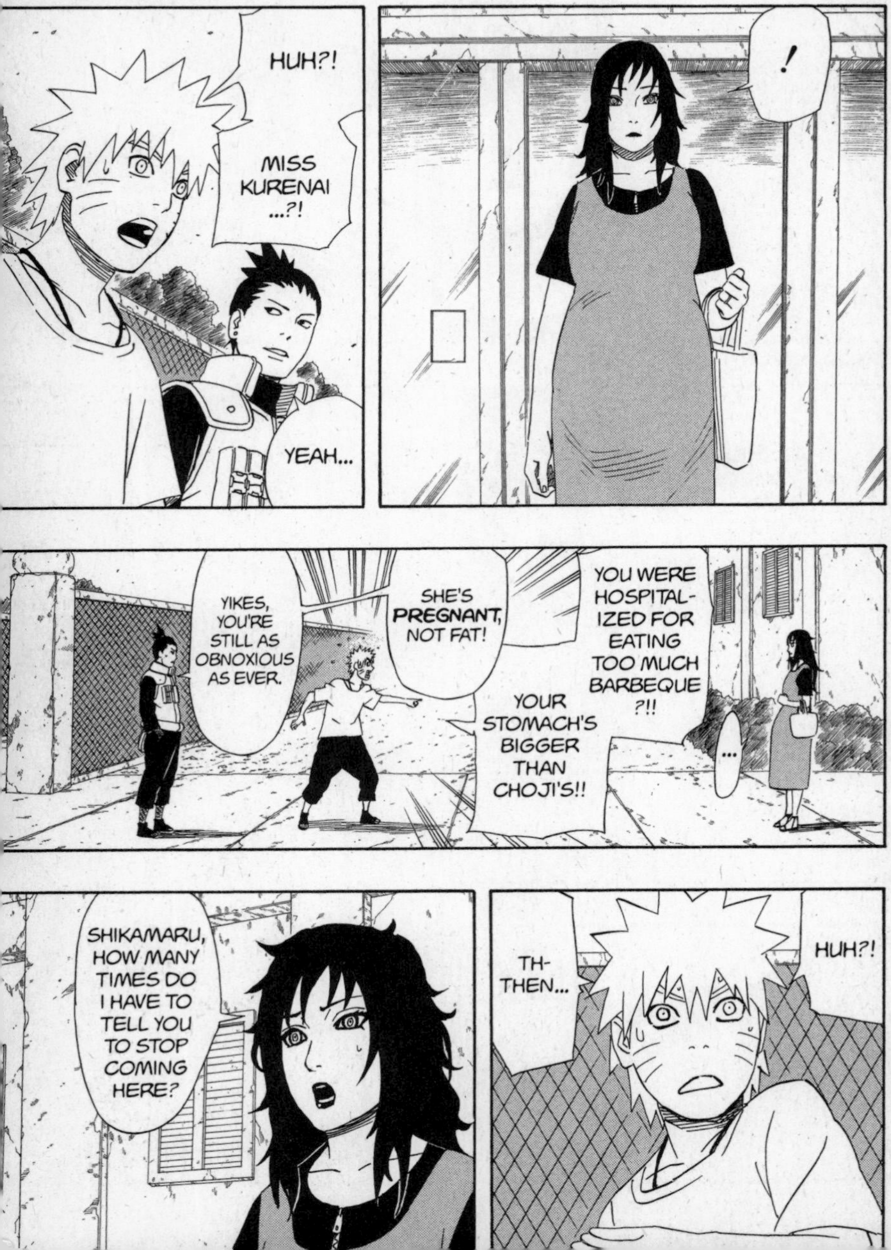
!
HUH?!
MISS KURENAI ...?!
YEAH...
...
YOU WERE HOSPITAL-IZED FOR EATING TOO MUCH BARBEQUE ?!!
YOUR STOMACH'S BIGGER THAN CHOJI'S!!
SHE'S **PREGNANT,** NOT FAT!
YIKES, YOU'RE STILL AS OBNOXIOUS AS EVER.
HUH?!
TH-THEN...
SHIKAMARU, HOW MANY TIMES DO I HAVE TO TELL YOU TO STOP COMING HERE?

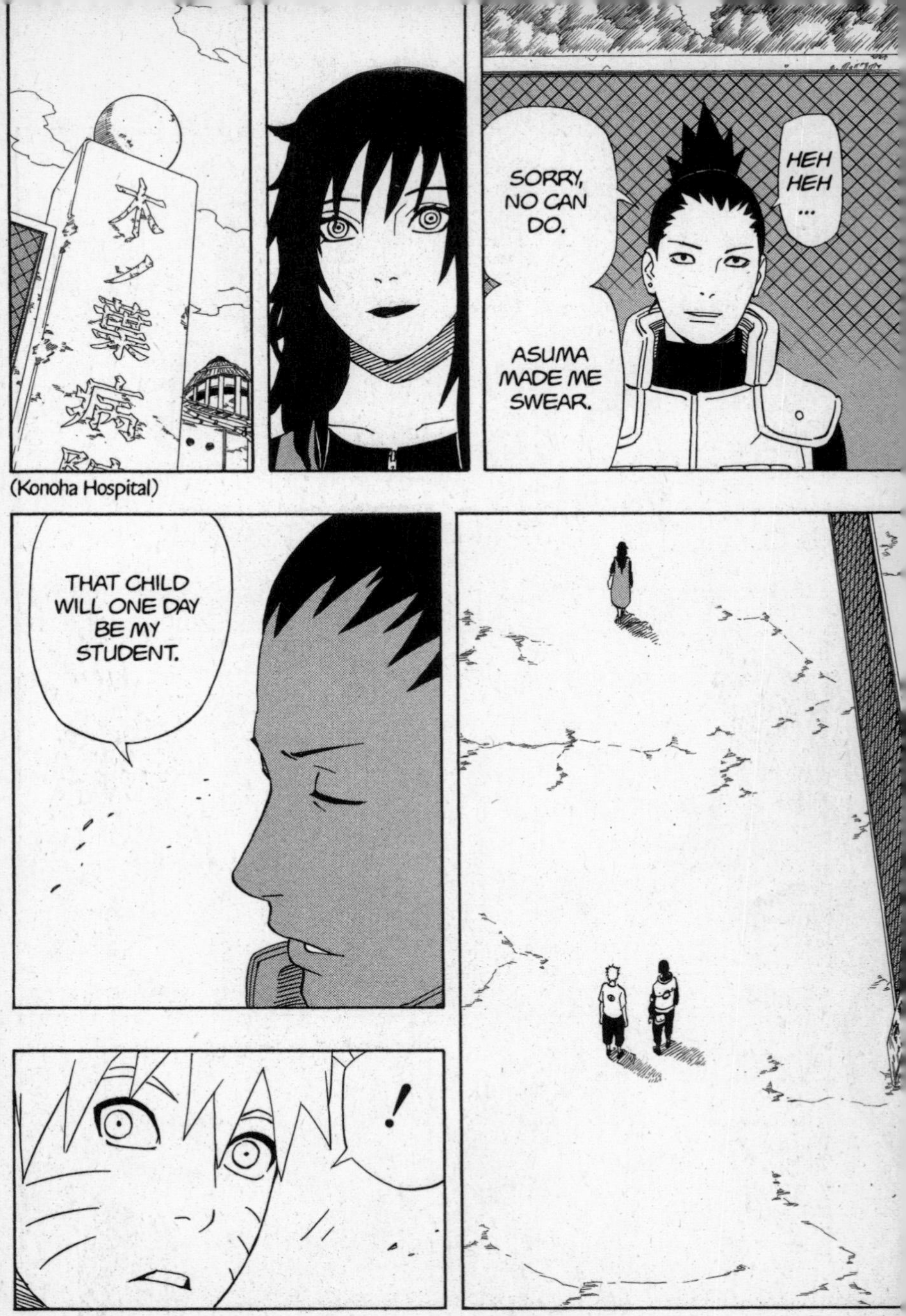
HEH HEH ...
SORRY, NO CAN DO.
ASUMA MADE ME SWEAR.
(Konoha Hospital)
THAT CHILD WILL ONE DAY BE MY STUDENT.
!

READ THIS WAY

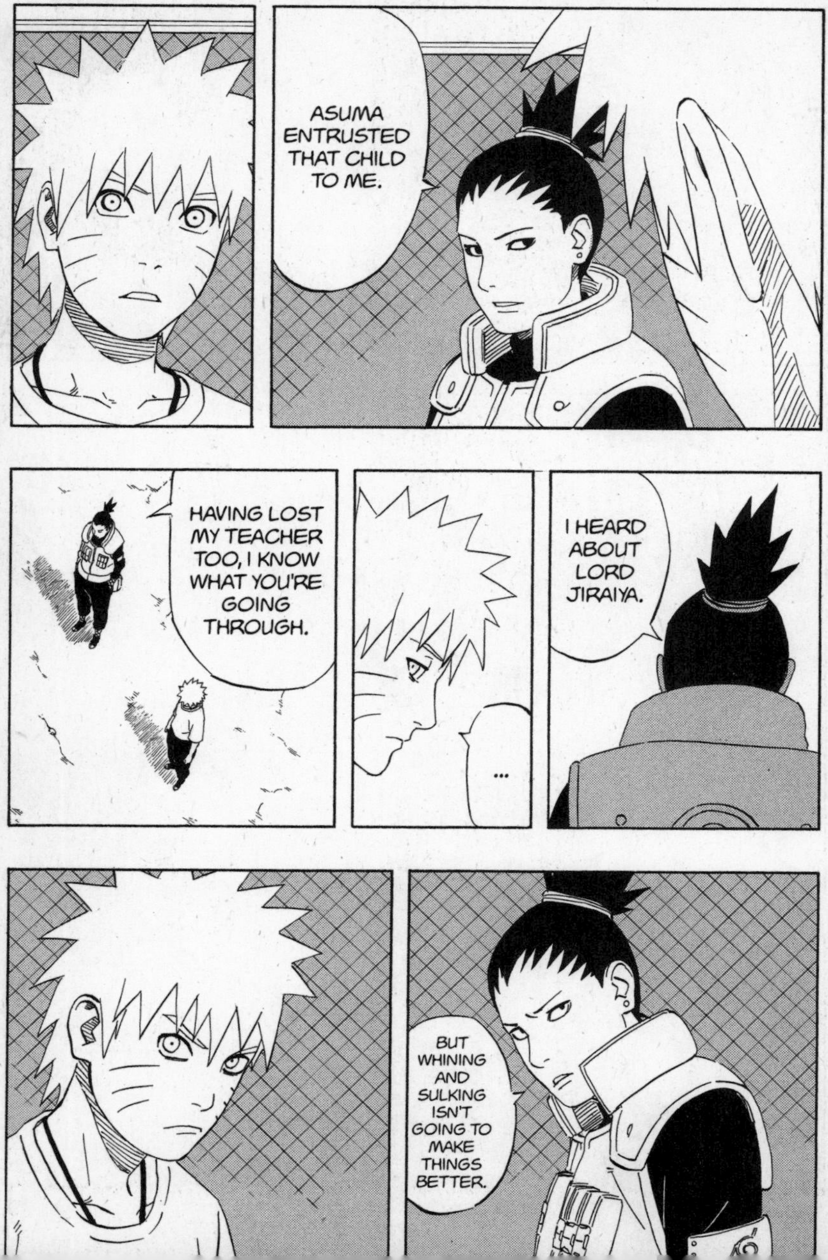
ASUMA ENTRUSTED THAT CHILD TO ME.
I HEARD ABOUT LORD JIRAIYA.
...
HAVING LOST MY TEACHER TOO, I KNOW WHAT YOU'RE GOING THROUGH.
BUT WHINING AND SULKING ISN'T GOING TO MAKE THINGS BETTER.

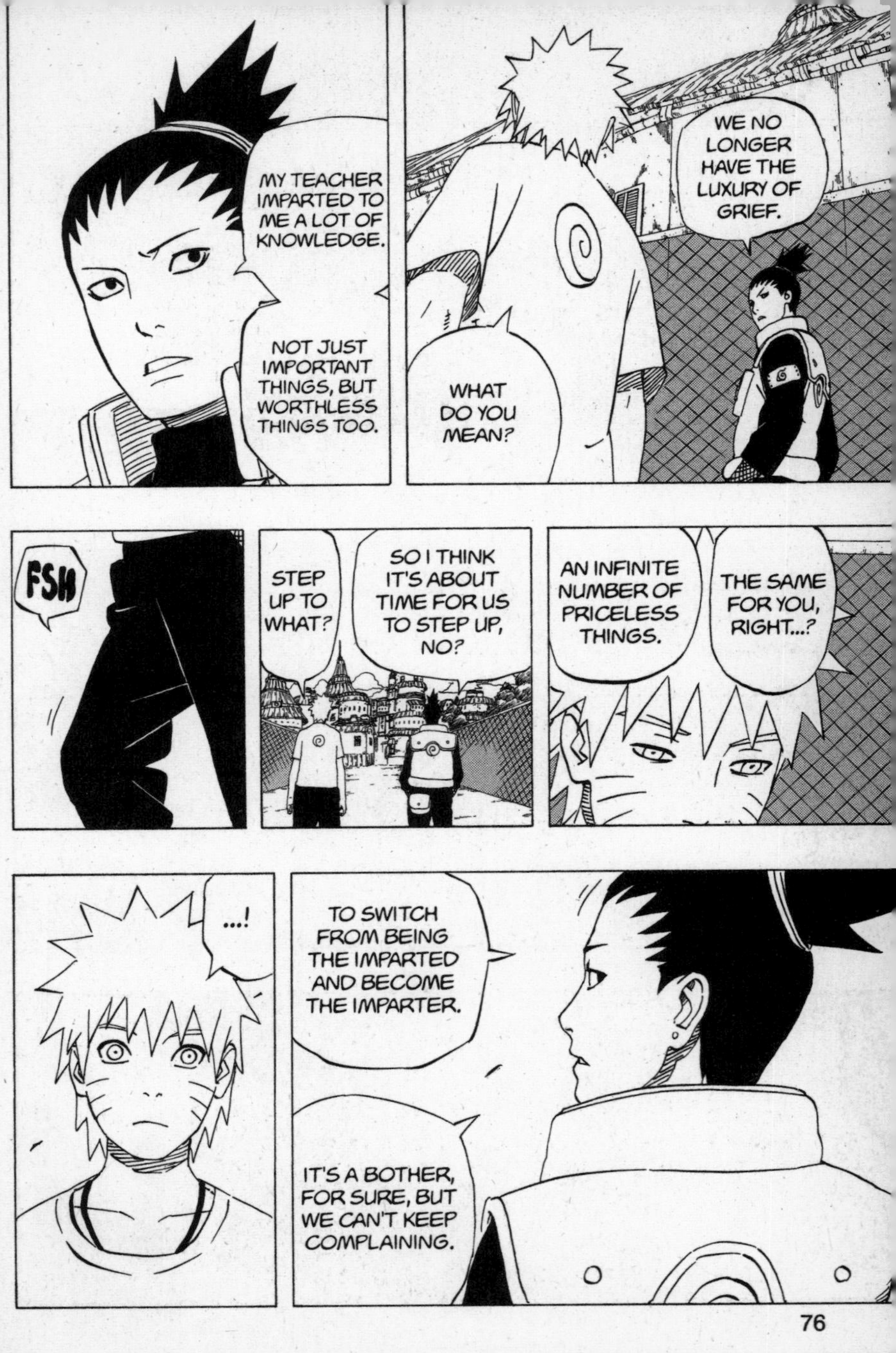
WE NO LONGER HAVE THE LUXURY OF GRIEF.
WHAT DO YOU MEAN?
MY TEACHER IMPARTED TO ME A LOT OF KNOWLEDGE.
NOT JUST IMPORTANT THINGS, BUT WORTHLESS THINGS TOO.
THE SAME FOR YOU, RIGHT...?
AN INFINITE NUMBER OF PRICELESS THINGS.
SO I THINK IT'S ABOUT TIME FOR US TO STEP UP, NO?
STEP UP TO WHAT?
FSH
TO SWITCH FROM BEING THE IMPARTED AND BECOME THE IMPARTER.
IT'S A BOTHER, FOR SURE, BUT WE CAN'T KEEP COMPLAINING.
...!

READ THIS WAY

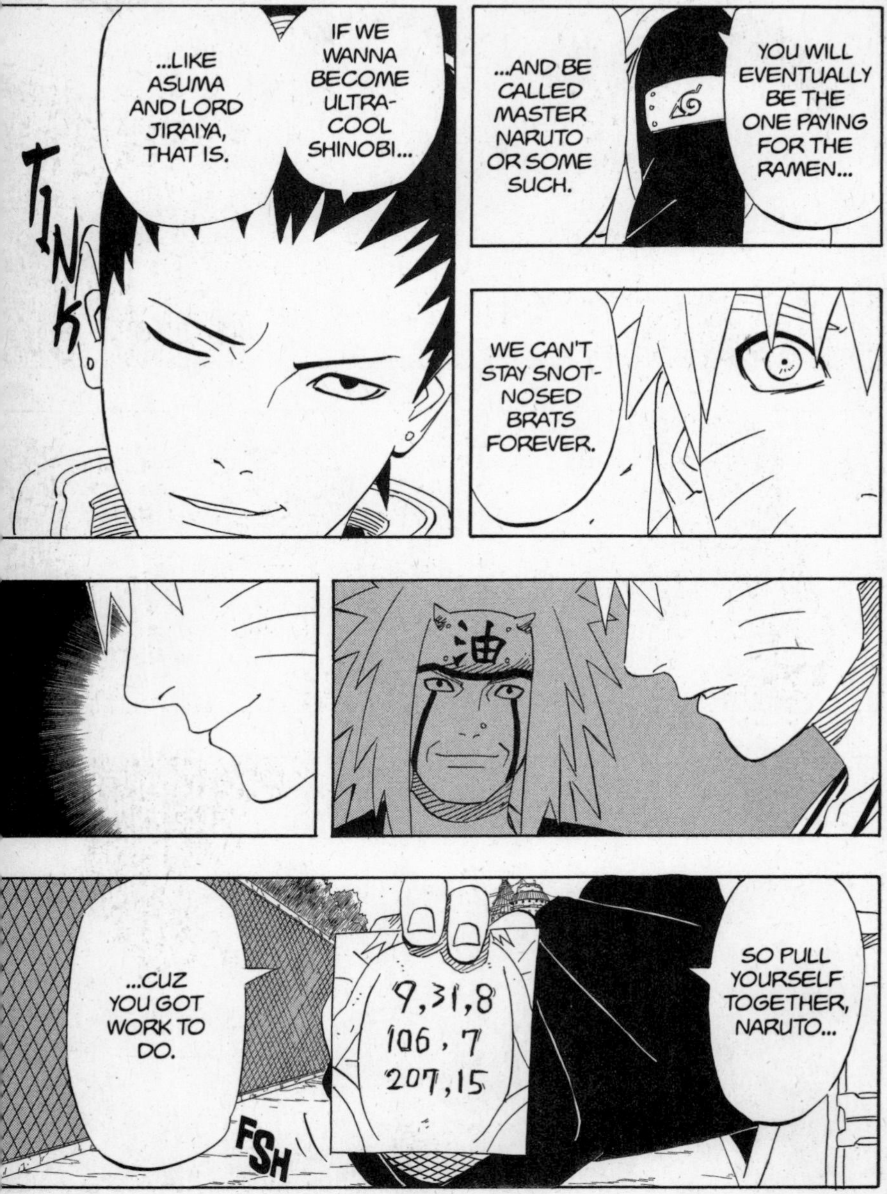

YOU WILL EVENTUALLY BE THE ONE PAYING FOR THE RAMEN...
...AND BE CALLED MASTER NARUTO OR SOME SUCH.
WE CAN'T STAY SNOT-NOSED BRATS FOREVER.
IF WE WANNA BECOME ULTRA-COOL SHINOBI...
...LIKE ASUMA AND LORD JIRAIYA, THAT IS.
TINK
SO PULL YOURSELF TOGETHER, NARUTO...
9,31,8
106,7
207,15
...CUZ YOU GOT WORK TO DO.
FSH

NARUTO

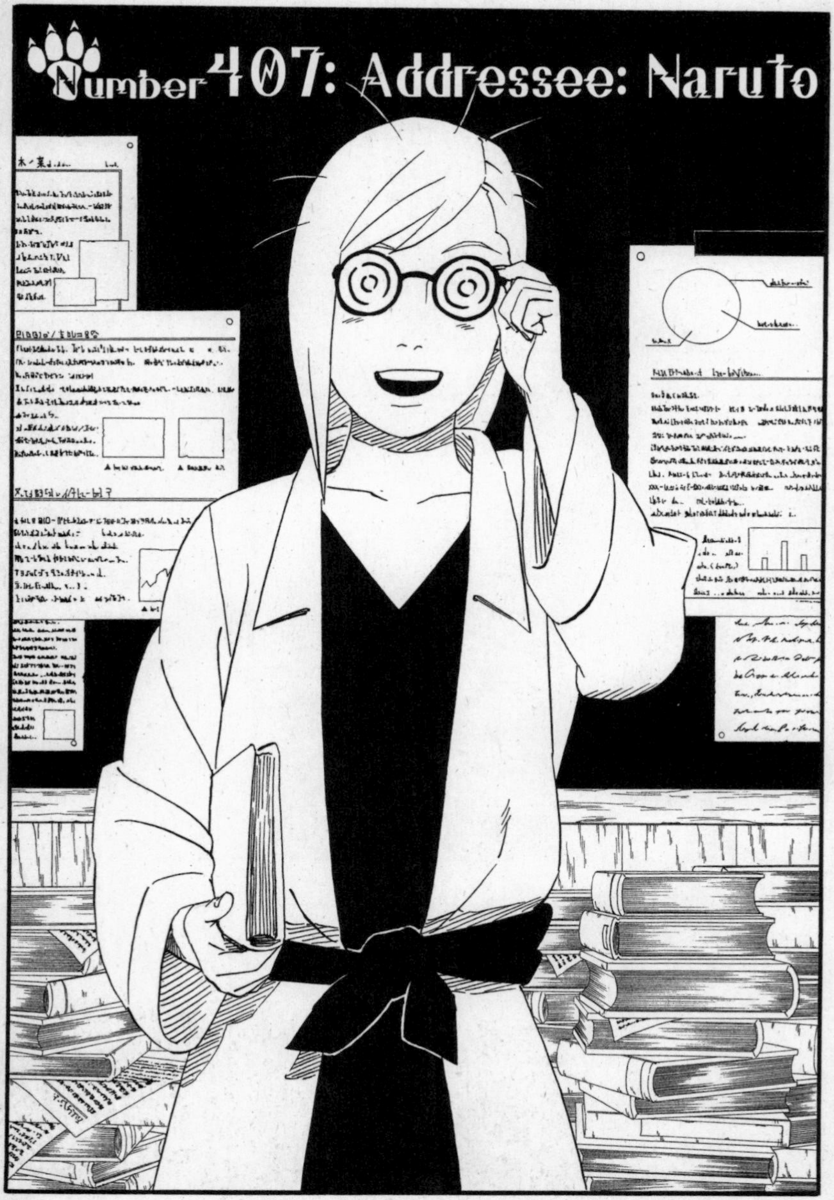
Number 407: Addressee: Naruto

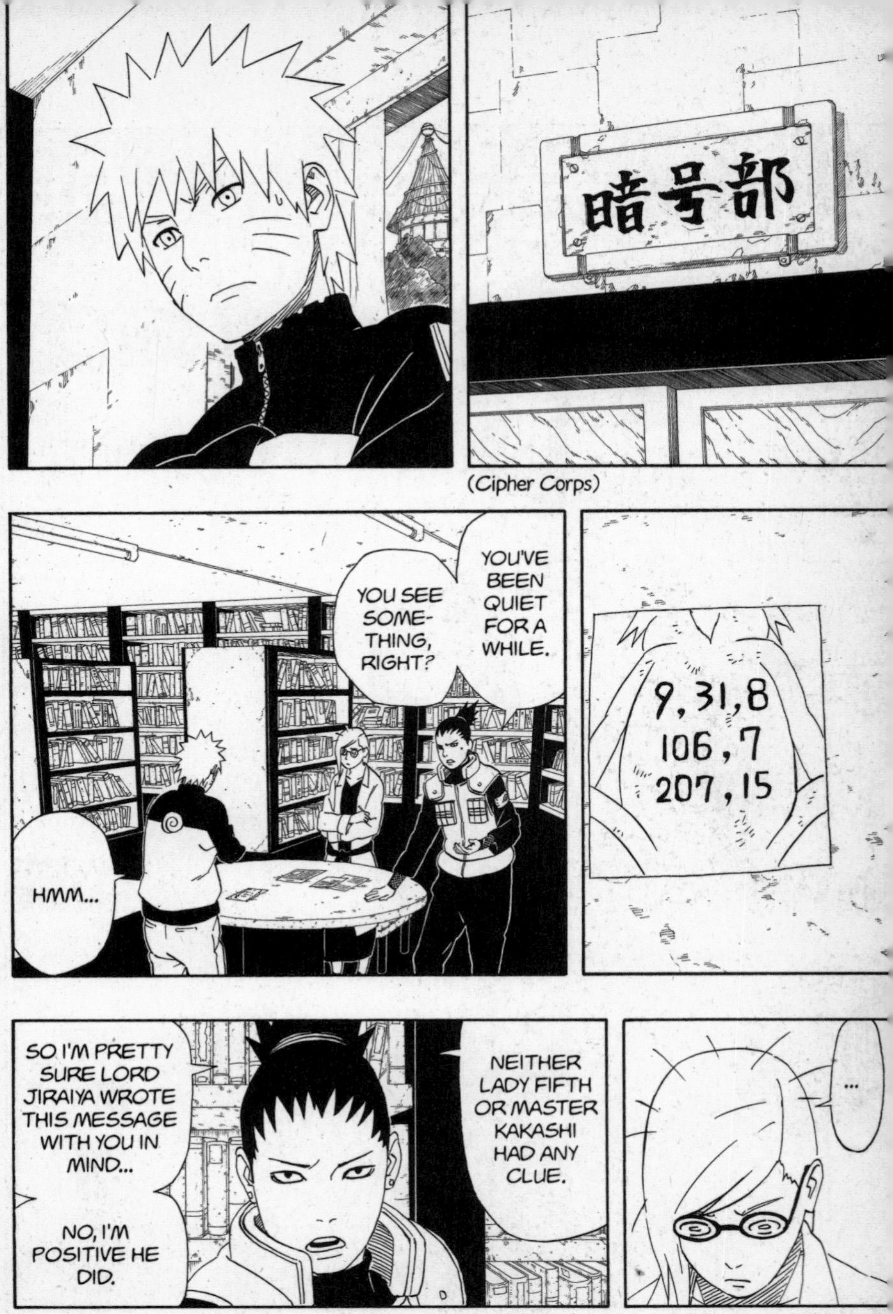

暗号部
(Cipher Corps)
9,31,8
106,7
207,15
YOU'VE BEEN QUIET FOR A WHILE.
YOU SEE SOME-THING, RIGHT?
HMM...
...
NEITHER LADY FIFTH OR MASTER KAKASHI HAD ANY CLUE.
SO I'M PRETTY SURE LORD JIRAIYA WROTE THIS MESSAGE WITH YOU IN MIND...
NO, I'M POSITIVE HE DID.

READ THIS WAY

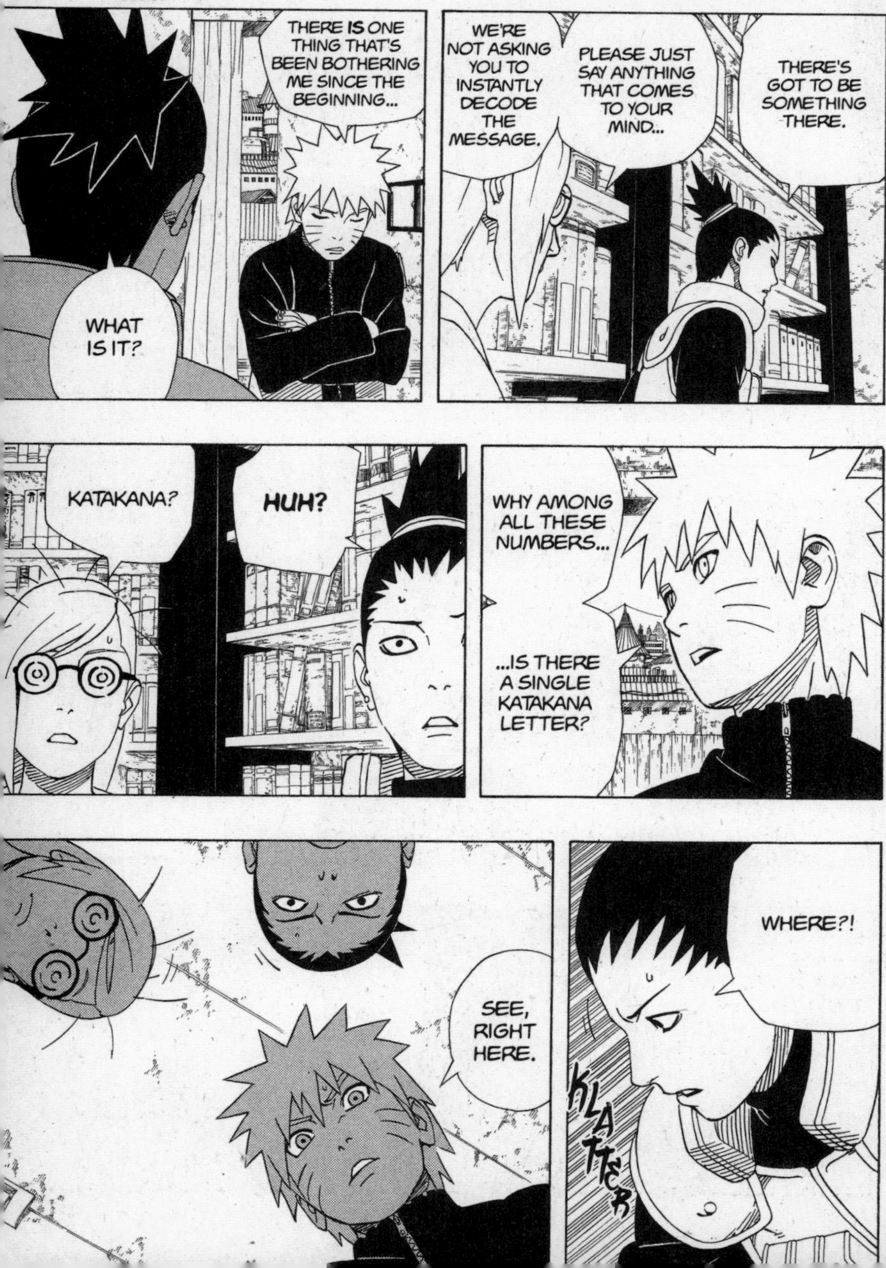
THERE'S GOT TO BE SOMETHING THERE.
PLEASE JUST SAY ANYTHING THAT COMES TO YOUR MIND...
WE'RE NOT ASKING YOU TO INSTANTLY DECODE THE MESSAGE.
THERE **IS** ONE THING THAT'S BEEN BOTHERING ME SINCE THE BEGINNING...
WHAT IS IT?
WHY AMONG ALL THESE NUMBERS...
...IS THERE A SINGLE KATAKANA LETTER?
HUH?
KATAKANA?
WHERE?!
KLATTER
SEE, RIGHT HERE.

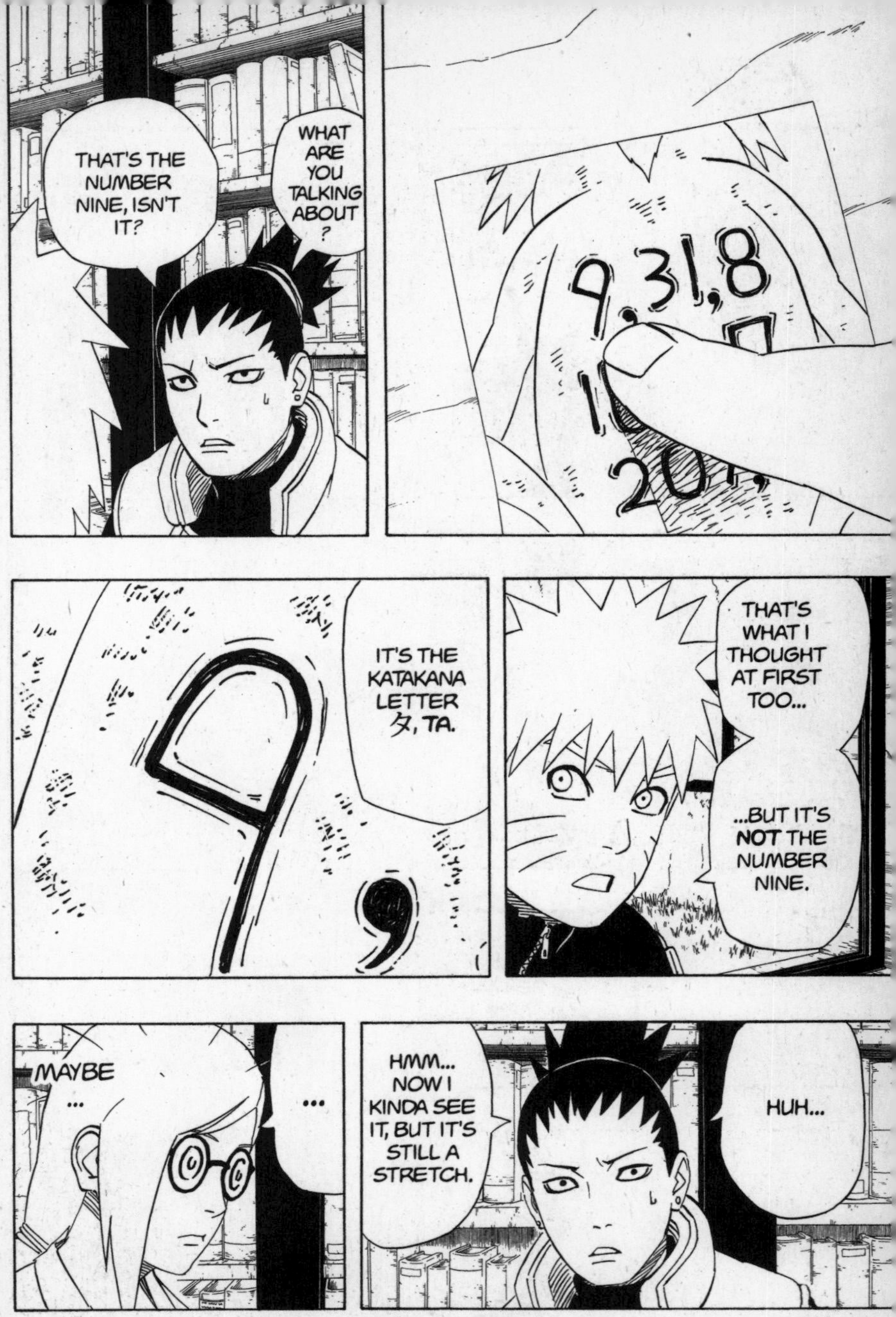
9,31,8
WHAT ARE YOU TALKING ABOUT?
THAT'S THE NUMBER NINE, ISN'T IT?
THAT'S WHAT I THOUGHT AT FIRST TOO...
...BUT IT'S **NOT** THE NUMBER NINE.
IT'S THE KATAKANA LETTER タ, TA.
HUH...
HMM... NOW I KINDA SEE IT, BUT IT'S STILL A STRETCH.
...
MAYBE ...

READ THIS WAY

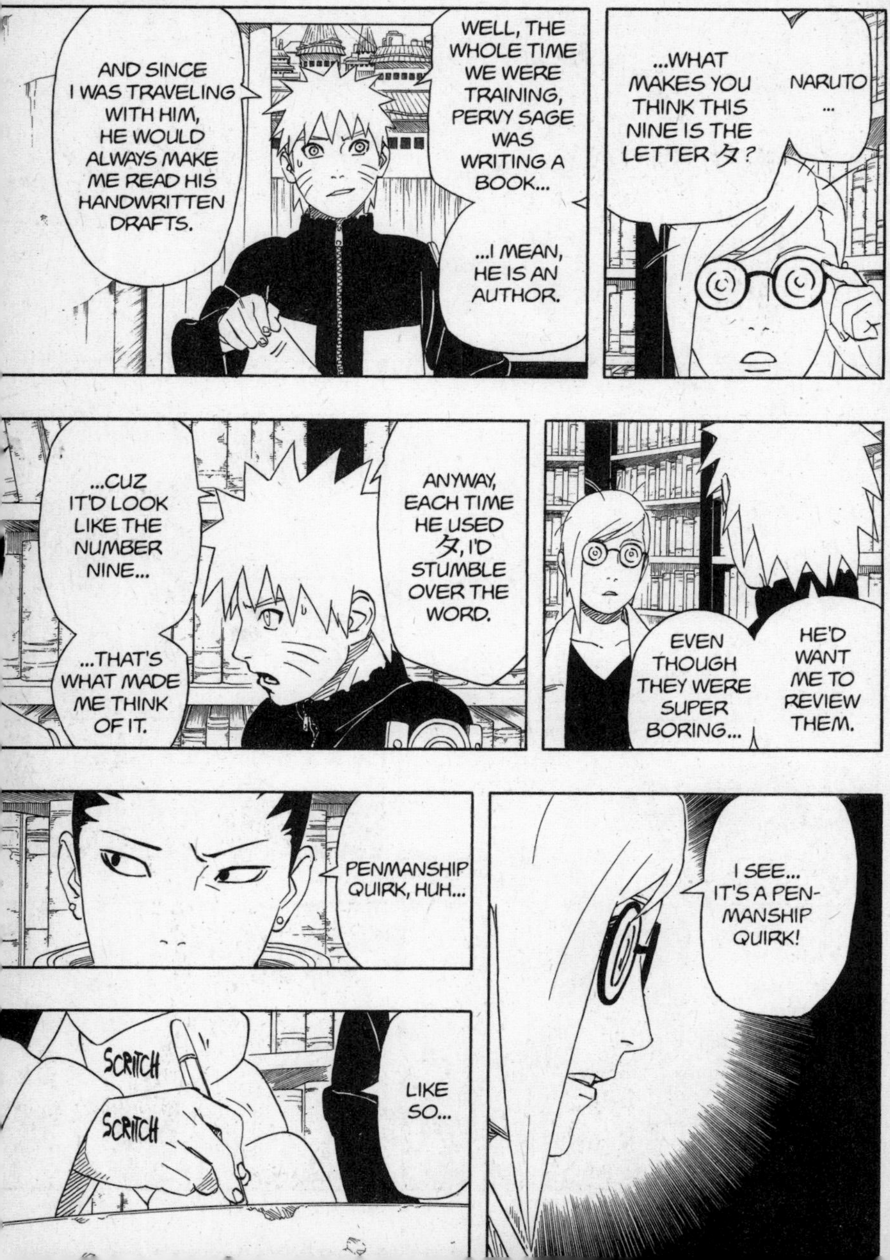
NARUTO ...
...WHAT MAKES YOU THINK THIS NINE IS THE LETTER 夕?
WELL, THE WHOLE TIME WE WERE TRAINING, PERVY SAGE WAS WRITING A BOOK...
...I MEAN, HE IS AN AUTHOR.
AND SINCE I WAS TRAVELING WITH HIM, HE WOULD ALWAYS MAKE ME READ HIS HANDWRITTEN DRAFTS.
HE'D WANT ME TO REVIEW THEM.
EVEN THOUGH THEY WERE SUPER BORING...
ANYWAY, EACH TIME HE USED 夕, I'D STUMBLE OVER THE WORD.
...CUZ IT'D LOOK LIKE THE NUMBER NINE...
...THAT'S WHAT MADE ME THINK OF IT.
I SEE... IT'S A PEN-MANSHIP QUIRK!
PENMANSHIP QUIRK, HUH...
LIKE SO...
SCRITCH
SCRITCH

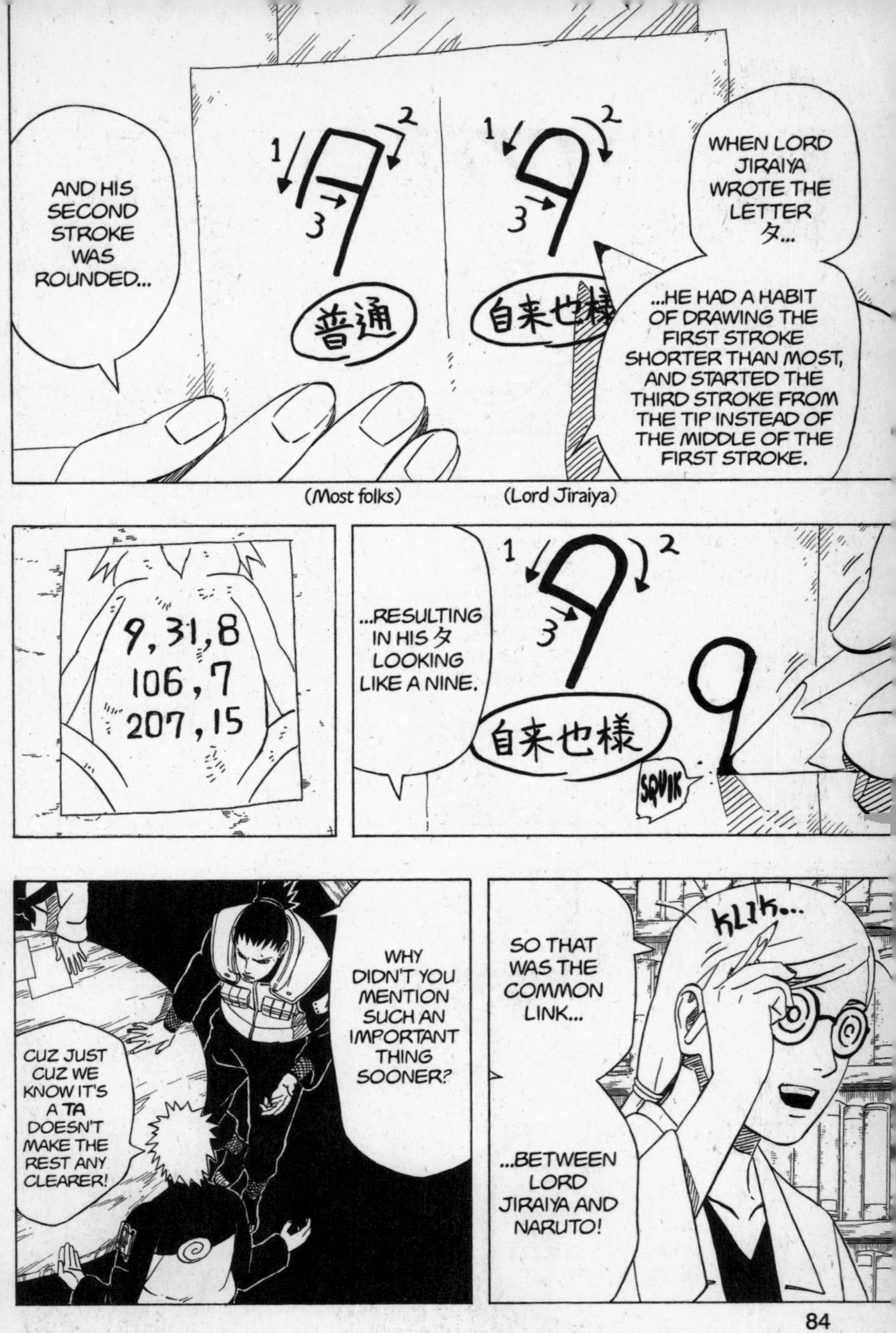
WHEN LORD JIRAIYA WROTE THE LETTER タ...
...HE HAD A HABIT OF DRAWING THE FIRST STROKE SHORTER THAN MOST, AND STARTED THE THIRD STROKE FROM THE TIP INSTEAD OF THE MIDDLE OF THE FIRST STROKE.
1 2 3
自来也様
1 2 3
普通
AND HIS SECOND STROKE WAS ROUNDED...
(Most folks)
(Lord Jiraiya)
1 2 3
...RESULTING IN HIS タ LOOKING LIKE A NINE.
自来也様
9
SQUIK
9, 31, 8
106, 7
207, 15
KLIK...
SO THAT WAS THE COMMON LINK...
...BETWEEN LORD JIRAIYA AND NARUTO!
WHY DIDN'T YOU MENTION SUCH AN IMPORTANT THING SOONER?
CUZ JUST CUZ WE KNOW IT'S A TA DOESN'T MAKE THE REST ANY CLEARER!

READ THIS WAY

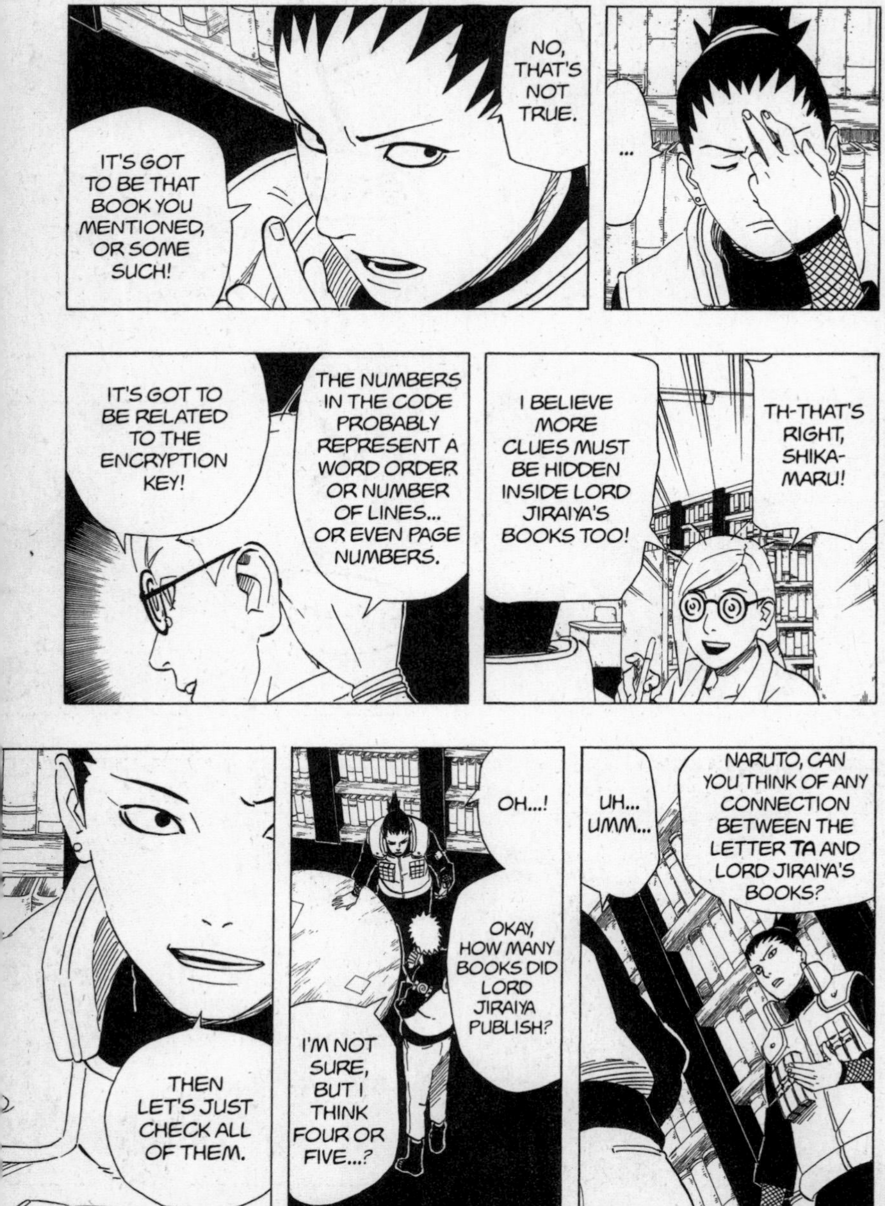
...
NO, THAT'S NOT TRUE.
IT'S GOT TO BE THAT BOOK YOU MENTIONED, OR SOME SUCH!
TH-THAT'S RIGHT, SHIKAMARU!
I BELIEVE MORE CLUES MUST BE HIDDEN INSIDE LORD JIRAIYA'S BOOKS TOO!
THE NUMBERS IN THE CODE PROBABLY REPRESENT A WORD ORDER OR NUMBER OF LINES... OR EVEN PAGE NUMBERS.
IT'S GOT TO BE RELATED TO THE ENCRYPTION KEY!
NARUTO, CAN YOU THINK OF ANY CONNECTION BETWEEN THE LETTER TA AND LORD JIRAIYA'S BOOKS?
UH... UMM...
OH...!
OKAY, HOW MANY BOOKS DID LORD JIRAIYA PUBLISH?
I'M NOT SURE, BUT I THINK FOUR OR FIVE...?
THEN LET'S JUST CHECK ALL OF THEM.

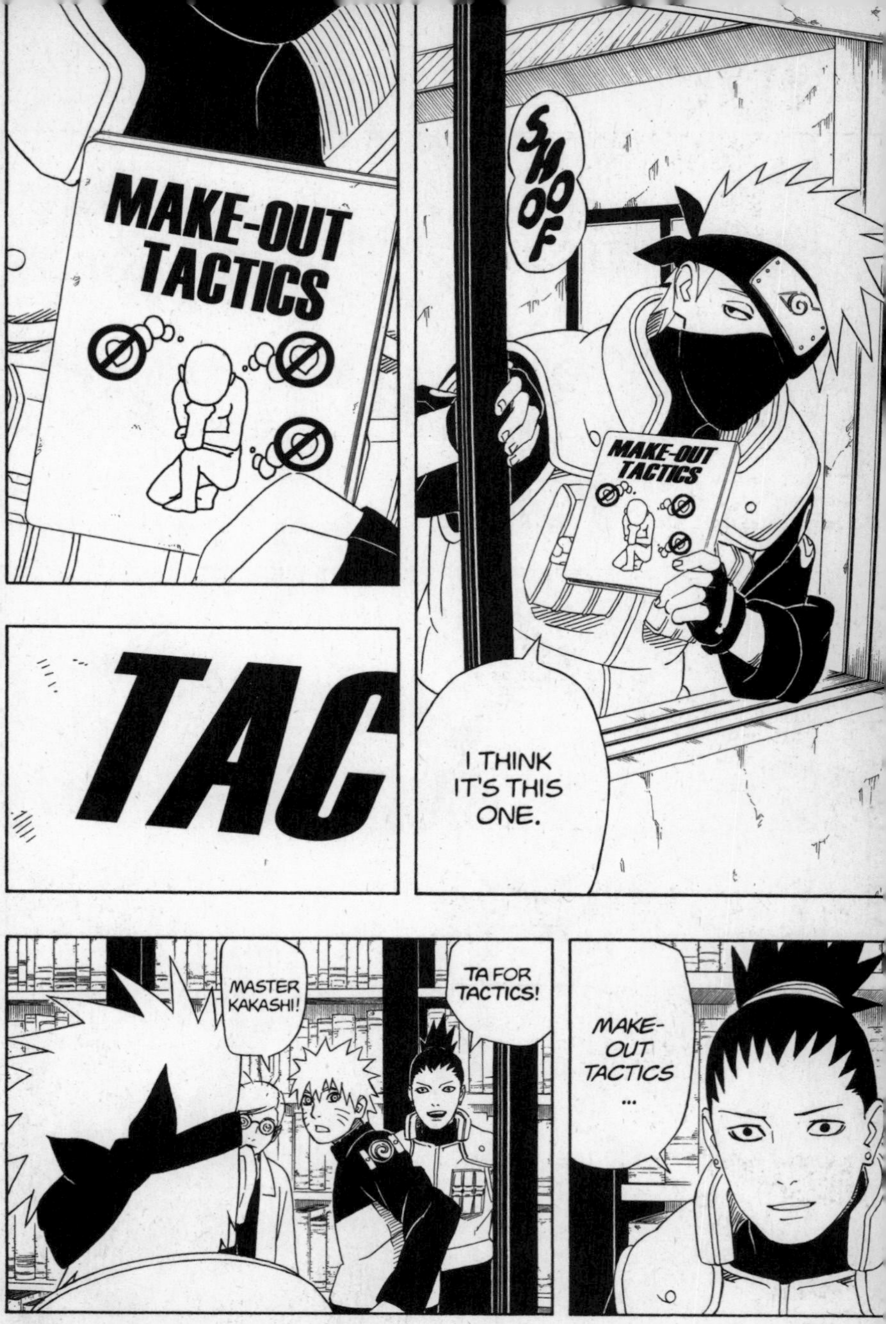
SHOOF
MAKE-OUT TACTICS
I THINK IT'S THIS ONE.
MAKE-OUT TACTICS
TAC
MAKE-OUT TACTICS ...
TA FOR TACTICS!
MASTER KAKASHI!

READ THIS WAY

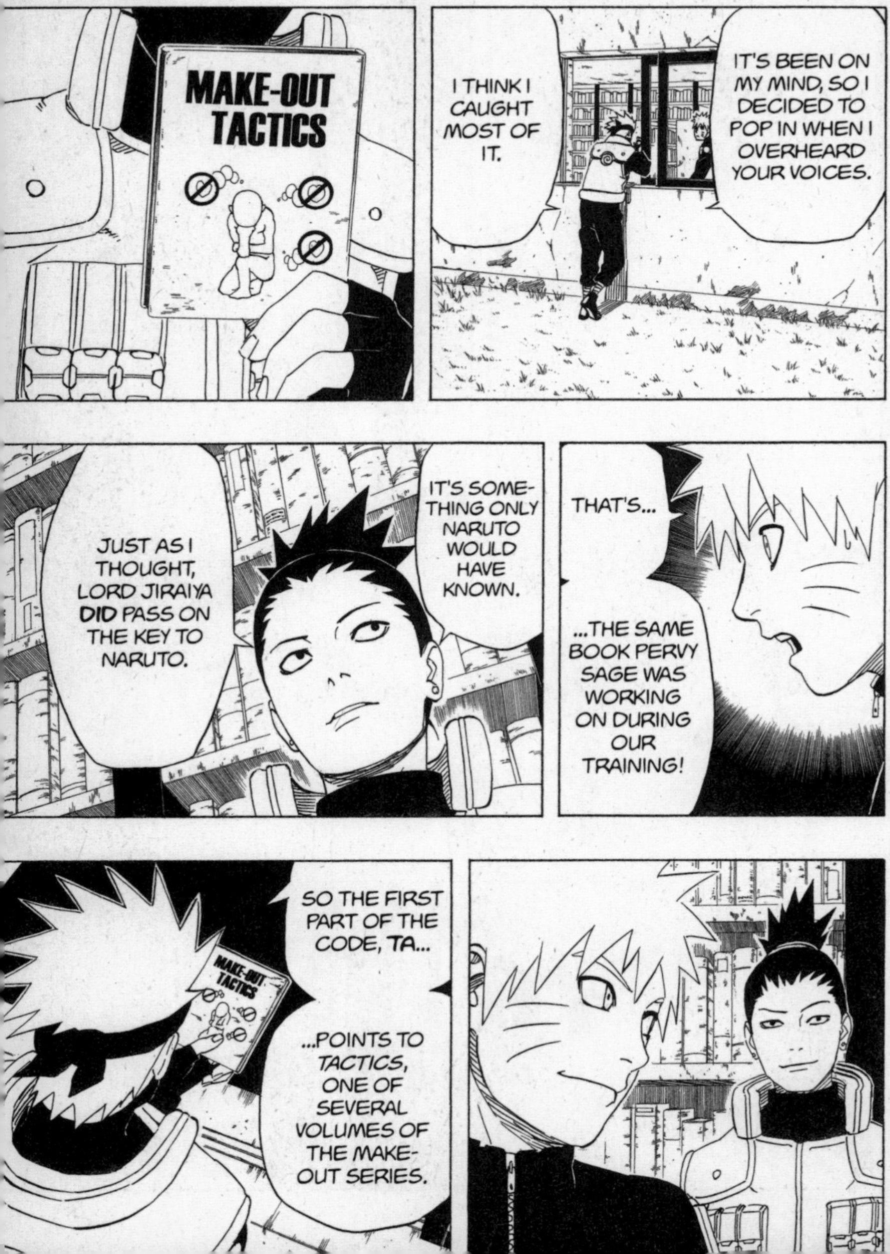
IT'S BEEN ON MY MIND, SO I DECIDED TO POP IN WHEN I OVERHEARD YOUR VOICES.
I THINK I CAUGHT MOST OF IT.
MAKE-OUT TACTICS
THAT'S...
...THE SAME BOOK PERVY SAGE WAS WORKING ON DURING OUR TRAINING!
IT'S SOME-THING ONLY NARUTO WOULD HAVE KNOWN.
JUST AS I THOUGHT, LORD JIRAIYA DID PASS ON THE KEY TO NARUTO.
SO THE FIRST PART OF THE CODE, TA...
MAKE-OUT TACTICS
...POINTS TO TACTICS, ONE OF SEVERAL VOLUMES OF THE MAKE-OUT SERIES.

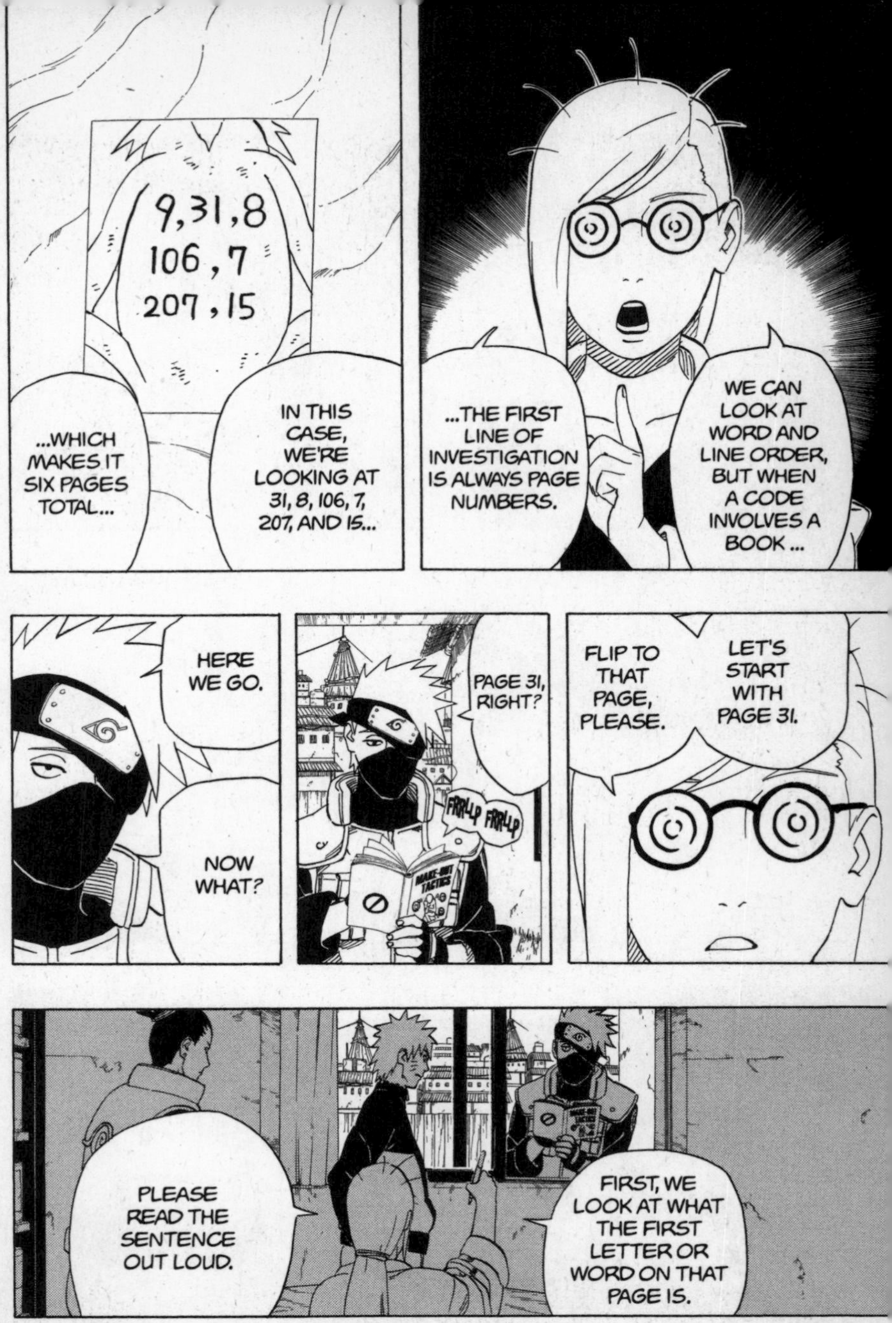
WE CAN LOOK AT WORD AND LINE ORDER, BUT WHEN A CODE INVOLVES A BOOK...
...THE FIRST LINE OF INVESTIGATION IS ALWAYS PAGE NUMBERS.
9,31,8
106,7
207,15
IN THIS CASE, WE'RE LOOKING AT 31, 8, 106, 7, 207, AND 15...
...WHICH MAKES IT SIX PAGES TOTAL...
LET'S START WITH PAGE 31.
FLIP TO THAT PAGE, PLEASE.
PAGE 31, RIGHT?
FRRLLP FRRLLP
MAKE-OUT TACTICS
HERE WE GO.
NOW WHAT?
FIRST, WE LOOK AT WHAT THE FIRST LETTER OR WORD ON THAT PAGE IS.
PLEASE READ THE SENTENCE OUT LOUD.

READ THIS WAY

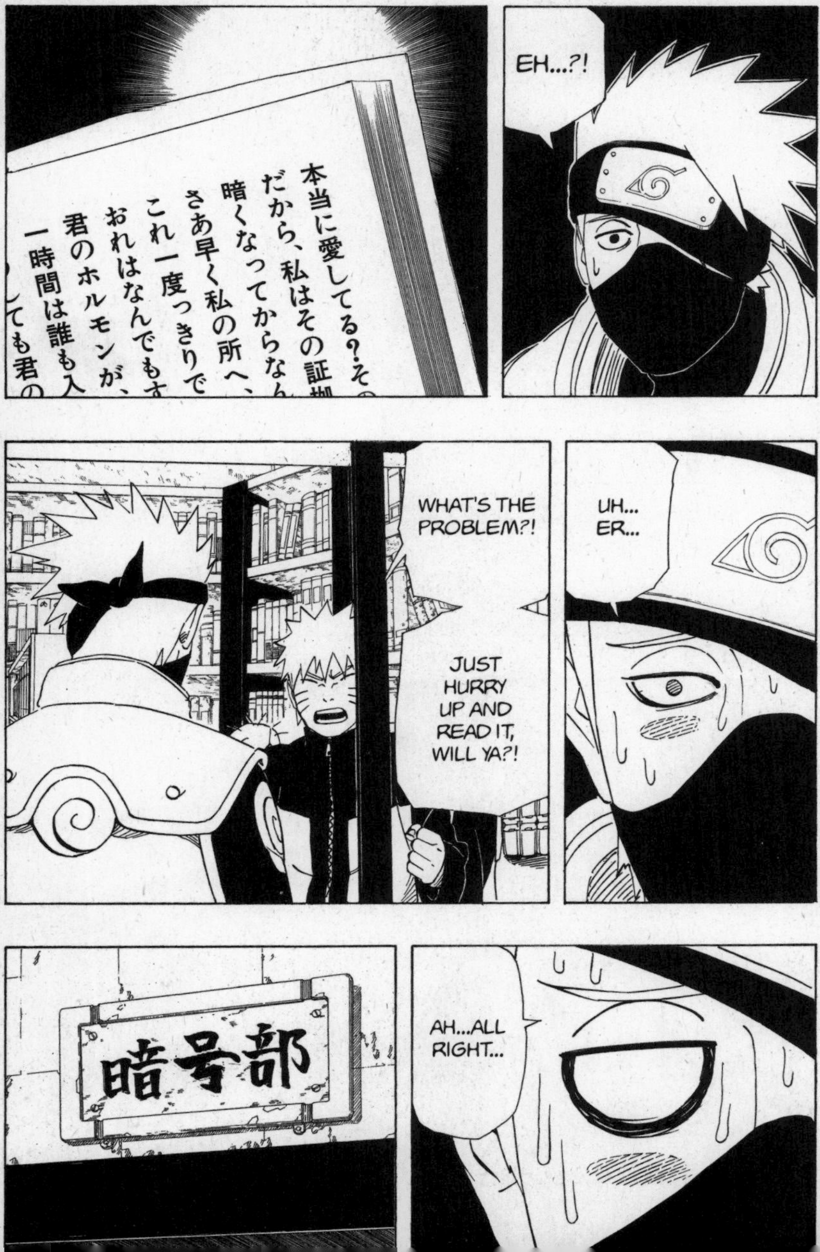
EH...?!
本当に愛してる?そ
だから、私はその証
暗くなってからな
さあ早く私の所へ、
これ一度っきりで
おれはなんでも
君のホルモンが、
一時間は誰も
ても君
UH... ER...
WHAT'S THE PROBLEM?!
JUST HURRY UP AND READ IT, WILL YA?!
AH...ALL RIGHT...
暗号部

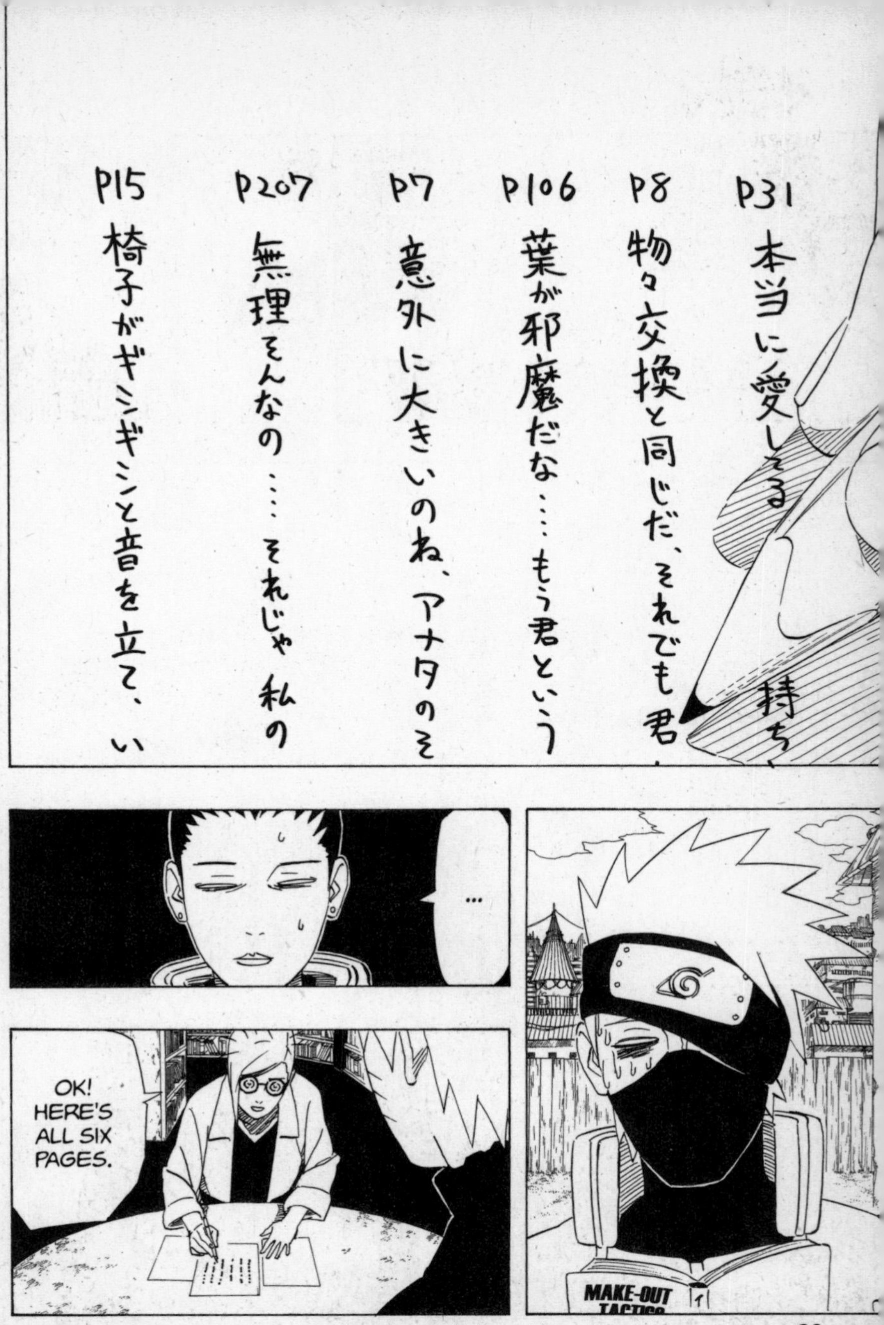
P31 本当に愛してる 持ち、
P8 物々交換と同じだ、それでも君
P106 葉が邪魔だな…もう君という
P7 意外に大きいのね、アナタのそ
P207 無理そんなの…それじゃ私の
P15 椅子がギシギシと音を立て、い
MAKE-OUT
...
OK! HERE'S ALL SIX PAGES.

READ THIS WAY

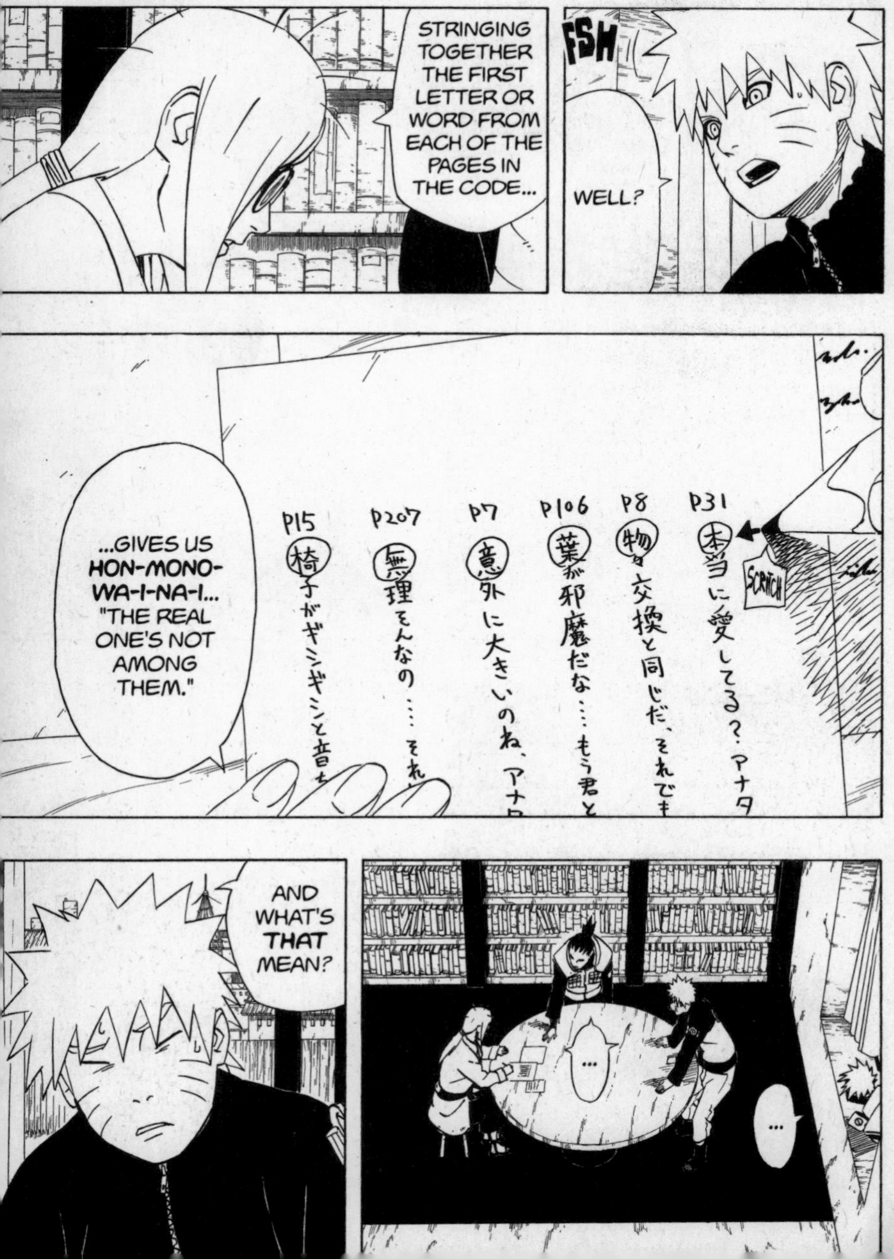
FSH
WELL?
STRINGING TOGETHER THE FIRST LETTER OR WORD FROM EACH OF THE PAGES IN THE CODE...
P31 本当に愛してる？アナタ
P8 物々交換と同じだ、それで
P106 葉が邪魔だな…もう君と
P7 意外に大きいのね、アナ
P207 無理をんなの…… それ
P15 椅子がギシギシと音
SCRATCH
...GIVES US HON-MONO-WA-I-NA-I... "THE REAL ONE'S NOT AMONG THEM."
...
...
AND WHAT'S THAT MEAN?

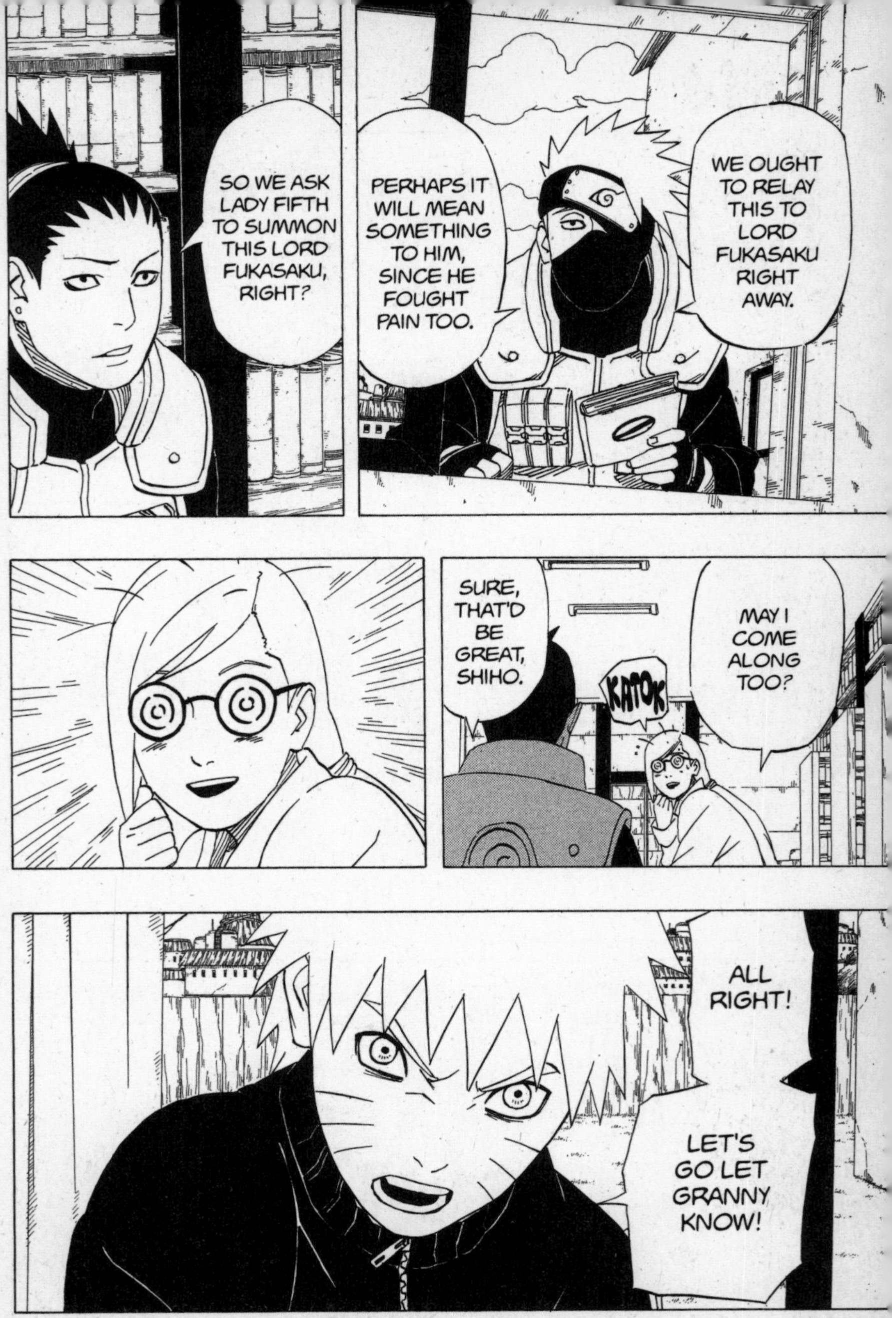

WE OUGHT TO RELAY THIS TO LORD FUKASAKU RIGHT AWAY.
PERHAPS IT WILL MEAN SOMETHING TO HIM, SINCE HE FOUGHT PAIN TOO.
SO WE ASK LADY FIFTH TO SUMMON THIS LORD FUKASAKU, RIGHT?
MAY I COME ALONG TOO?
KATOK
SURE, THAT'D BE GREAT, SHIHO.
ALL RIGHT!
LET'S GO LET GRANNY KNOW!

READ THIS WAY

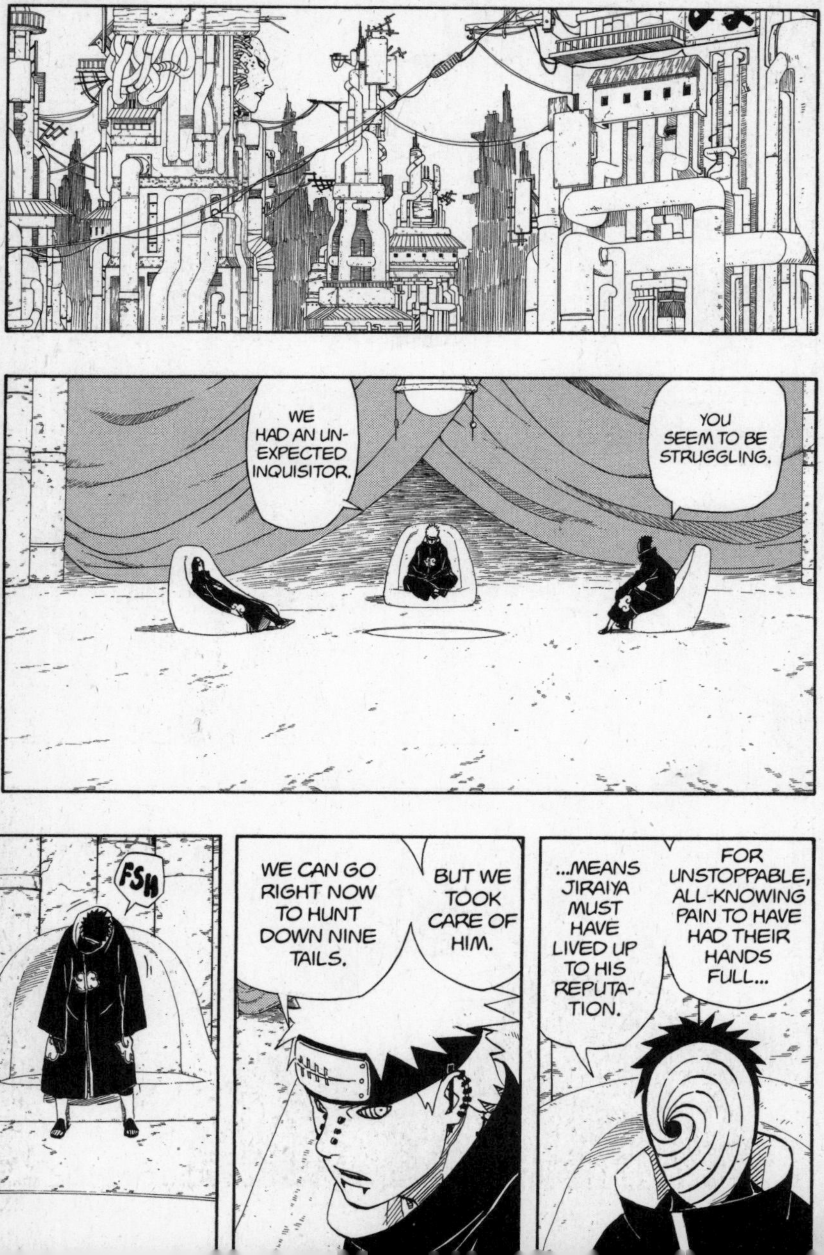
YOU SEEM TO BE STRUGGLING.
WE HAD AN UN-EXPECTED INQUISITOR.
FOR UNSTOPPABLE, ALL-KNOWING PAIN TO HAVE HAD THEIR HANDS FULL...
...MEANS JIRAIYA MUST HAVE LIVED UP TO HIS REPUTA-TION.
BUT WE TOOK CARE OF HIM.
WE CAN GO RIGHT NOW TO HUNT DOWN NINE TAILS.
FSH

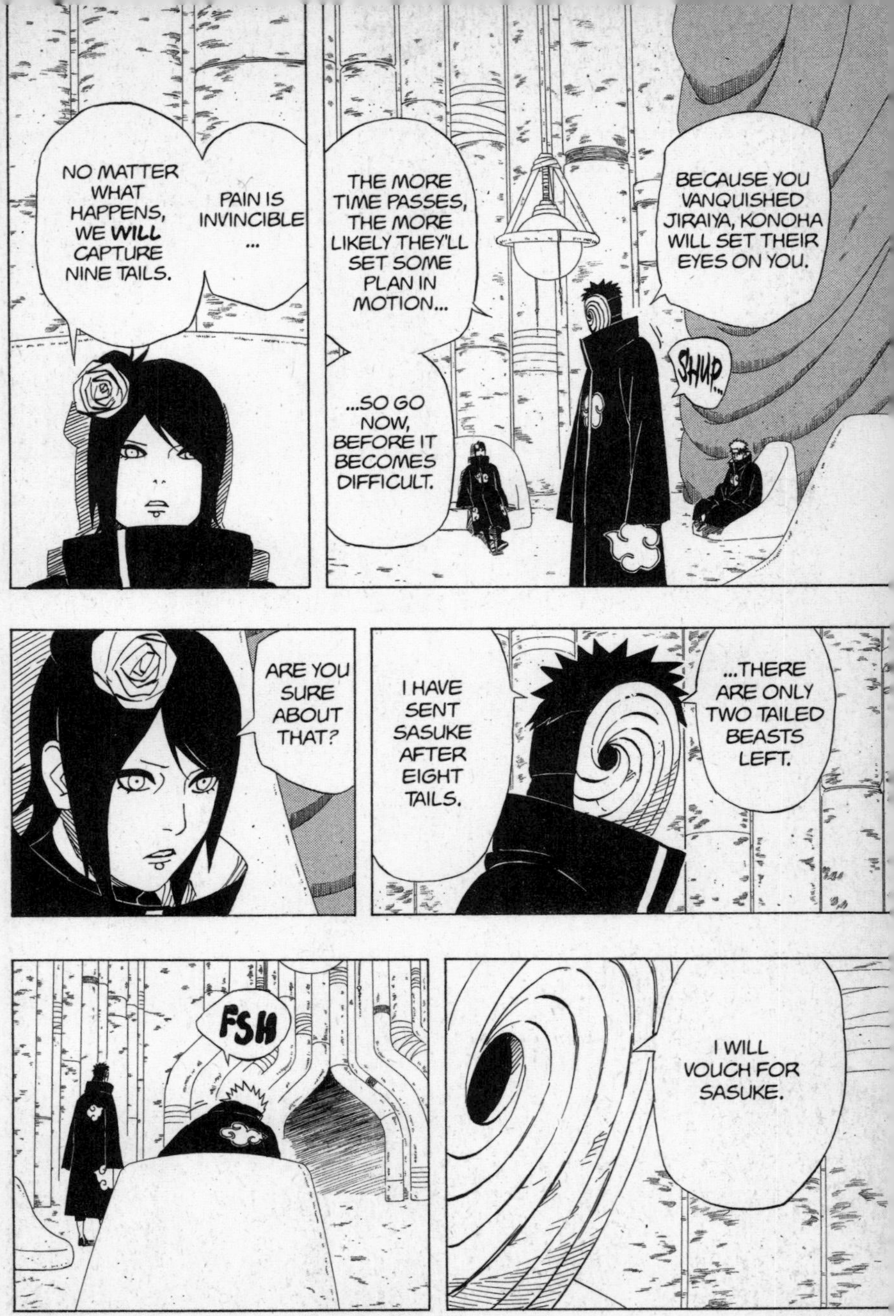
BECAUSE YOU VANQUISHED JIRAIYA, KONOHA WILL SET THEIR EYES ON YOU.
SHUP...
THE MORE TIME PASSES, THE MORE LIKELY THEY'LL SET SOME PLAN IN MOTION...
...SO GO NOW, BEFORE IT BECOMES DIFFICULT.
PAIN IS INVINCIBLE ...
NO MATTER WHAT HAPPENS, WE **WILL** CAPTURE NINE TAILS.
...THERE ARE ONLY TWO TAILED BEASTS LEFT.
I HAVE SENT SASUKE AFTER EIGHT TAILS.
ARE YOU SURE ABOUT THAT?
I WILL VOUCH FOR SASUKE.
FSH

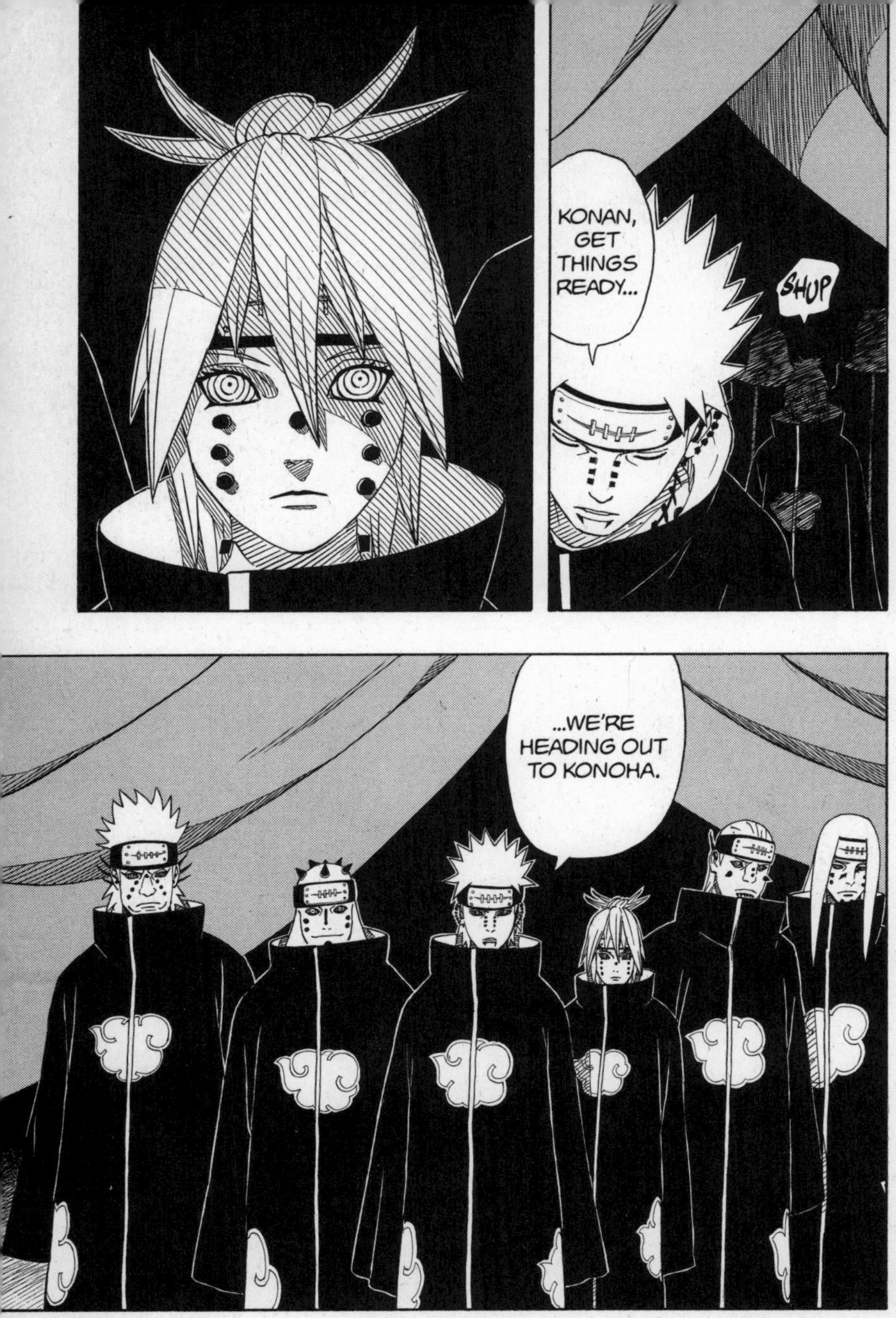
KONAN, GET THINGS READY...
SHUP
...WE'RE HEADING OUT TO KONOHA.

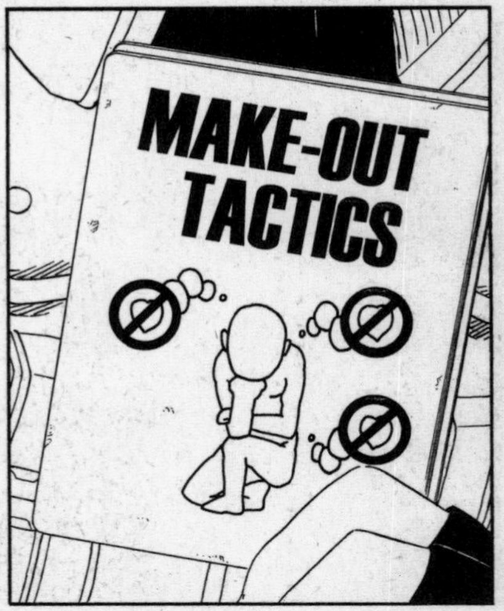
MAKE-OUT
TACTICS

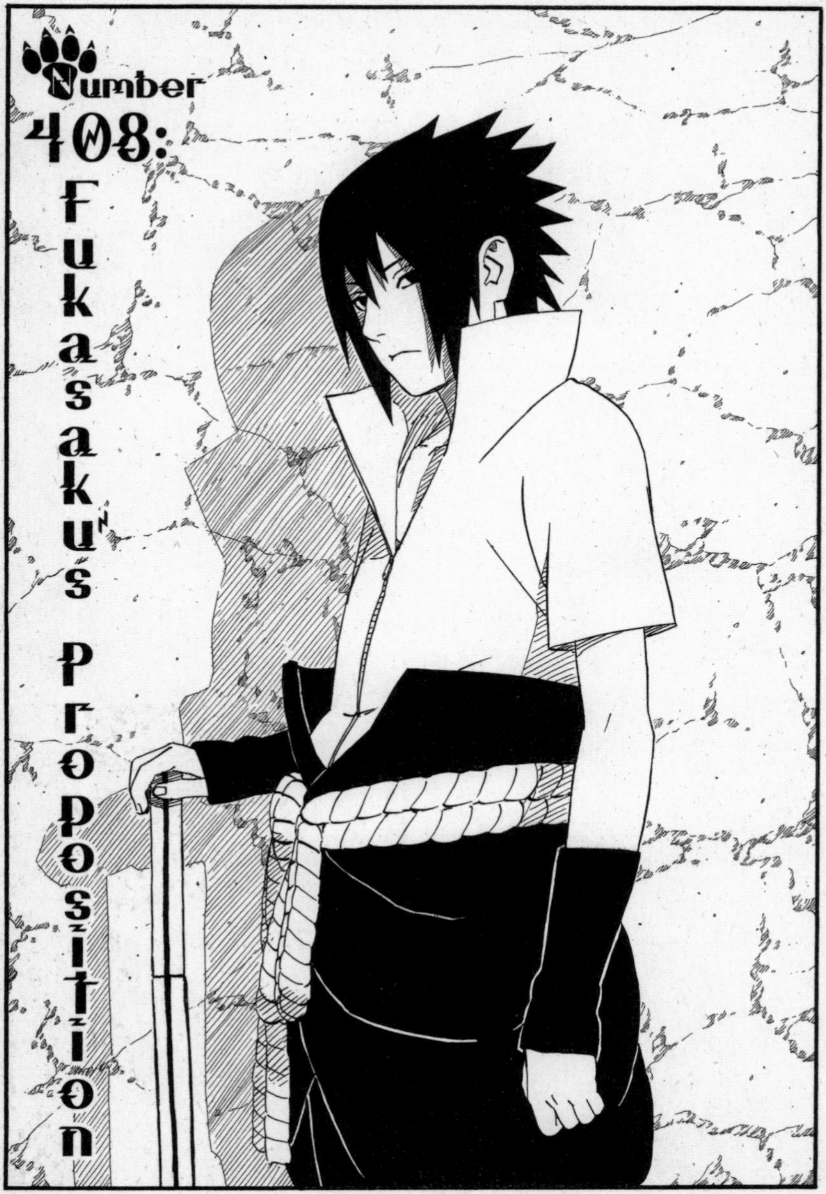
Number 408: Fukasaku's Proposition

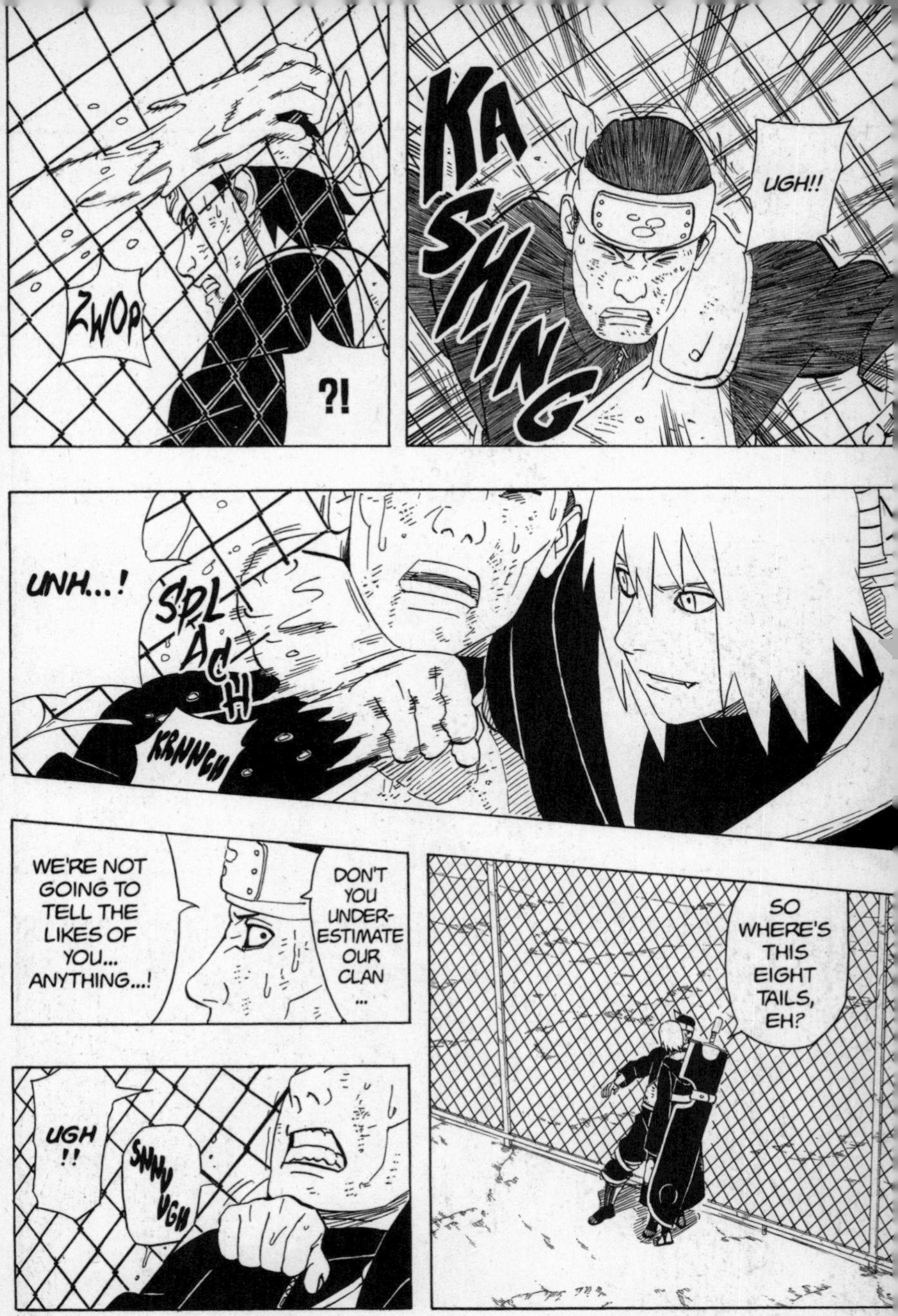
UGH!!
KASHING
ZWOP
?!
SPLACH
UNH...!
KRNNCH
SO WHERE'S THIS EIGHT TAILS, EH?
DON'T YOU UNDER-ESTIMATE OUR CLAN...
WE'RE NOT GOING TO TELL THE LIKES OF YOU... ANYTHING...!
SNNNUGH
UGH!!

READ THIS WAY

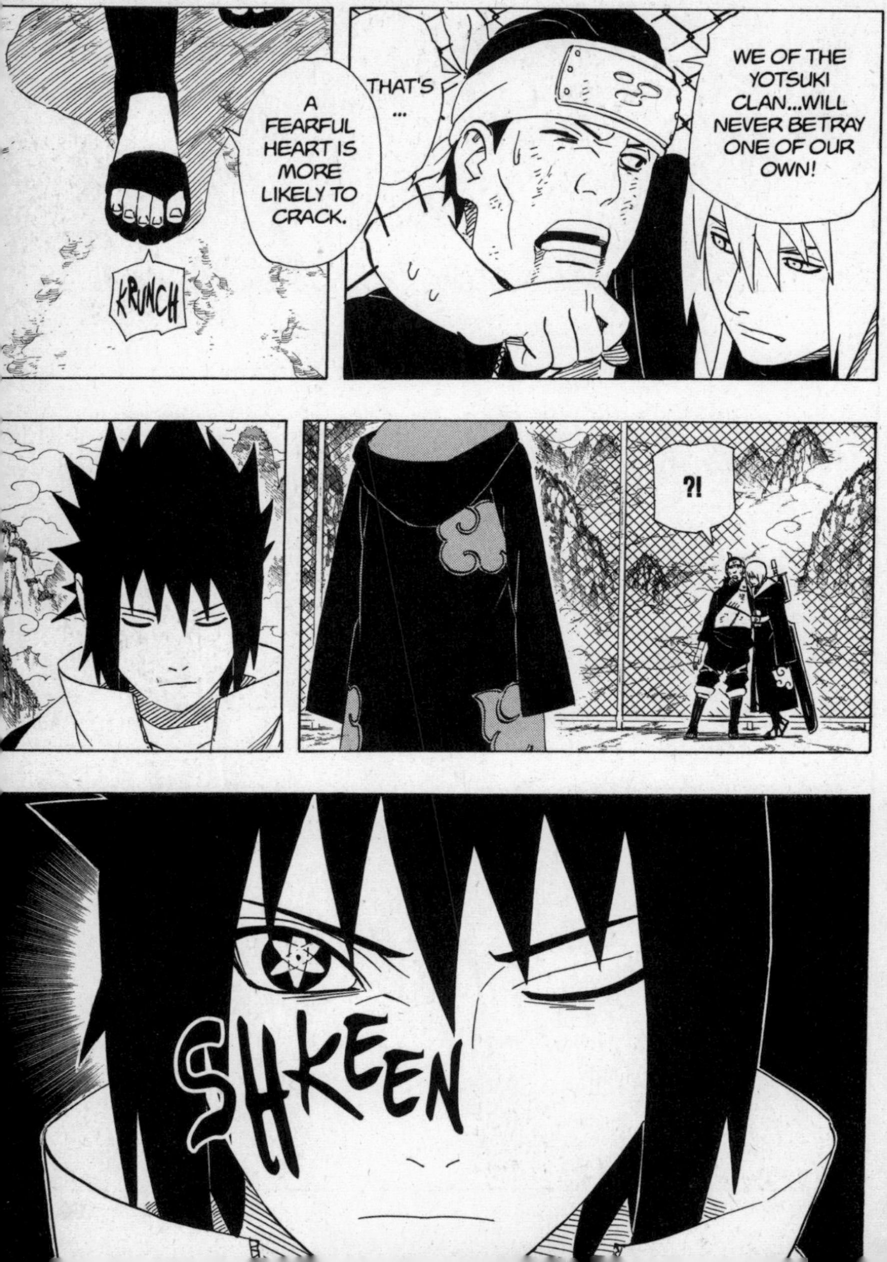
WE OF THE YOTSUKI CLAN...WILL NEVER BETRAY ONE OF OUR OWN!
THAT'S ...
A FEARFUL HEART IS MORE LIKELY TO CRACK.
KRUNCH
?!
SHKEEN

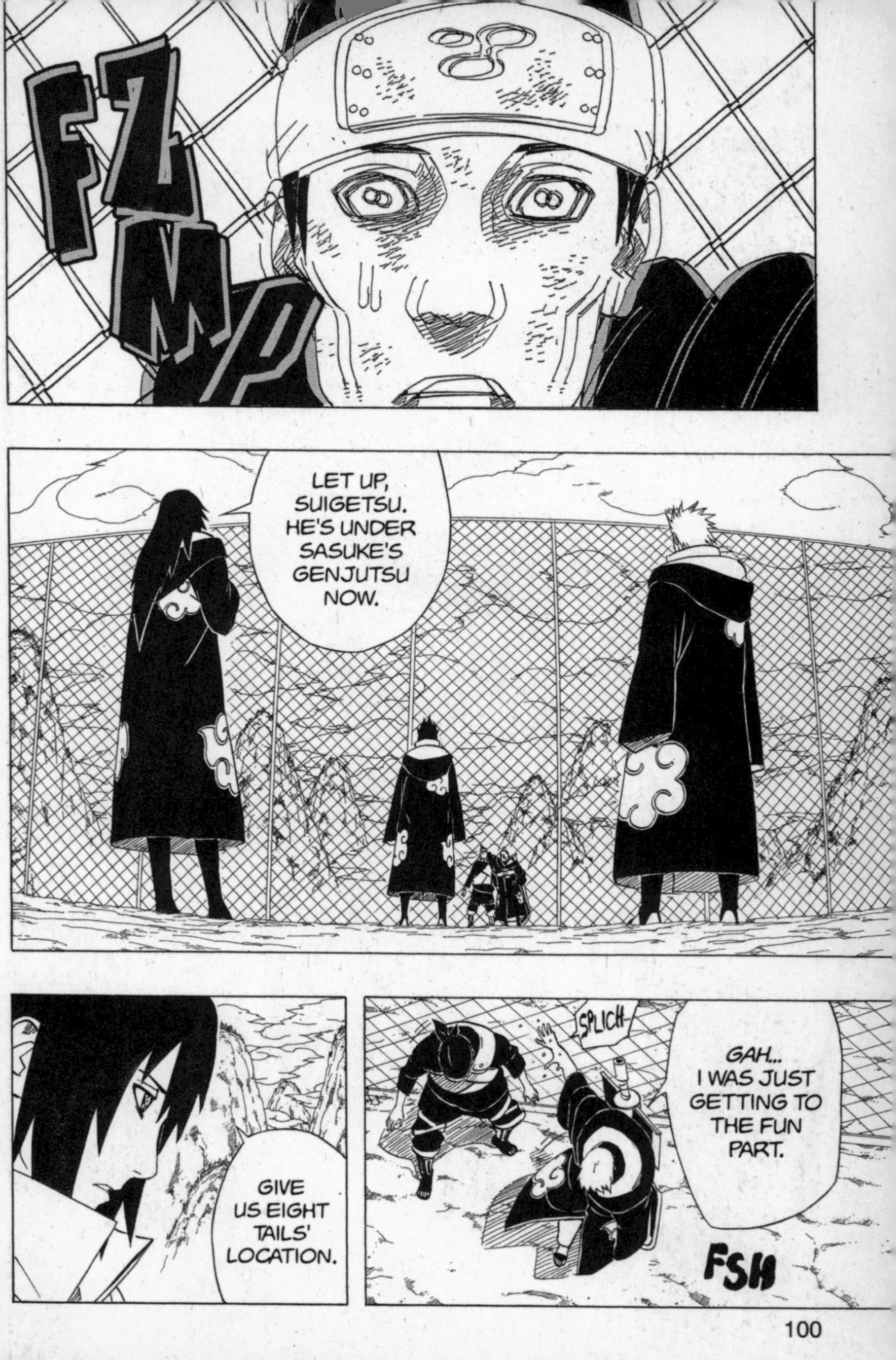
FZMP
LET UP, SUIGETSU. HE'S UNDER SASUKE'S GENJUTSU NOW.
SPLICH...
GAH... I WAS JUST GETTING TO THE FUN PART.
FSH
GIVE US EIGHT TAILS' LOCATION.

READ THIS WAY

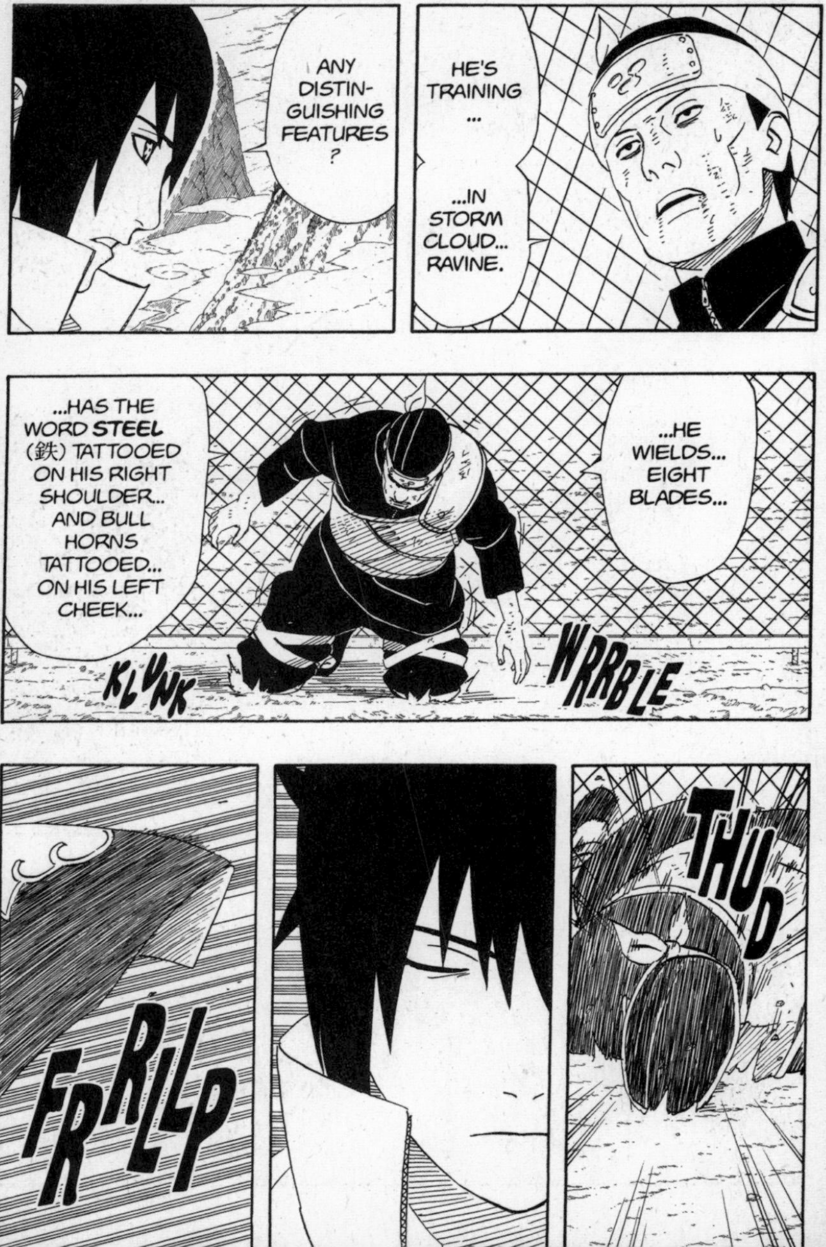
HE'S TRAINING ...
...IN STORM CLOUD... RAVINE.
ANY DISTIN-GUISHING FEATURES ?
...HE WIELDS... EIGHT BLADES...
...HAS THE WORD **STEEL** (鉄) TATTOOED ON HIS RIGHT SHOULDER... AND BULL HORNS TATTOOED... ON HIS LEFT CHEEK...
WRRBLE
KLUNK
THUD
FRRLLP

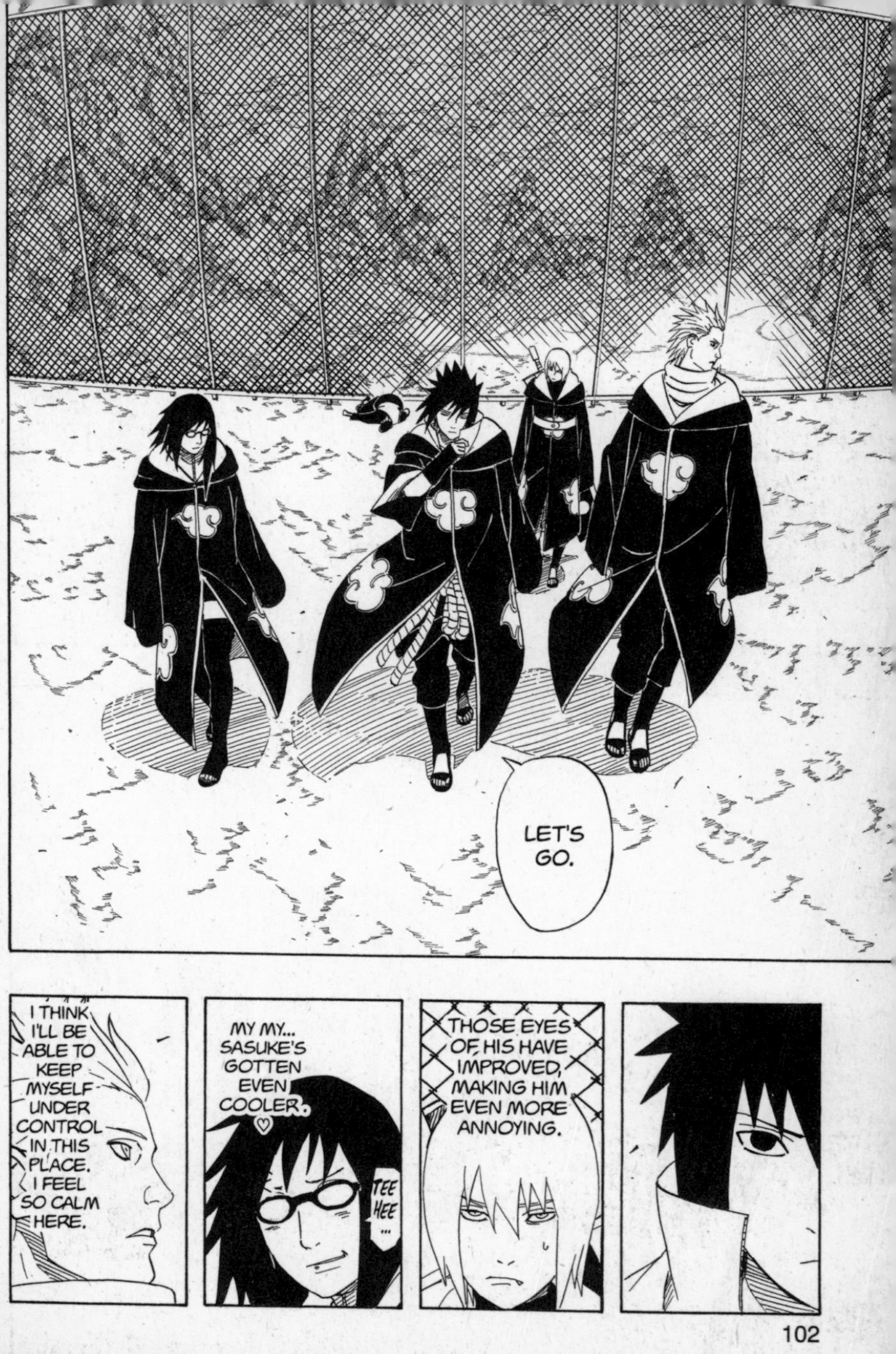
LET'S GO.
THOSE EYES OF HIS HAVE IMPROVED, MAKING HIM EVEN MORE ANNOYING.
MY MY... SASUKE'S GOTTEN EVEN COOLER. ♡
TEE HEE ...
I THINK I'LL BE ABLE TO KEEP MYSELF UNDER CONTROL IN THIS PLACE. I FEEL SO CALM HERE.

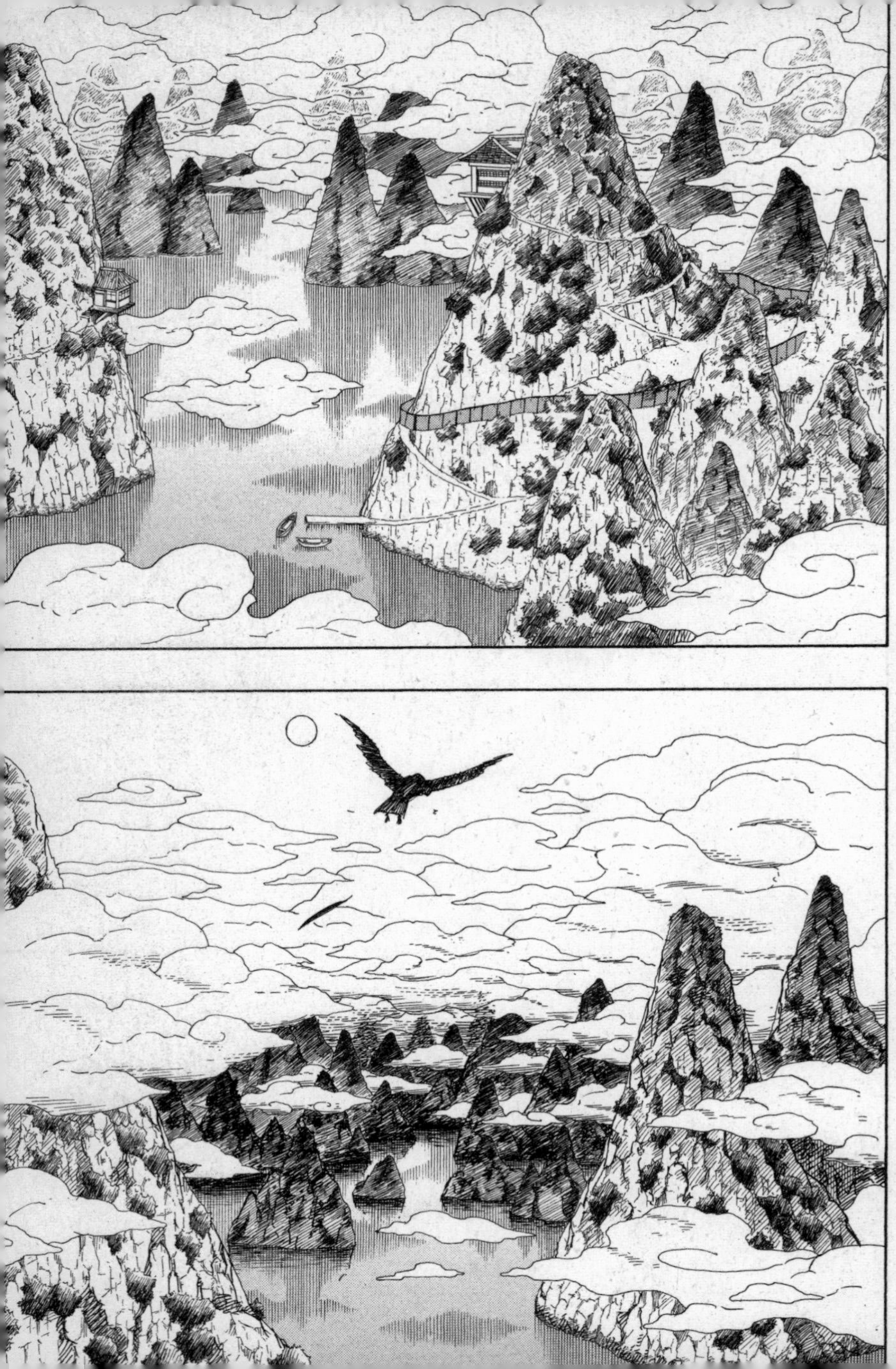

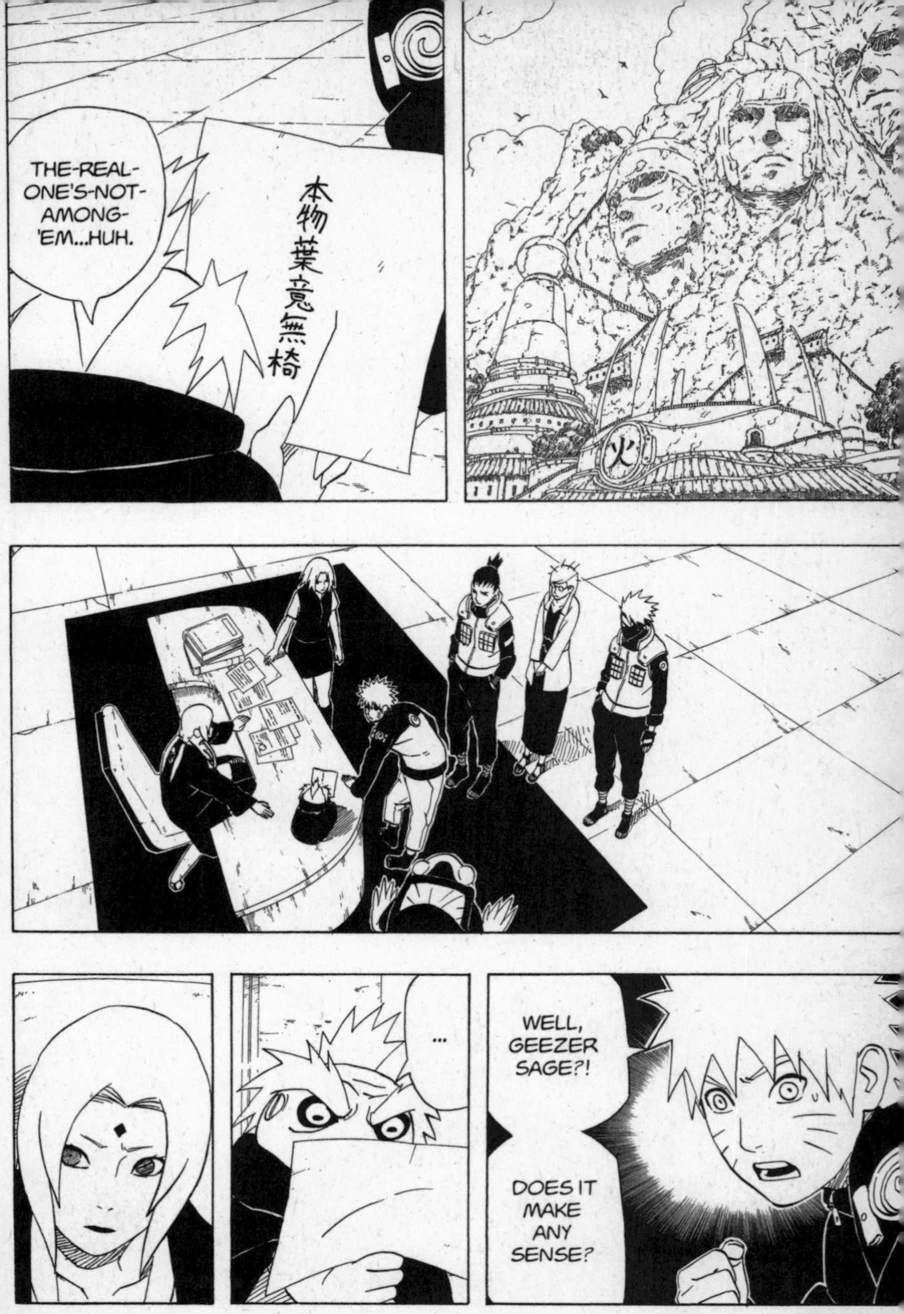
THE-REAL-ONE'S-NOT-AMONG-'EM...HUH.
本物葉竟無椅
WELL, GEEZER SAGE?!
DOES IT MAKE ANY SENSE?
...

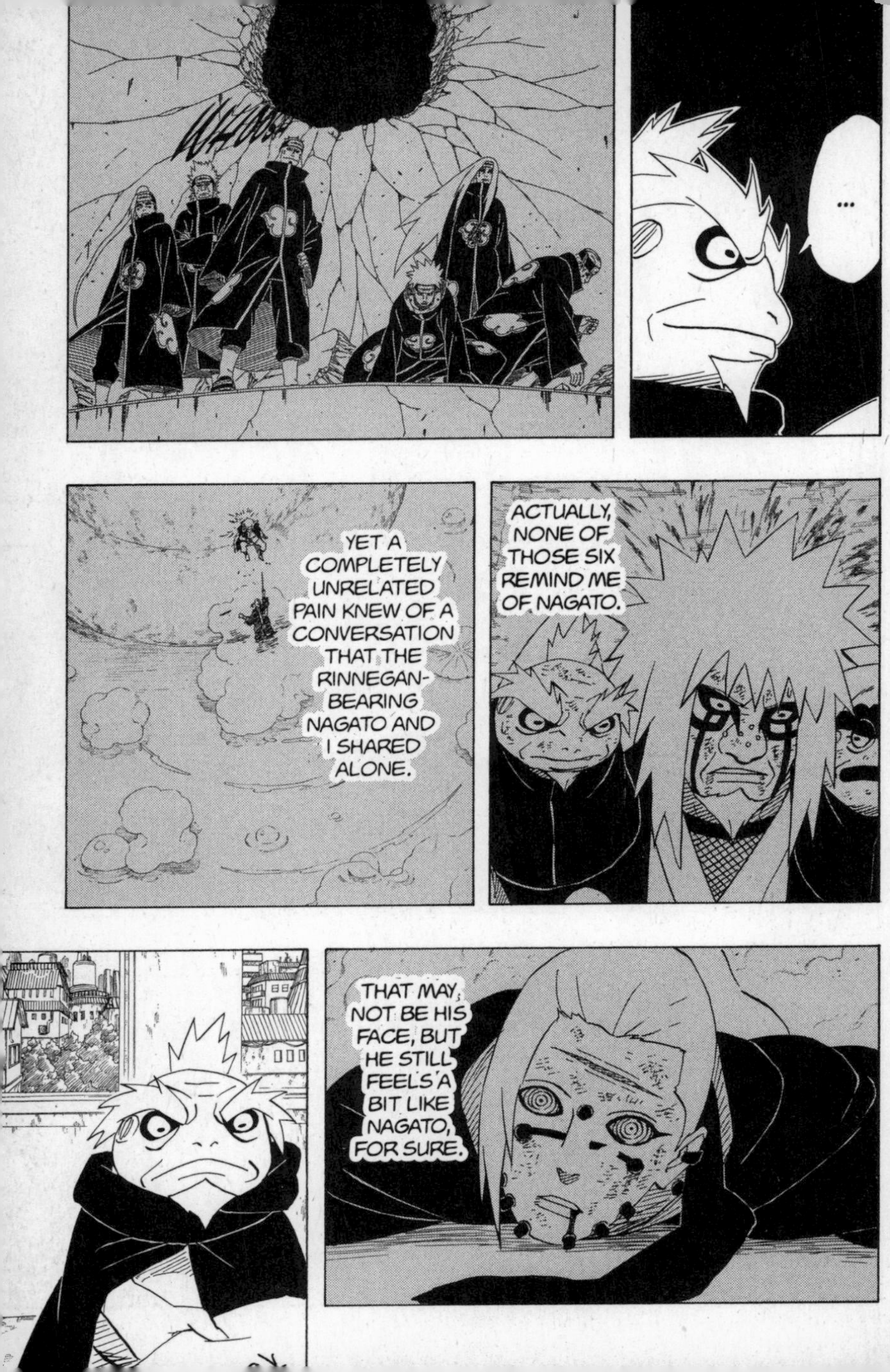
...
ACTUALLY, NONE OF THOSE SIX REMIND ME OF NAGATO.
YET A COMPLETELY UNRELATED PAIN KNEW OF A CONVERSATION THAT THE RINNEGAN-BEARING NAGATO AND I SHARED ALONE.
THAT MAY NOT BE HIS FACE, BUT HE STILL FEELS A BIT LIKE NAGATO, FOR SURE.

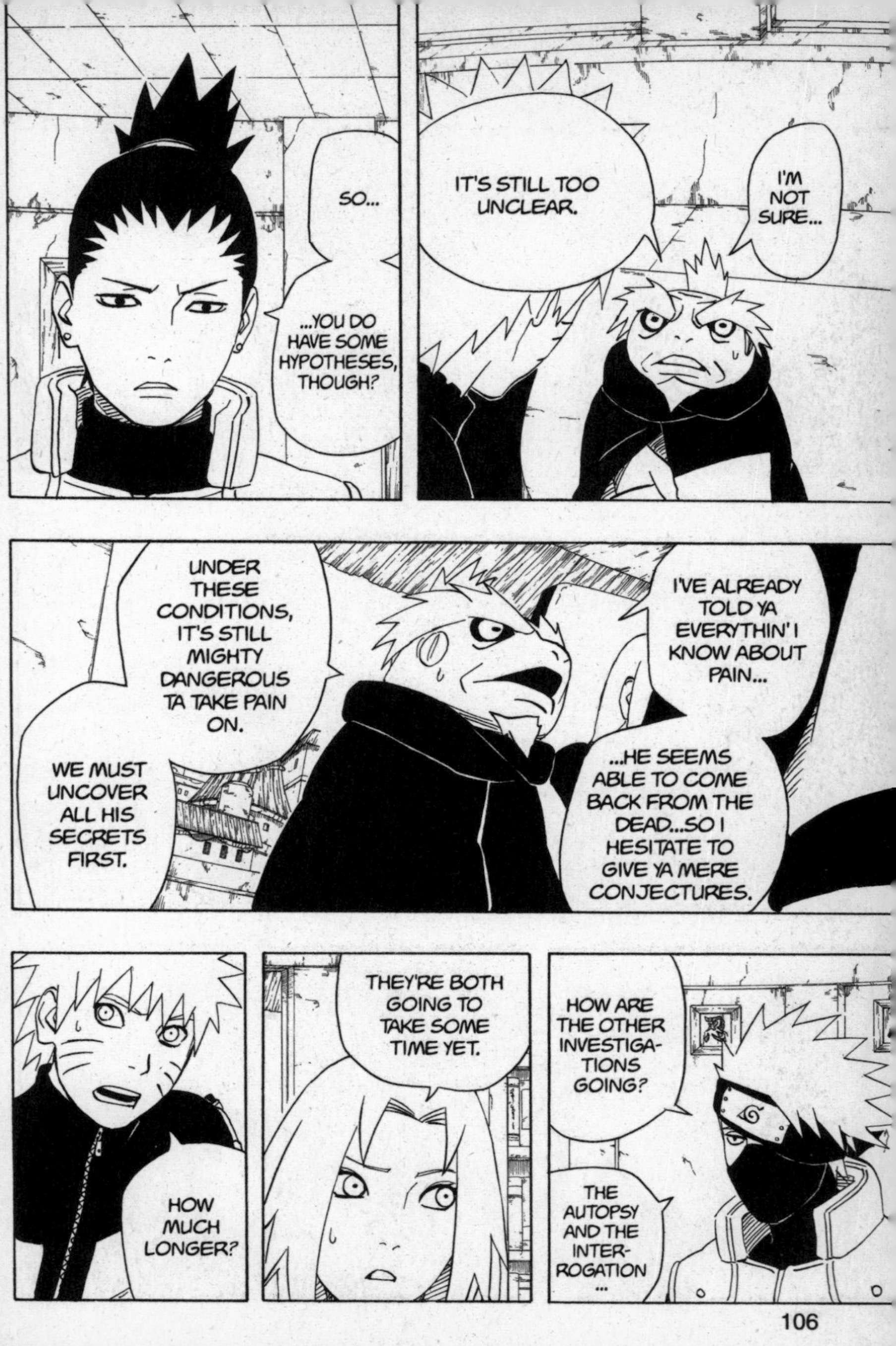
I'M NOT SURE...
IT'S STILL TOO UNCLEAR.
SO...
...YOU DO HAVE SOME HYPOTHESES, THOUGH?
I'VE ALREADY TOLD YA EVERYTHIN' I KNOW ABOUT PAIN...
...HE SEEMS ABLE TO COME BACK FROM THE DEAD...SO I HESITATE TO GIVE YA MERE CONJECTURES.
UNDER THESE CONDITIONS, IT'S STILL MIGHTY DANGEROUS TA TAKE PAIN ON.
WE MUST UNCOVER ALL HIS SECRETS FIRST.
HOW ARE THE OTHER INVESTIGA-TIONS GOING?
THE AUTOPSY AND THE INTER-ROGATION ...
THEY'RE BOTH GOING TO TAKE SOME TIME YET.
HOW MUCH LONGER?

READ THIS WAY

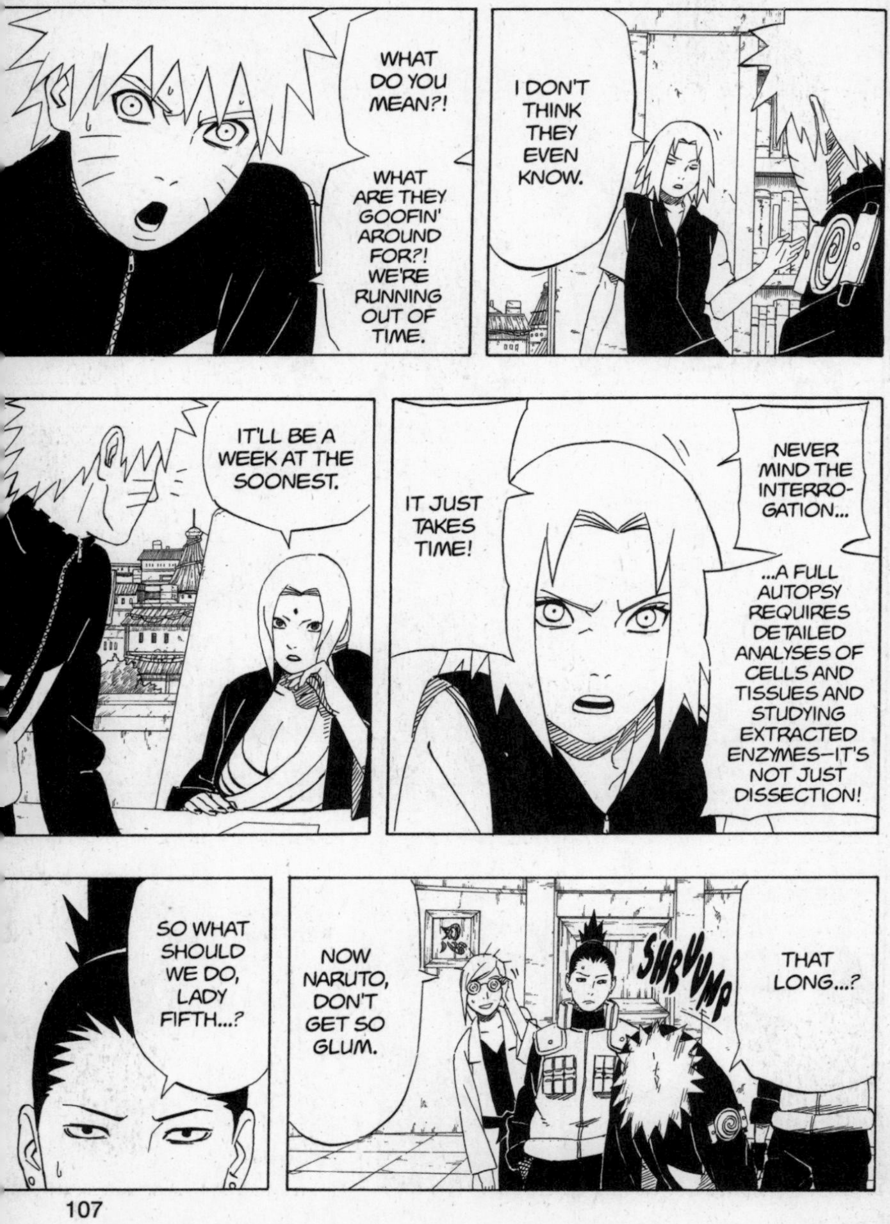
I DON'T THINK THEY EVEN KNOW.
WHAT DO YOU MEAN?!
WHAT ARE THEY GOOFIN' AROUND FOR?! WE'RE RUNNING OUT OF TIME.
NEVER MIND THE INTERROGATION...
...A FULL AUTOPSY REQUIRES DETAILED ANALYSES OF CELLS AND TISSUES AND STUDYING EXTRACTED ENZYMES--IT'S NOT JUST DISSECTION!
IT JUST TAKES TIME!
IT'LL BE A WEEK AT THE SOONEST.
THAT LONG...?
SHRVUMP
NOW NARUTO, DON'T GET SO GLUM.
SO WHAT SHOULD WE DO, LADY FIFTH...?

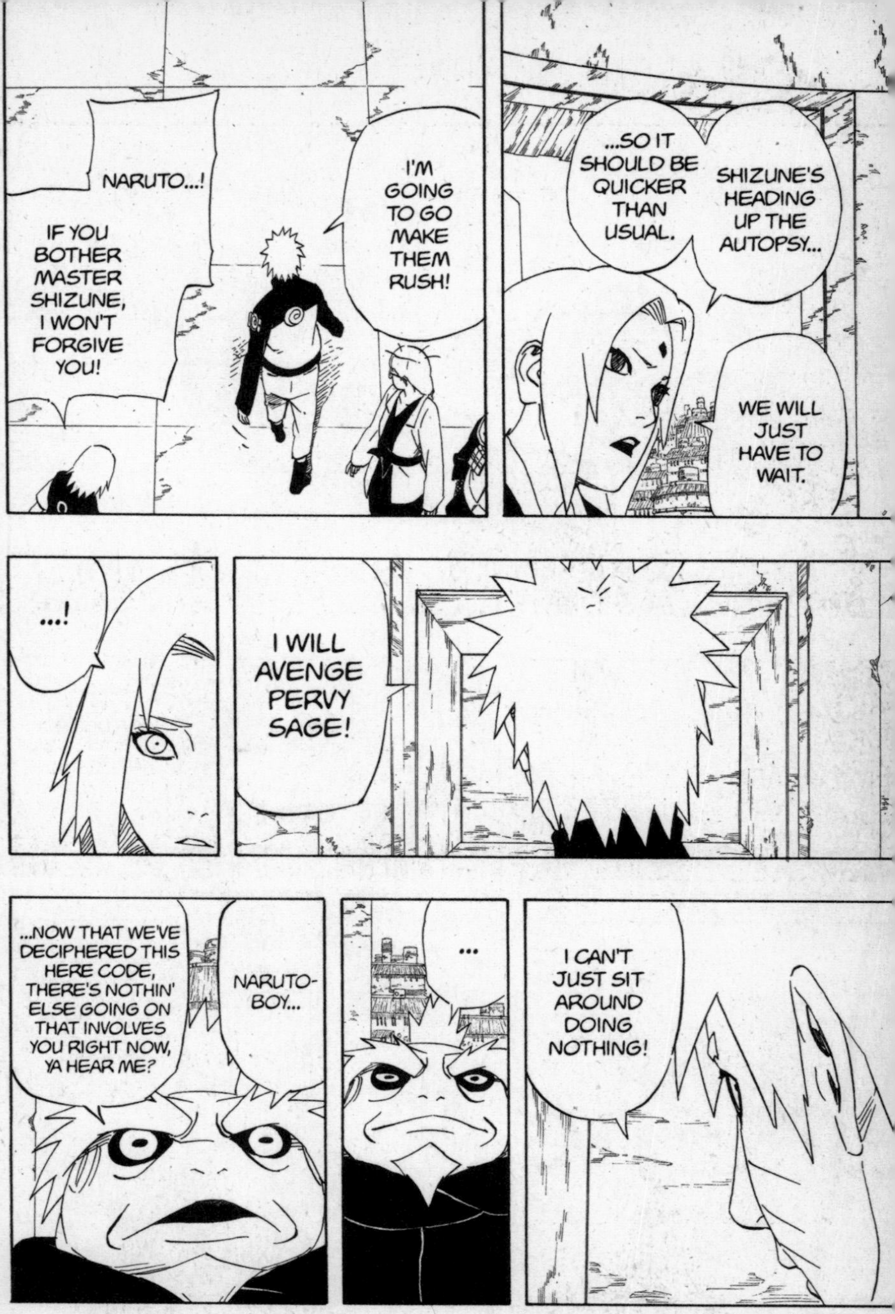
SHIZUNE'S HEADING UP THE AUTOPSY...
...SO IT SHOULD BE QUICKER THAN USUAL.
WE WILL JUST HAVE TO WAIT.
I'M GOING TO GO MAKE THEM RUSH!
NARUTO...!
IF YOU BOTHER MASTER SHIZUNE, I WON'T FORGIVE YOU!
I WILL AVENGE PERVY SAGE!
...!
I CAN'T JUST SIT AROUND DOING NOTHING!
...
NARUTO-BOY...
...NOW THAT WE'VE DECIPHERED THIS HERE CODE, THERE'S NOTHIN' ELSE GOING ON THAT INVOLVES YOU RIGHT NOW, YA HEAR ME?

READ THIS WAY

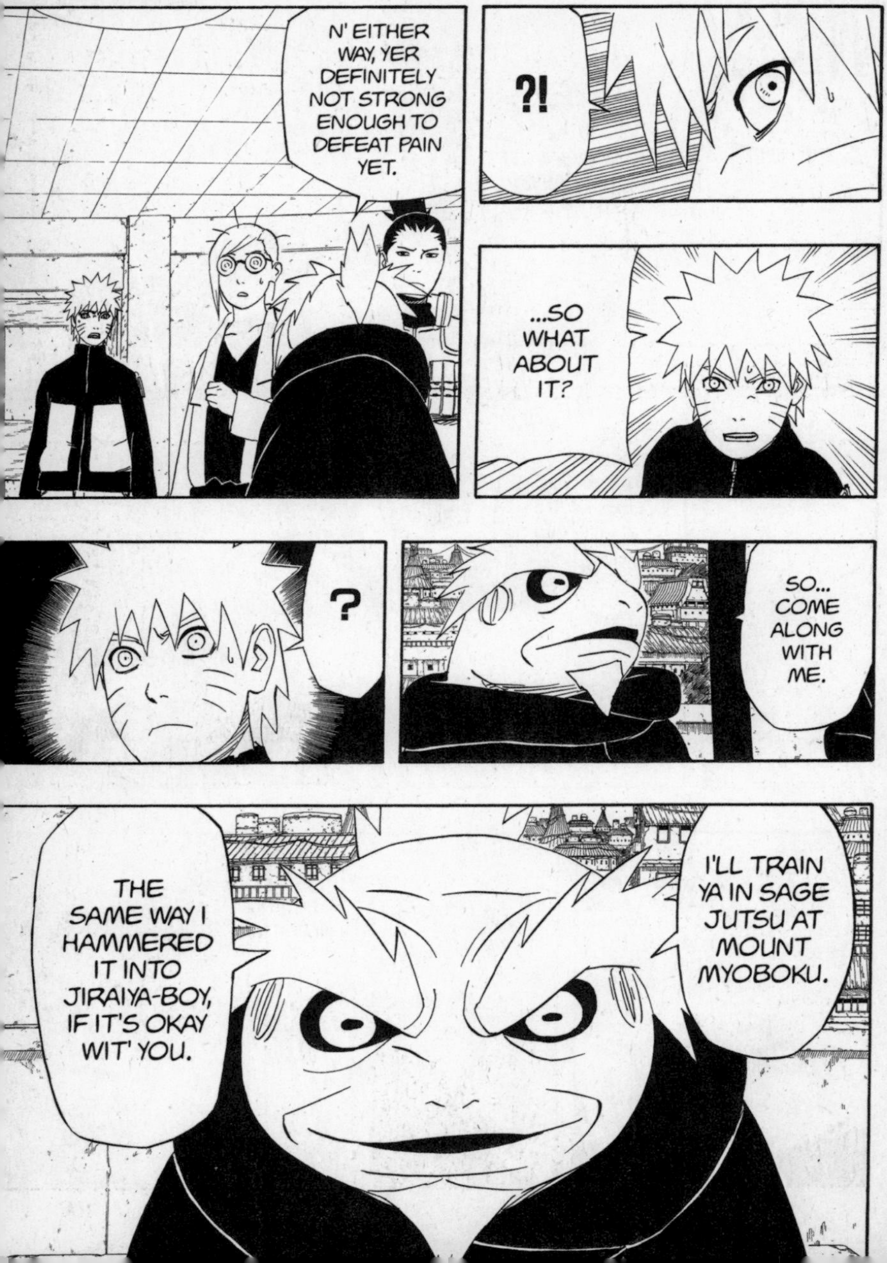
?!
...SO WHAT ABOUT IT?
N' EITHER WAY, YER DEFINITELY NOT STRONG ENOUGH TO DEFEAT PAIN YET.
SO... COME ALONG WITH ME.
?
I'LL TRAIN YA IN SAGE JUTSU AT MOUNT MYOBOKU.
THE SAME WAY I HAMMERED IT INTO JIRAIYA-BOY, IF IT'S OKAY WIT' YOU.

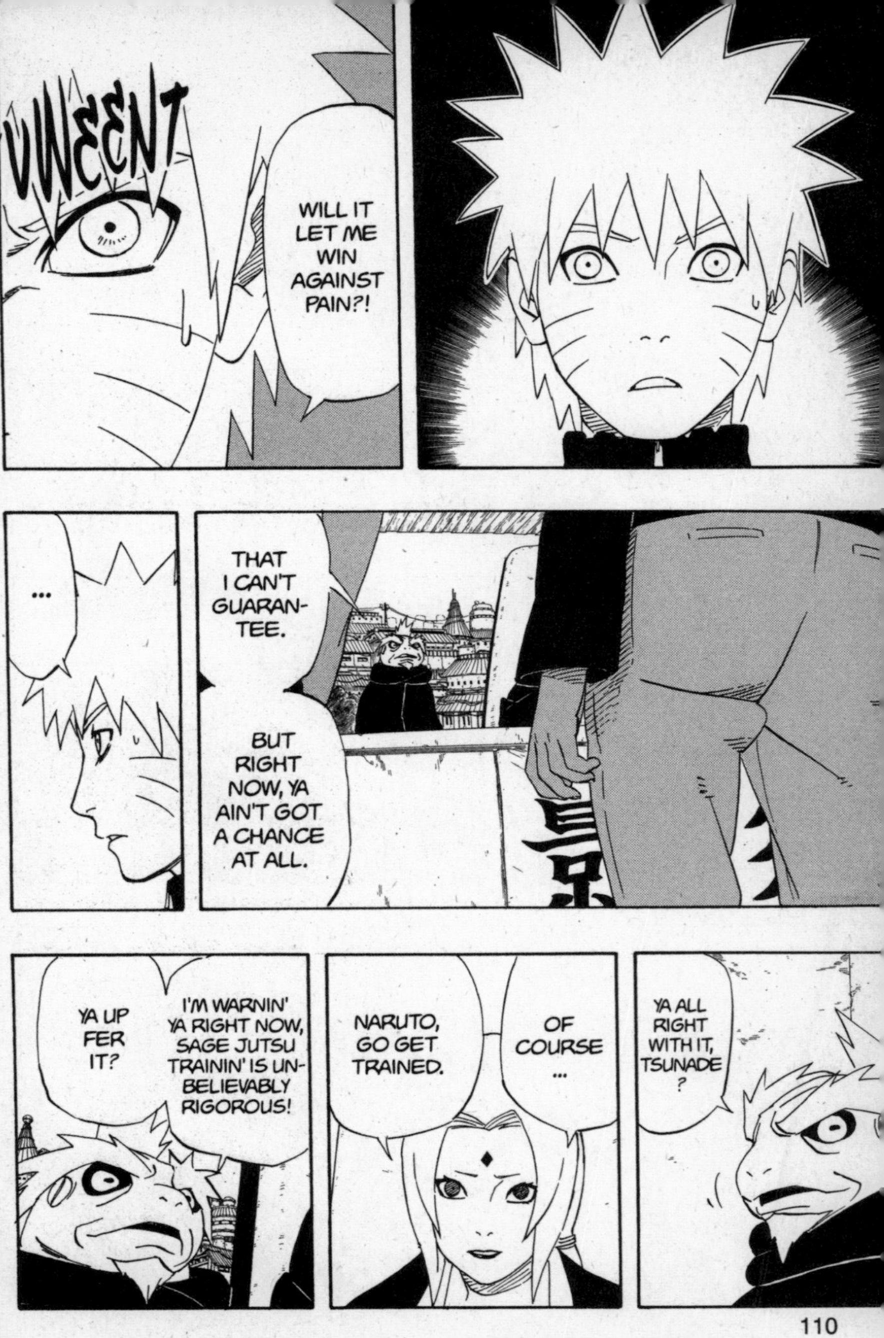
WILL IT LET ME WIN AGAINST PAIN?!
VWEENT
THAT I CAN'T GUARAN-TEE.
BUT RIGHT NOW, YA AIN'T GOT A CHANCE AT ALL.
...
YA ALL RIGHT WITH IT, TSUNADE?
OF COURSE...
NARUTO, GO GET TRAINED.
I'M WARNIN' YA RIGHT NOW, SAGE JUTSU TRAININ' IS UN-BELIEVABLY RIGOROUS!
YA UP FER IT?

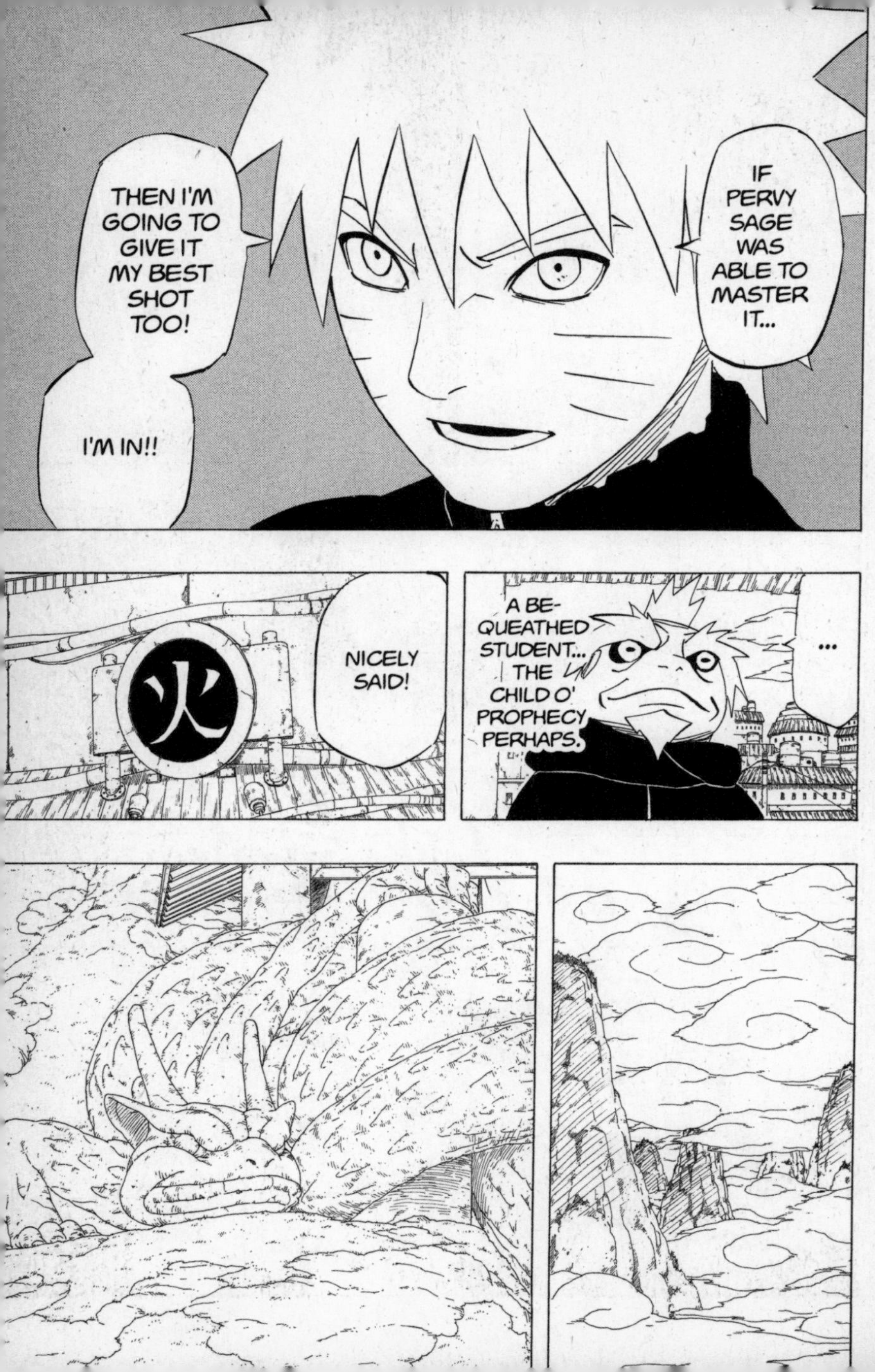

IF PERVY SAGE WAS ABLE TO MASTER IT...
THEN I'M GOING TO GIVE IT MY BEST SHOT TOO!
I'M IN!!
...
A BE-QUEATHED STUDENT... THE CHILD O' PROPHECY PERHAPS.
NICELY SAID!

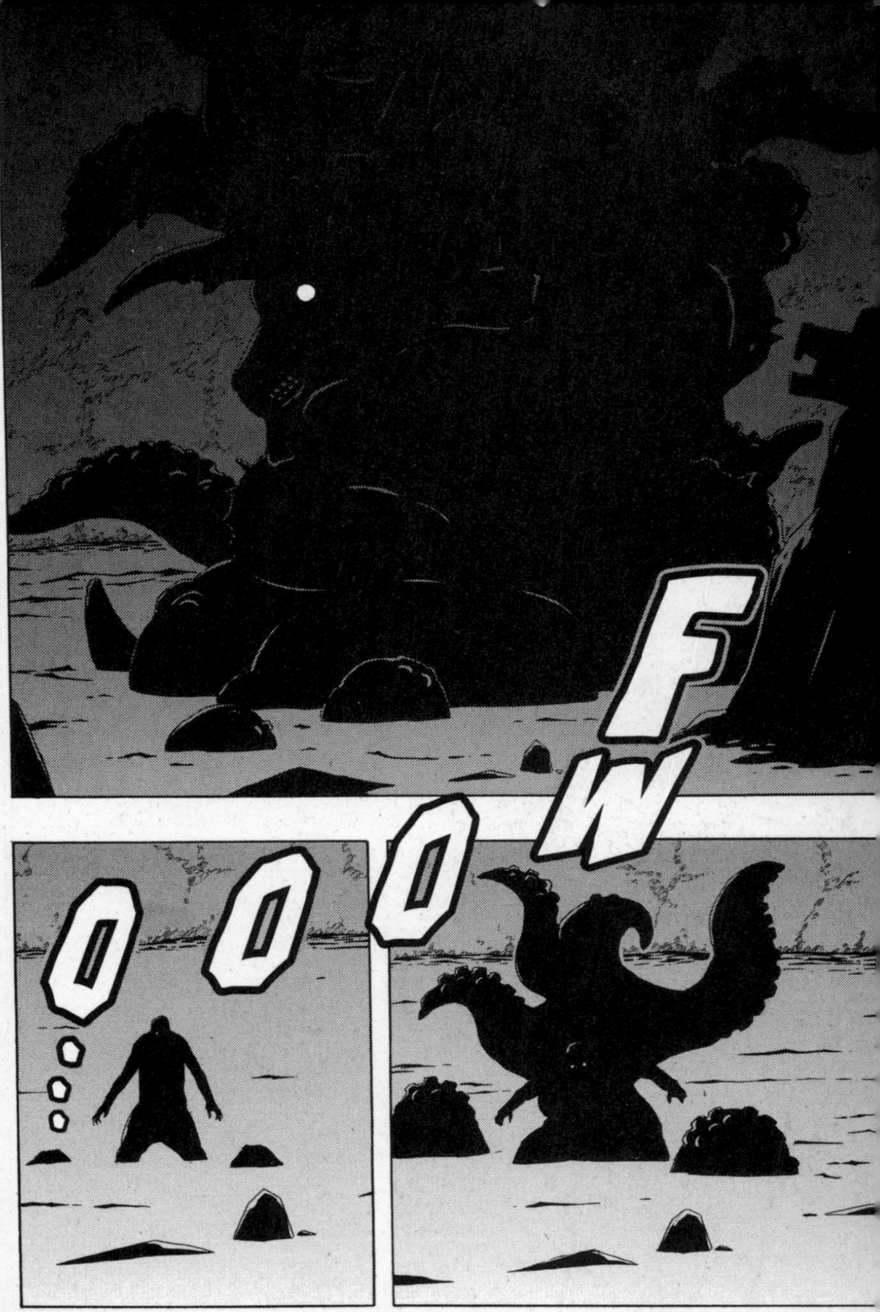
FWOOOO...

READ THIS WAY

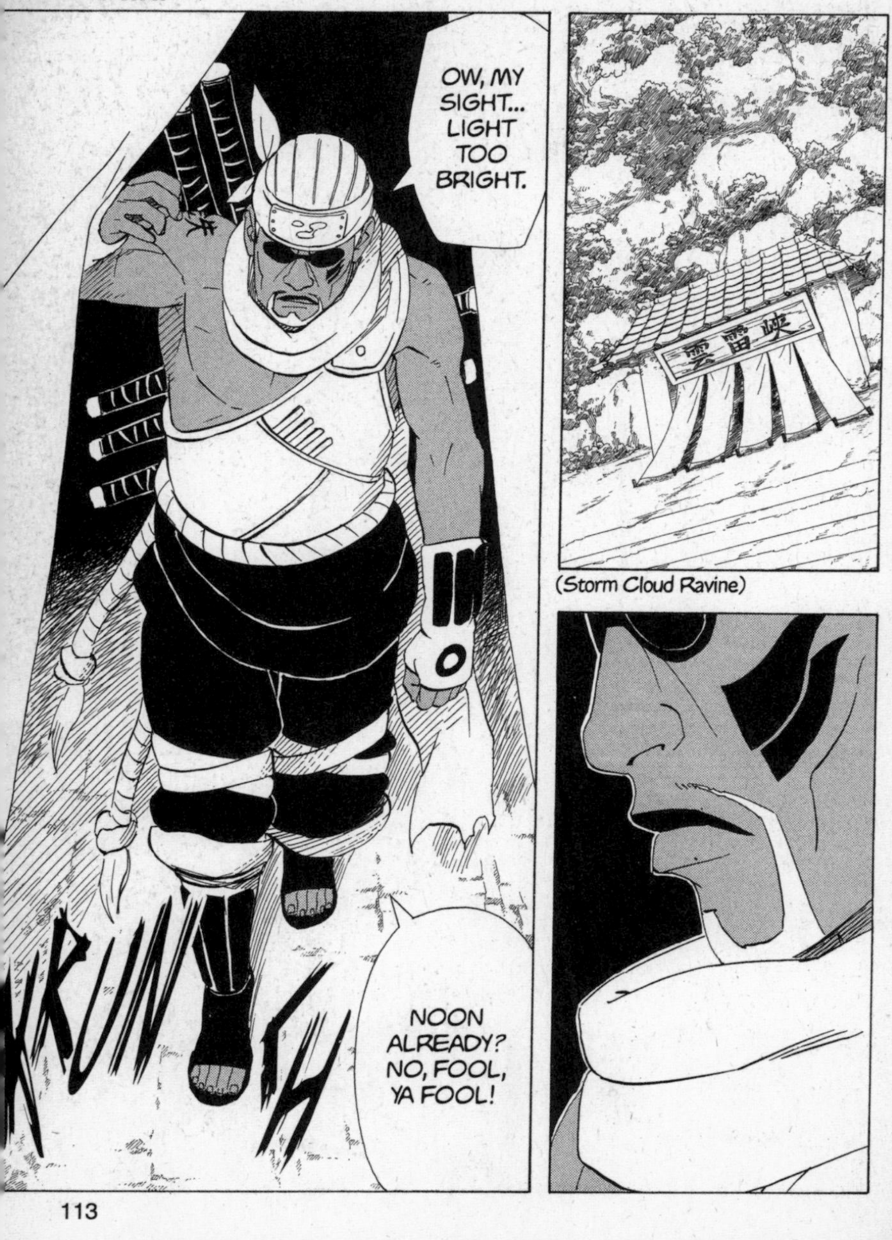
雲雷峡
(Storm Cloud Ravine)
OW, MY SIGHT... LIGHT TOO BRIGHT.
NOON ALREADY? NO, FOOL, YA FOOL!
KRUNCH

NARUTO

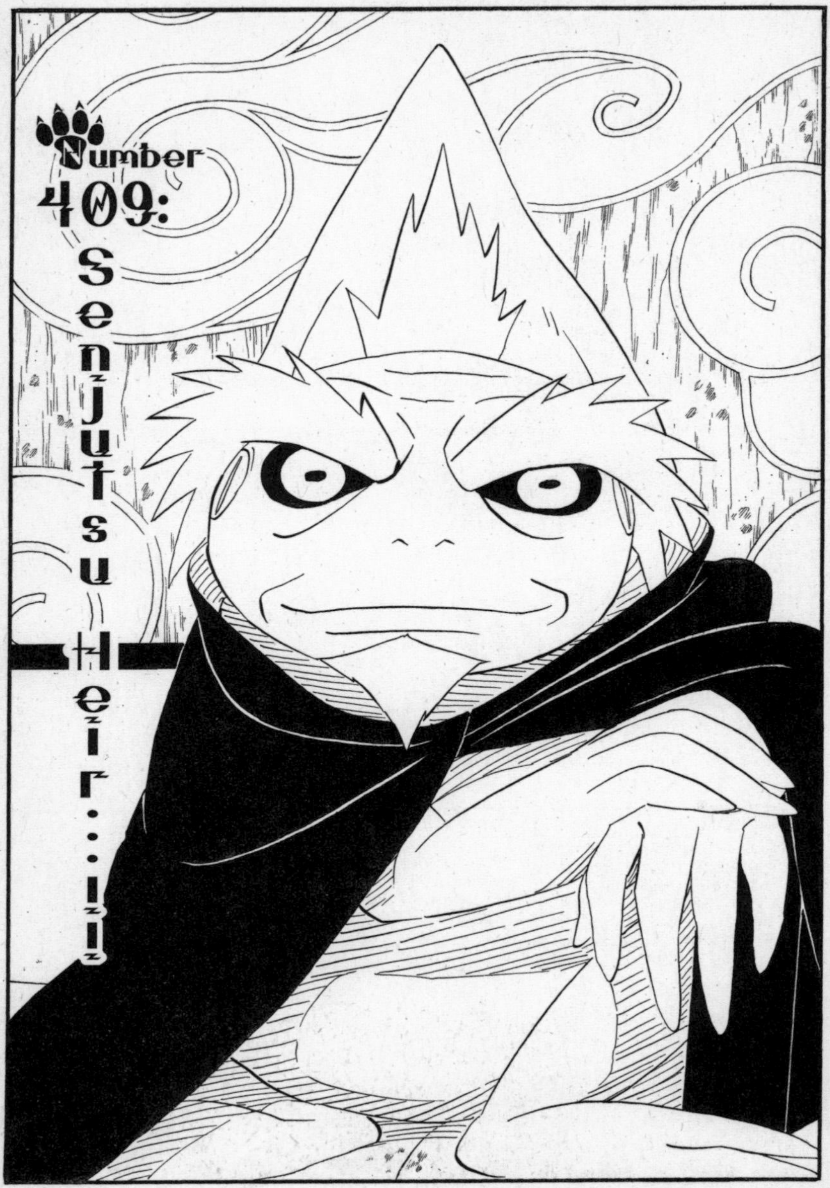
Number 409: Senjutsu Heir...!!

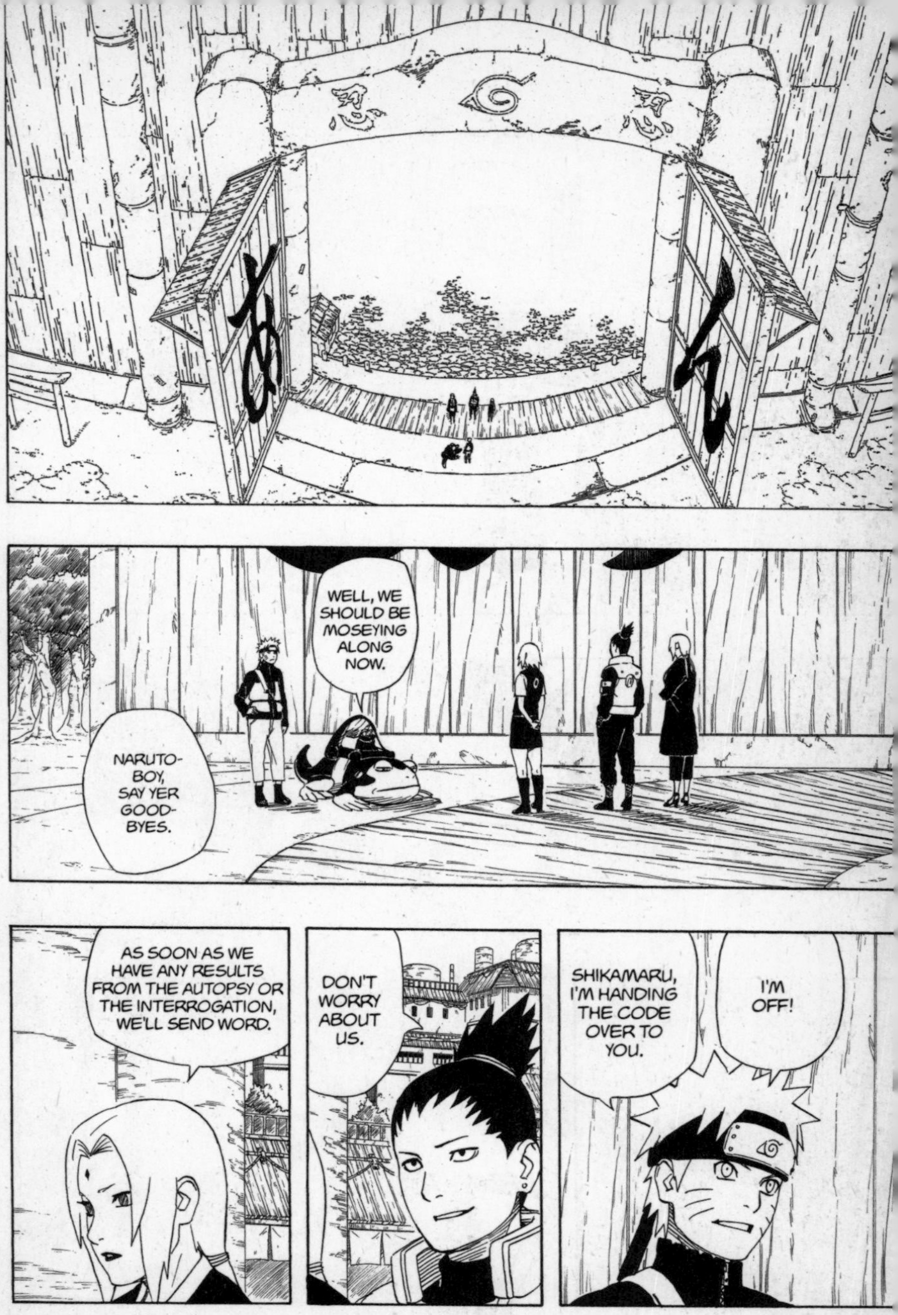
WELL, WE SHOULD BE MOSEYING ALONG NOW.
NARUTO-BOY, SAY YER GOOD-BYES.
I'M OFF!
SHIKAMARU, I'M HANDING THE CODE OVER TO YOU.
DON'T WORRY ABOUT US.
AS SOON AS WE HAVE ANY RESULTS FROM THE AUTOPSY OR THE INTERROGATION, WE'LL SEND WORD.

READ THIS WAY

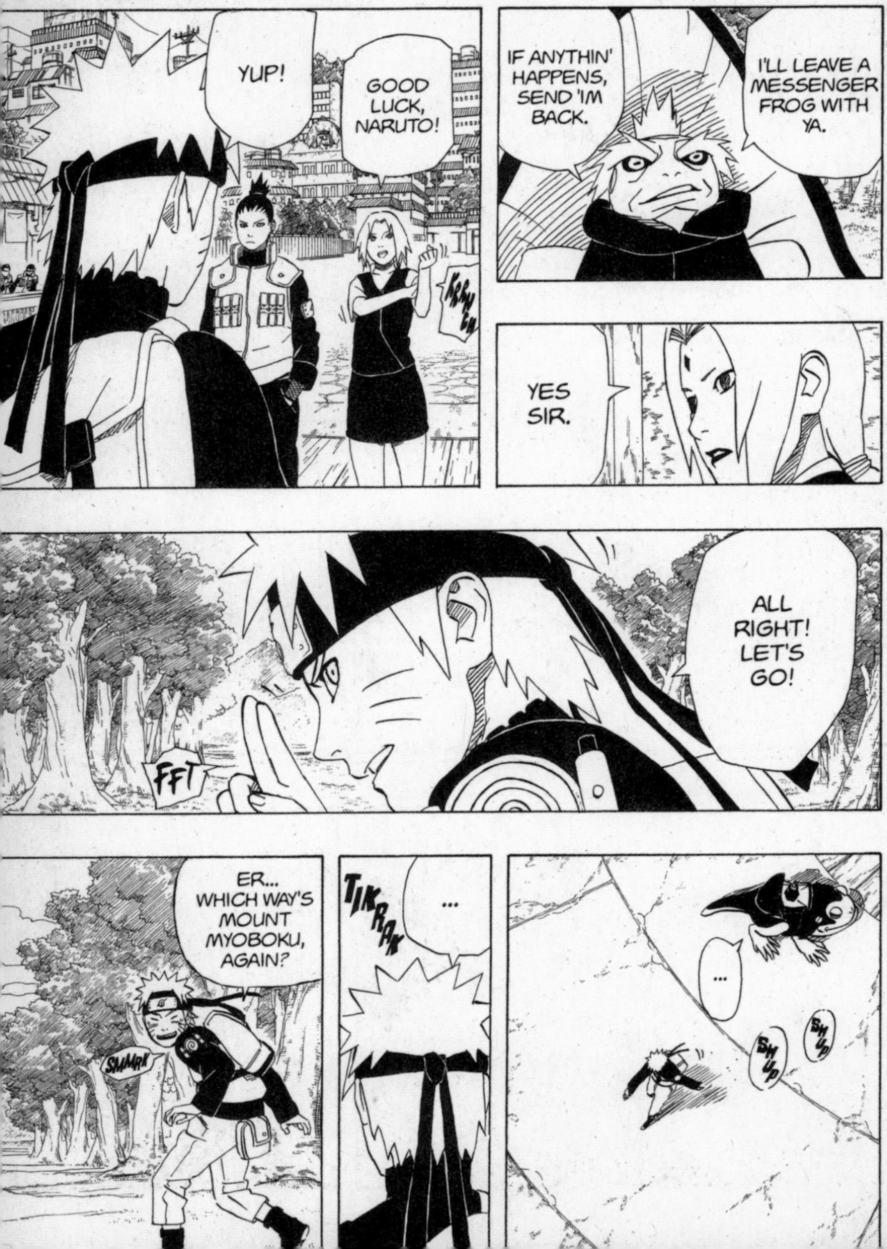
I'LL LEAVE A MESSENGER FROG WITH YA.
IF ANYTHIN' HAPPENS, SEND 'IM BACK.
YES SIR.
GOOD LUCK, NARUTO!
YUP!
KRRUNCH
ALL RIGHT! LET'S GO!
FFT
...
SHUP
SHUP
TIKRAK
...
ER... WHICH WAY'S MOUNT MYOBOKU, AGAIN?
SMMRK

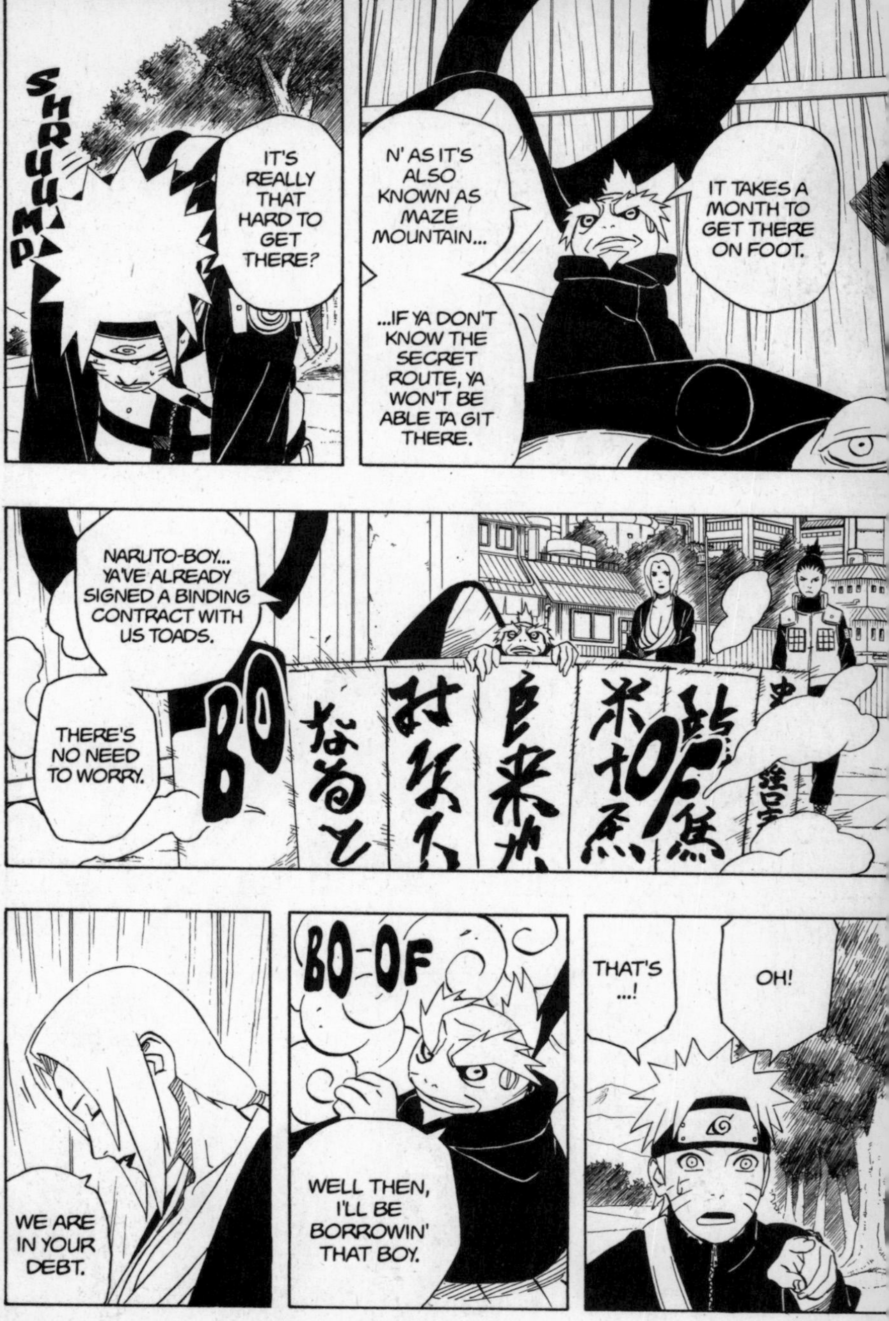
IT TAKES A MONTH TO GET THERE ON FOOT.
N' AS IT'S ALSO KNOWN AS MAZE MOUNTAIN...
...IF YA DON'T KNOW THE SECRET ROUTE, YA WON'T BE ABLE TA GIT THERE.
IT'S REALLY THAT HARD TO GET THERE?
SHRUUMP
NARUTO-BOY... YA'VE ALREADY SIGNED A BINDING CONTRACT WITH US TOADS.
THERE'S NO NEED TO WORRY.
BO
OF
OH!
THAT'S ...!
BO-OF
WELL THEN, I'LL BE BORROWIN' THAT BOY.
WE ARE IN YOUR DEBT.

READ THIS WAY

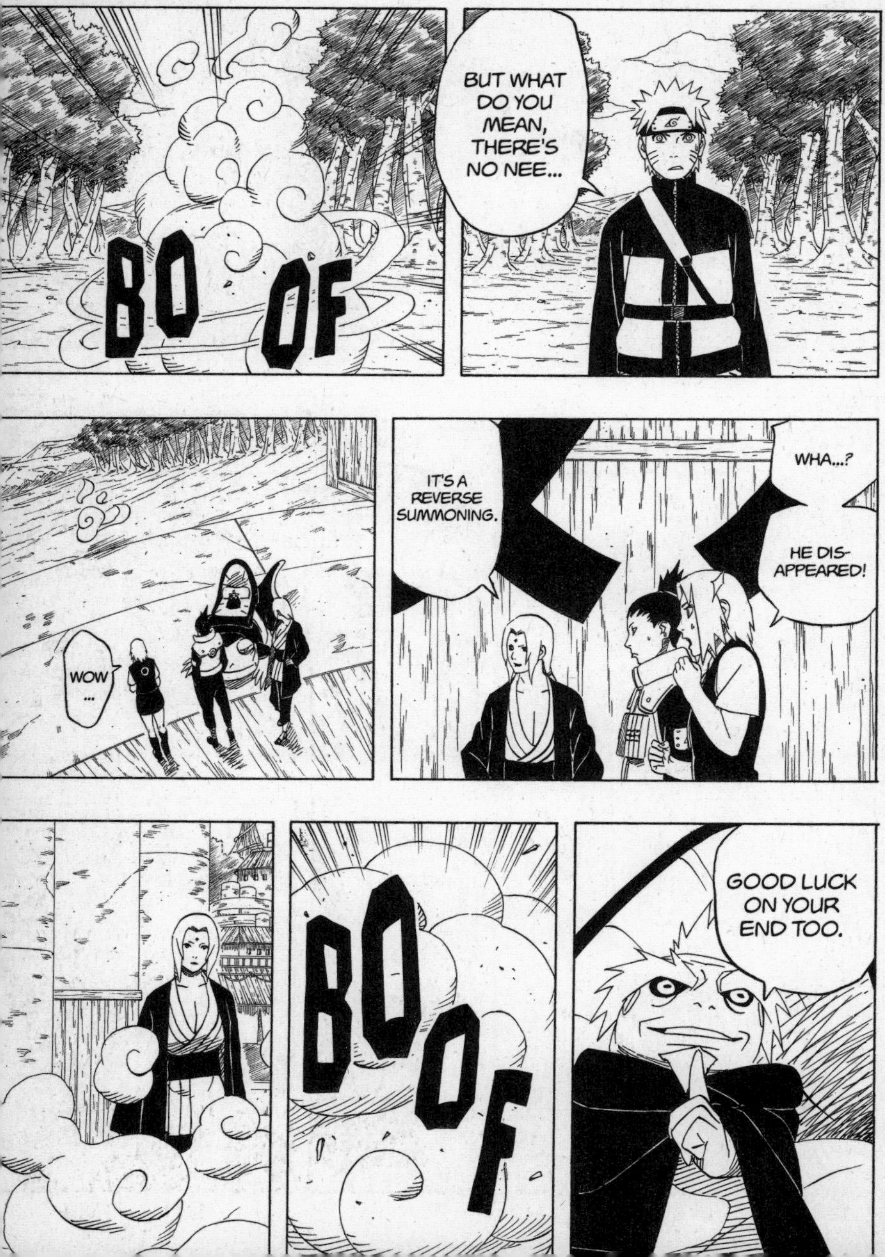
BUT WHAT DO YOU MEAN, THERE'S NO NEE...
BO OF
WHA...?
HE DIS-APPEARED!
IT'S A REVERSE SUMMONING.
WOW ...
GOOD LUCK ON YOUR END TOO.
BO O OF

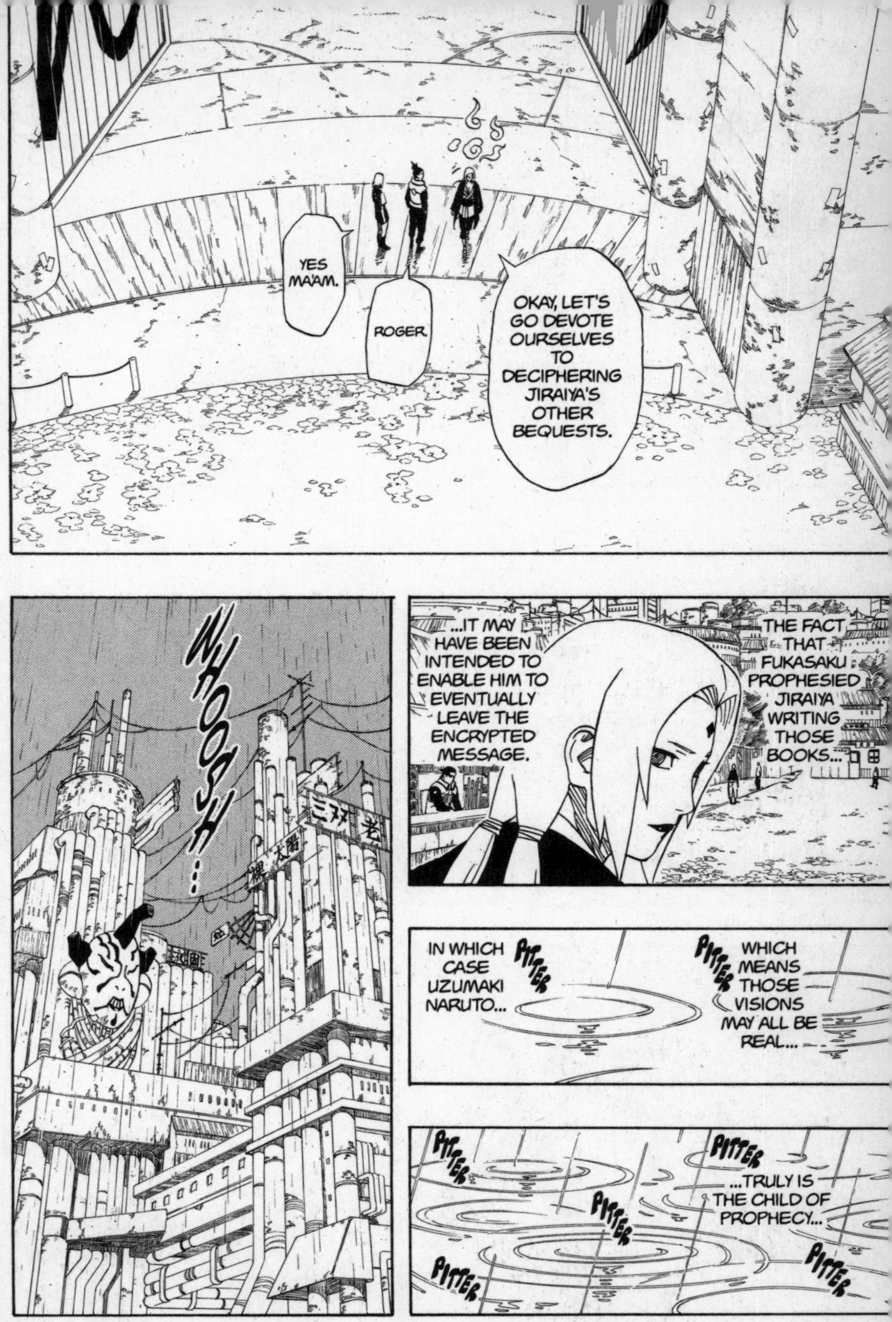
OKAY, LET'S GO DEVOTE OURSELVES TO DECIPHERING JIRAIYA'S OTHER BEQUESTS.
ROGER.
YES MA'AM.
THE FACT THAT FUKASAKU PROPHESIED JIRAIYA WRITING THOSE BOOKS...
...IT MAY HAVE BEEN INTENDED TO ENABLE HIM TO EVENTUALLY LEAVE THE ENCRYPTED MESSAGE.
PITTER
WHICH MEANS THOSE VISIONS MAY ALL BE REAL...
PITTER
IN WHICH CASE UZUMAKI NARUTO...
PITTER
...TRULY IS THE CHILD OF PROPHECY...
PITTER
PITTER
PITTER
PITTER
WHOOSH...

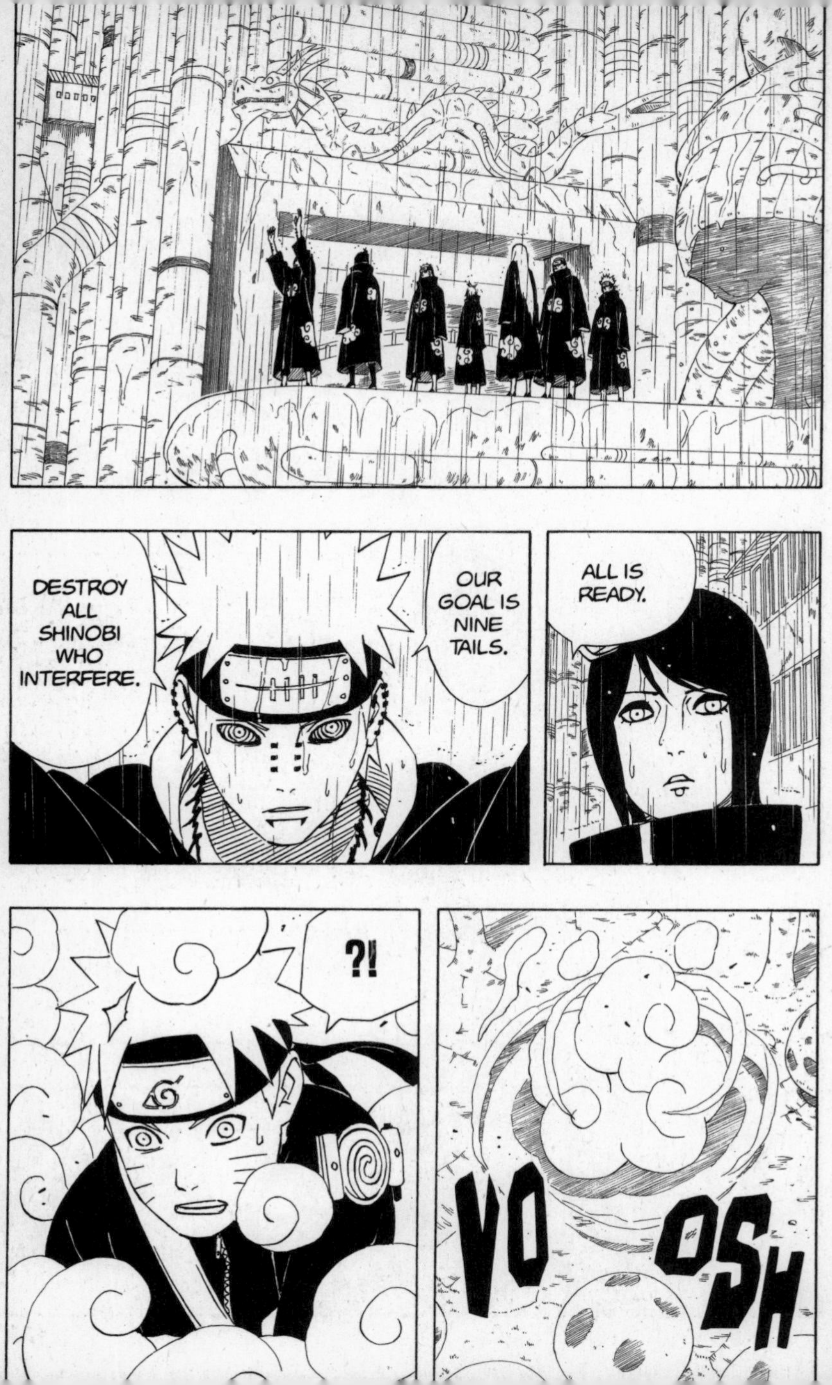
ALL IS READY.
OUR GOAL IS NINE TAILS.
DESTROY ALL SHINOBI WHO INTERFERE.
VOOSH
?!

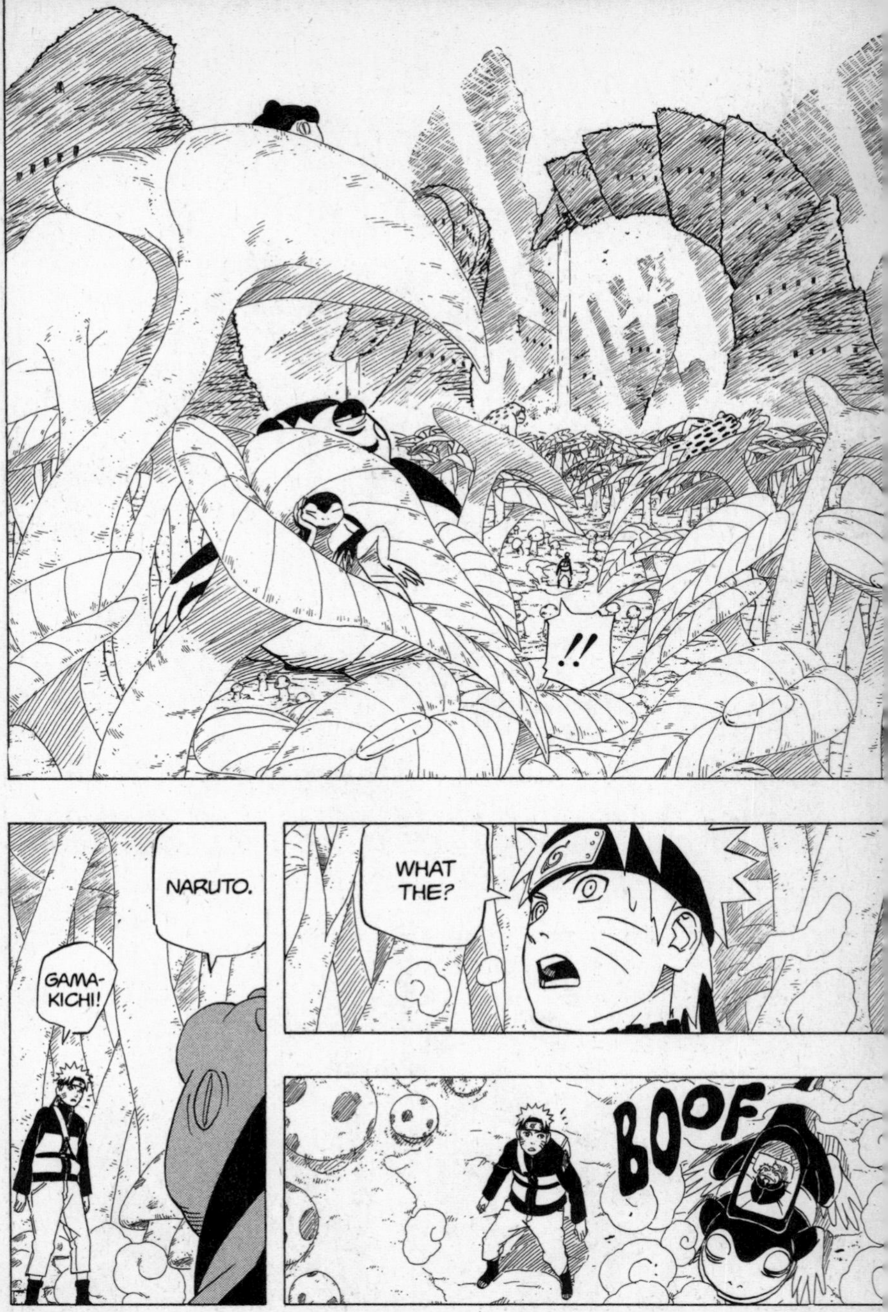
!!
WHAT THE?
BOOF
NARUTO.
GAMA-KICHI!

READ THIS WAY

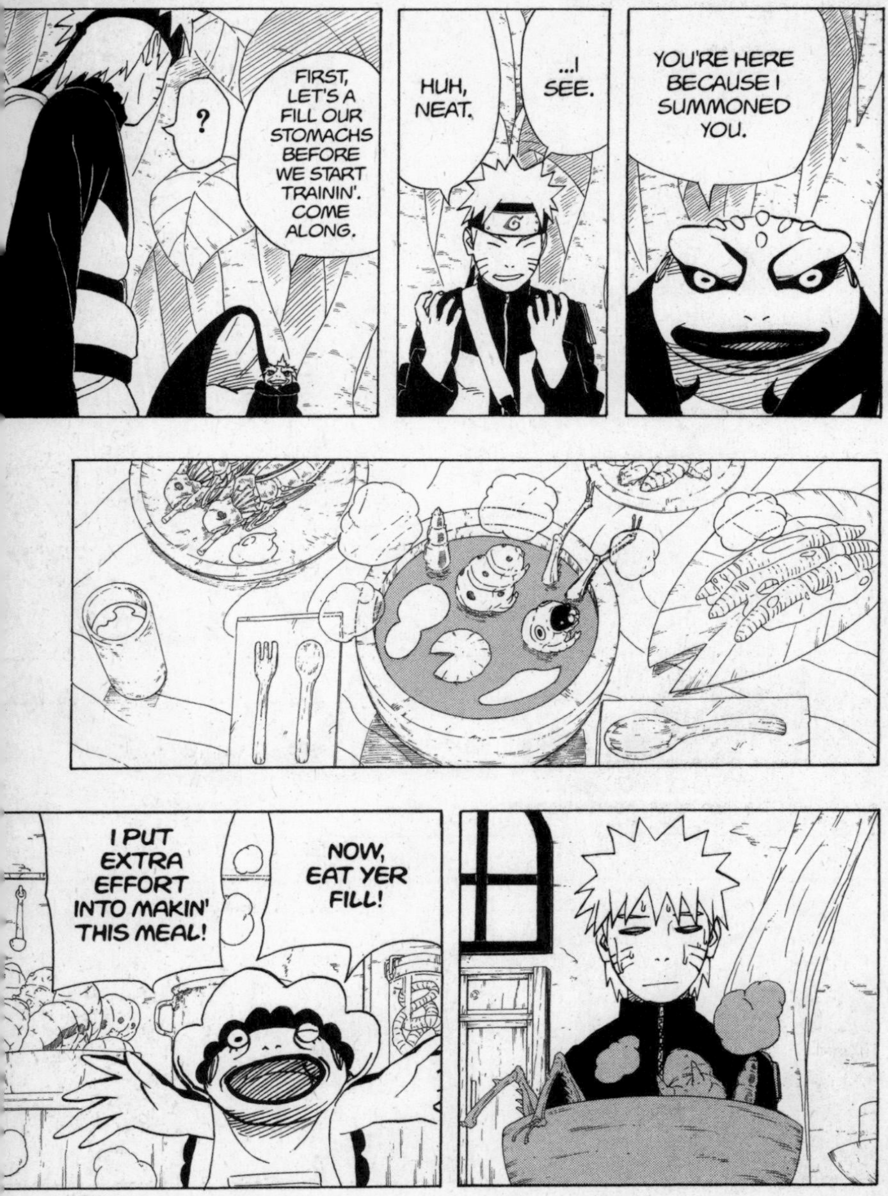

YOU'RE HERE BECAUSE I SUMMONED YOU.
...I SEE.
HUH, NEAT.
FIRST, LET'S A FILL OUR STOMACHS BEFORE WE START TRAININ'. COME ALONG.
?
I PUT EXTRA EFFORT INTO MAKIN' THIS MEAL!
NOW, EAT YER FILL!

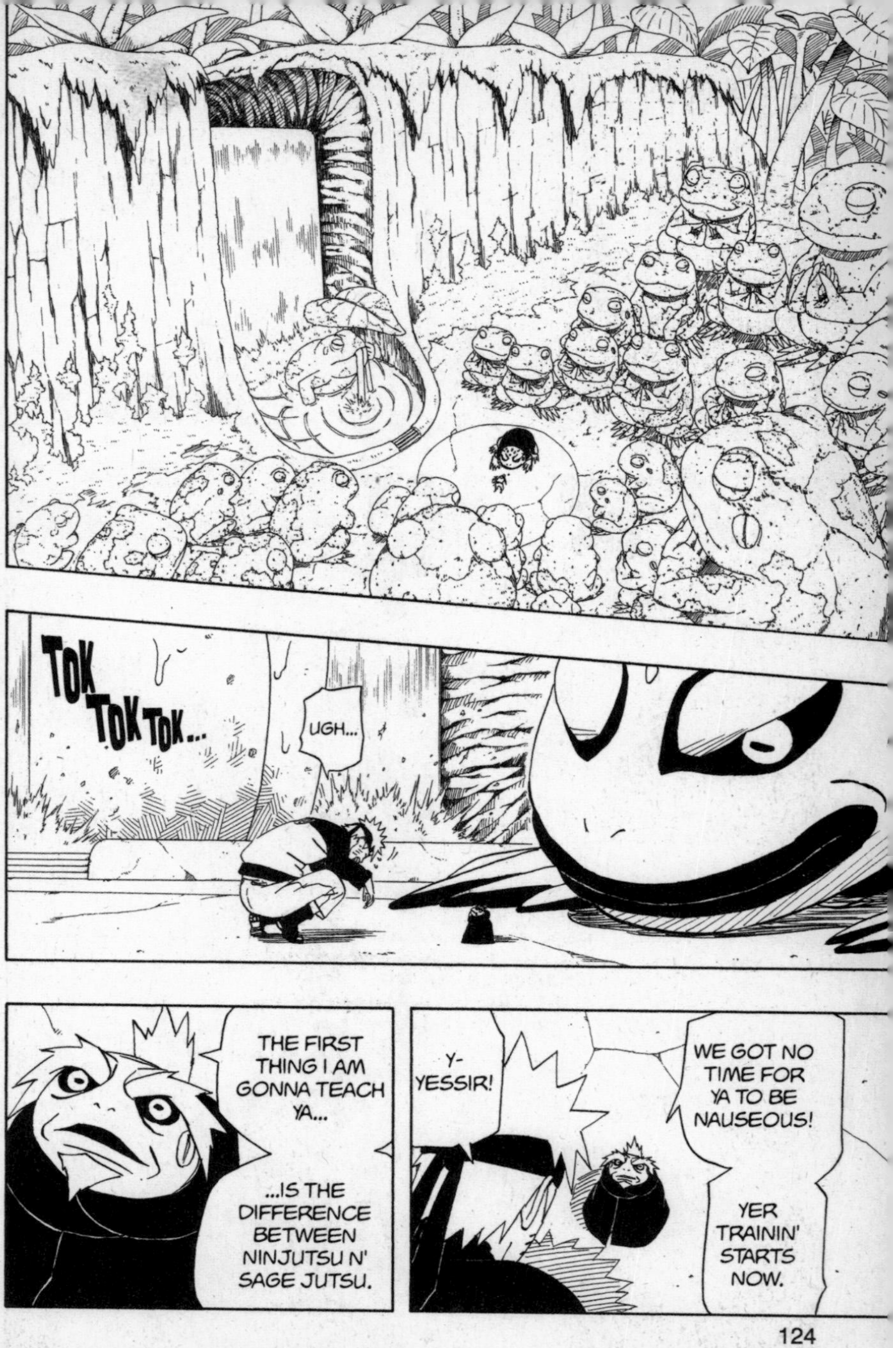
TOK TOK TOK...
UGH...
THE FIRST THING I AM GONNA TEACH YA...
...IS THE DIFFERENCE BETWEEN NINJUTSU N' SAGE JUTSU.
WE GOT NO TIME FOR YA TO BE NAUSEOUS!
YER TRAININ' STARTS NOW.
Y-YESSIR!

READ THIS WAY

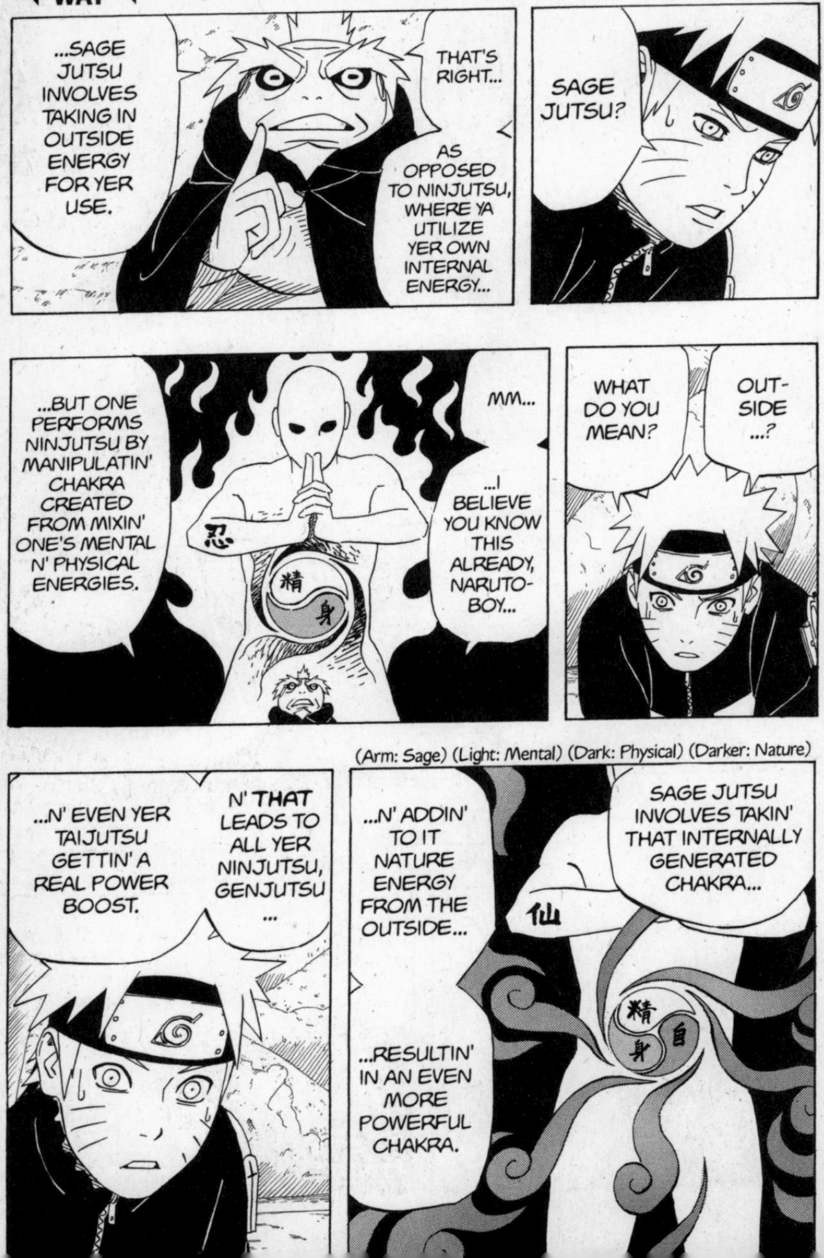
SAGE JUTSU?
THAT'S RIGHT...
...SAGE JUTSU INVOLVES TAKING IN OUTSIDE ENERGY FOR YER USE.
AS OPPOSED TO NINJUTSU, WHERE YA UTILIZE YER OWN INTERNAL ENERGY...
OUT-SIDE ...?
WHAT DO YOU MEAN?
MM...
...I BELIEVE YOU KNOW THIS ALREADY, NARUTO-BOY...
...BUT ONE PERFORMS NINJUTSU BY MANIPULATIN' CHAKRA CREATED FROM MIXIN' ONE'S MENTAL N' PHYSICAL ENERGIES.
忍
精
身
(Arm: Sage) (Light: Mental) (Dark: Physical) (Darker: Nature)
SAGE JUTSU INVOLVES TAKIN' THAT INTERNALLY GENERATED CHAKRA...
仙
...N' ADDIN' TO IT NATURE ENERGY FROM THE OUTSIDE...
精
自
身
...RESULTIN' IN AN EVEN MORE POWERFUL CHAKRA.
N' THAT LEADS TO ALL YER NINJUTSU, GENJUTSU ...
...N' EVEN YER TAIJUTSU GETTIN' A REAL POWER BOOST.

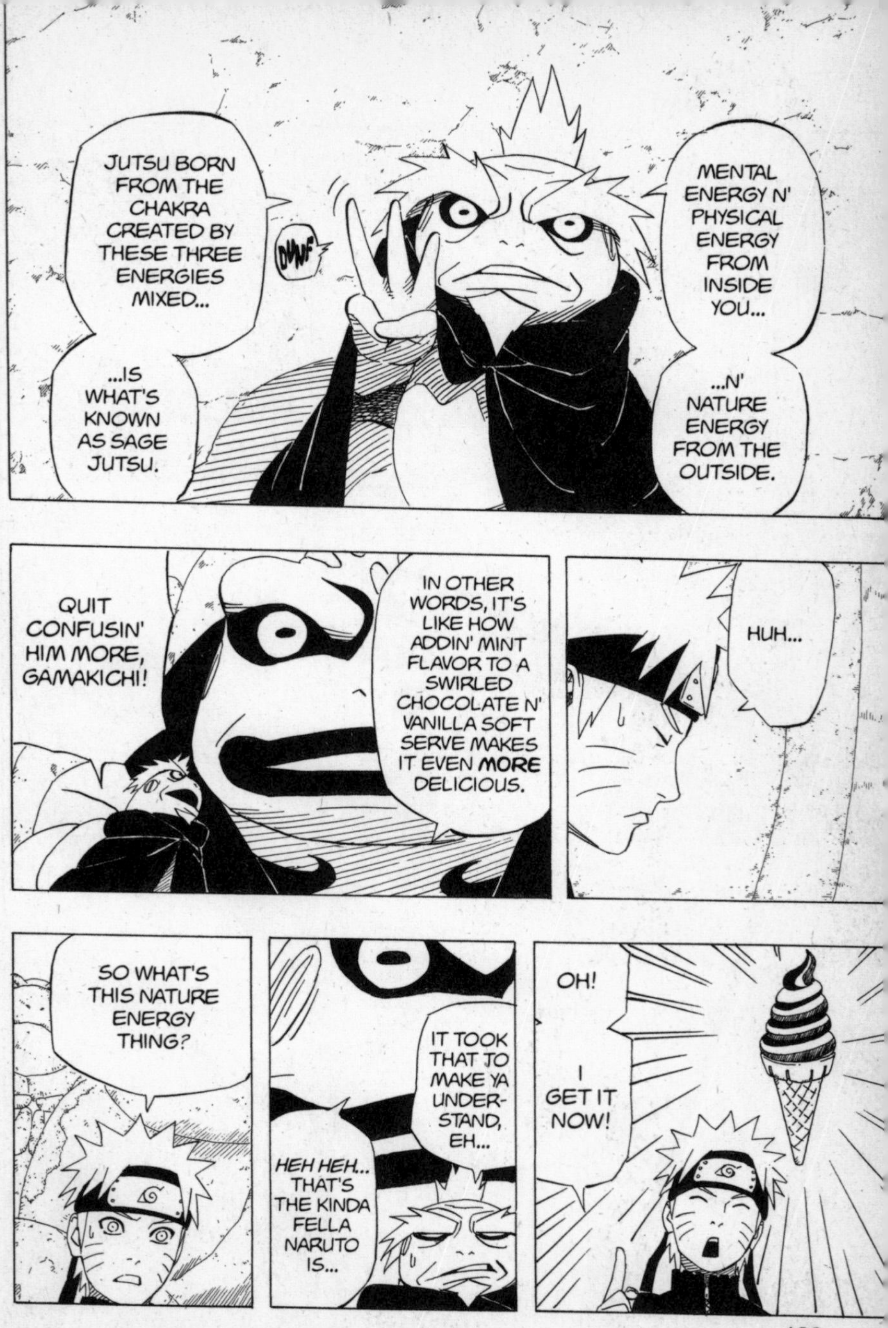
MENTAL ENERGY N' PHYSICAL ENERGY FROM INSIDE YOU...
...N' NATURE ENERGY FROM THE OUTSIDE.
JUTSU BORN FROM THE CHAKRA CREATED BY THESE THREE ENERGIES MIXED...
...IS WHAT'S KNOWN AS SAGE JUTSU.
HUH...
IN OTHER WORDS, IT'S LIKE HOW ADDIN' MINT FLAVOR TO A SWIRLED CHOCOLATE N' VANILLA SOFT SERVE MAKES IT EVEN **MORE** DELICIOUS.
QUIT CONFUSIN' HIM MORE, GAMAKICHI!
OH!
I GET IT NOW!
IT TOOK THAT TO MAKE YA UNDER-STAND, EH...
HEH HEH... THAT'S THE KINDA FELLA NARUTO IS...
SO WHAT'S THIS NATURE ENERGY THING?

READ THIS WAY

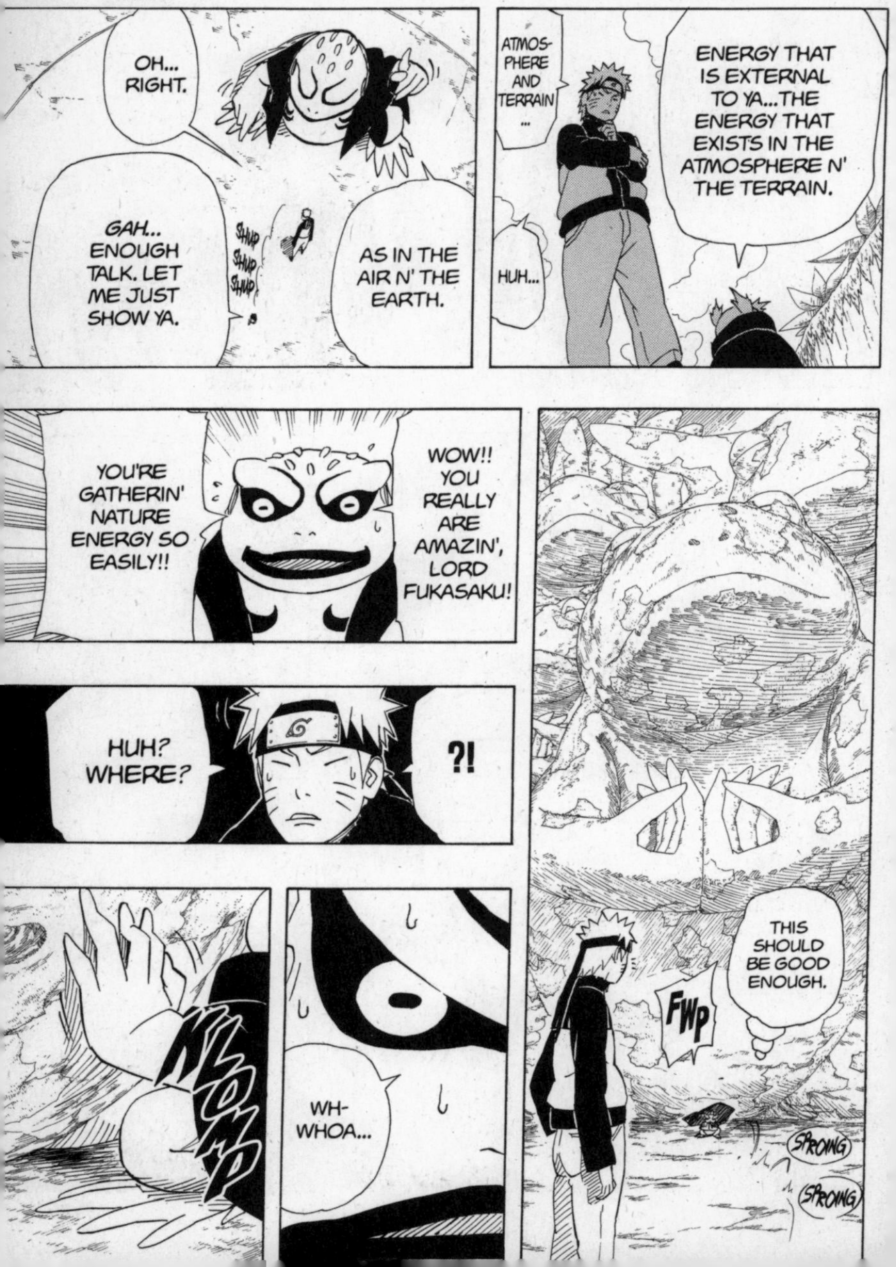
ENERGY THAT IS EXTERNAL TO YA...THE ENERGY THAT EXISTS IN THE ATMOSPHERE N' THE TERRAIN.
ATMOSPHERE AND TERRAIN...
HUH...
AS IN THE AIR N' THE EARTH.
OH... RIGHT.
GAH... ENOUGH TALK. LET ME JUST SHOW YA.
SHUP SHUP SHUP
THIS SHOULD BE GOOD ENOUGH.
FWP
SPROING
SPROING
WOW!! YOU REALLY ARE AMAZIN', LORD FUKASAKU!
YOU'RE GATHERIN' NATURE ENERGY SO EASILY!!
?!
HUH? WHERE?
WH- WHOA...
WOMP

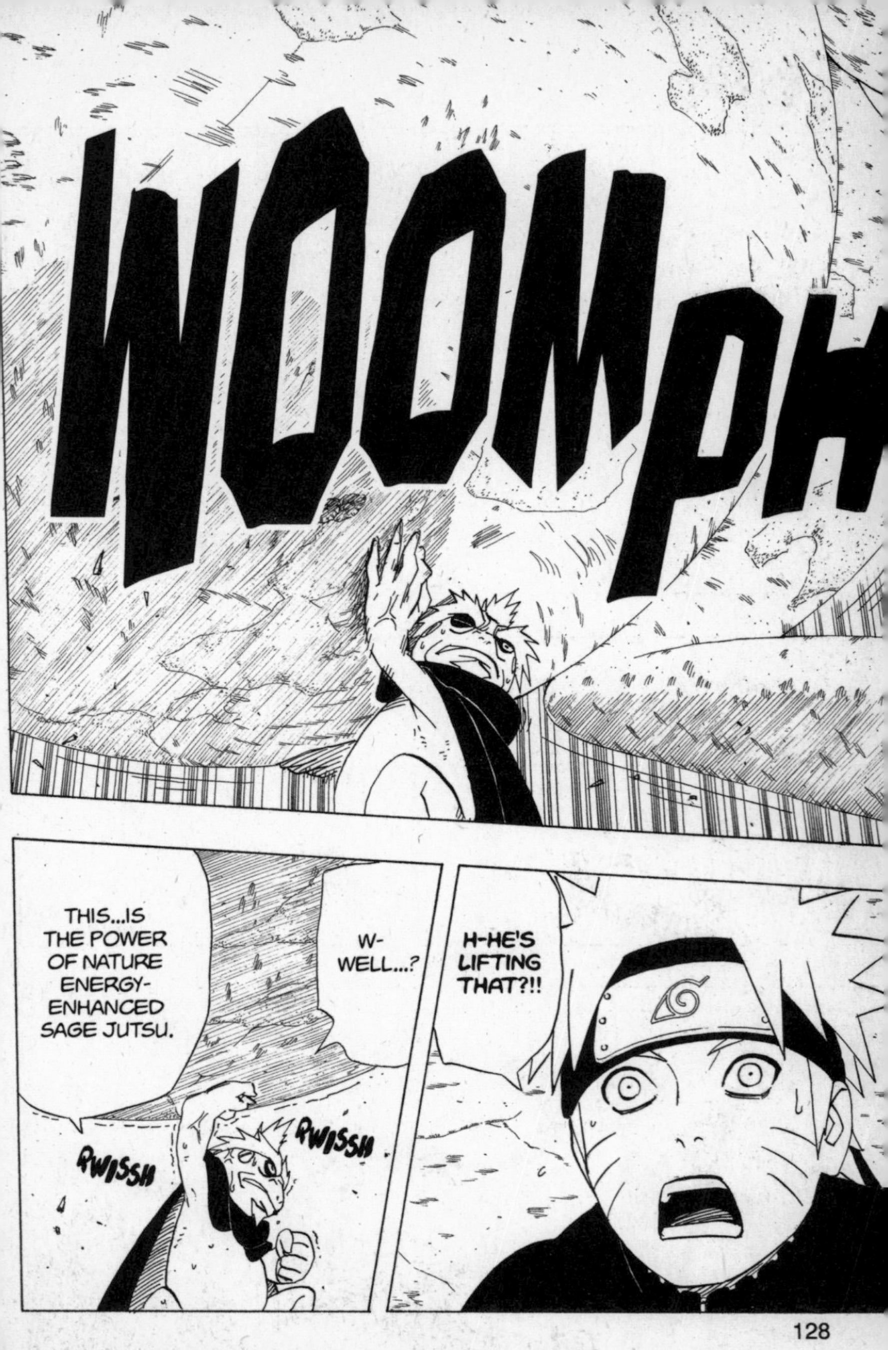
WOOMPH
H-HE'S LIFTING THAT?!!
W-WELL...?
THIS...IS THE POWER OF NATURE ENERGY-ENHANCED SAGE JUTSU.
RWISSH
RWISSH

READ THIS WAY

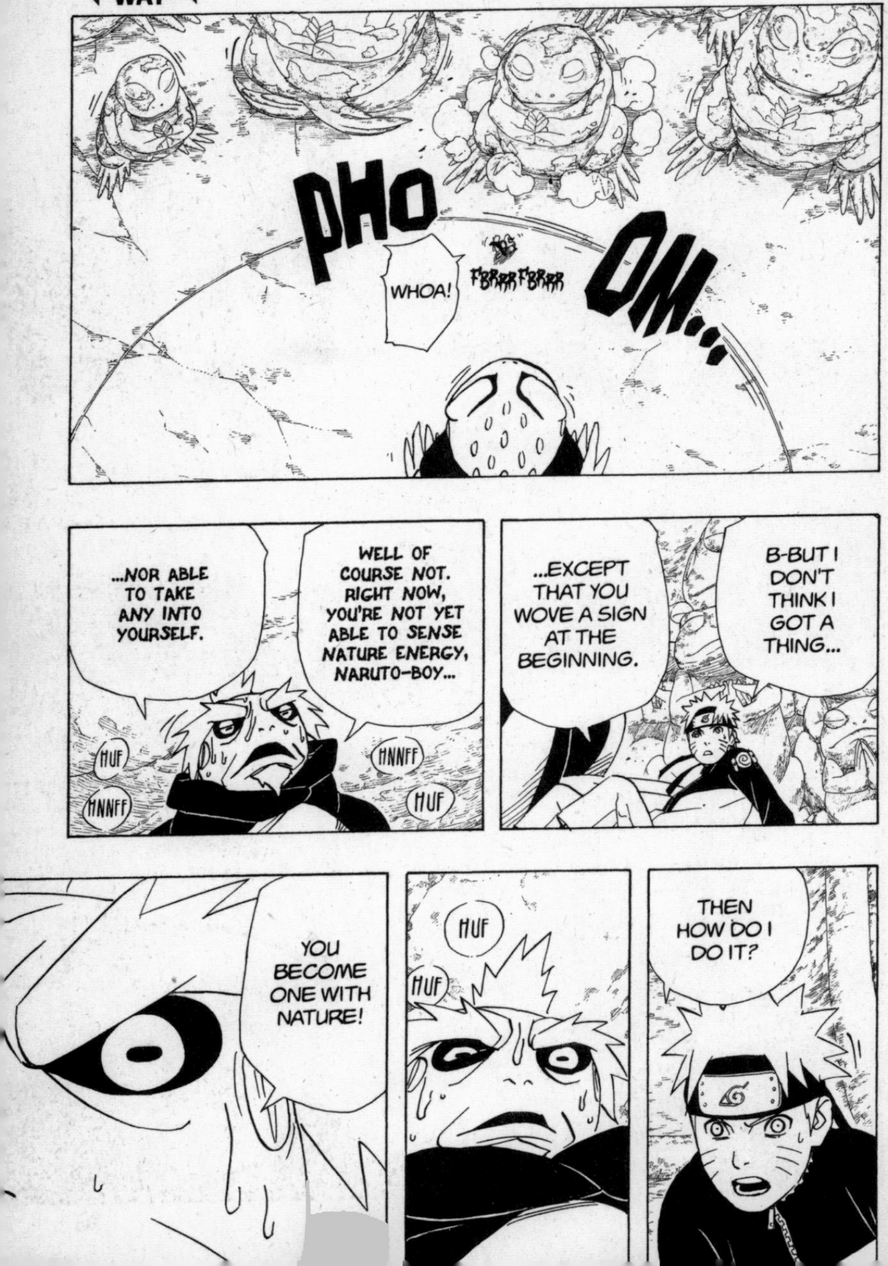
PHO
OM...
WHOA!
FBRRR FBRRR
B-BUT I DON'T THINK I GOT A THING...
...EXCEPT THAT YOU WOVE A SIGN AT THE BEGINNING.
WELL OF COURSE NOT. RIGHT NOW, YOU'RE NOT YET ABLE TO SENSE NATURE ENERGY, NARUTO-BOY...
HNNFF
HUF
...NOR ABLE TO TAKE ANY INTO YOURSELF.
HUF
HNNFF
THEN HOW DO I DO IT?
HUF
HUF
YOU BECOME ONE WITH NATURE!

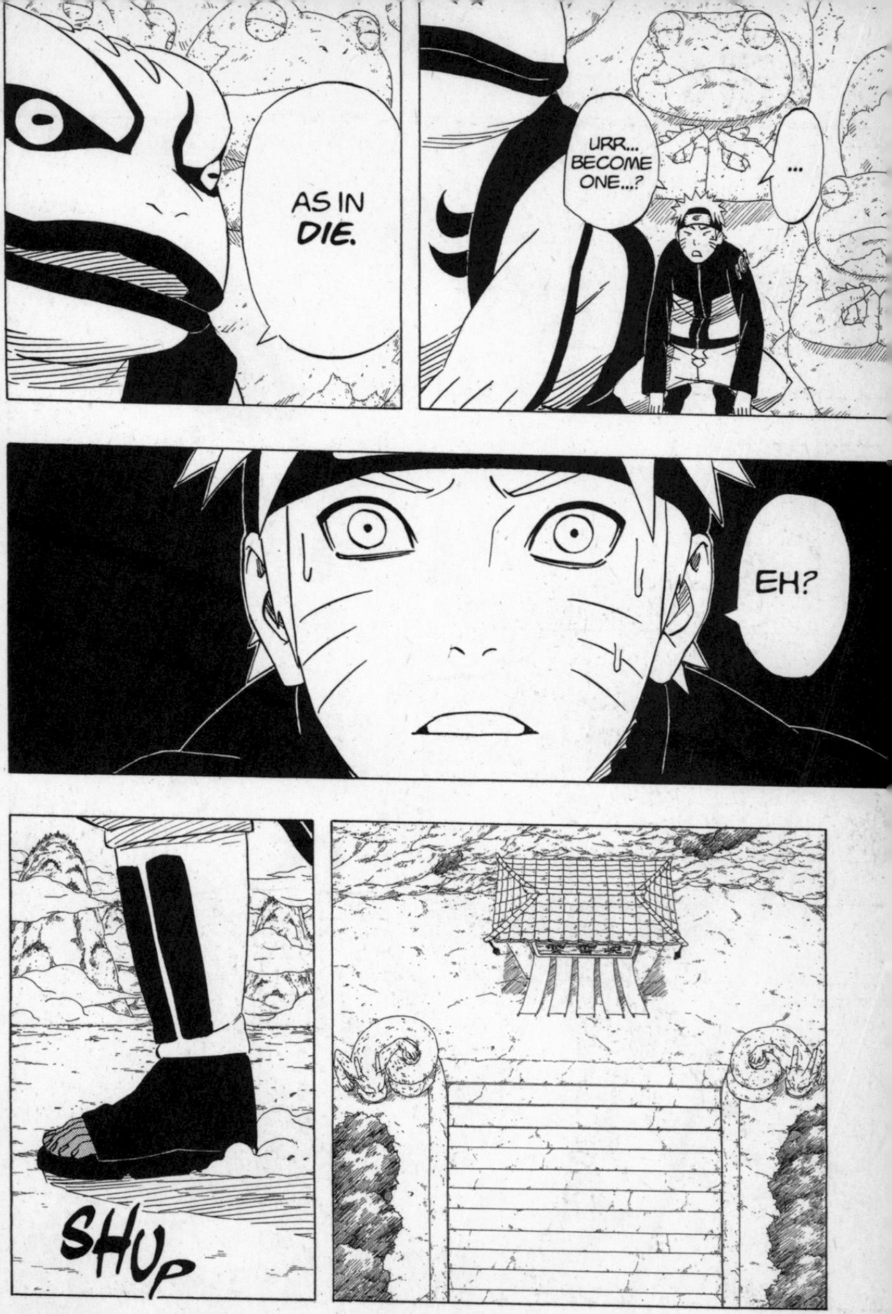
...
URR... BECOME ONE...?
AS IN DIE.
EH?
SHUP

READ THIS WAY

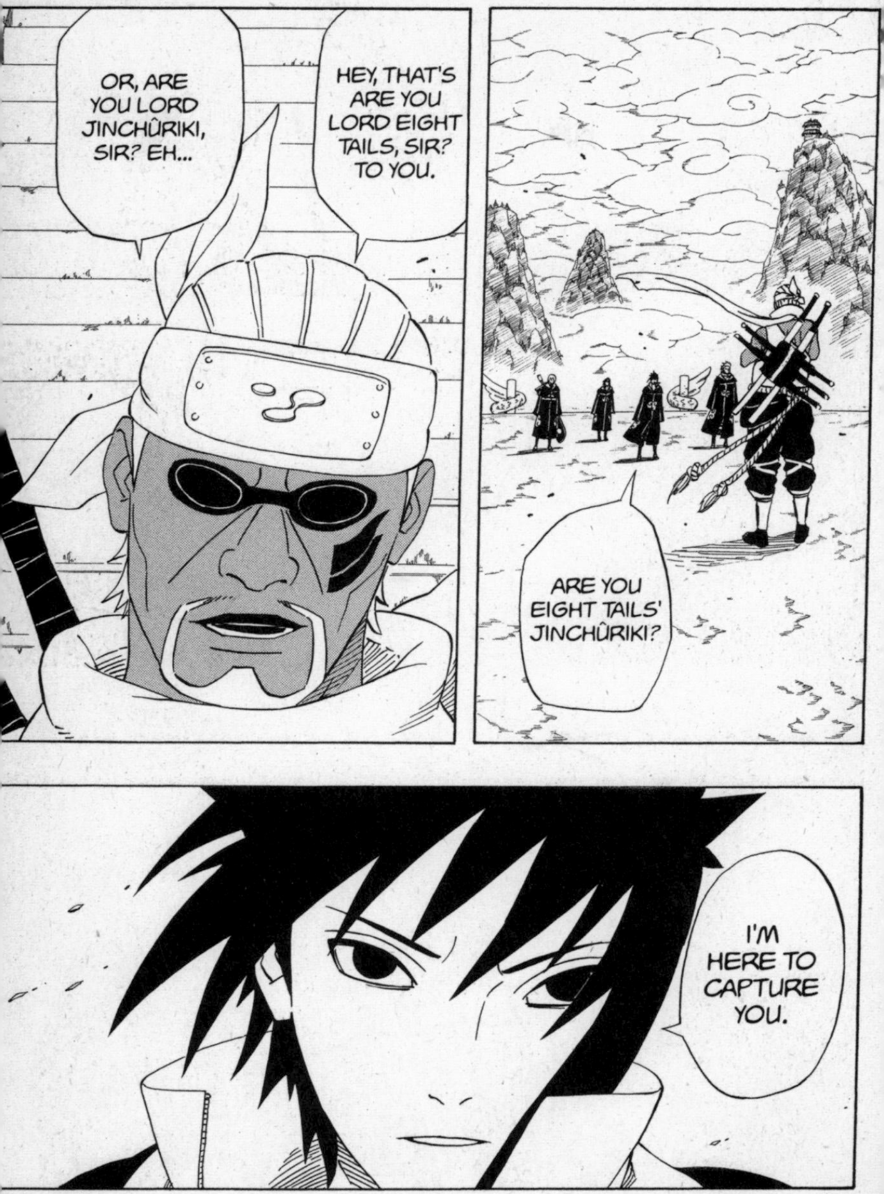
ARE YOU EIGHT TAILS' JINCHŪRIKI?
HEY, THAT'S ARE YOU LORD EIGHT TAILS, SIR? TO YOU.
OR, ARE YOU LORD JINCHŪRIKI, SIR? EH...
I'M HERE TO CAPTURE YOU.

NARUTO

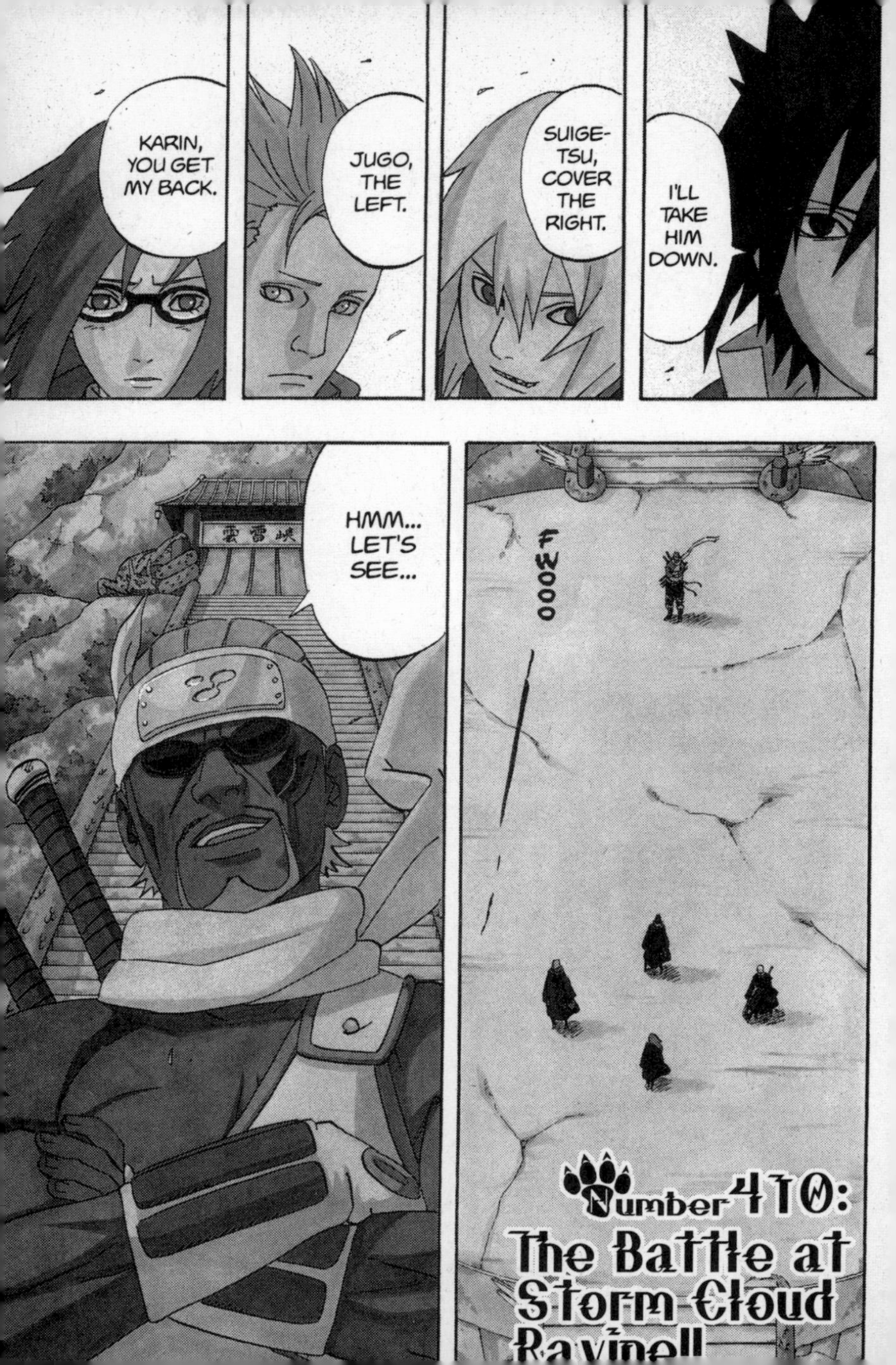
KARIN, YOU GET MY BACK.
JUGO, THE LEFT.
SUIGE-TSU, COVER THE RIGHT.
I'LL TAKE HIM DOWN.
HMM... LET'S SEE...
FWOOO
Number 410: The Battle at Storm Cloud Ravine!!

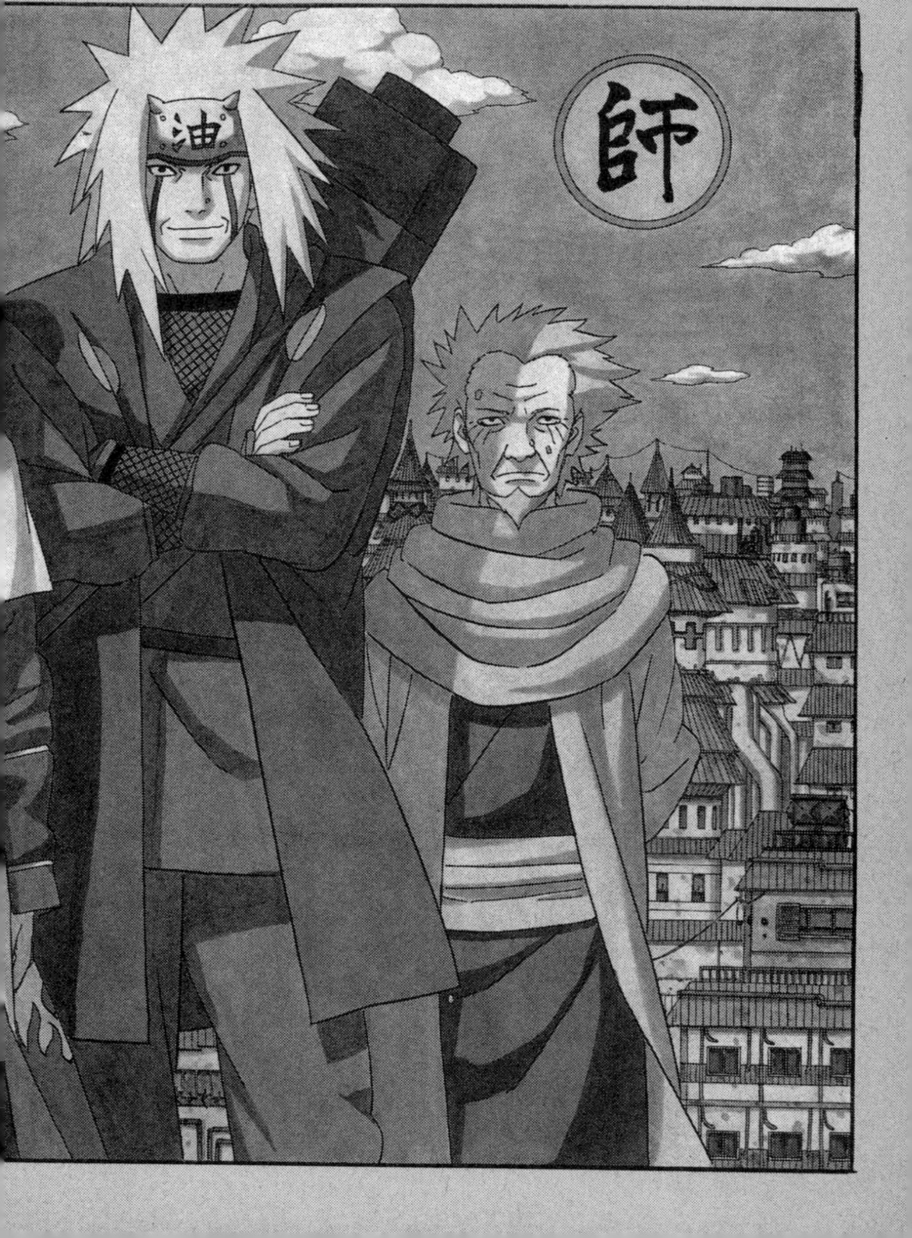
師

Number 410: The Battle at Storm Cloud Ravine!!

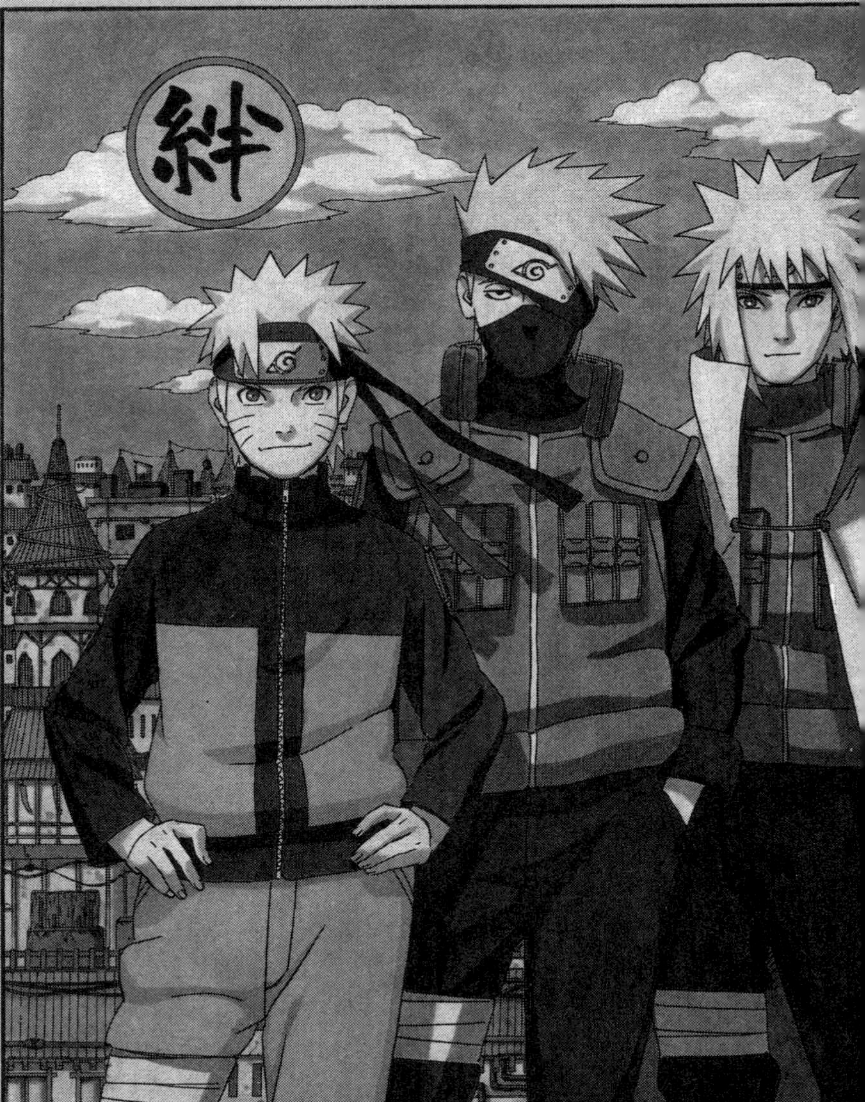
絆

NARUTO
-ナルト-

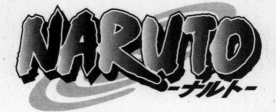

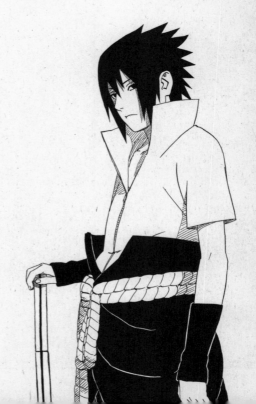

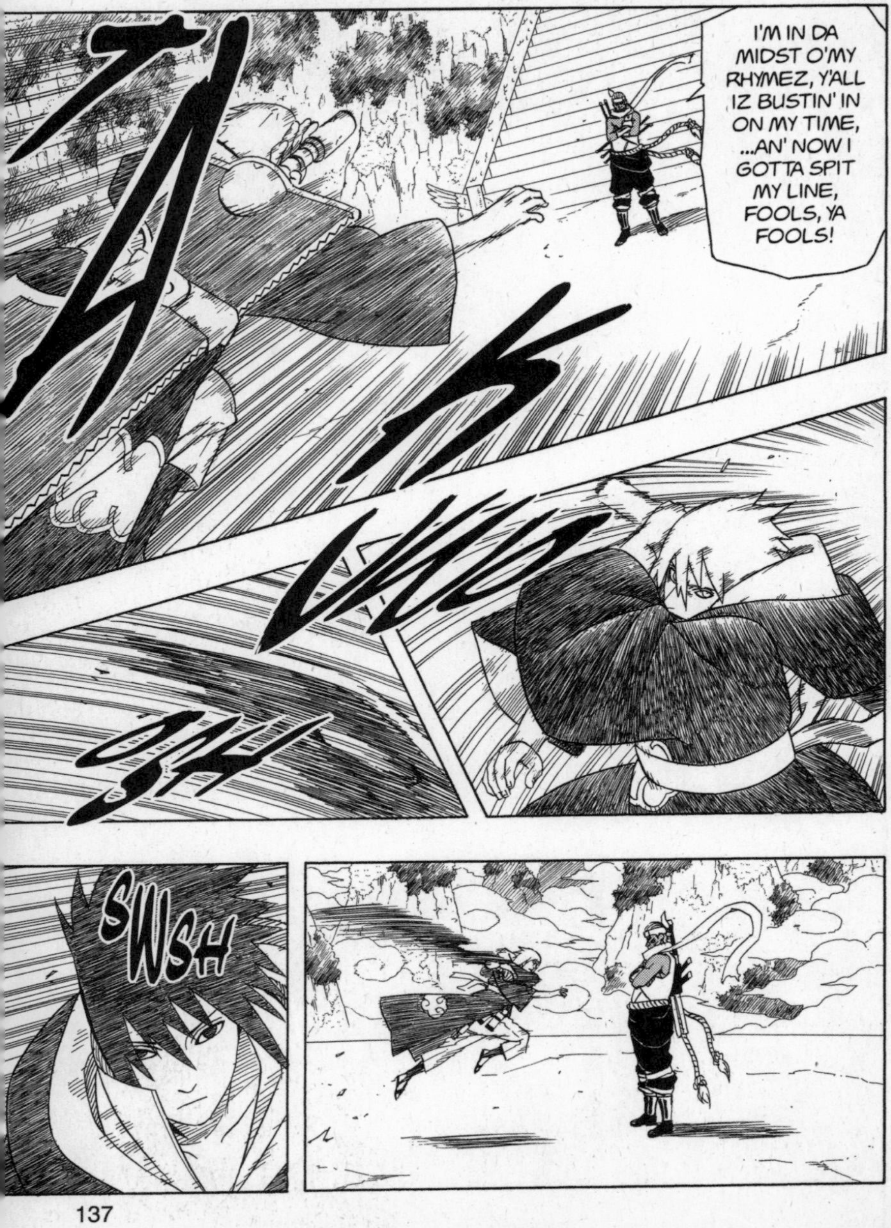
I'M IN DA MIDST O'MY RHYMEZ, Y'ALL IZ BUSTIN' IN ON MY TIME, ...AN' NOW I GOTTA SPIT MY LINE, FOOLS, YA FOOLS!
WHO
OSH
SWSH

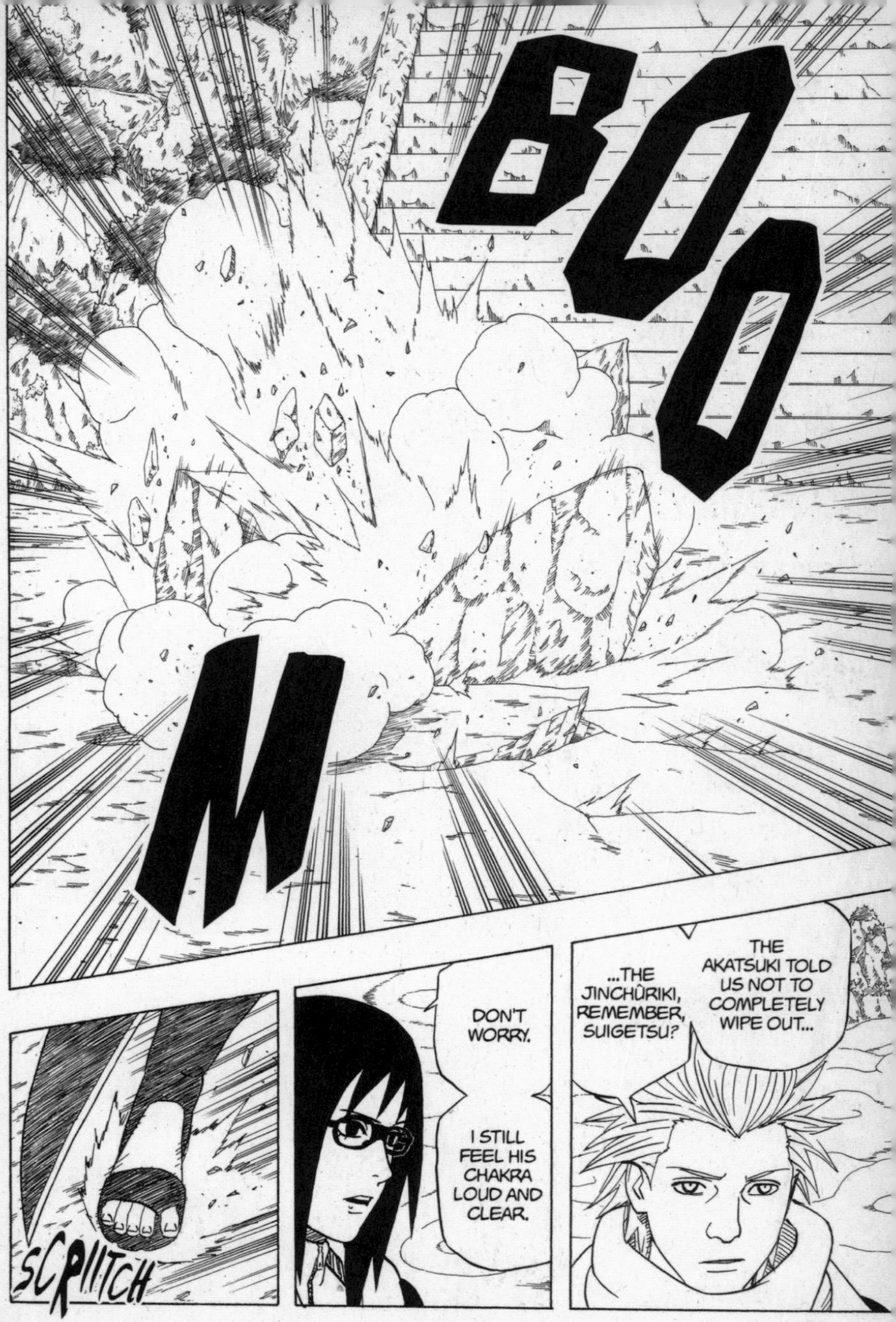
BOOM
THE AKATSUKI TOLD US NOT TO COMPLETELY WIPE OUT...
...THE JINCHÛRIKI, REMEMBER, SUIGETSU?
DON'T WORRY.
I STILL FEEL HIS CHAKRA LOUD AND CLEAR.
SCRIITCH

SHEESH, WHAT A FLASHY DIVERSION.

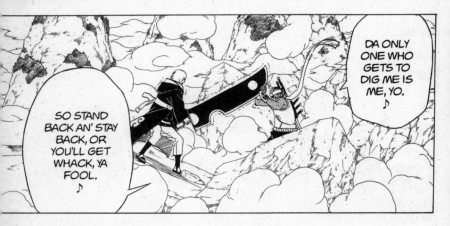

DA ONLY ONE WHO GETS TO DIG ME IS ME, YO. ♪

SO STAND BACK AN' STAY BACK, OR YOU'LL GET WHACK, YA FOOL. ♪

STEP BACK, SUIGETSU...

SHUP

WHORL

UGH!

FWAP

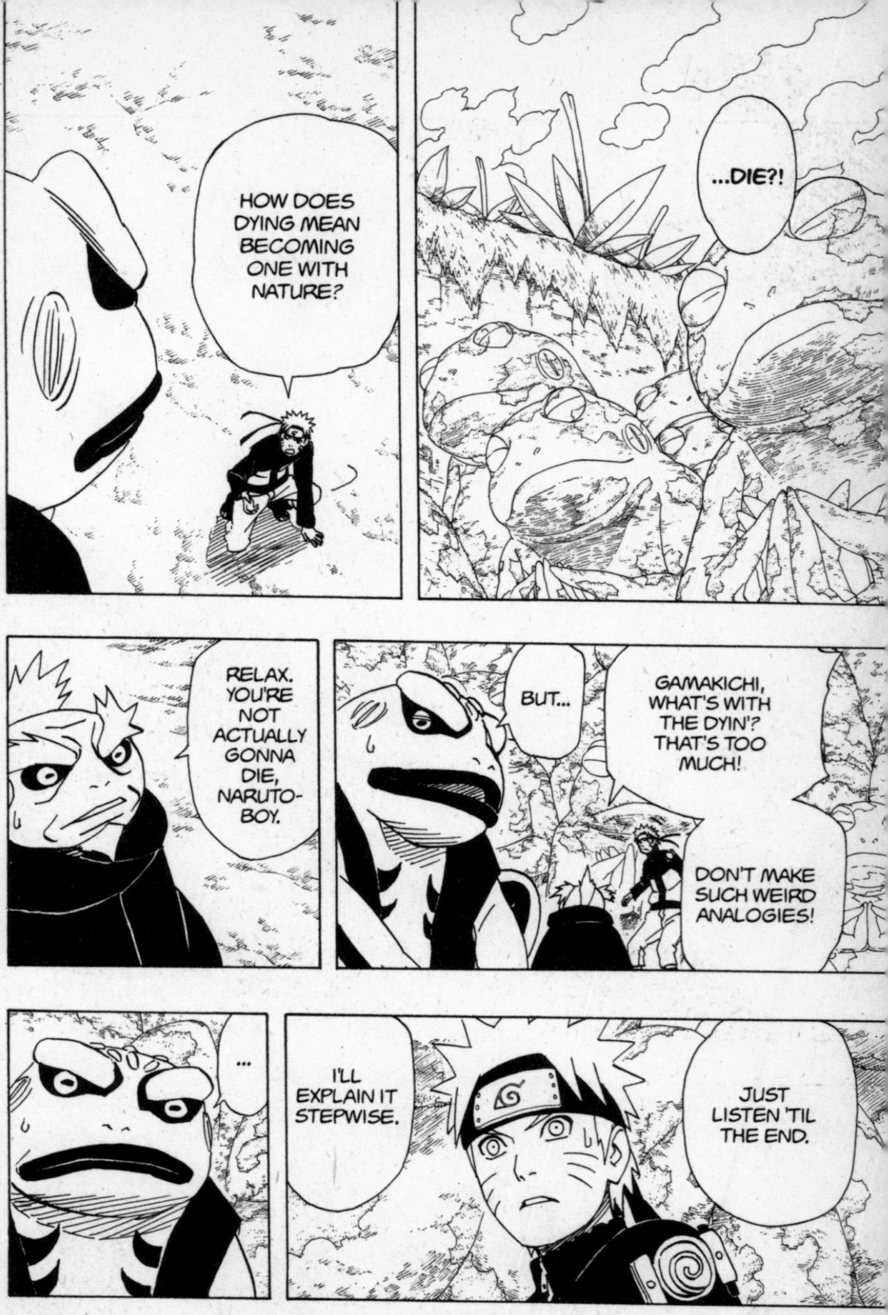
...DIE?!
HOW DOES DYING MEAN BECOMING ONE WITH NATURE?
GAMAKICHI, WHAT'S WITH THE DYIN'? THAT'S TOO MUCH!
DON'T MAKE SUCH WEIRD ANALOGIES!
BUT...
RELAX. YOU'RE NOT ACTUALLY GONNA DIE, NARUTO-BOY.
JUST LISTEN 'TIL THE END.
I'LL EXPLAIN IT STEPWISE.
...

READ THIS WAY

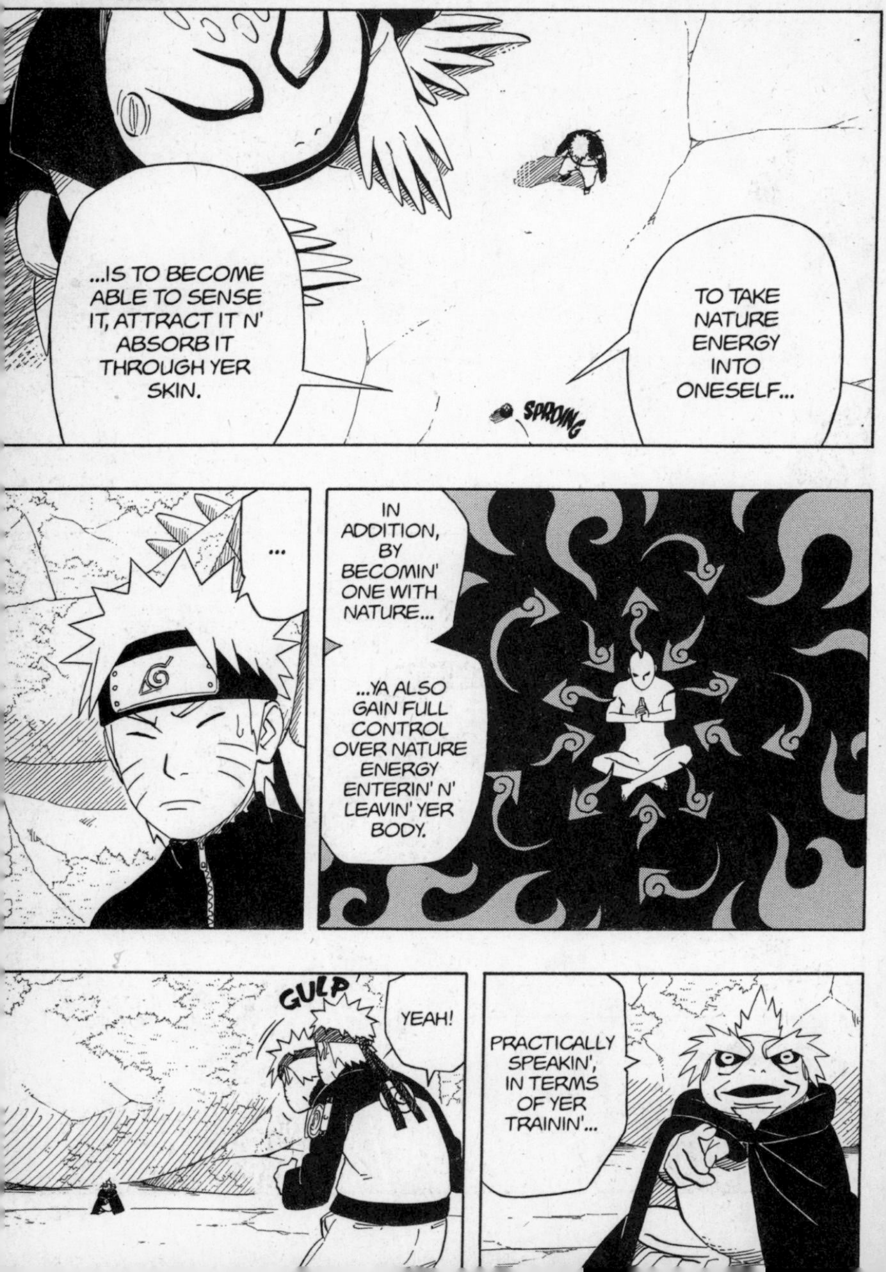
TO TAKE NATURE ENERGY INTO ONESELF...
SPROING
...IS TO BECOME ABLE TO SENSE IT, ATTRACT IT N' ABSORB IT THROUGH YER SKIN.
IN ADDITION, BY BECOMIN' ONE WITH NATURE...
...YA ALSO GAIN FULL CONTROL OVER NATURE ENERGY ENTERIN' N' LEAVIN' YER BODY.
...
PRACTICALLY SPEAKIN', IN TERMS OF YER TRAININ'...
YEAH!
GULP

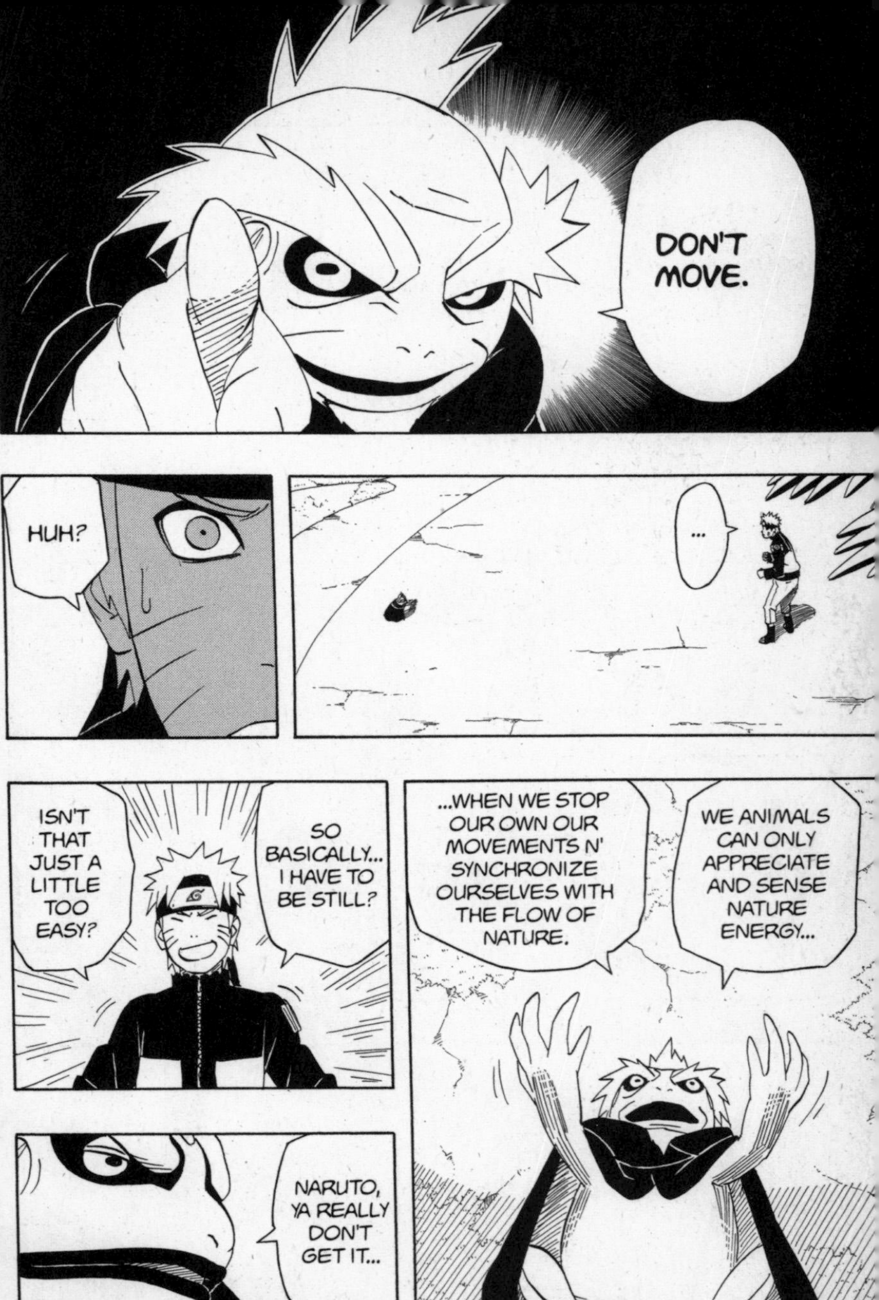
DON'T MOVE.
...
HUH?
WE ANIMALS CAN ONLY APPRECIATE AND SENSE NATURE ENERGY...
...WHEN WE STOP OUR OWN OUR MOVEMENTS N' SYNCHRONIZE OURSELVES WITH THE FLOW OF NATURE.
SO BASICALLY... I HAVE TO BE STILL?
ISN'T THAT JUST A LITTLE TOO EASY?
NARUTO, YA REALLY DON'T GET IT...

READ THIS WAY

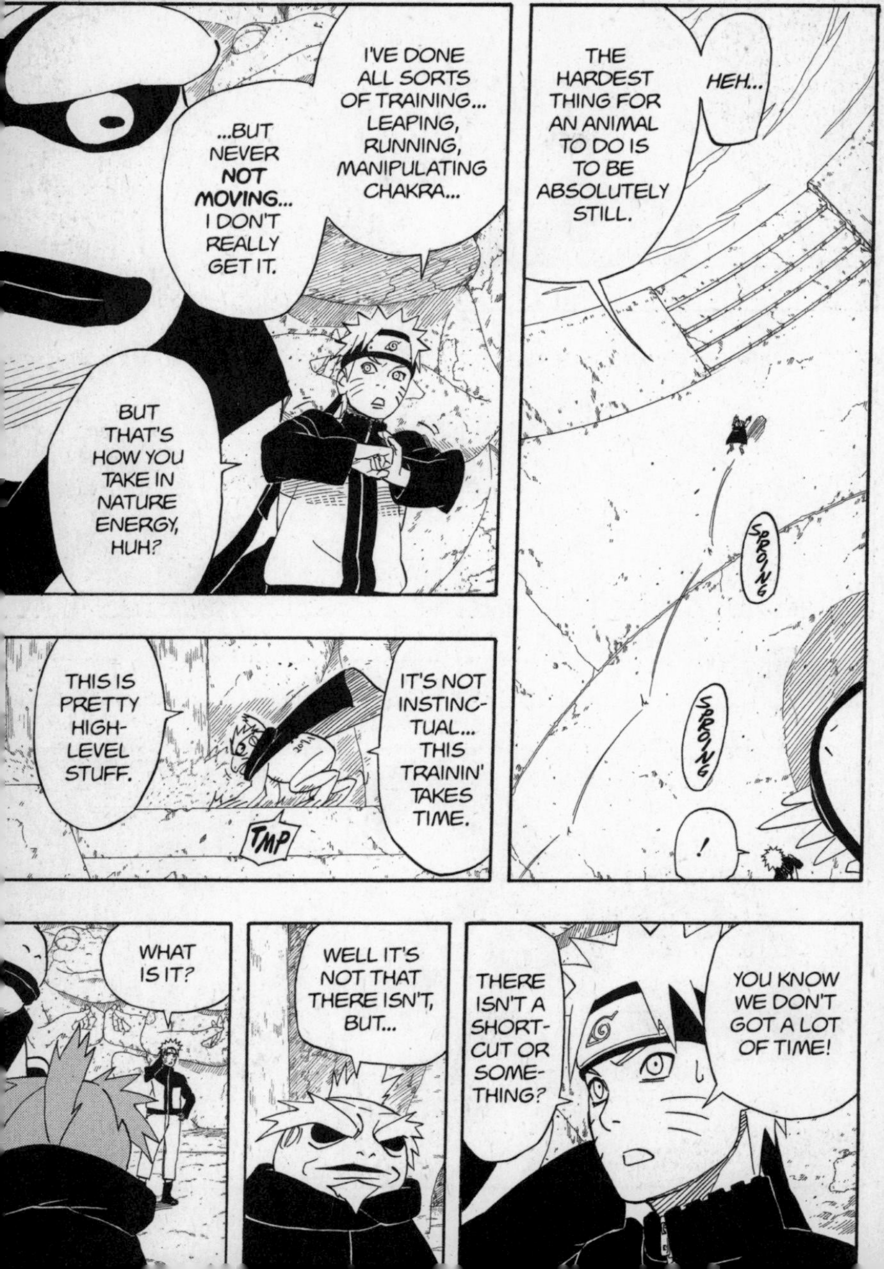
HEH...
THE HARDEST THING FOR AN ANIMAL TO DO IS TO BE ABSOLUTELY STILL.
SPROING
SPROING
!
I'VE DONE ALL SORTS OF TRAINING... LEAPING, RUNNING, MANIPULATING CHAKRA...
...BUT NEVER **NOT MOVING...** I DON'T REALLY GET IT.
BUT THAT'S HOW YOU TAKE IN NATURE ENERGY, HUH?
IT'S NOT INSTINCTUAL... THIS TRAININ' TAKES TIME.
THIS IS PRETTY HIGH-LEVEL STUFF.
TMP
YOU KNOW WE DON'T GOT A LOT OF TIME!
THERE ISN'T A SHORTCUT OR SOMETHING?
WELL IT'S NOT THAT THERE ISN'T, BUT...
WHAT IS IT?

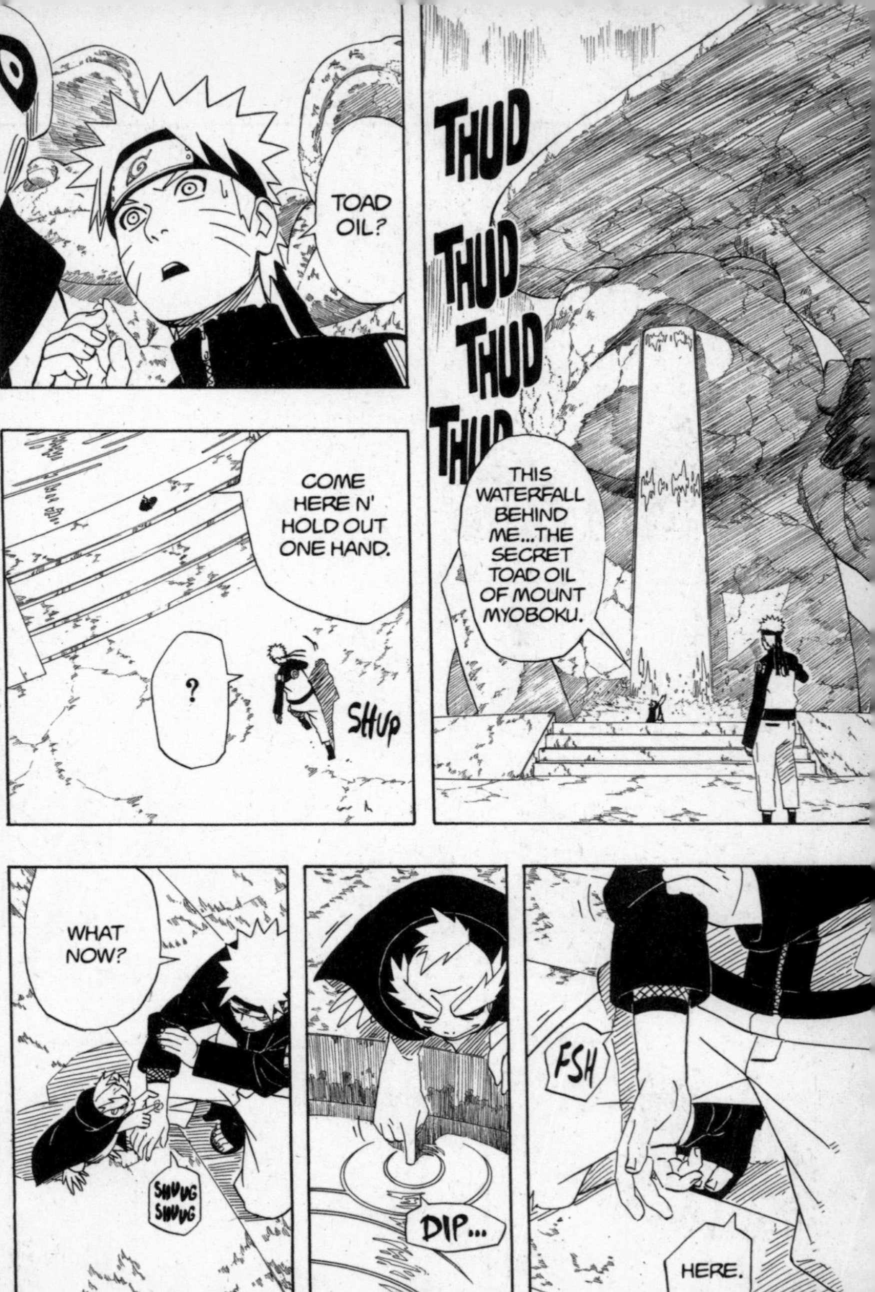
THUD
THUD
THUD
THUD
THIS WATERFALL BEHIND ME...THE SECRET TOAD OIL OF MOUNT MYOBOKU.
TOAD OIL?
COME HERE N' HOLD OUT ONE HAND.
?
SHUP
FSH
HERE.
DIP...
WHAT NOW?
SHUG SHUG

READ THIS WAY

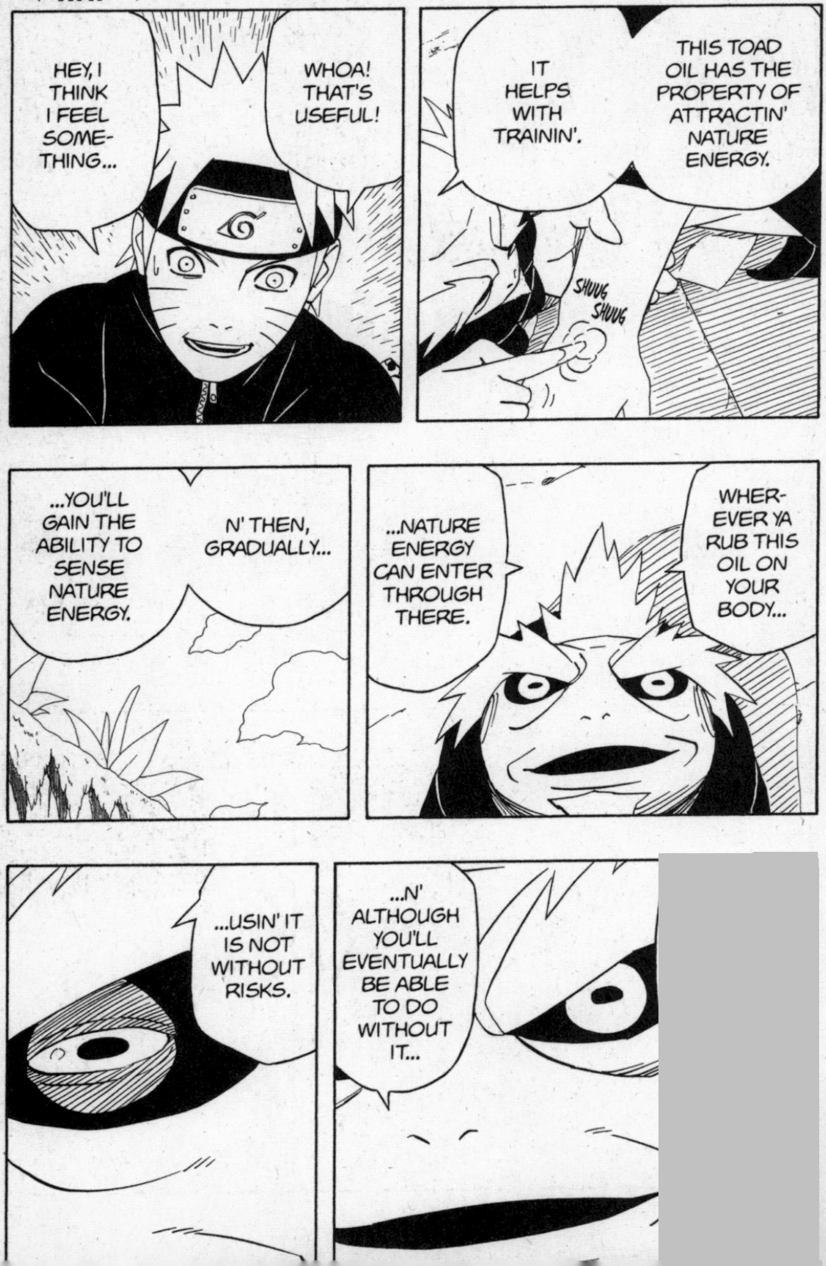
THIS TOAD OIL HAS THE PROPERTY OF ATTRACTIN' NATURE ENERGY.
IT HELPS WITH TRAININ'.
SHUUG SHUUG
WHOA! THAT'S USEFUL!
HEY, I THINK I FEEL SOME-THING...
WHER-EVER YA RUB THIS OIL ON YOUR BODY...
...NATURE ENERGY CAN ENTER THROUGH THERE.
N' THEN, GRADUALLY...
...YOU'LL GAIN THE ABILITY TO SENSE NATURE ENERGY.
...N' ALTHOUGH YOU'LL EVENTUALLY BE ABLE TO DO WITHOUT IT...
...USIN' IT IS NOT WITHOUT RISKS.

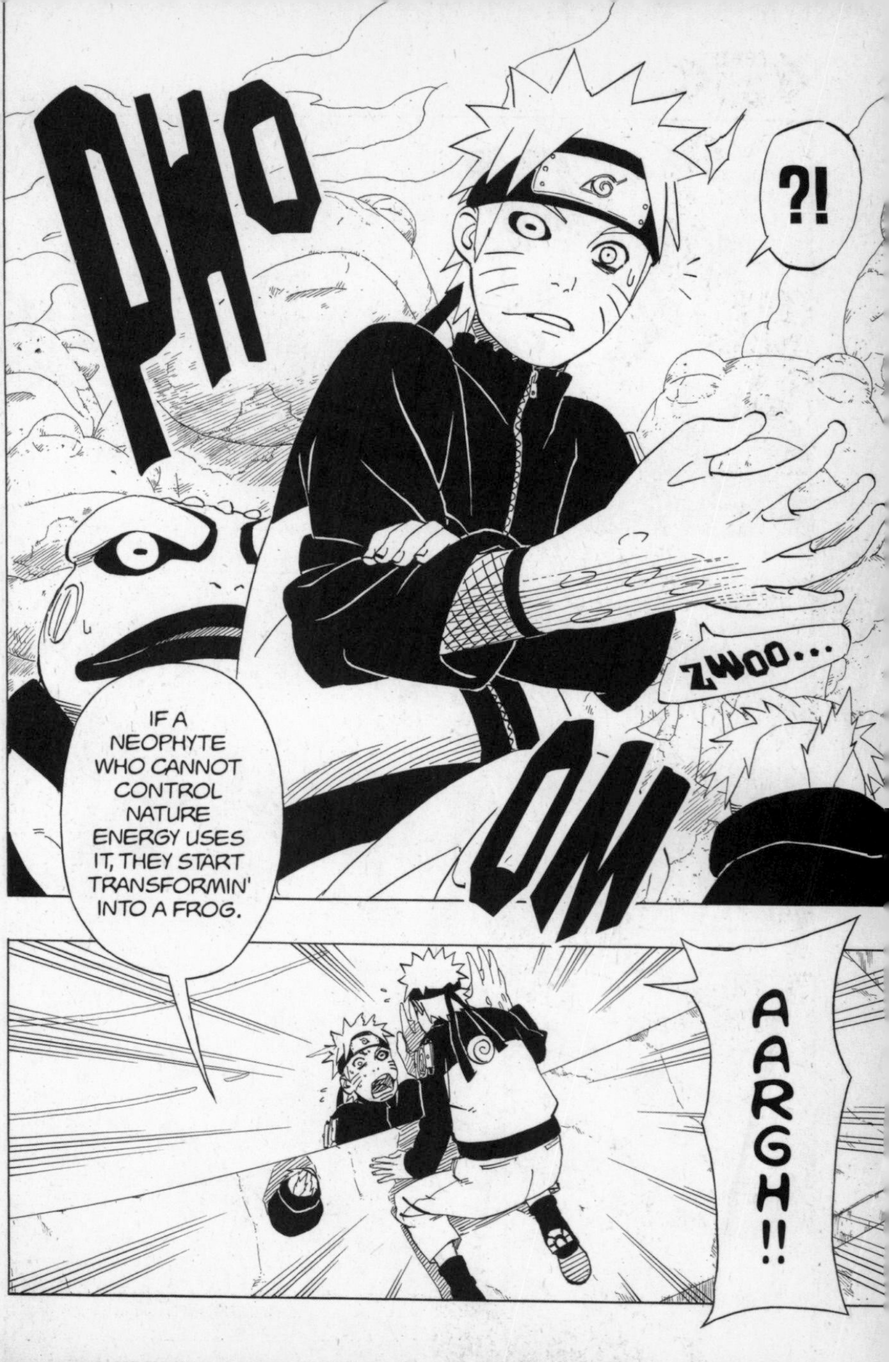
?!
ZWOO...
PHO
OM
IF A NEOPHYTE WHO CANNOT CONTROL NATURE ENERGY USES IT, THEY START TRANSFORMIN' INTO A FROG.
AARGH!!

READ THIS WAY

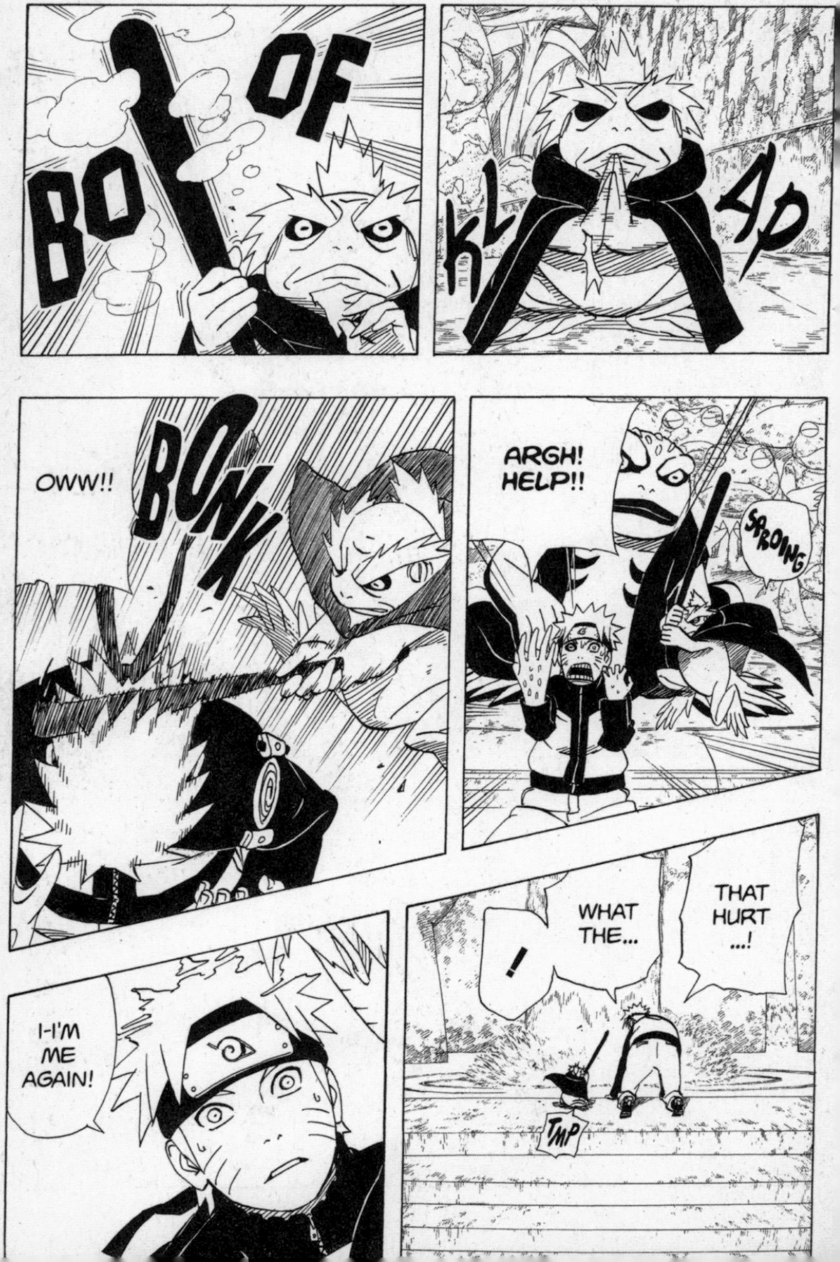
KLAP
BOOF
SPROING
ARGH! HELP!!
BONK
OWW!!
THAT HURT ...!
WHAT THE...
!
TMP
I-I'M ME AGAIN!

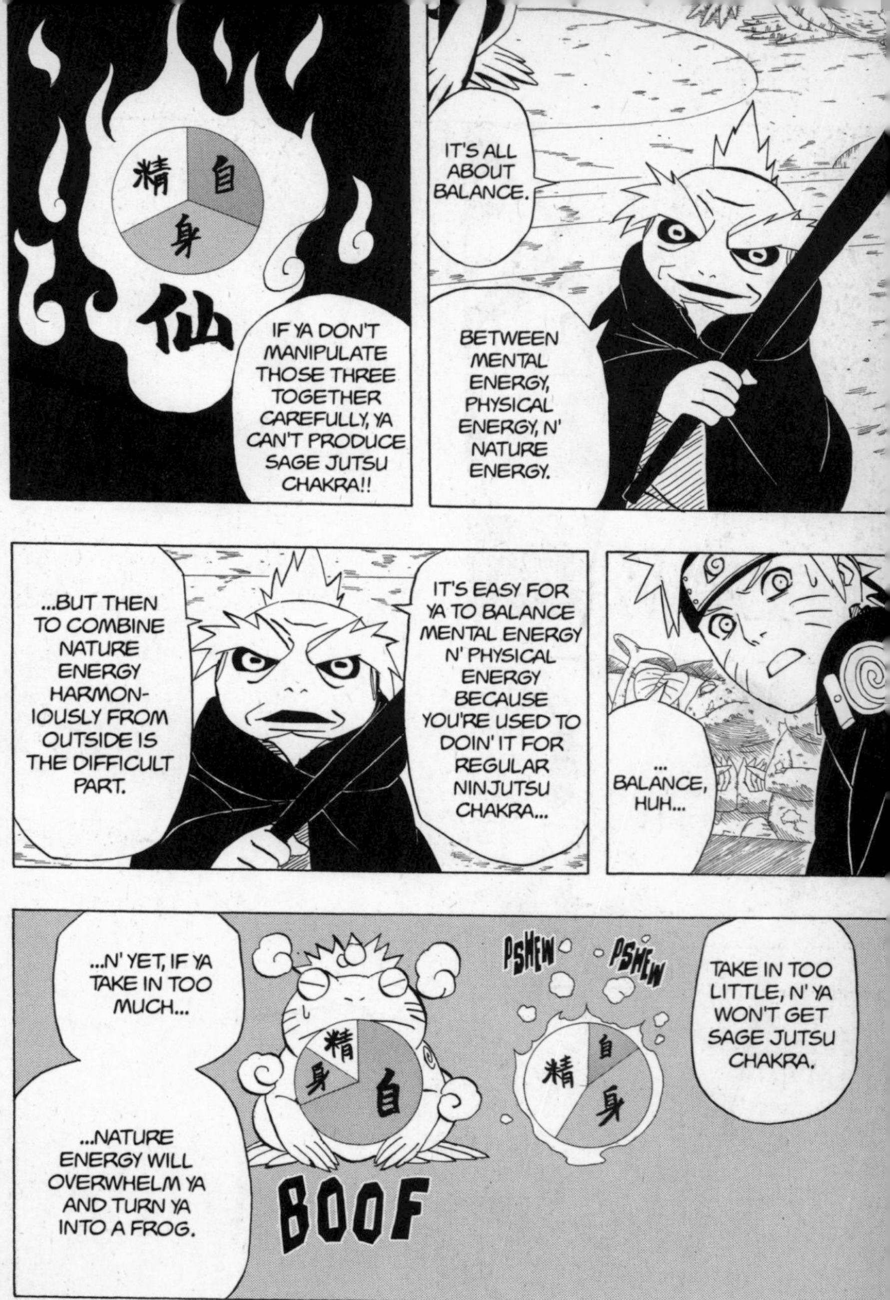
IT'S ALL ABOUT BALANCE.
BETWEEN MENTAL ENERGY, PHYSICAL ENERGY, N' NATURE ENERGY.
精
自
身
仙
IF YA DON'T MANIPULATE THOSE THREE TOGETHER CAREFULLY, YA CAN'T PRODUCE SAGE JUTSU CHAKRA!!
... BALANCE, HUH...
IT'S EASY FOR YA TO BALANCE MENTAL ENERGY N' PHYSICAL ENERGY BECAUSE YOU'RE USED TO DOIN' IT FOR REGULAR NINJUTSU CHAKRA...
...BUT THEN TO COMBINE NATURE ENERGY HARMONIOUSLY FROM OUTSIDE IS THE DIFFICULT PART.
TAKE IN TOO LITTLE, N' YA WON'T GET SAGE JUTSU CHAKRA.
PSHEW
PSHEW
自
精
身
...N' YET, IF YA TAKE IN TOO MUCH...
精
身
自
...NATURE ENERGY WILL OVERWHELM YA AND TURN YA INTO A FROG.
BOOF

READ THIS WAY

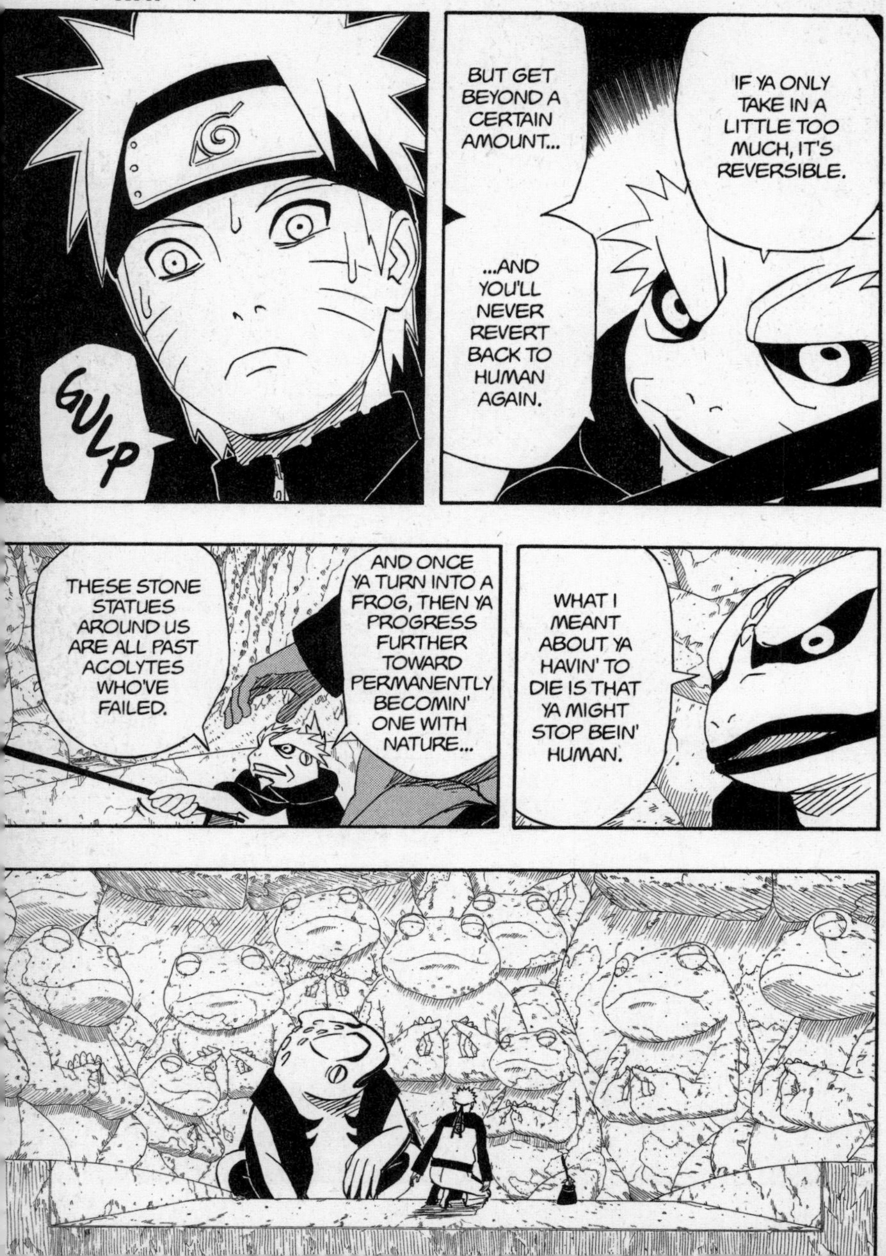
IF YA ONLY TAKE IN A LITTLE TOO MUCH, IT'S REVERSIBLE.
BUT GET BEYOND A CERTAIN AMOUNT...
...AND YOU'LL NEVER REVERT BACK TO HUMAN AGAIN.
GULP
WHAT I MEANT ABOUT YA HAVIN' TO DIE IS THAT YA MIGHT STOP BEIN' HUMAN.
AND ONCE YA TURN INTO A FROG, THEN YA PROGRESS FURTHER TOWARD PERMANENTLY BECOMIN' ONE WITH NATURE...
THESE STONE STATUES AROUND US ARE ALL PAST ACOLYTES WHO'VE FAILED.

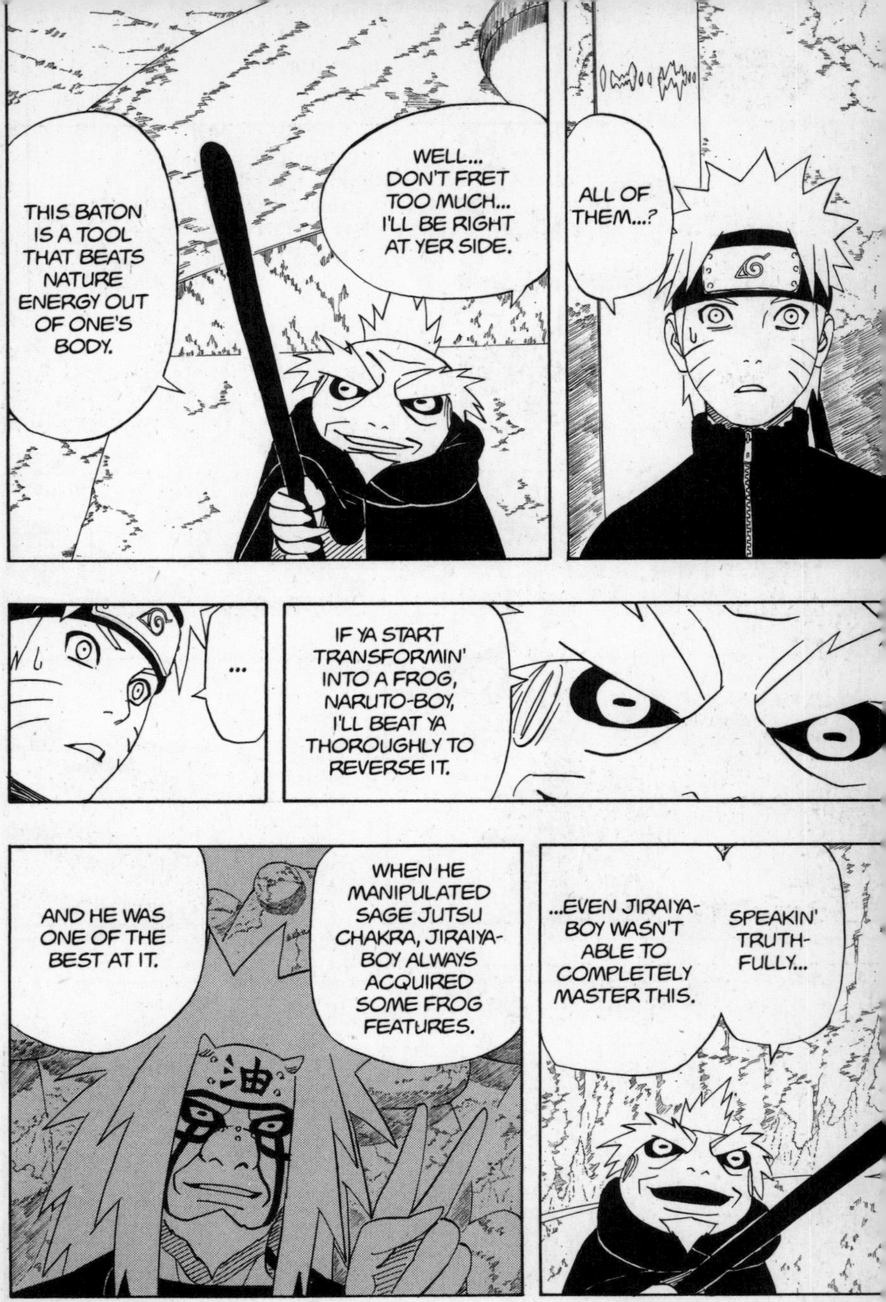
ALL OF THEM...?
WELL... DON'T FRET TOO MUCH... I'LL BE RIGHT AT YER SIDE.
THIS BATON IS A TOOL THAT BEATS NATURE ENERGY OUT OF ONE'S BODY.
IF YA START TRANSFORMIN' INTO A FROG, NARUTO-BOY, I'LL BEAT YA THOROUGHLY TO REVERSE IT.
...
SPEAKIN' TRUTHFULLY...
...EVEN JIRAIYA-BOY WASN'T ABLE TO COMPLETELY MASTER THIS.
WHEN HE MANIPULATED SAGE JUTSU CHAKRA, JIRAIYA-BOY ALWAYS ACQUIRED SOME FROG FEATURES.
AND HE WAS ONE OF THE BEST AT IT.

READ THIS WAY

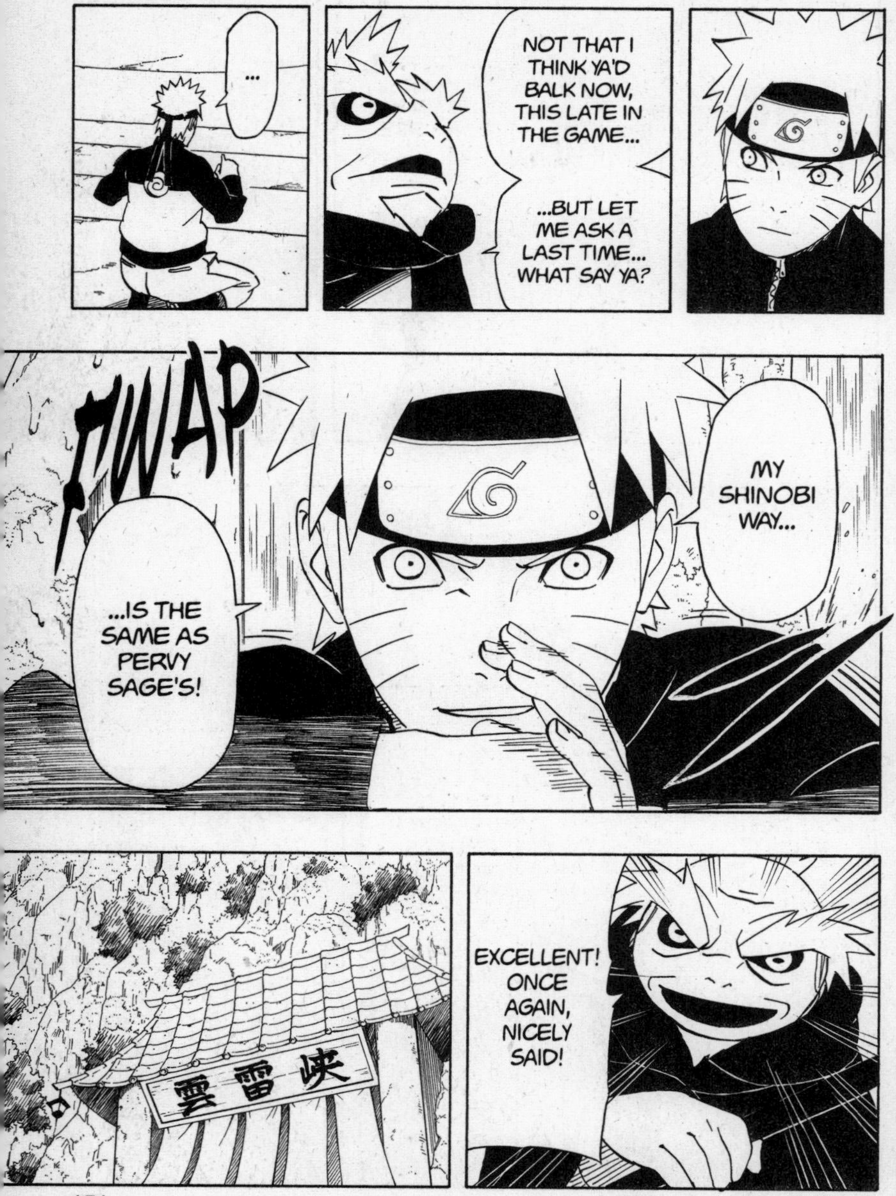
NOT THAT I THINK YA'D BALK NOW, THIS LATE IN THE GAME...
...BUT LET ME ASK A LAST TIME... WHAT SAY YA?
...
MY SHINOBI WAY...
FWAP
...IS THE SAME AS PERVY SAGE'S!
EXCELLENT! ONCE AGAIN, NICELY SAID!
雲雷峡

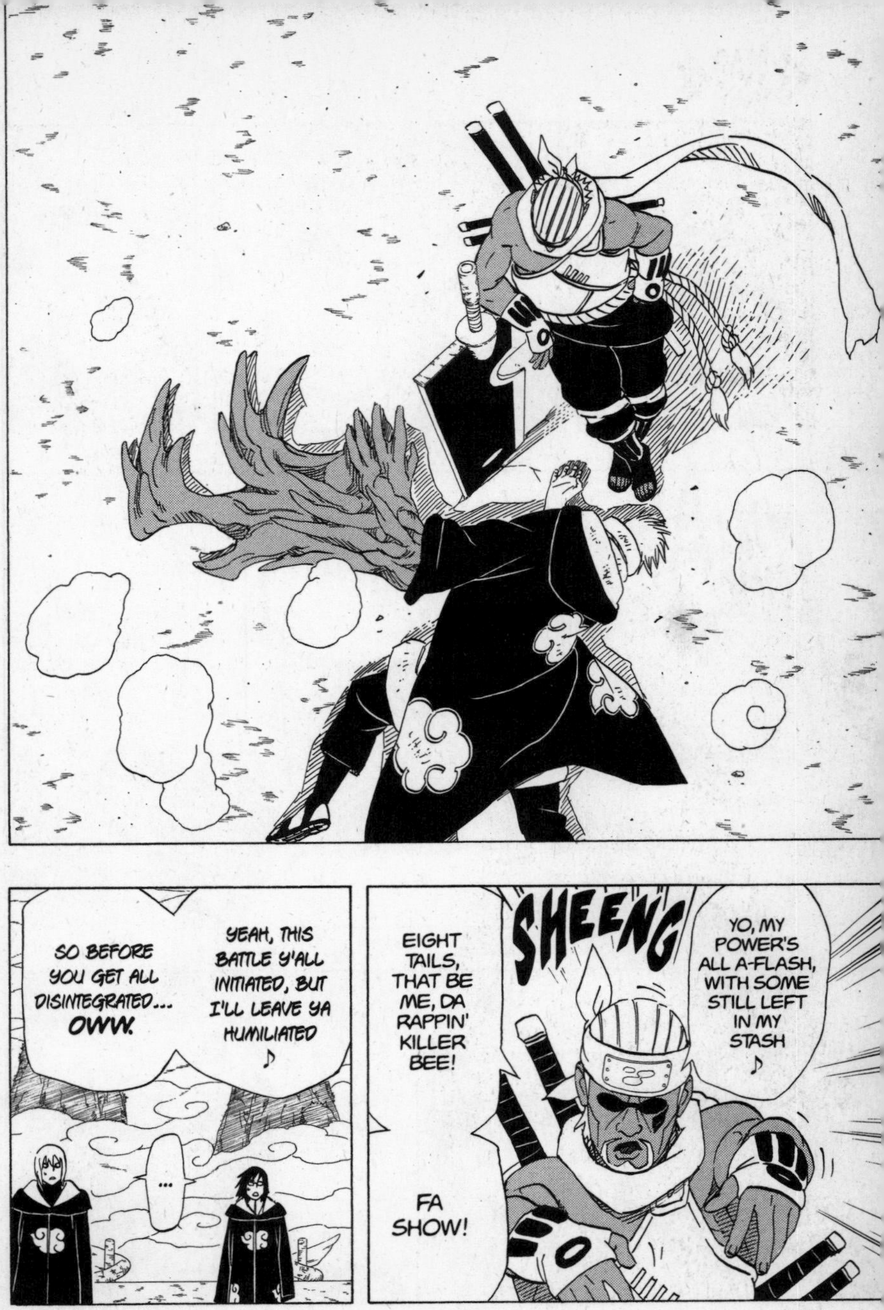
SHEENG
YO, MY POWER'S ALL A-FLASH, WITH SOME STILL LEFT IN MY STASH ♪
EIGHT TAILS, THAT BE ME, DA RAPPIN' KILLER BEE!
FA SHOW!
YEAH, THIS BATTLE Y'ALL INITIATED, BUT I'LL LEAVE YA HUMILIATED ♪
SO BEFORE YOU GET ALL DISINTEGRATED... **OWW.**
...

READ THIS WAY

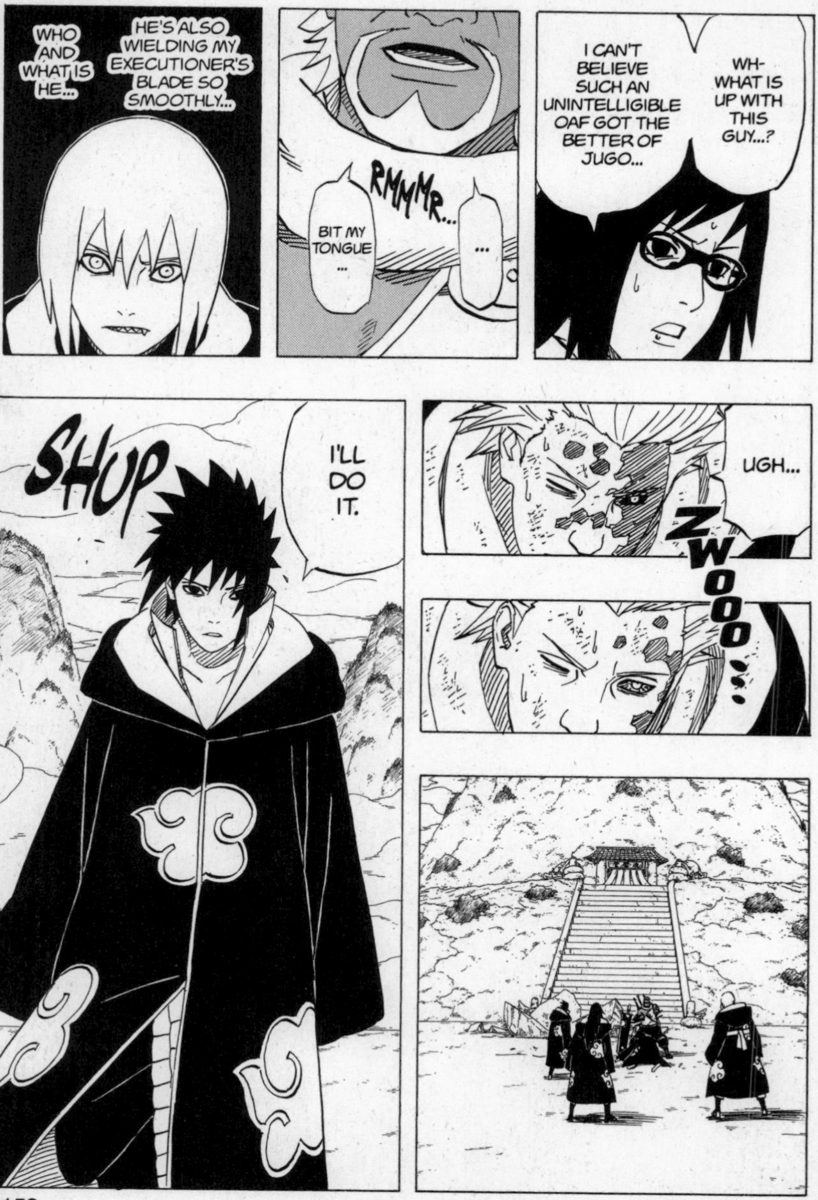
WH- WHAT IS UP WITH THIS GUY...?
I CAN'T BELIEVE SUCH AN UNINTELLIGIBLE OAF GOT THE BETTER OF JUGO...
...
RMMMR...
BIT MY TONGUE ...
HE'S ALSO WIELDING MY EXECUTIONER'S BLADE SO SMOOTHLY...
WHO AND WHAT IS HE...
UGH...
ZWOOO
I'LL DO IT.
SHUP

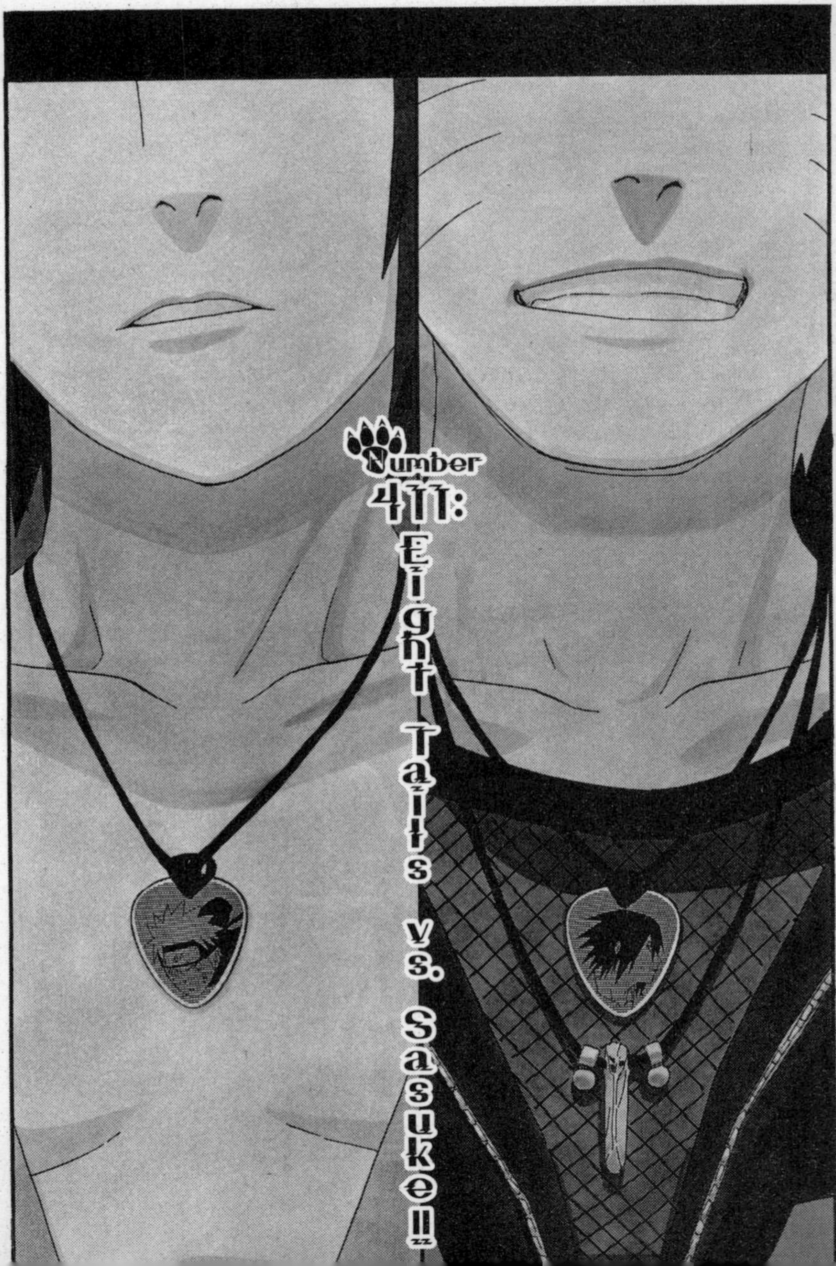
Number 411: Eight Tails vs. Sasuke!!

READ THIS WAY

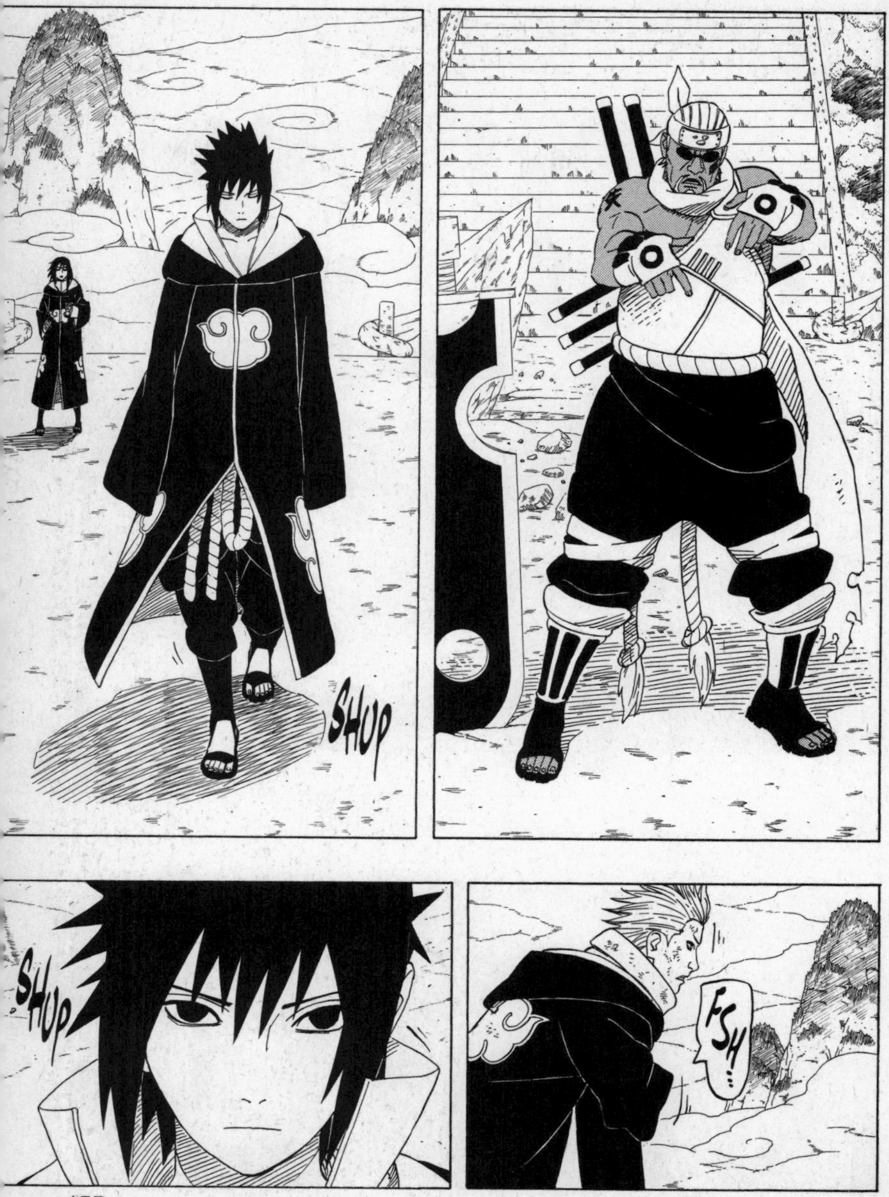
SHUP
FSH...
SHUP

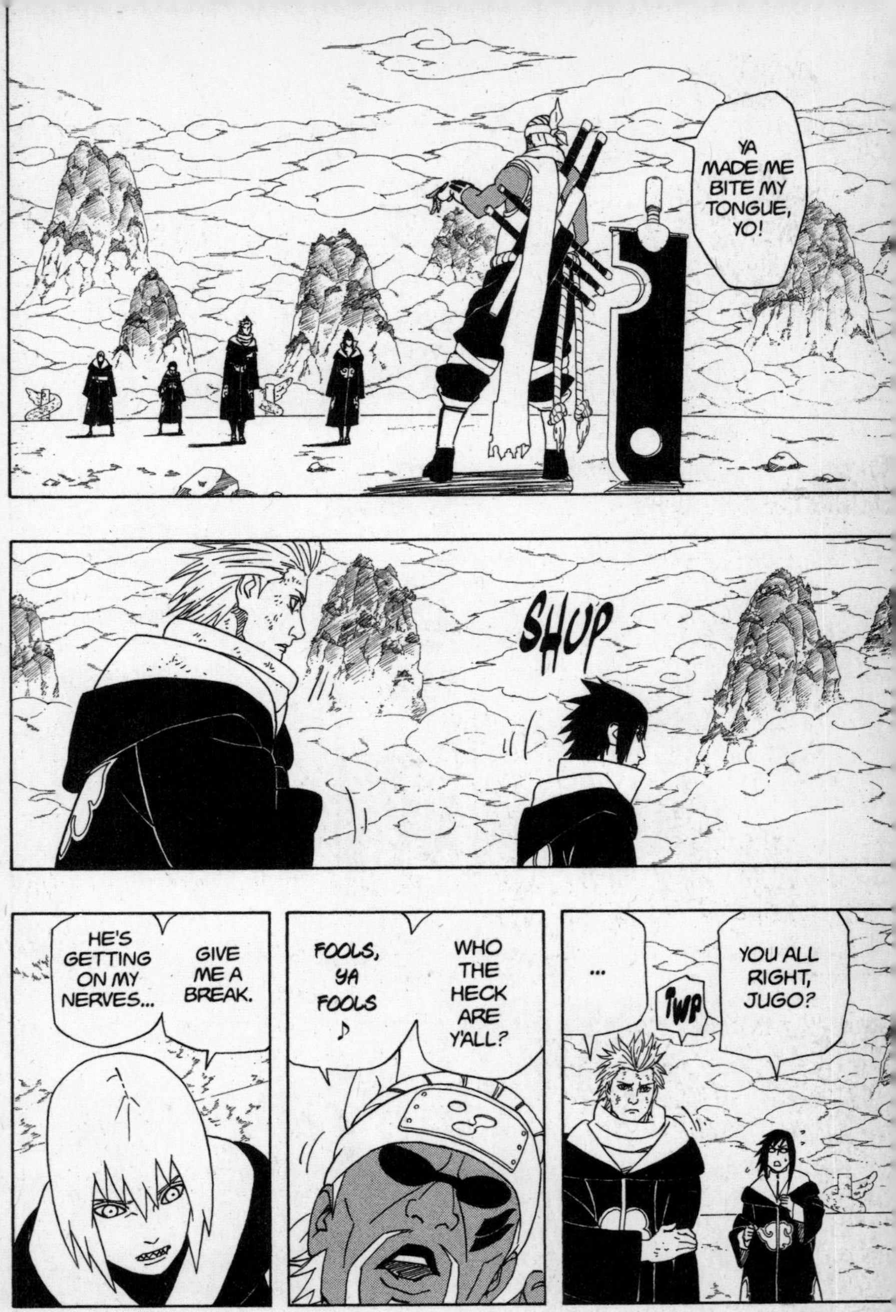
YA MADE ME BITE MY TONGUE, YO!
SHUP
YOU ALL RIGHT, JUGO?
TWP
...
WHO THE HECK ARE Y'ALL?
FOOLS, YA FOOLS ♪
GIVE ME A BREAK.
HE'S GETTING ON MY NERVES...

READ THIS WAY

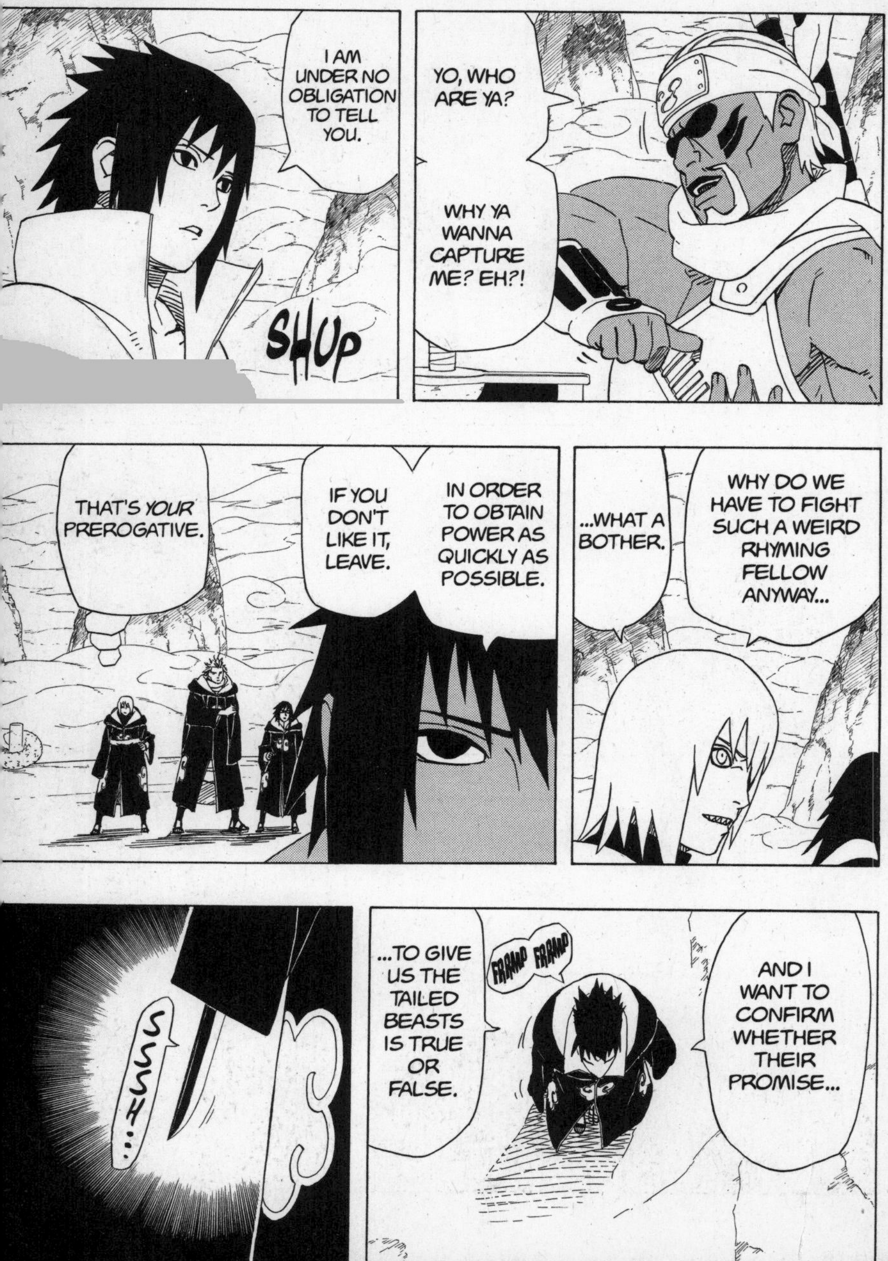
YO, WHO ARE YA?
WHY YA WANNA CAPTURE ME? EH?!
I AM UNDER NO OBLIGATION TO TELL YOU.
SHUP
WHY DO WE HAVE TO FIGHT SUCH A WEIRD RHYMING FELLOW ANYWAY...
...WHAT A BOTHER.
IN ORDER TO OBTAIN POWER AS QUICKLY AS POSSIBLE.
IF YOU DON'T LIKE IT, LEAVE.
THAT'S *YOUR* PREROGATIVE.
AND I WANT TO CONFIRM WHETHER THEIR PROMISE...
FRAMP FRAMP
...TO GIVE US THE TAILED BEASTS IS TRUE OR FALSE.
SSSH...

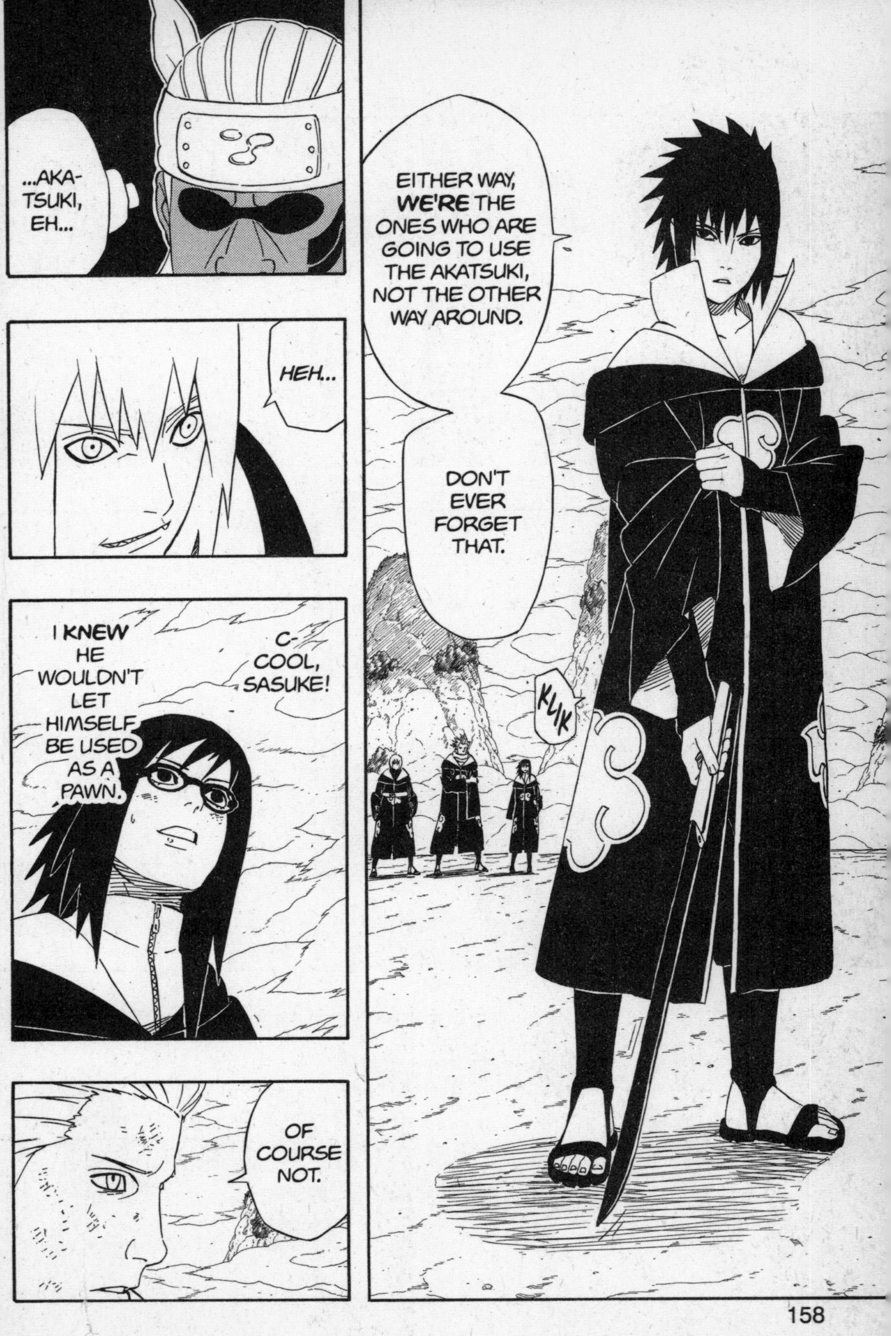
EITHER WAY, WE'RE THE ONES WHO ARE GOING TO USE THE AKATSUKI, NOT THE OTHER WAY AROUND.
DON'T EVER FORGET THAT.
KLIK
...AKA-TSUKI, EH...
HEH...
C-COOL, SASUKE!
I KNEW HE WOULDN'T LET HIMSELF BE USED AS A PAWN.
OF COURSE NOT.

READ THIS WAY

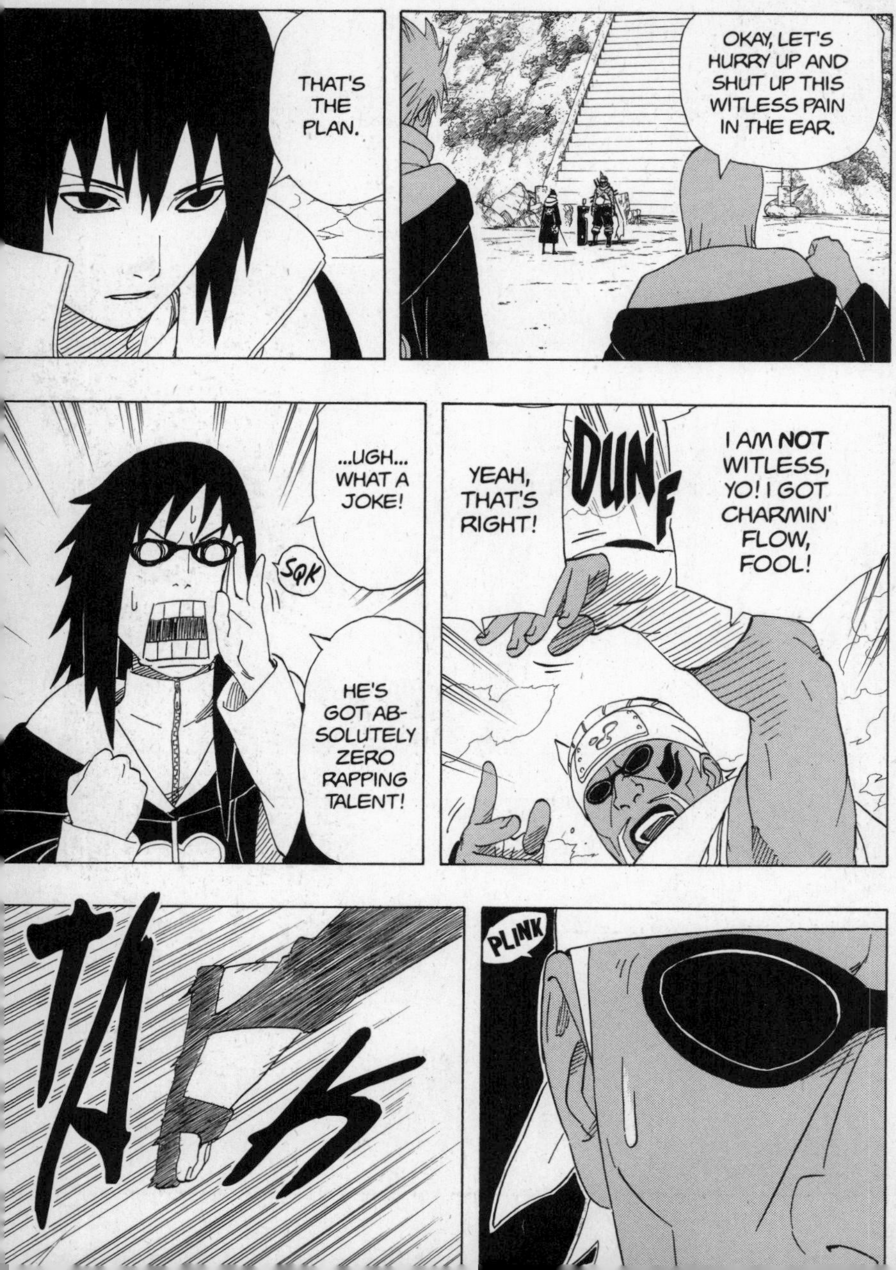
OKAY, LET'S HURRY UP AND SHUT UP THIS WITLESS PAIN IN THE EAR.
THAT'S THE PLAN.
I AM NOT WITLESS, YO! I GOT CHARMIN' FLOW, FOOL!
DUNF
YEAH, THAT'S RIGHT!
...UGH... WHAT A JOKE!
SQK
HE'S GOT AB-SOLUTELY ZERO RAPPING TALENT!
PLINK

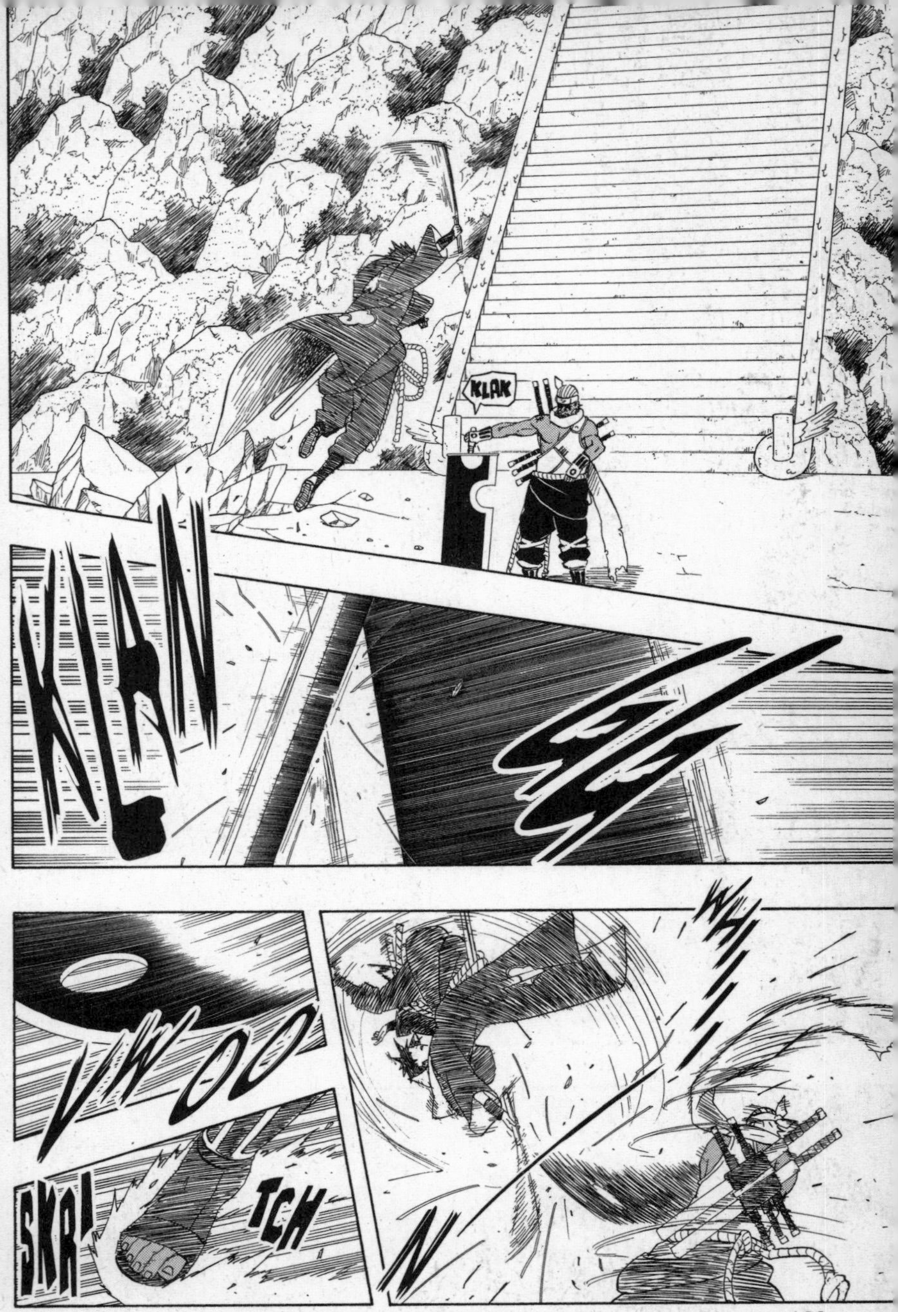
KLAK
KLAN
VWOO
SKRITCH

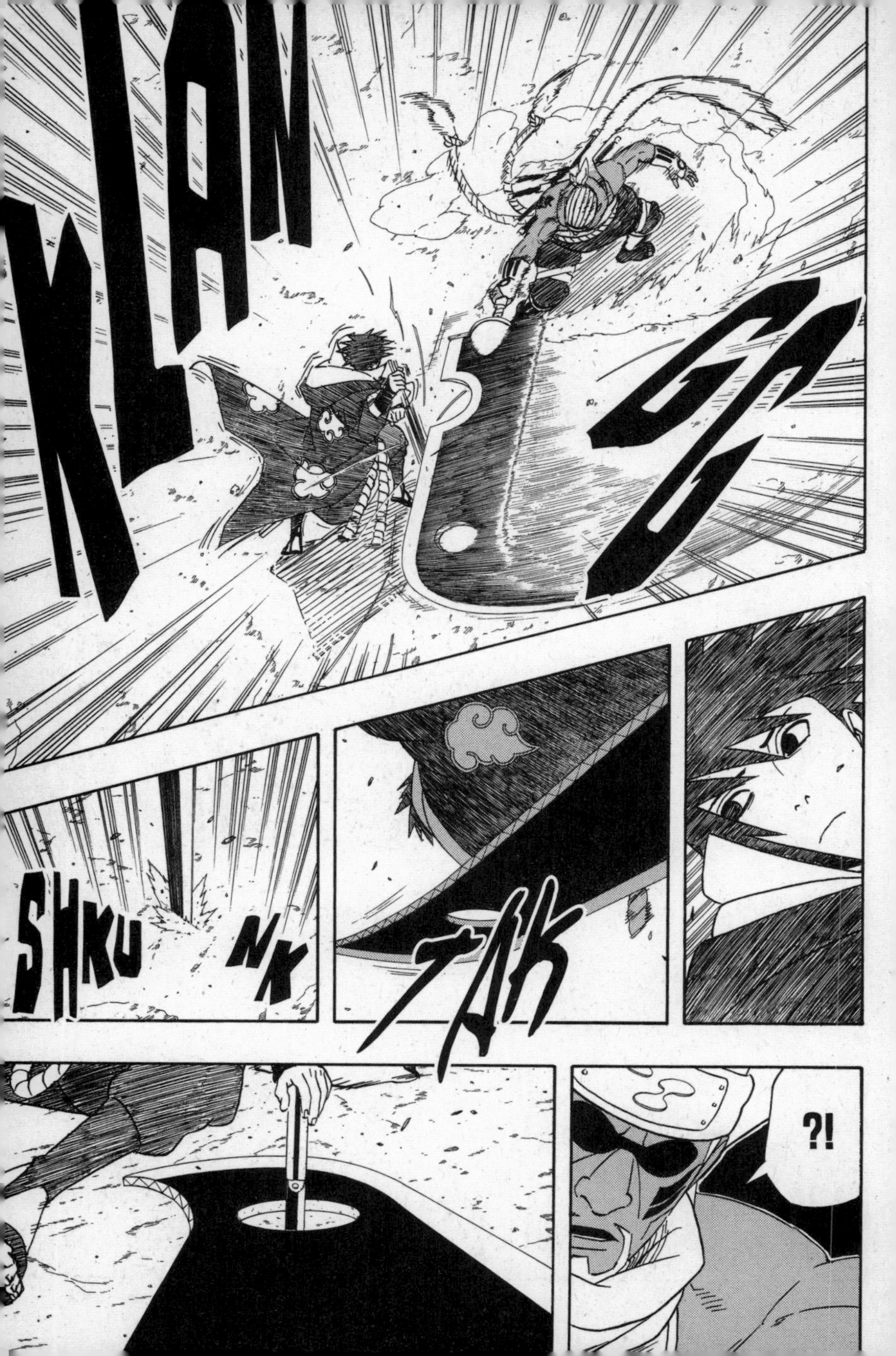
KLAN
TAK
SHKU
NK
?!

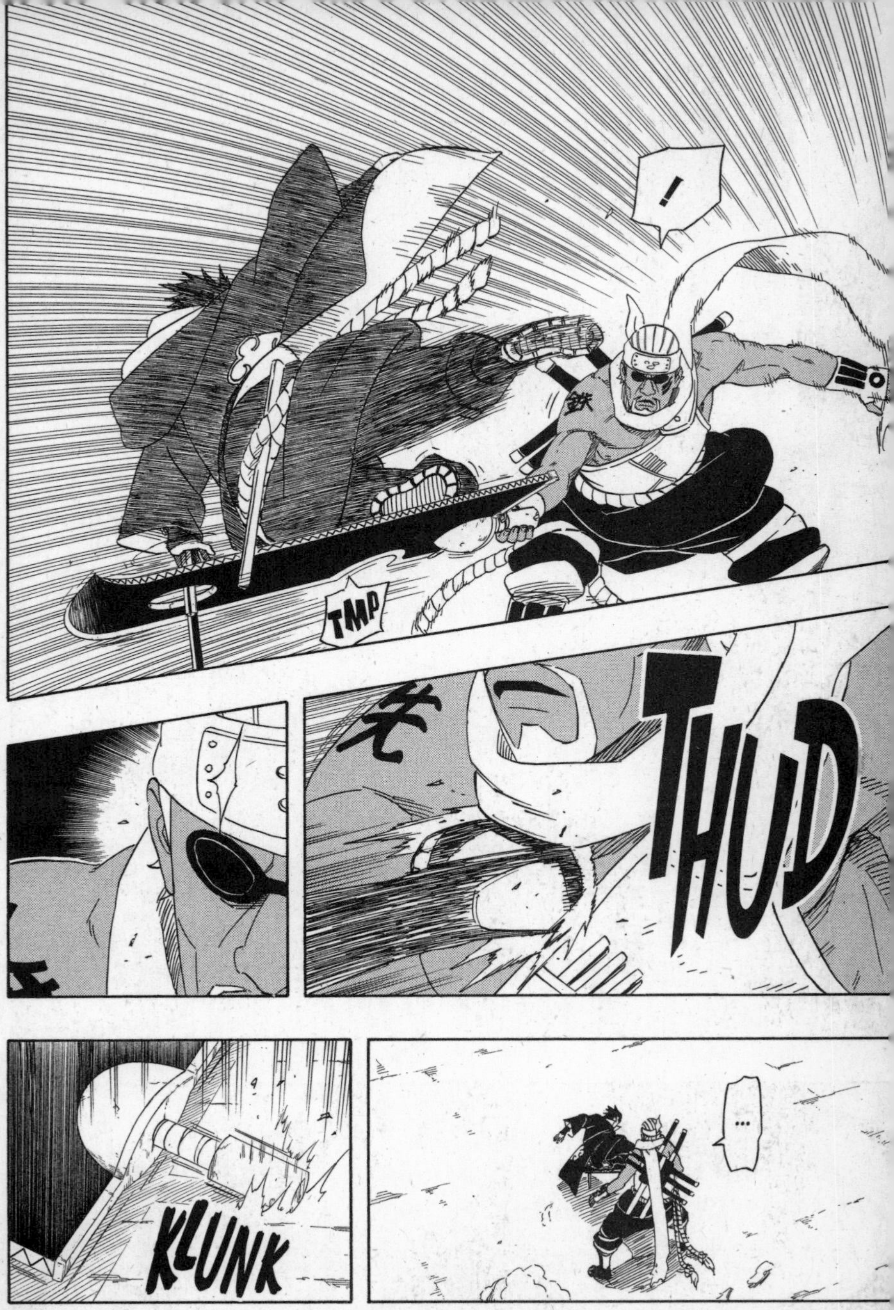
!
TMP
THUD
...
KLUNK

READ THIS WAY

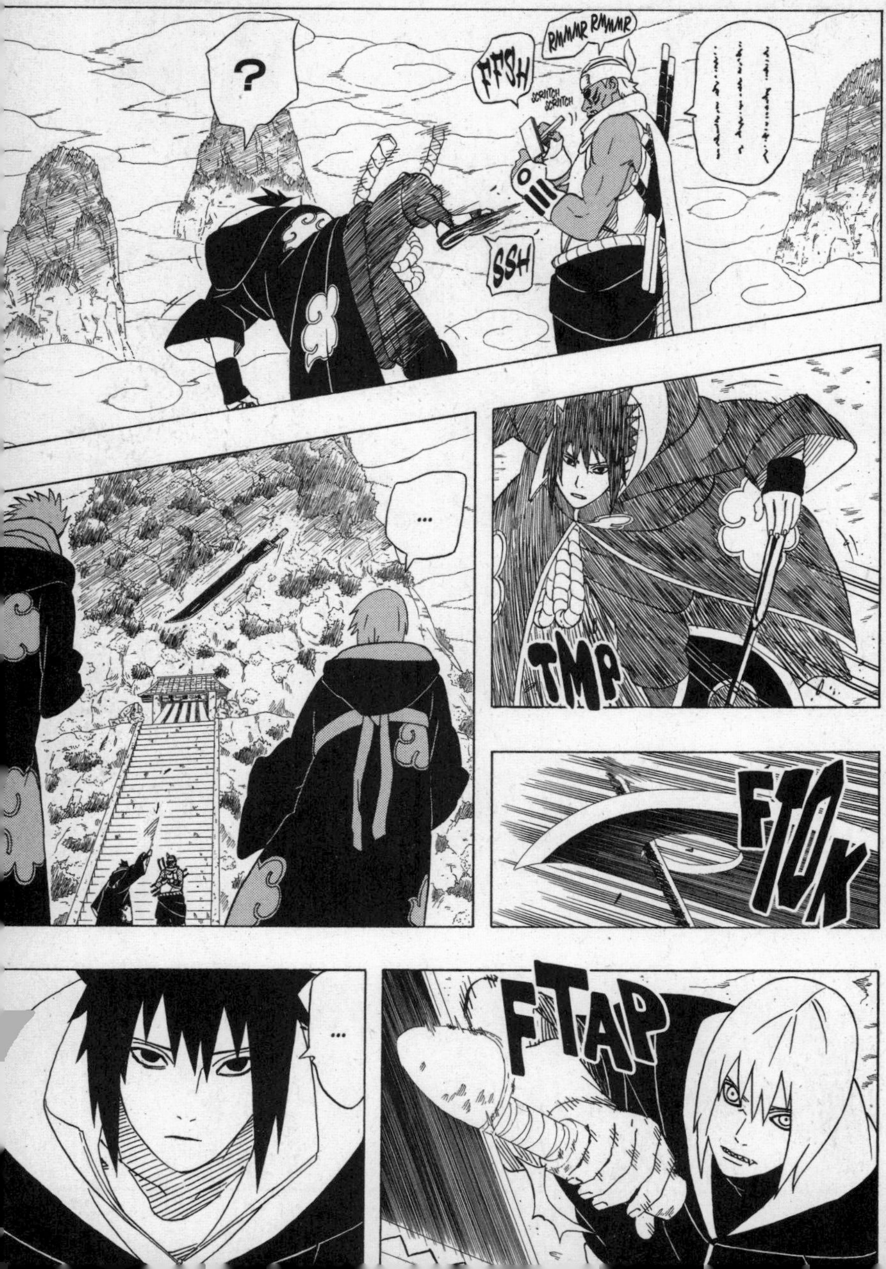

RMMMR RMMMR
FFSH
SCRITCH SCRITCH
?
SSH
TMP
FTOK
...
FTAP
...

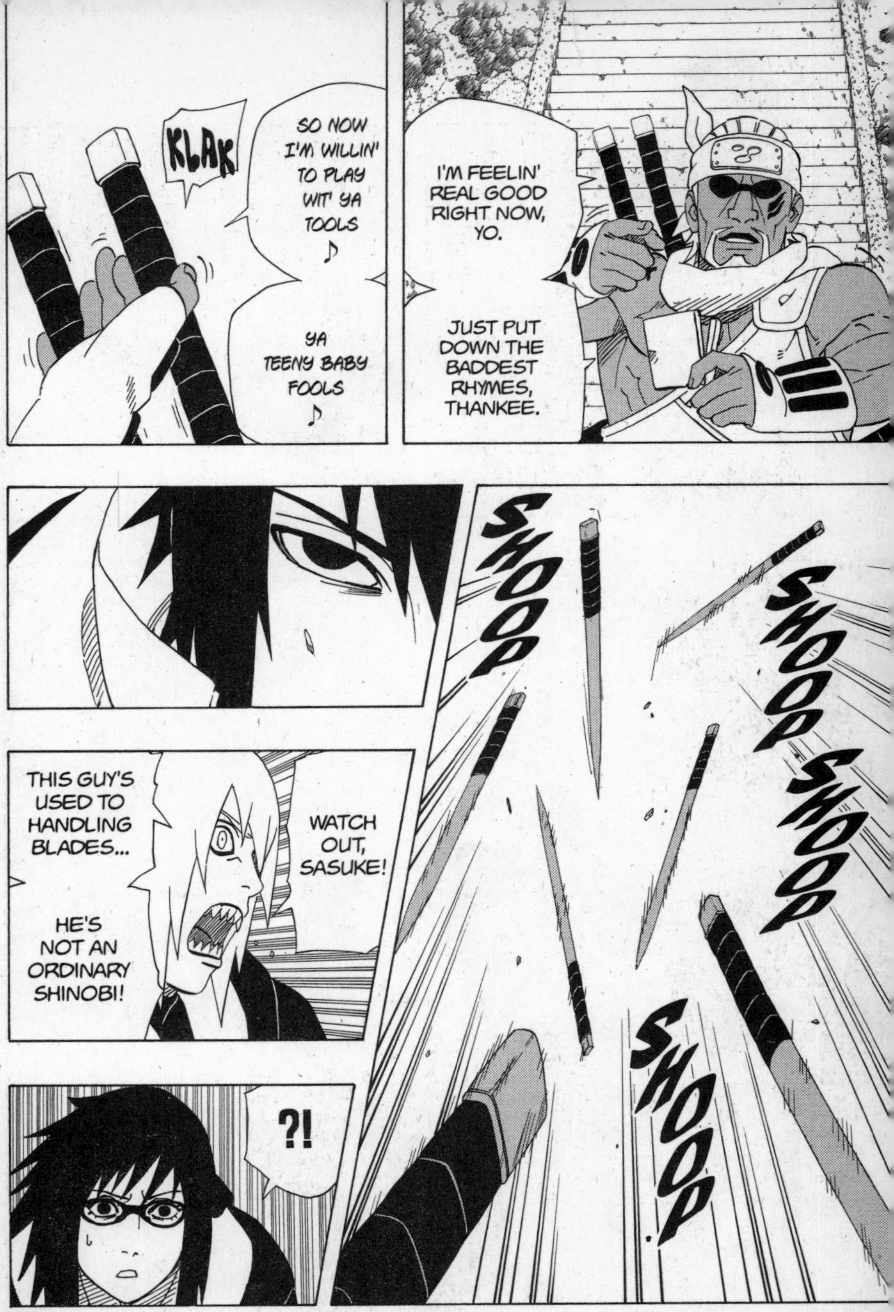
I'M FEELIN' REAL GOOD RIGHT NOW, YO.
JUST PUT DOWN THE BADDEST RHYMES, THANKEE.
SO NOW I'M WILLIN' TO PLAY WIT' YA TOOLS ♪
KLAK
YA TEENY BABY FOOLS ♪
SHOOP SHOOP SHOOP
SHOOP
SHOOP
WATCH OUT, SASUKE!
THIS GUY'S USED TO HANDLING BLADES...
HE'S NOT AN ORDINARY SHINOBI!
?!

READ THIS WAY

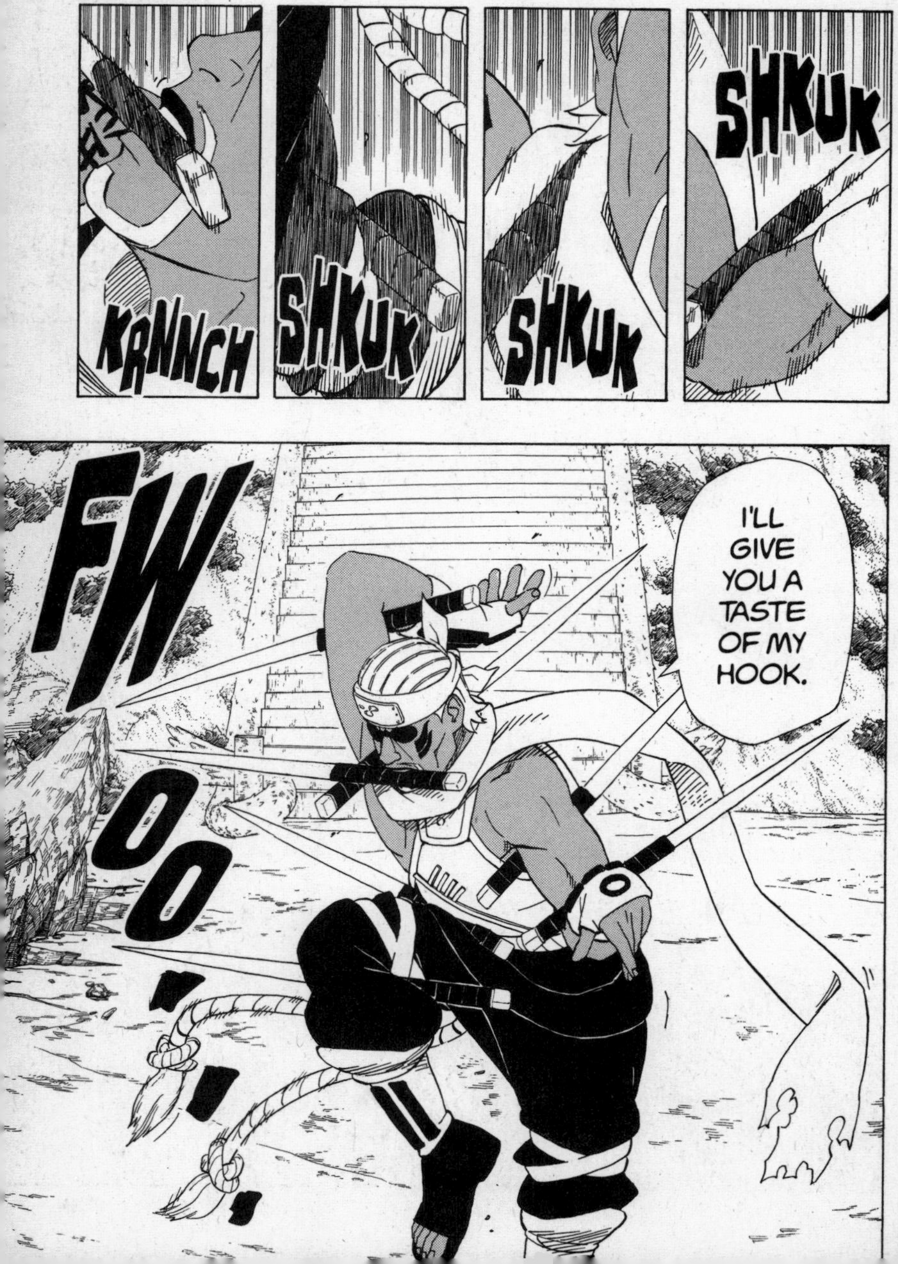
SHKUK
SHKUK
SHKUK
KRNNCH
I'LL GIVE YOU A TASTE OF MY HOOK.
FWOO

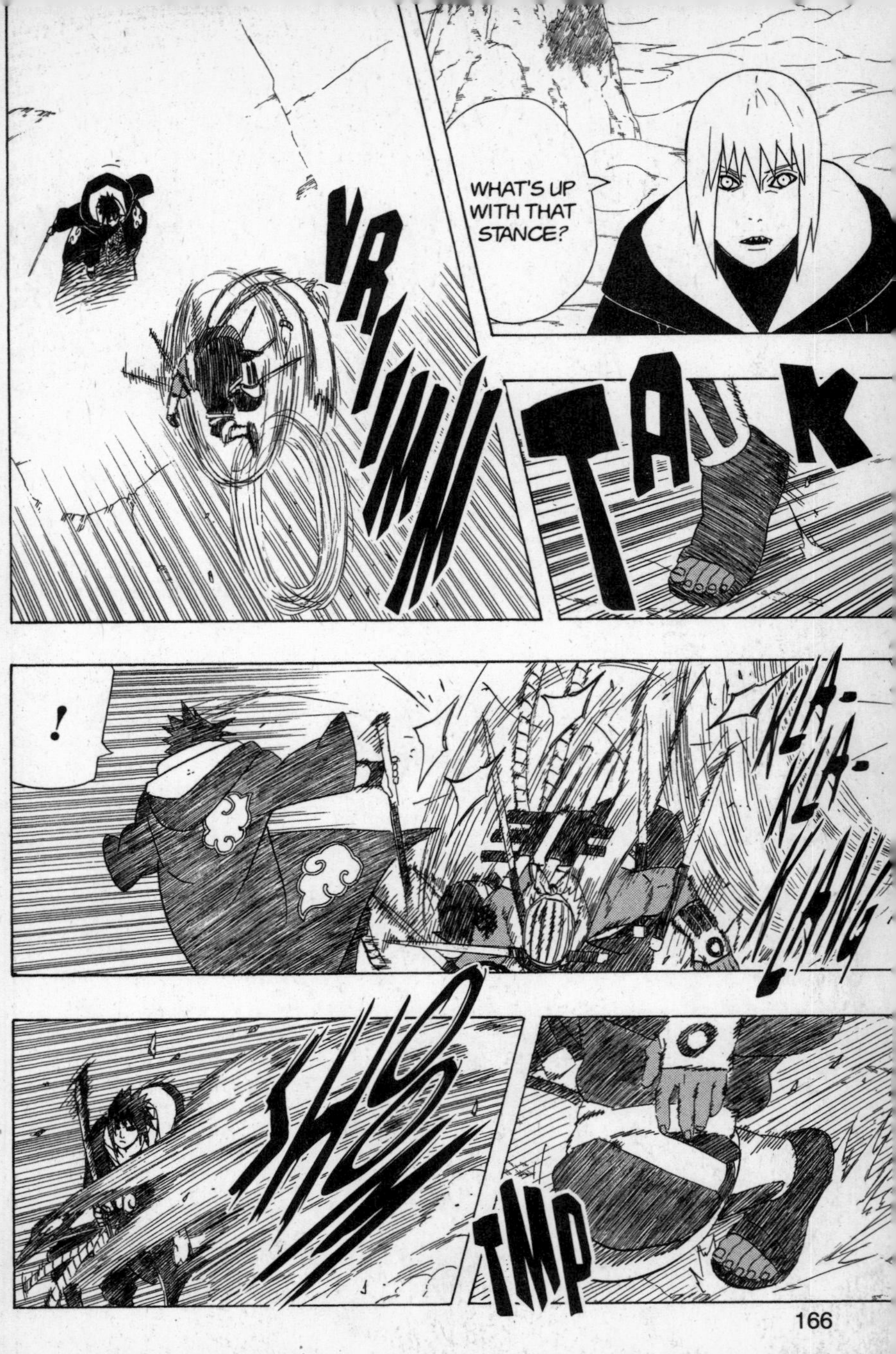
WHAT'S UP WITH THAT STANCE?
TAK
VRIIMM
KLA-KLA-KLANG
!
TMP
SHS

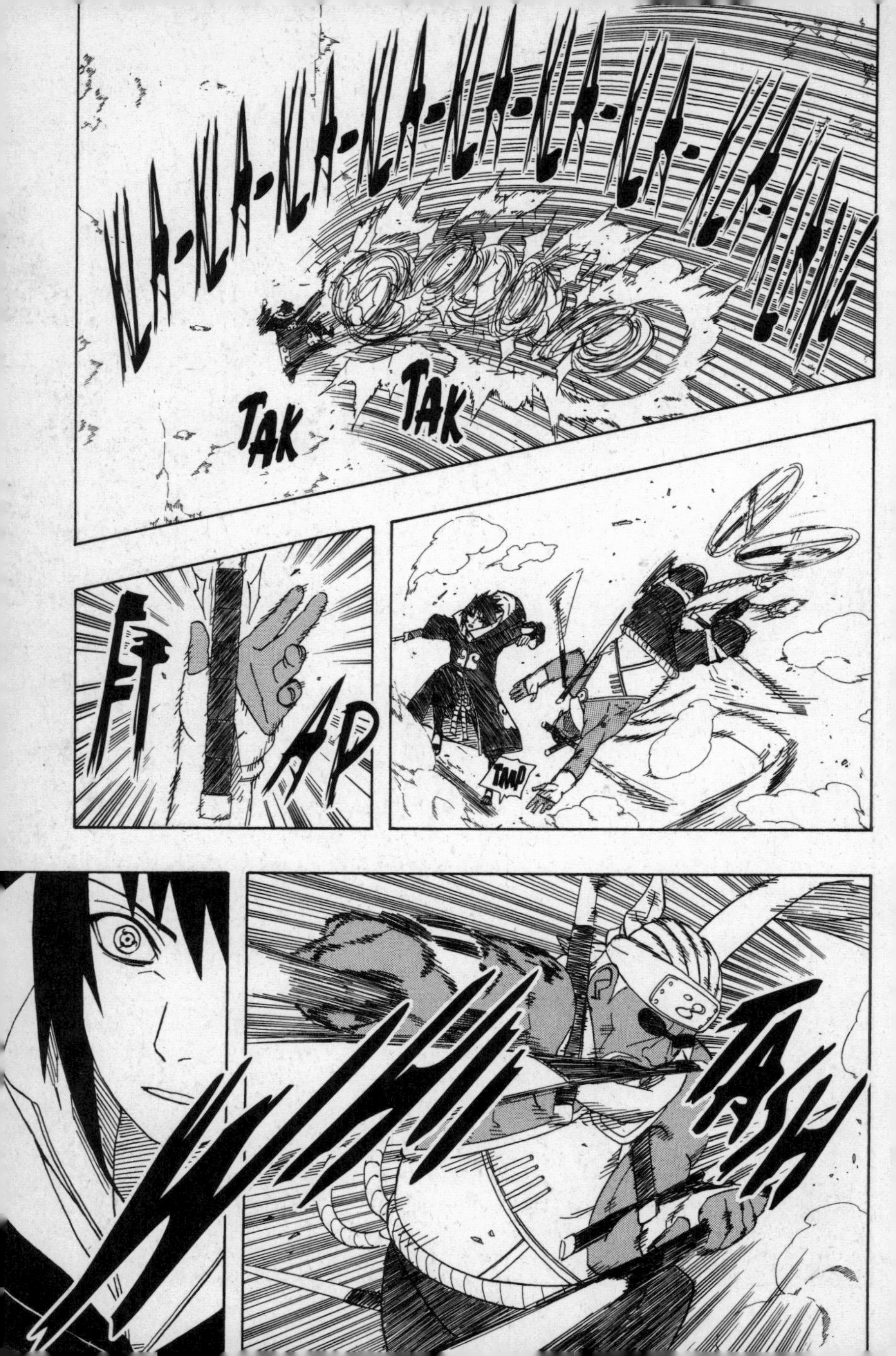
KLA-KLA-KLA-KLA-KLA-KLA-KLA-KLA-KLANG
TAK
TAK
TMP
FTAP
TASH

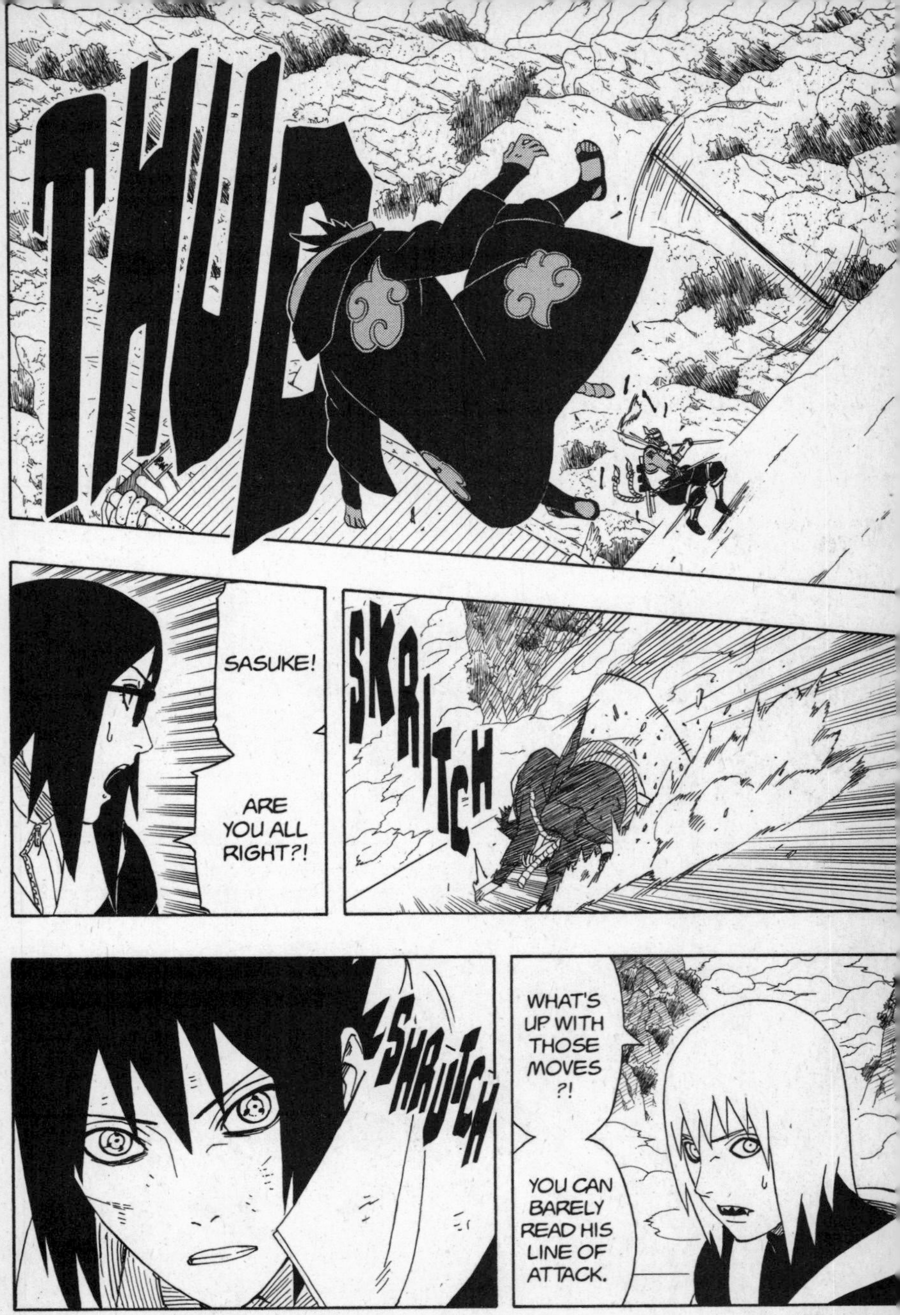
THUD
SKRITCH
SASUKE!
ARE YOU ALL RIGHT?!
WHAT'S UP WITH THOSE MOVES ?!
YOU CAN BARELY READ HIS LINE OF ATTACK.
SHRUTCH

READ THIS WAY

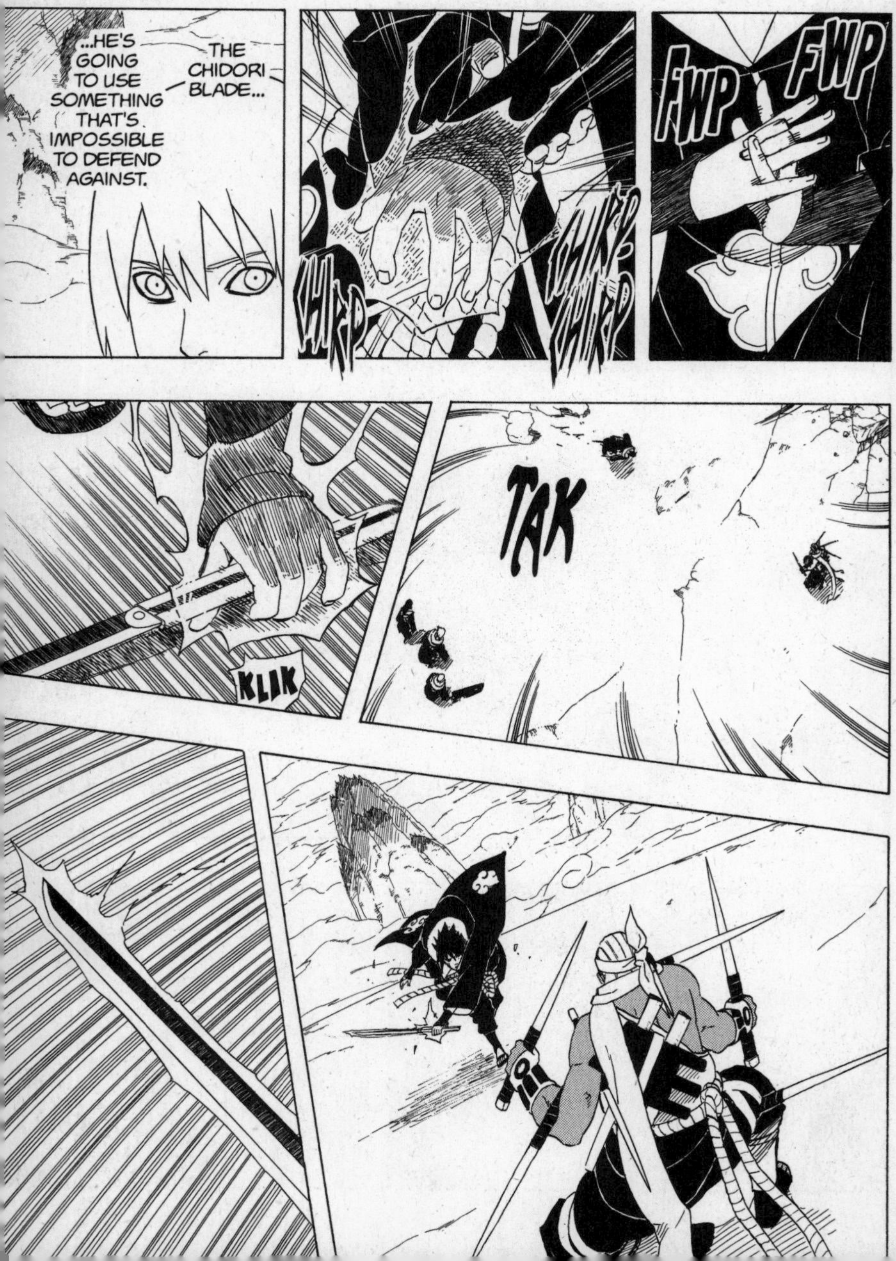
FWP FWP
THE CHIDORI BLADE...
...HE'S GOING TO USE SOMETHING THAT'S IMPOSSIBLE TO DEFEND AGAINST.
TAK
KLIK

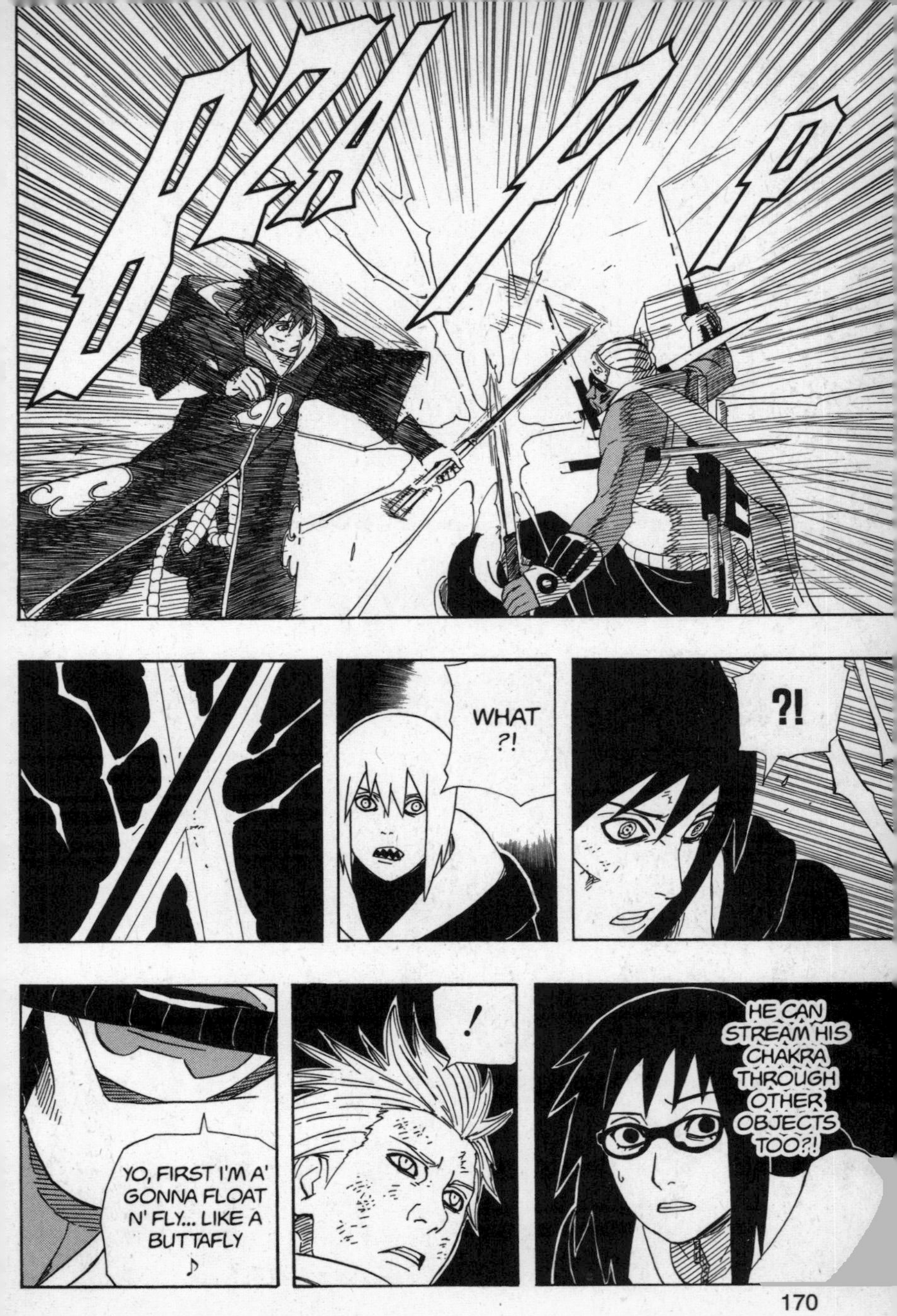
BZAPP
?!
WHAT ?!
HE CAN STREAM HIS CHAKRA THROUGH OTHER OBJECTS TOO?!
!
YO, FIRST I'M A' GONNA FLOAT N' FLY... LIKE A BUTTAFLY ♪

READ THIS WAY

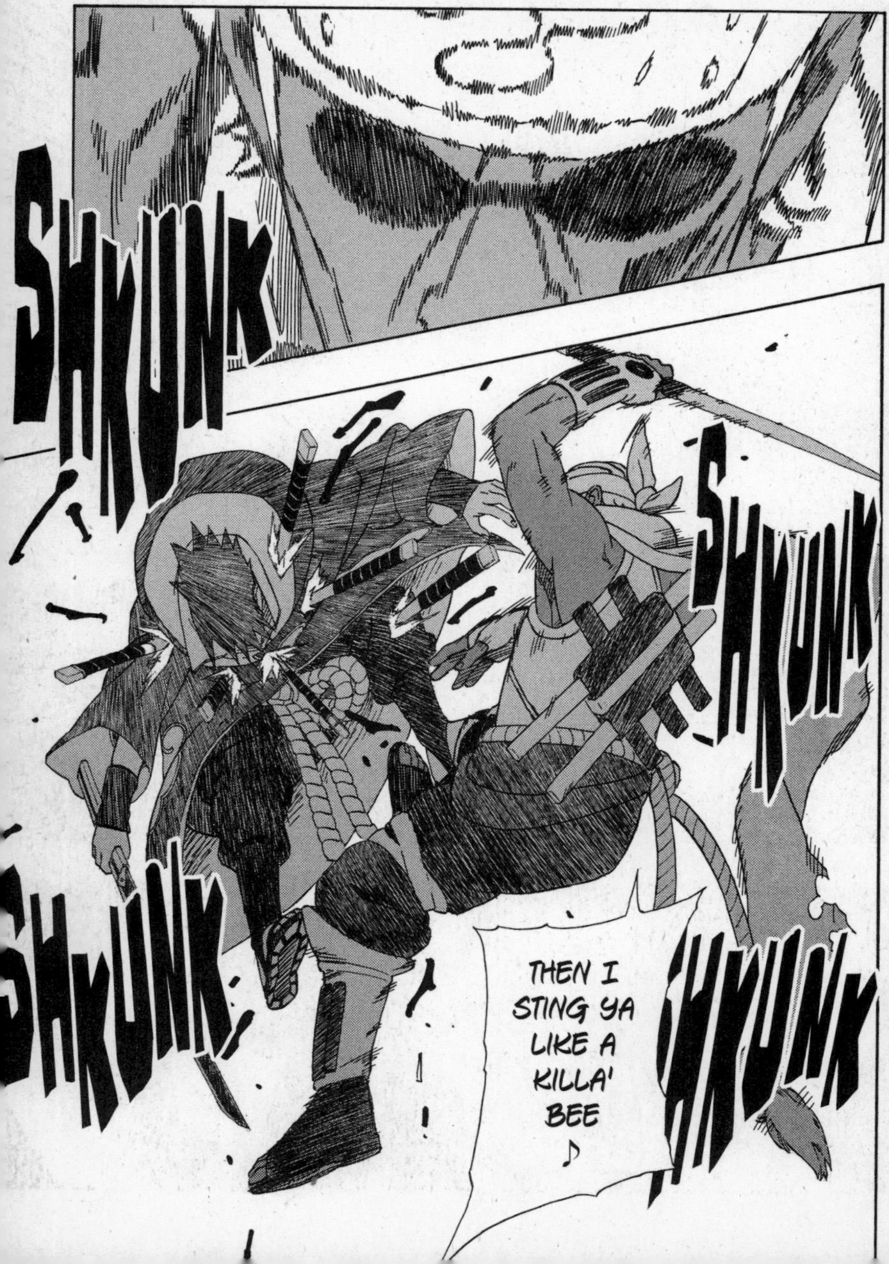
SHKUNK
SHKUNK
SHKUNK
THEN I STING YA LIKE A KILLA' BEE ♪
SHKUNK

NARUTO

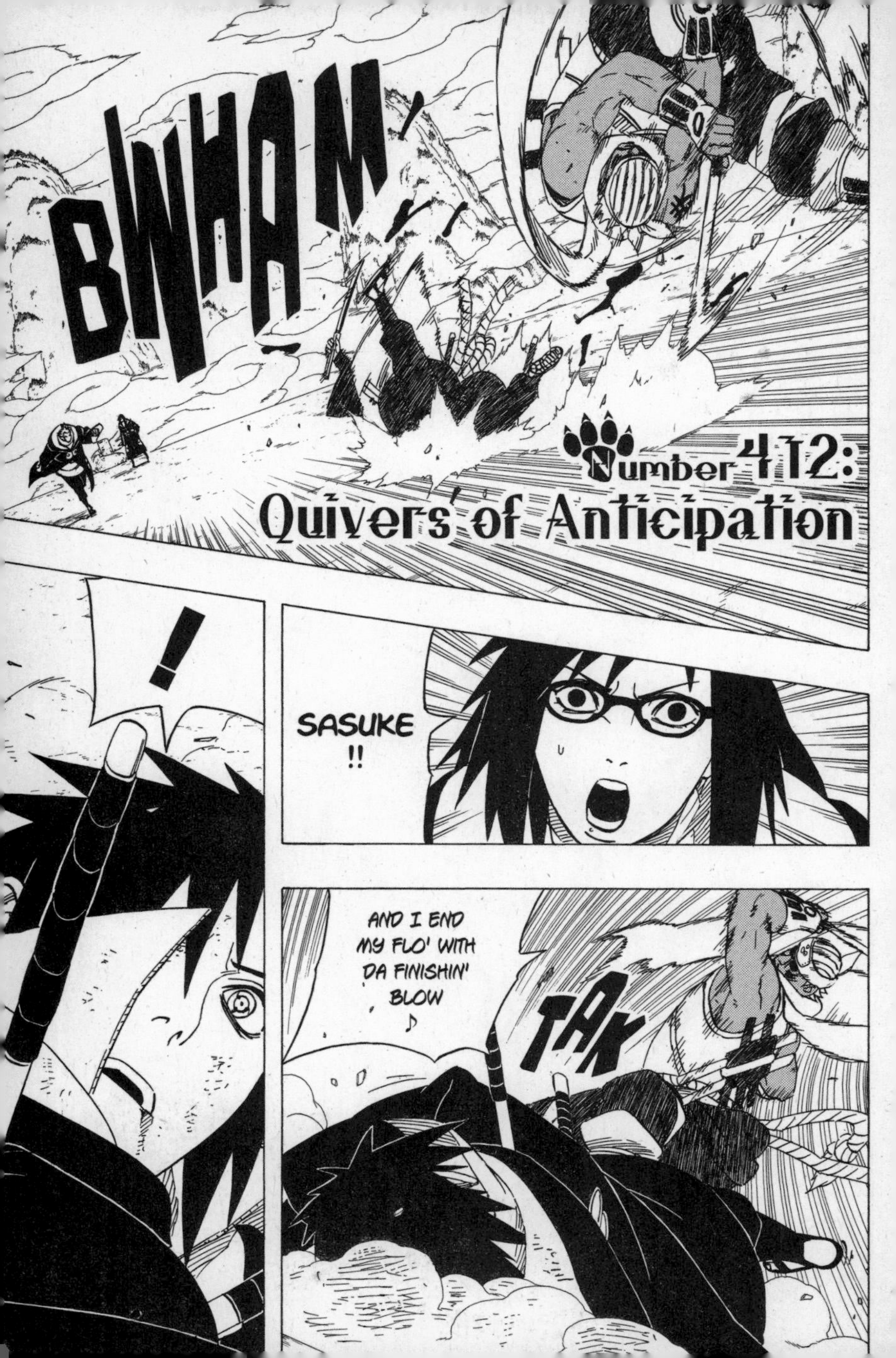
BWHAM
Number 412: Quivers of Anticipation
SASUKE !!
AND I END MY FLO' WITH DA FINISHIN' BLOW ♪
TAK
!

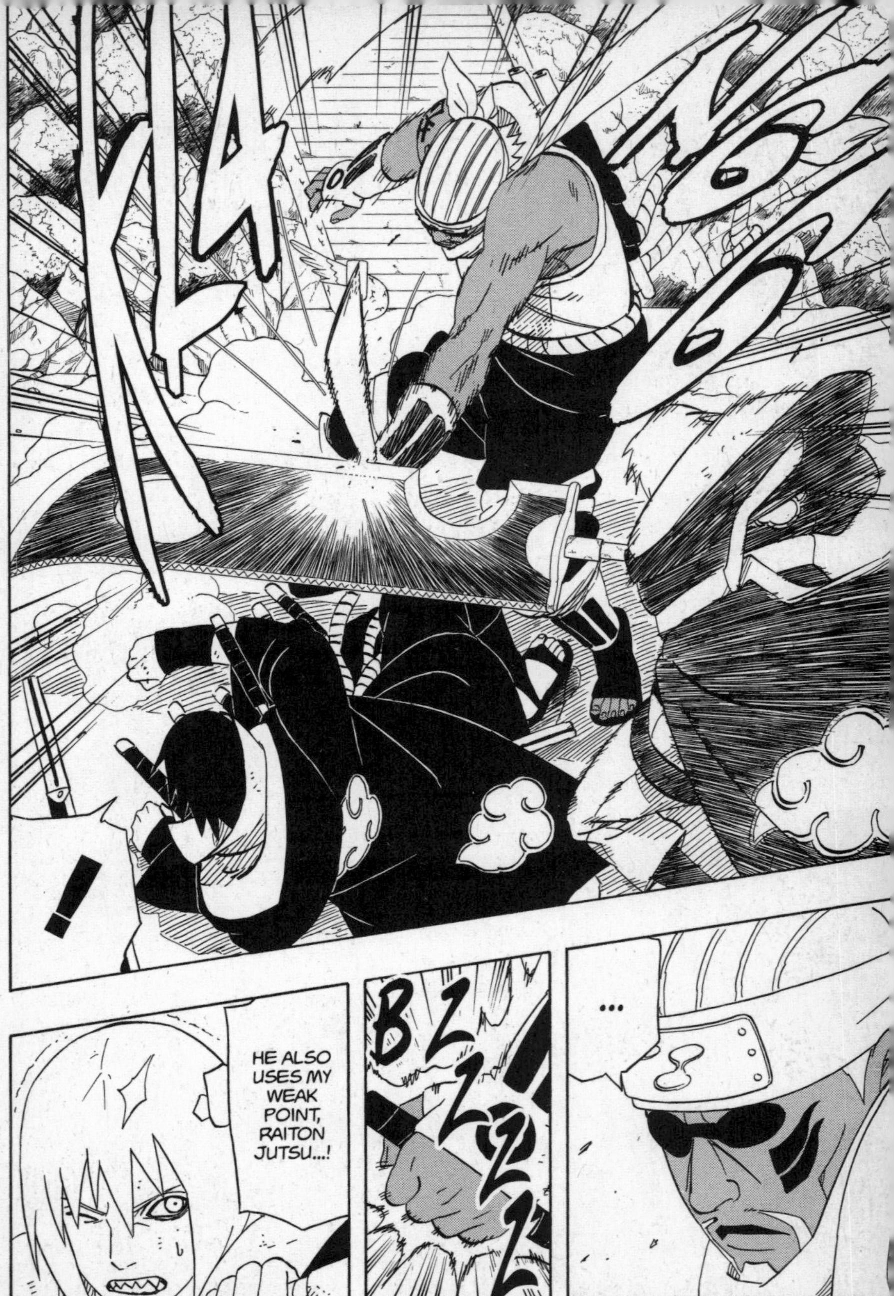
!
...
HE ALSO USES MY WEAK POINT, RAITON JUTSU...!

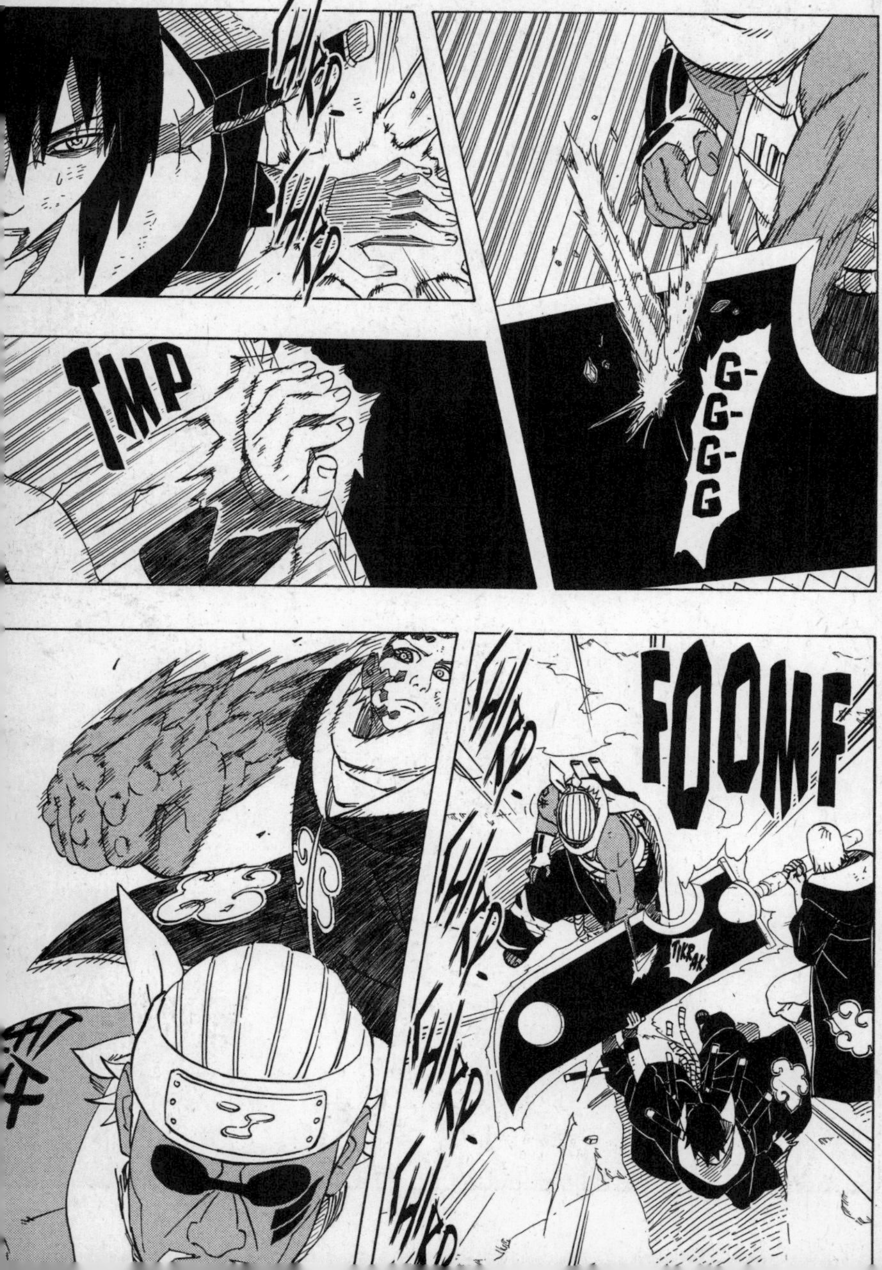
G-G-G-G
SHKP
SHKP
TMP
FOOMF
TIKRAK
SHKP
SHKP
SHKP
SHKP
SHKP

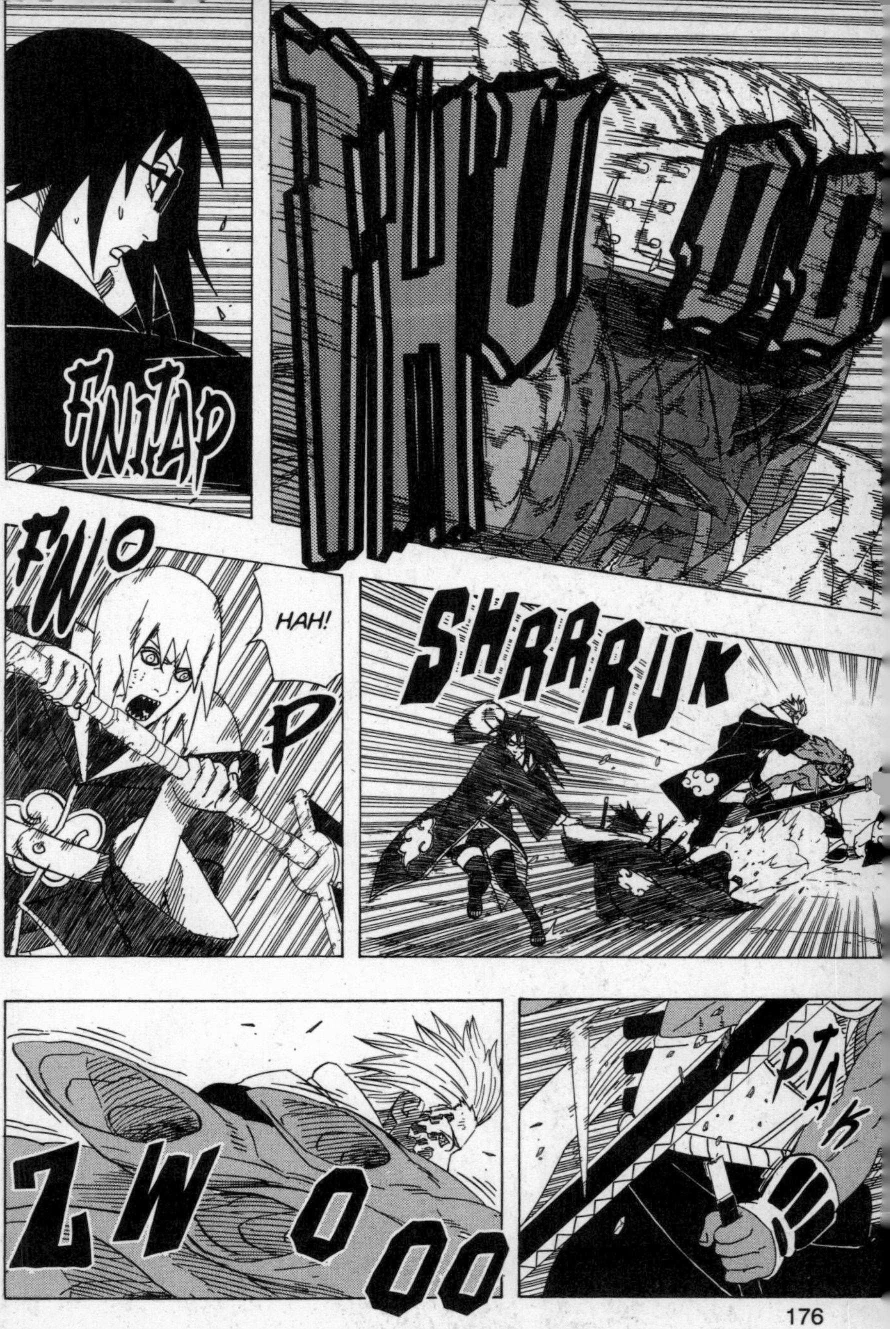
THUDD
FWIAP
SHRRRUK
FWO
P
HAH!
PTAK
ZWOOOO

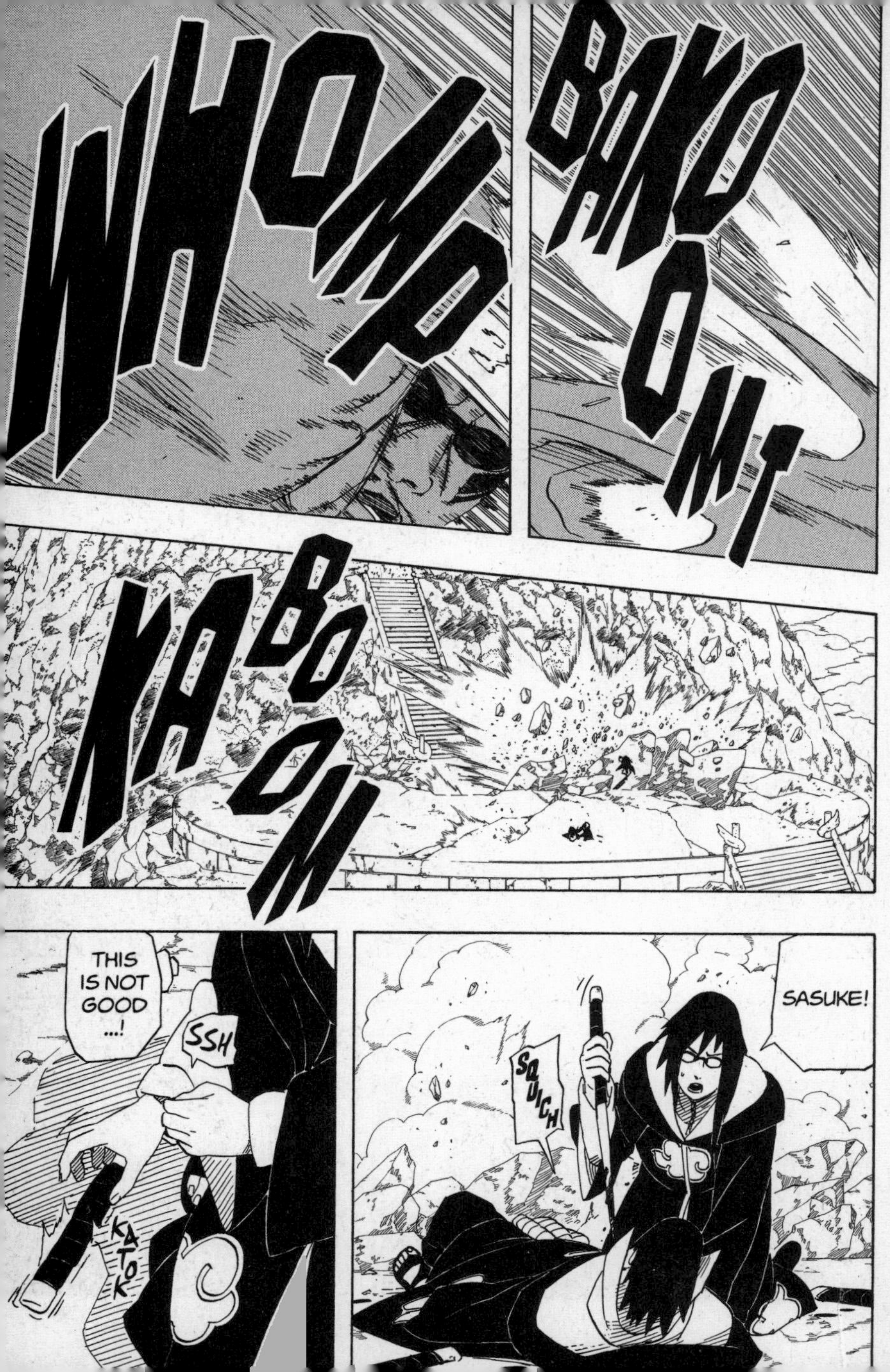
BAKOOM!
WHOMP
KABOOM
SASUKE!
SQUICH
THIS IS NOT GOOD ...!
SSH
KATOK

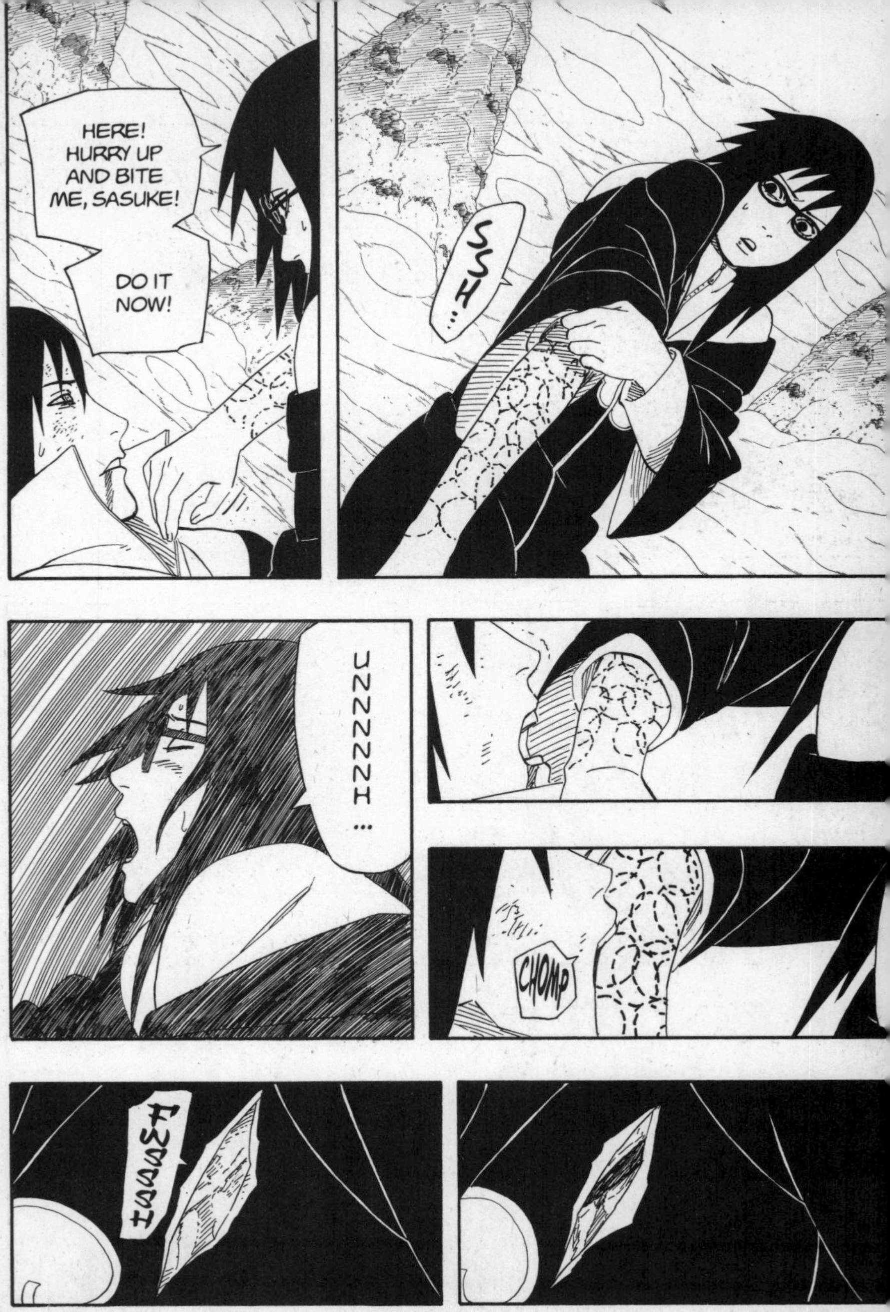
SSH...
HERE! HURRY UP AND BITE ME, SASUKE!
DO IT NOW!
CHOMP
UNNNNNH...
FWSSSH

READ THIS WAY

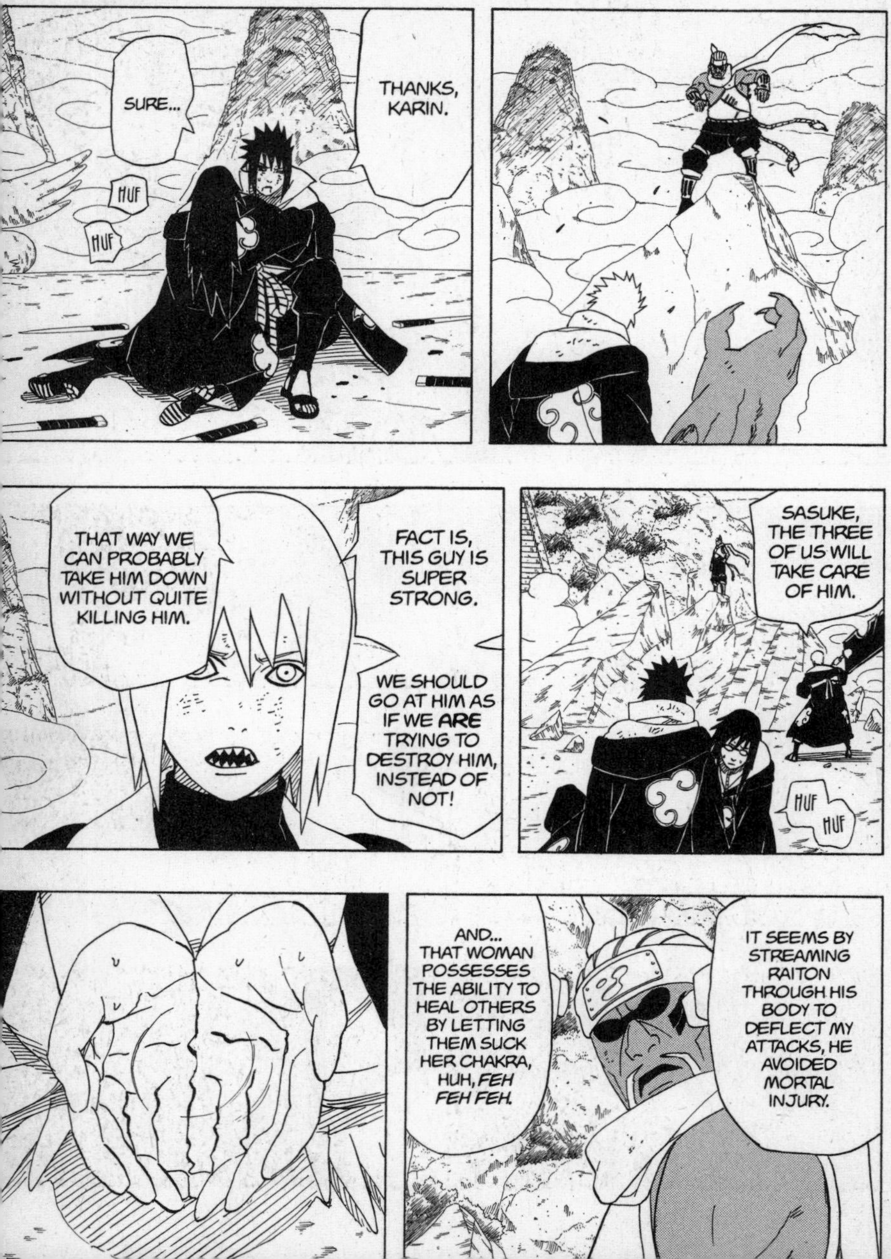
THANKS, KARIN.
SURE...
HUF
HUF
SASUKE, THE THREE OF US WILL TAKE CARE OF HIM.
HUF
HUF
FACT IS, THIS GUY IS SUPER STRONG.
WE SHOULD GO AT HIM AS IF WE **ARE** TRYING TO DESTROY HIM, INSTEAD OF NOT!
THAT WAY WE CAN PROBABLY TAKE HIM DOWN WITHOUT QUITE KILLING HIM.
IT SEEMS BY STREAMING RAITON THROUGH HIS BODY TO DEFLECT MY ATTACKS, HE AVOIDED MORTAL INJURY.
AND... THAT WOMAN POSSESSES THE ABILITY TO HEAL OTHERS BY LETTING THEM SUCK HER CHAKRA, HUH, *FEH FEH FEH.*

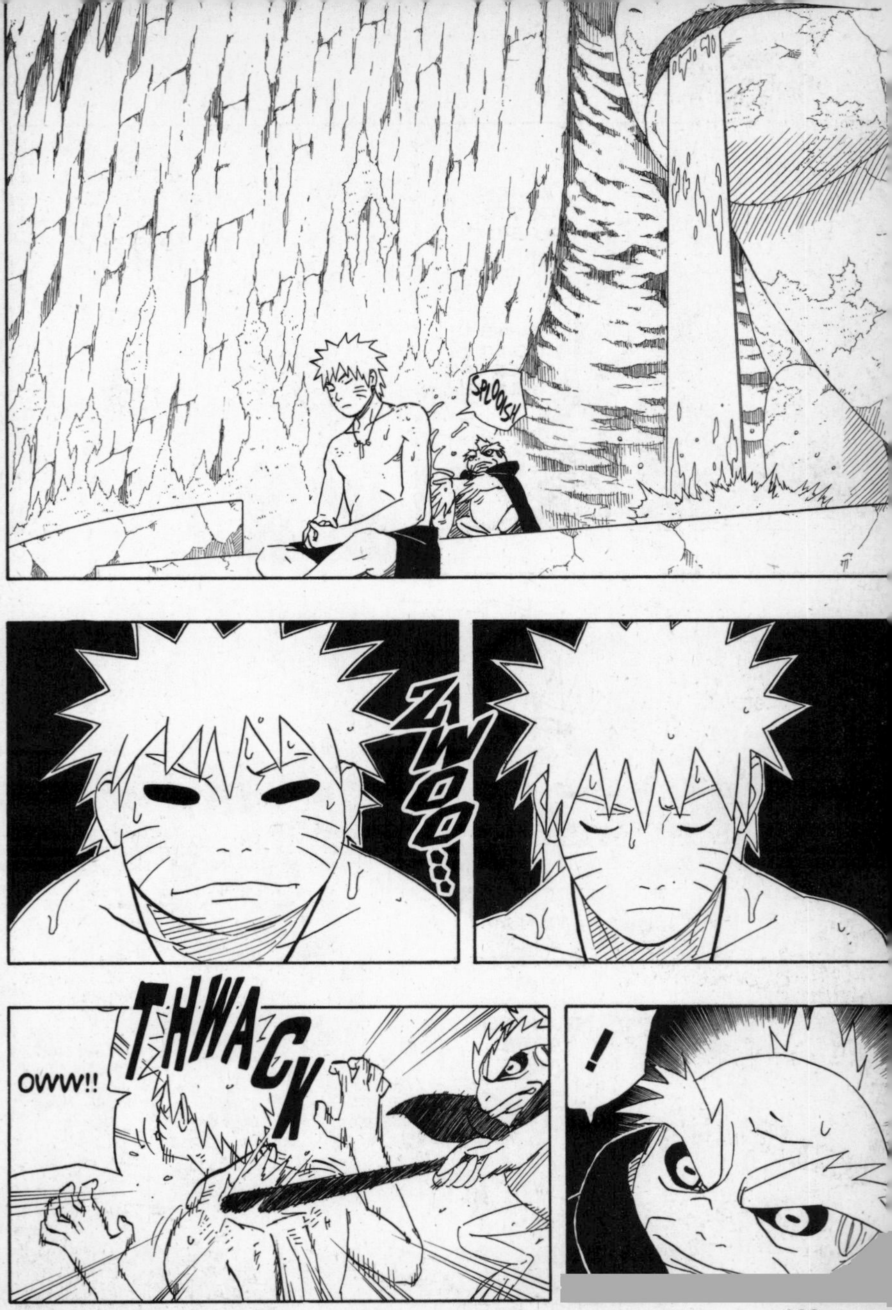
SPLOOSH
ZWOO...
!
THWACK
OWW!!

READ THIS WAY

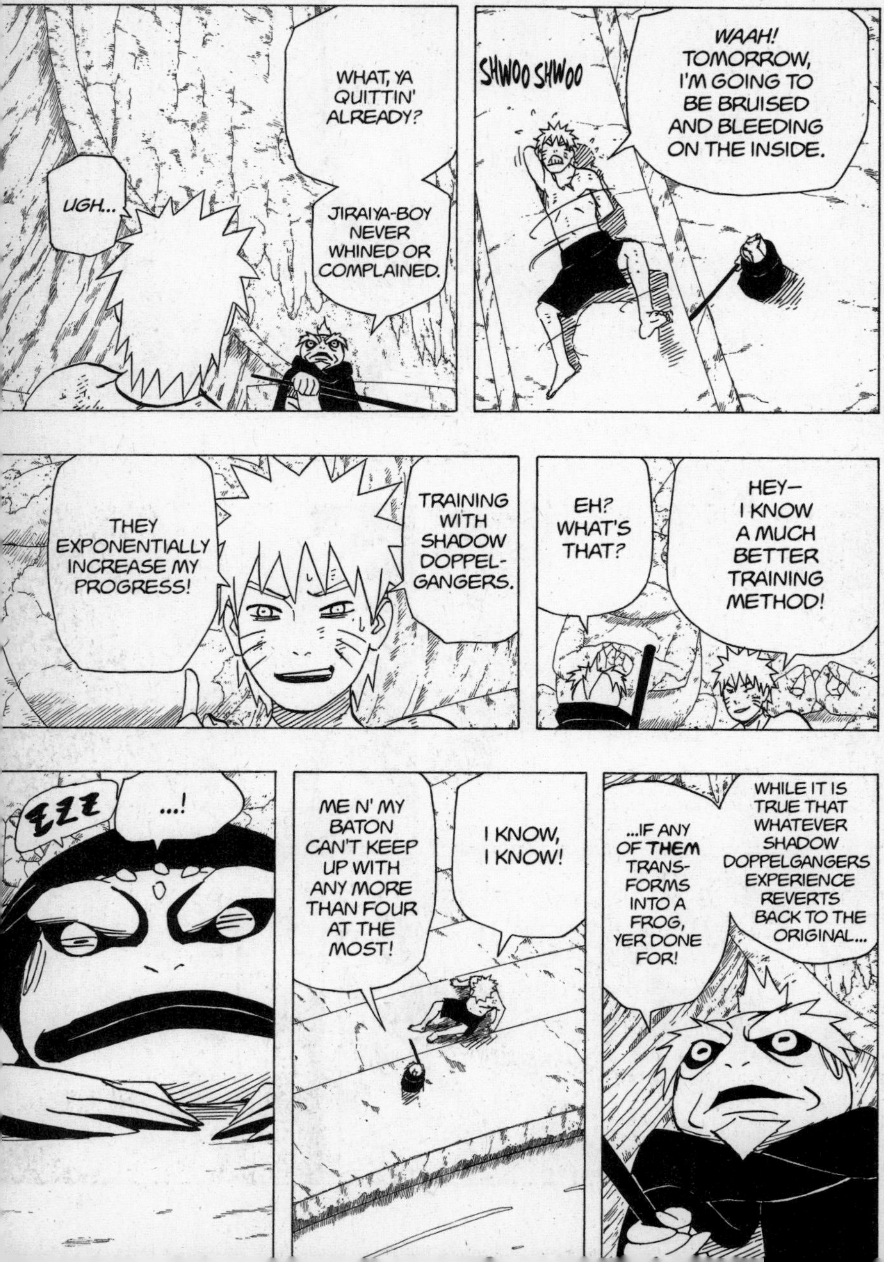
SHWOO SHWOO
WAAH! TOMORROW, I'M GOING TO BE BRUISED AND BLEEDING ON THE INSIDE.
WHAT, YA QUITTIN' ALREADY?
JIRAIYA-BOY NEVER WHINED OR COMPLAINED.
UGH...
HEY— I KNOW A MUCH BETTER TRAINING METHOD!
EH? WHAT'S THAT?
TRAINING WITH SHADOW DOPPEL-GANGERS.
THEY EXPONENTIALLY INCREASE MY PROGRESS!
WHILE IT IS TRUE THAT WHATEVER SHADOW DOPPELGANGERS EXPERIENCE REVERTS BACK TO THE ORIGINAL...
...IF ANY OF **THEM** TRANS-FORMS INTO A FROG, YER DONE FOR!
I KNOW, I KNOW!
ME N' MY BATON CAN'T KEEP UP WITH ANY MORE THAN FOUR AT THE MOST!
...!
ZZZ

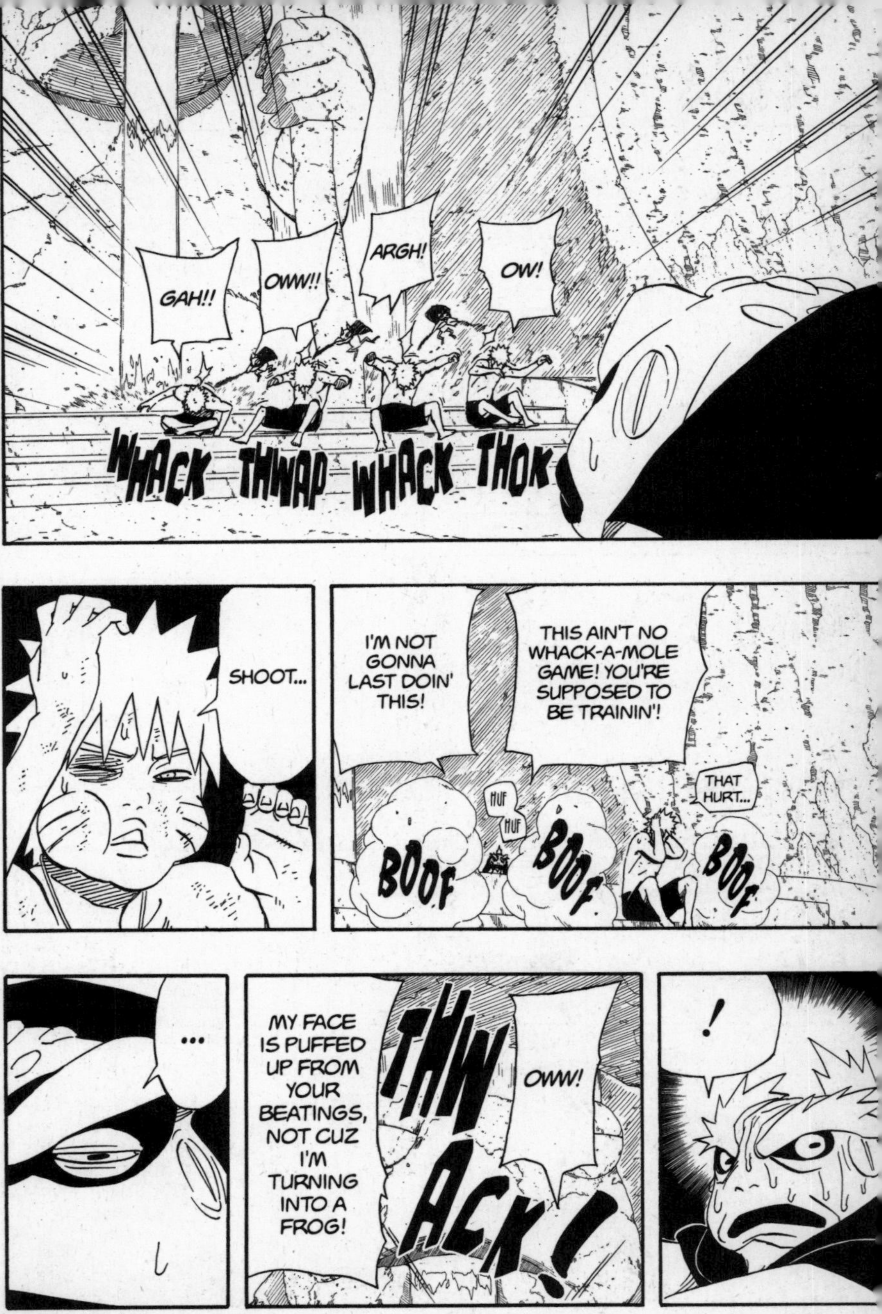
OW!
ARGH!
OWW!!
GAH!!
THOK
WHACK
THWAP
WHACK
THIS AIN'T NO WHACK-A-MOLE GAME! YOU'RE SUPPOSED TO BE TRAININ'!
I'M NOT GONNA LAST DOIN' THIS!
THAT HURT...
BOOF
HUF
HUF
BOOF
BOOF
SHOOT...
!
OWW!
THWACK!
MY FACE IS PUFFED UP FROM YOUR BEATINGS, NOT CUZ I'M TURNING INTO A FROG!
...

READ THIS WAY

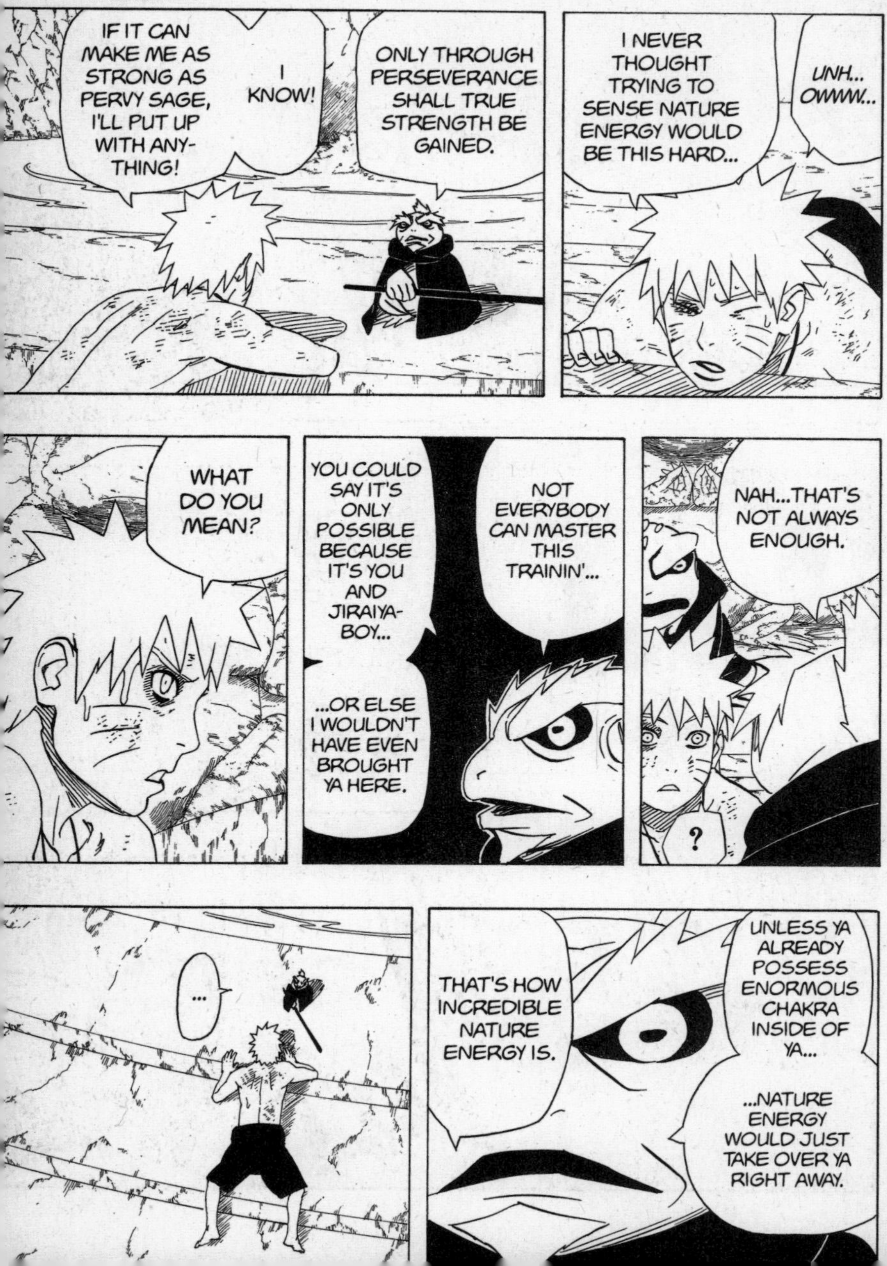
UNH... OWWW...
I NEVER THOUGHT TRYING TO SENSE NATURE ENERGY WOULD BE THIS HARD...
ONLY THROUGH PERSEVERANCE SHALL TRUE STRENGTH BE GAINED.
I KNOW!
IF IT CAN MAKE ME AS STRONG AS PERVY SAGE, I'LL PUT UP WITH ANY-THING!
NAH...THAT'S NOT ALWAYS ENOUGH.
NOT EVERYBODY CAN MASTER THIS TRAININ'...
YOU COULD SAY IT'S ONLY POSSIBLE BECAUSE IT'S YOU AND JIRAIYA-BOY...
...OR ELSE I WOULDN'T HAVE EVEN BROUGHT YA HERE.
?
WHAT DO YOU MEAN?
UNLESS YA ALREADY POSSESS ENORMOUS CHAKRA INSIDE OF YA...
...NATURE ENERGY WOULD JUST TAKE OVER YA RIGHT AWAY.
THAT'S HOW INCREDIBLE NATURE ENERGY IS.
...

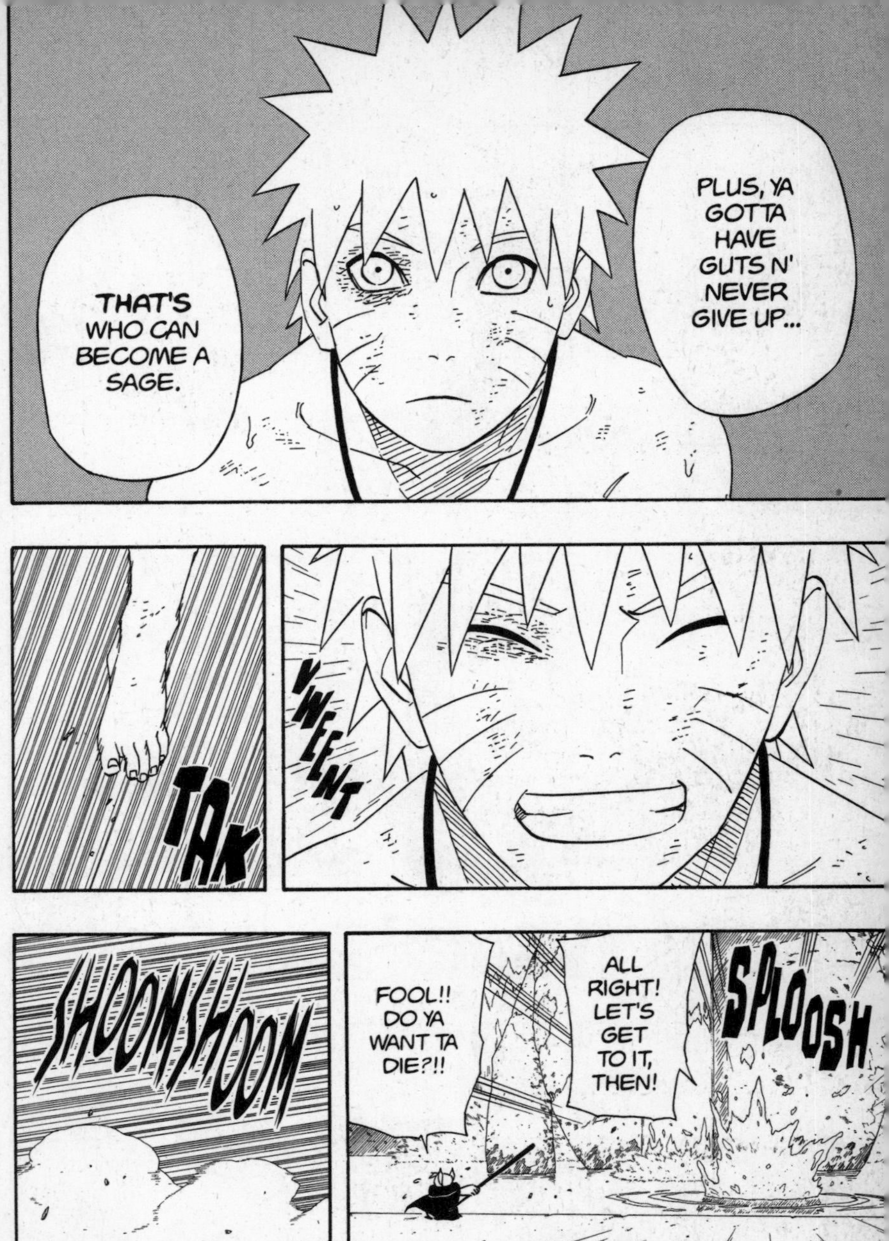
PLUS, YA GOTTA HAVE GUTS N' NEVER GIVE UP...
THAT'S WHO CAN BECOME A SAGE.
VWEENT
TAK
SPLOOSH
ALL RIGHT! LET'S GET TO IT, THEN!
FOOL!! DO YA WANT TA DIE?!!
SHOOM SHOOM

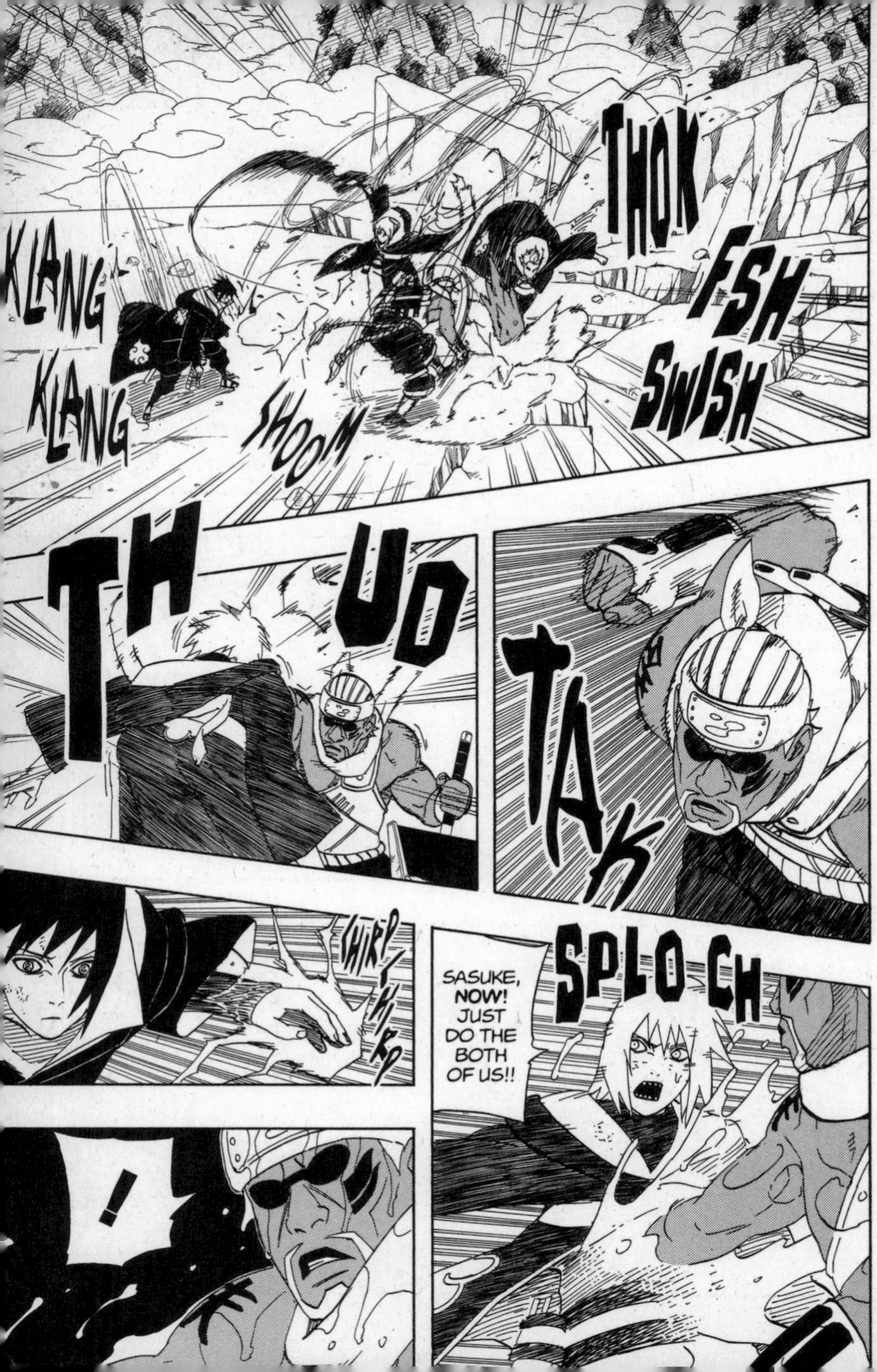
THOK
FSH
SWISH
SHOOM
KLANG
KLANG
TAK
THUD
SPLOCH
SASUKE, NOW! JUST DO THE BOTH OF US!!
SHIRP
SHIRP
!

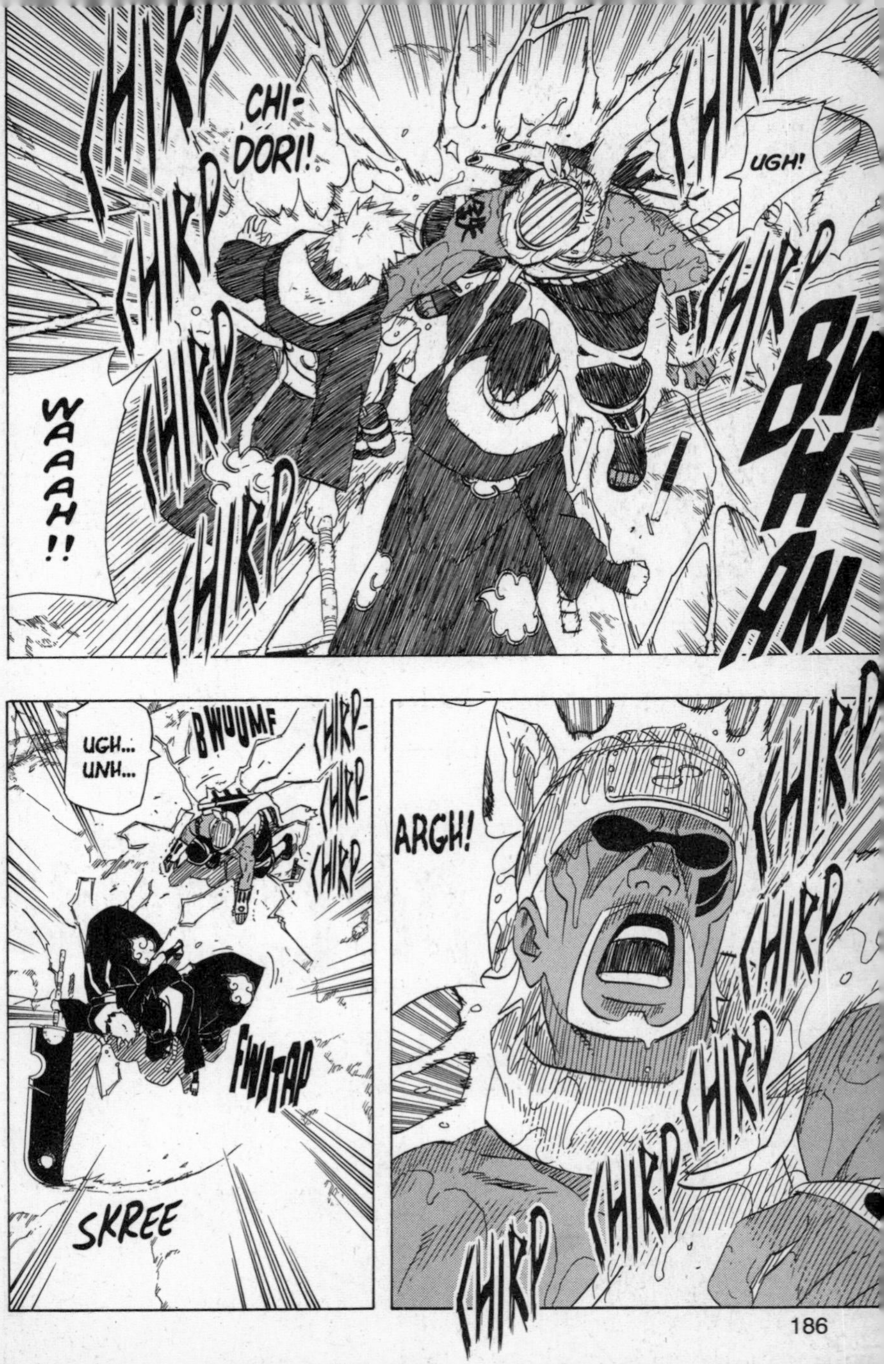
UGH!
CHIRP
CHIRP
BAAAM
CHIRP
CHI-DORI!!
CHIRP
CHIRP
CHIRP
WAAAAH!!
CHIRP
CHIRP
CHIRP
ARGH!
CHIRP
CHIRP
CHIRP
UGH... UNH...
BWUUMF
CHIRP-CHIRP-CHIRP
FWUTAP
SKREE

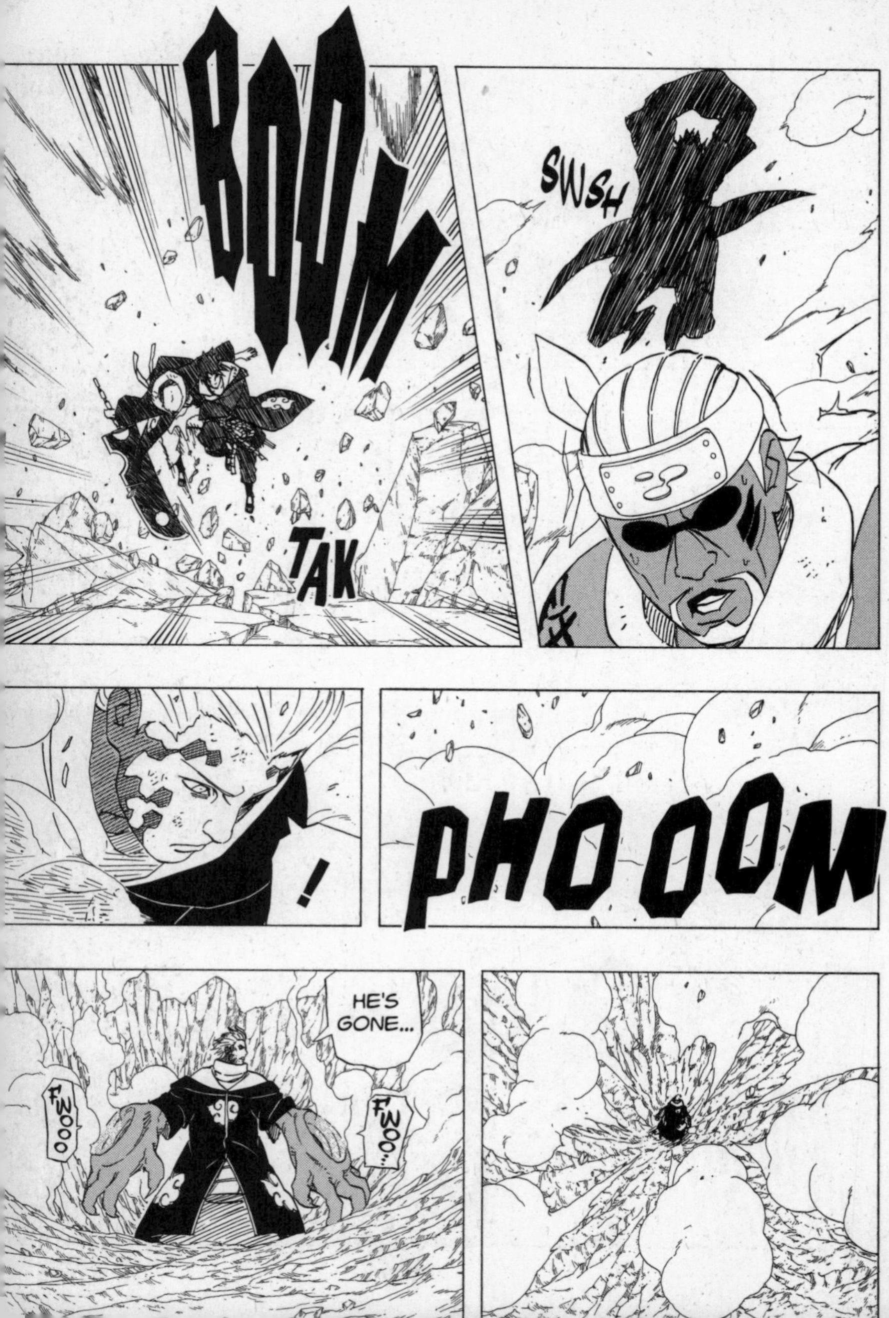
SWSH
BOOM
TAK
PHOOOM
!
HE'S GONE...
FWOO...
FWOOO

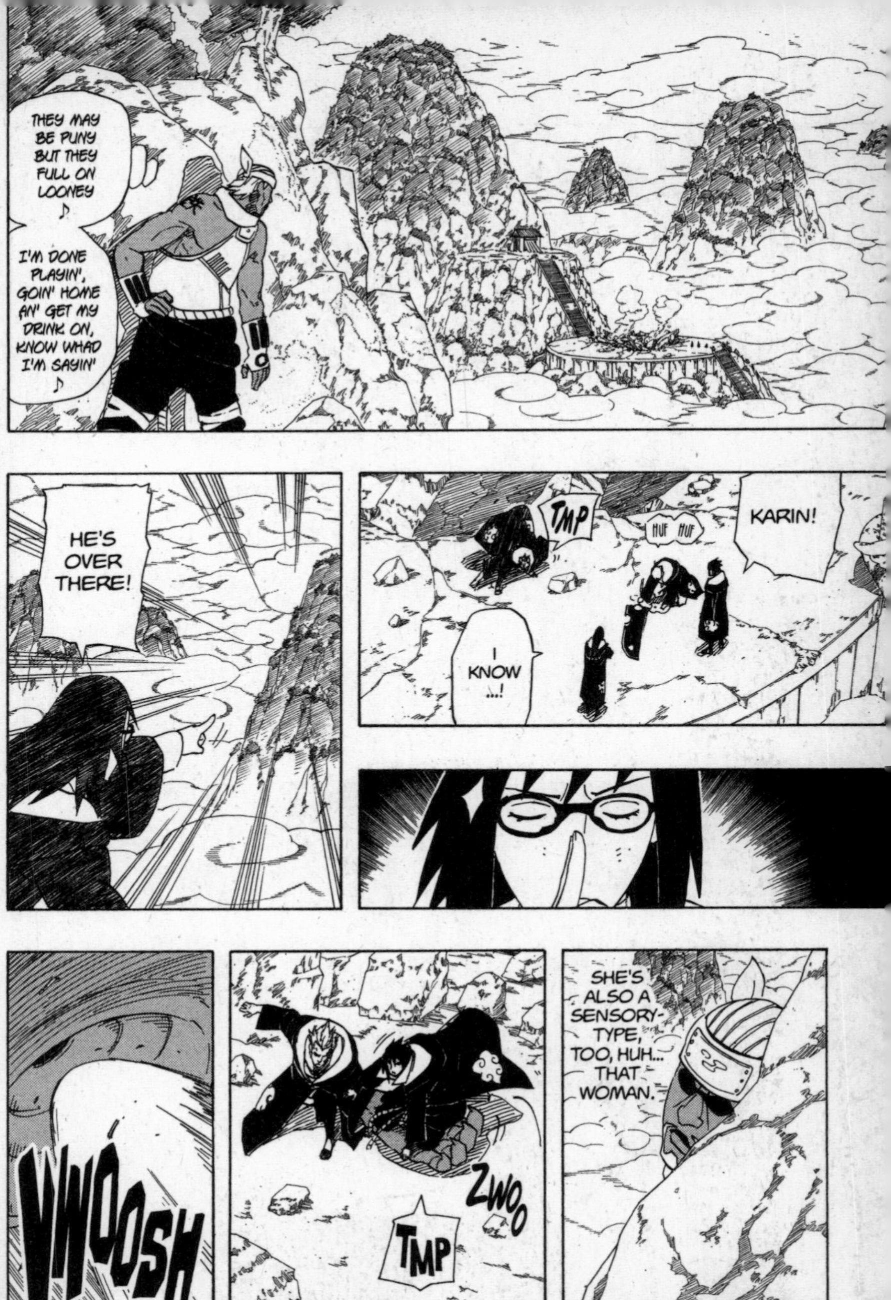
THEY MAY BE PUNY BUT THEY FULL ON LOONEY ♪
I'M DONE PLAYIN', GOIN' HOME AN' GET MY DRINK ON, KNOW WHAD I'M SAYIN' ♪
KARIN!
HUF HUF
TMP
I KNOW ...!
HE'S OVER THERE!
SHE'S ALSO A SENSORY-TYPE, TOO, HUH... THAT WOMAN.
ZWOO
TMP
VWOOSH

READ THIS WAY

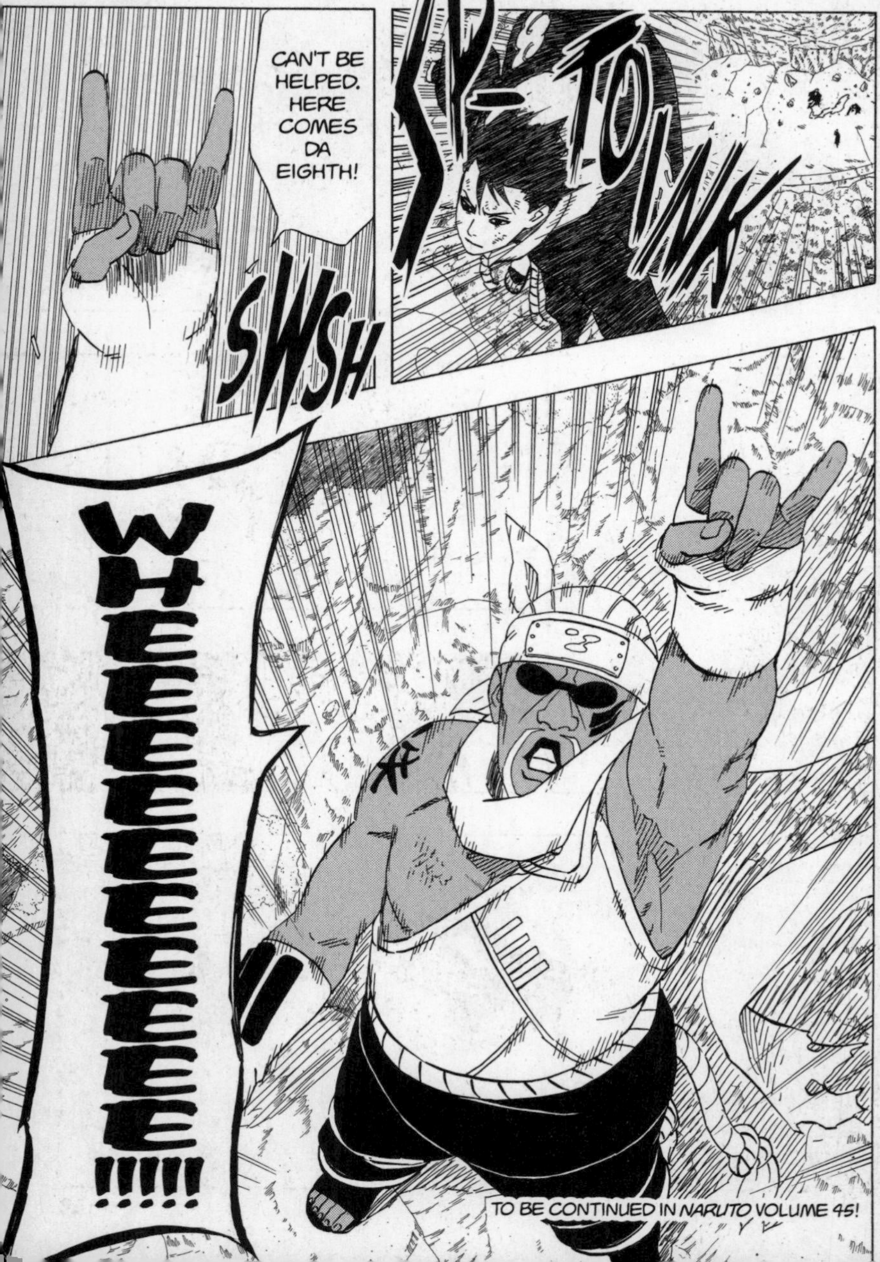
KP-TOWK
CAN'T BE HELPED. HERE COMES DA EIGHTH!
SWSH
WHEEEEEEEEEEE!!!!!
TO BE CONTINUED IN NARUTO VOLUME 45!

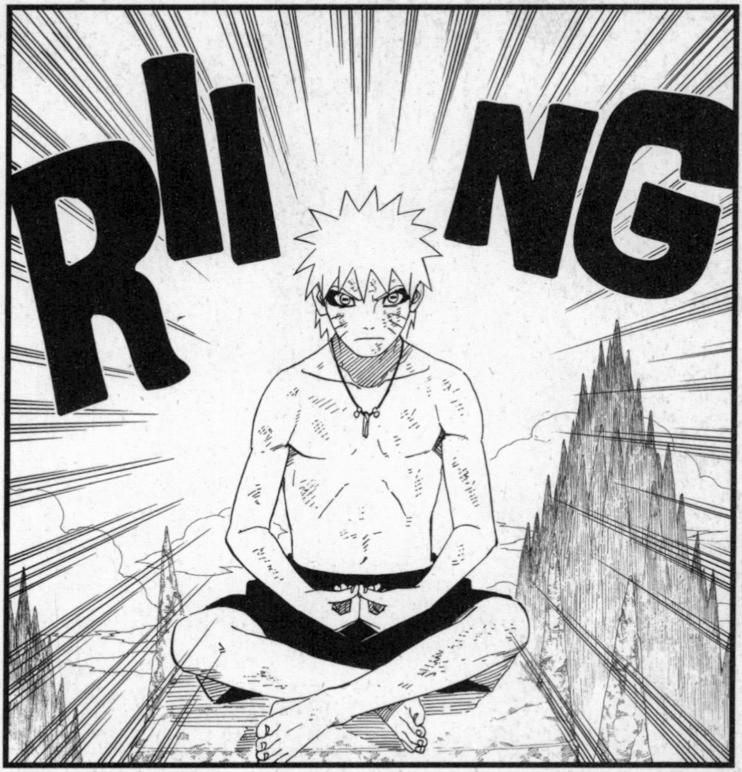
RII
NG

IN THE NEXT VOLUME...

BATTLEFIELD, KONOHA

Sasuke and Naruto find that their powers are ever-increasing. Sasuke can now use the Mangekyo Sharingan in multiple ways, and Naruto may have become even more powerful than his fallen sensei, Jiraiya! But is anyone powerful enough to stop the ultimate attack as the Pains of the Akatsuki launch their deadly strike against Naruto's home village?!

AVAILABLE JULY 2009!
READ IT FIRST IN SHONEN JUMP MAGAZINE!

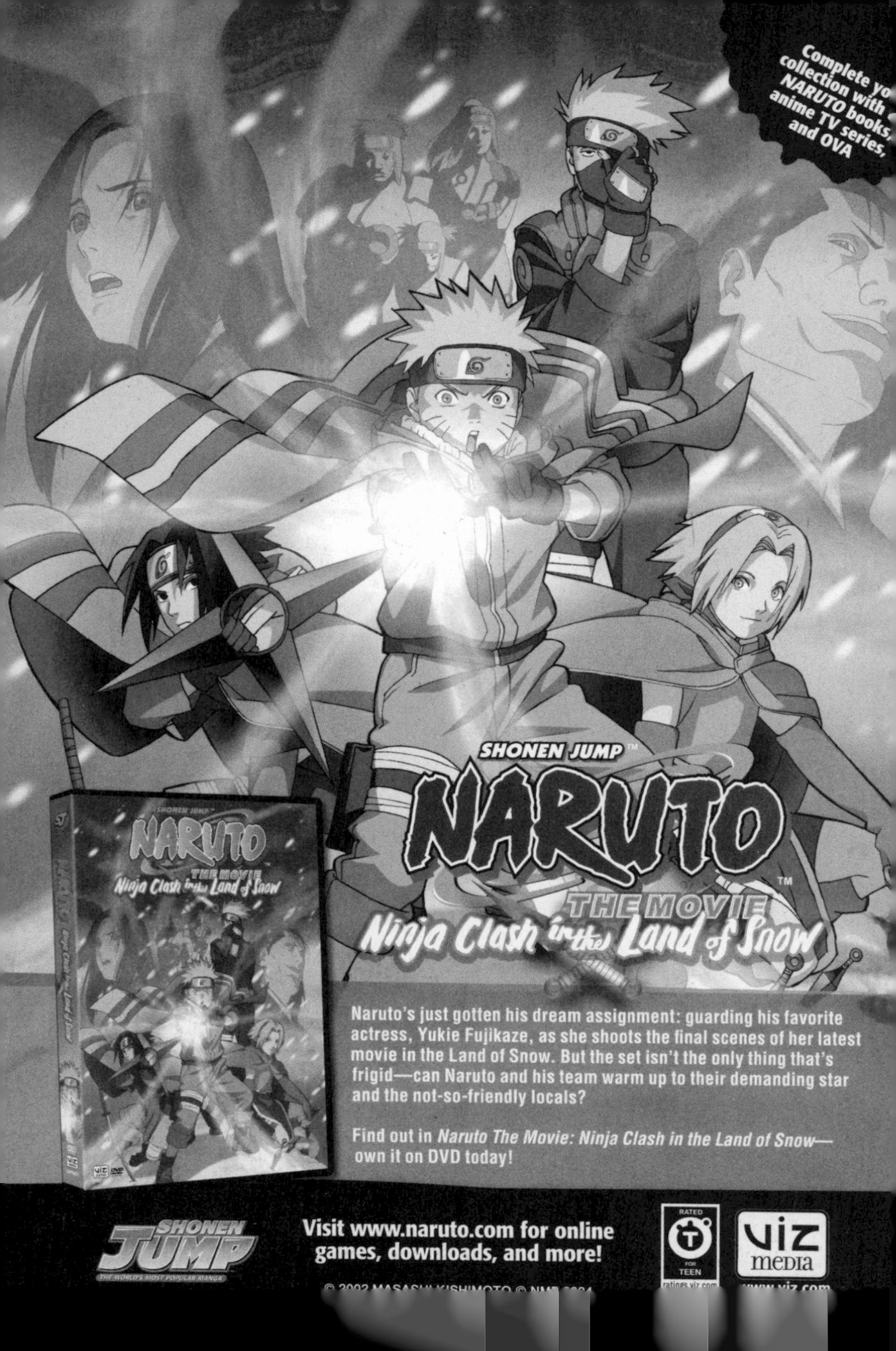

Complete yo
collection with
NARUTO books,
anime TV series,
and OVA
SHONEN JUMP™
NARUTO™
THE MOVIE
Ninja Clash in the Land of Snow
Naruto's just gotten his dream assignment: guarding his favorite actress, Yukie Fujikaze, as she shoots the final scenes of her latest movie in the Land of Snow. But the set isn't the only thing that's frigid—can Naruto and his team warm up to their demanding star and the not-so-friendly locals?
Find out in Naruto The Movie: Ninja Clash in the Land of Snow—own it on DVD today!
SHONEN JUMP
THE WORLD'S MOST POPULAR MANGA
Visit www.naruto.com for online games, downloads, and more!
RATED
T
FOR
TEEN
VIZ media

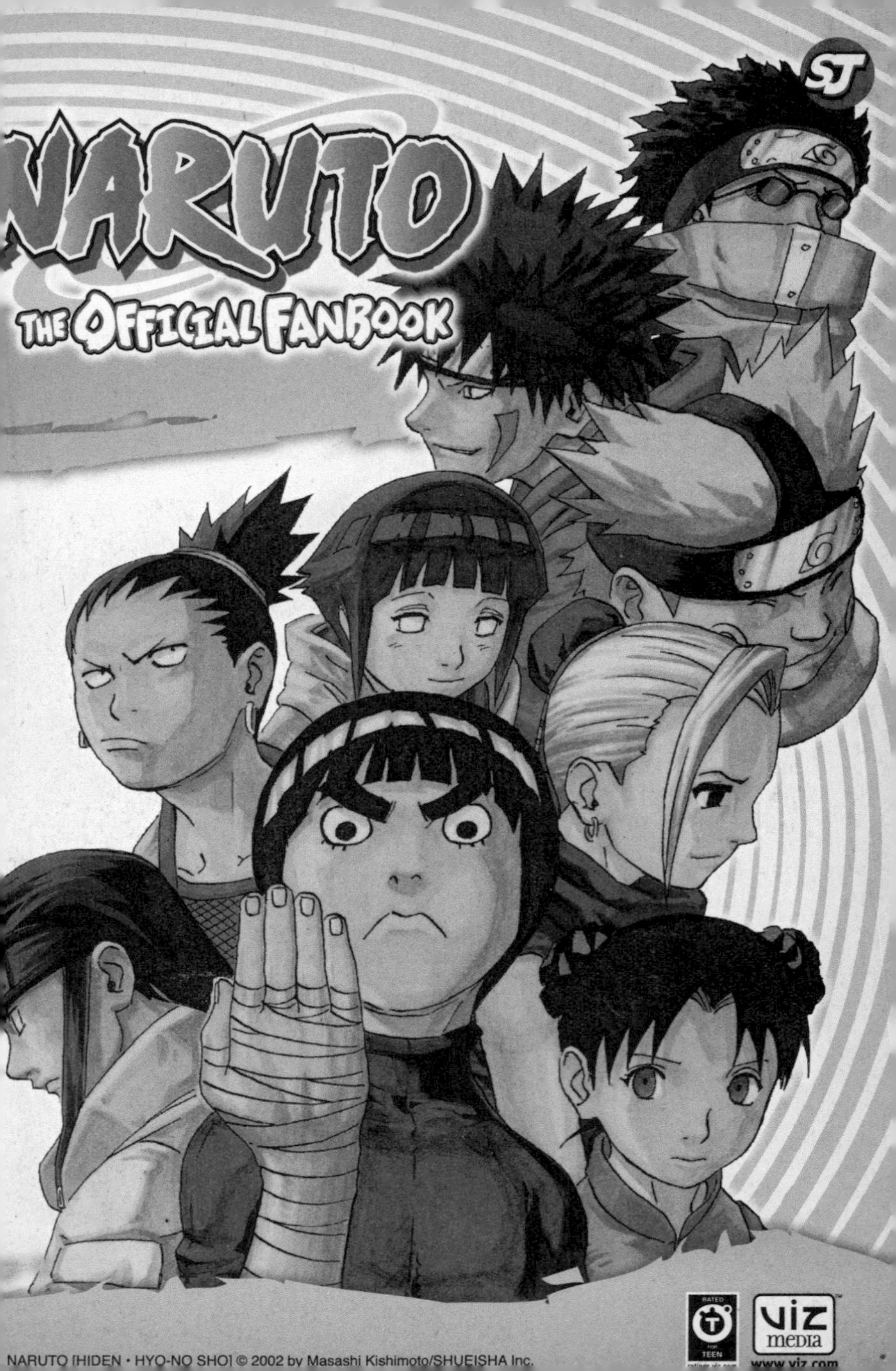
SJ
NARUTO
THE OFFICIAL FANBOOK
RATED T FOR TEEN
VIZ media
www.viz.com
NARUTO [HIDEN • HYO-NO SHO] © 2002 by Masashi Kishimoto/SHUEISHA Inc.

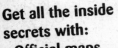

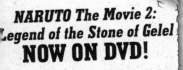

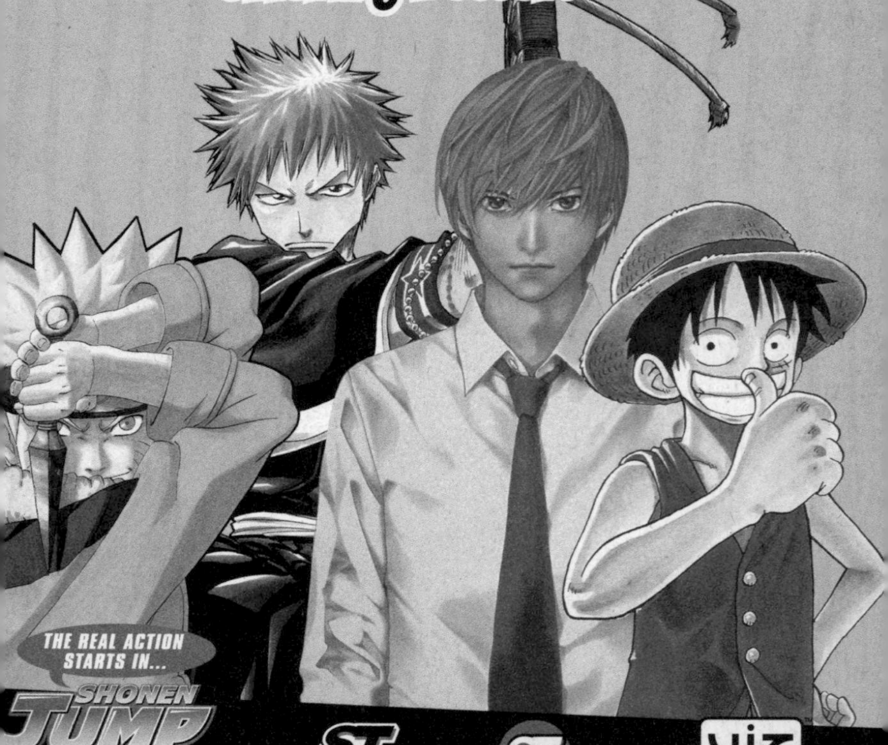

Save **50% OFF** the cover price!

SHONEN JUMP

THE WORLD'S MOST POPULAR MANGA

Over 300 pages per issue!

Each issue of SHONEN JUMP contains the coolest manga available in the U.S., anime news, and info on video & card games, toys AND more!

☑ **YES!** Please enter my one-year subscription (12 HUGE issues) to **SHONEN JUMP** at the LOW SUBSCRIPTION RATE of **$29.95!**

NAME _____

ADDRESS _____

CITY _____ **STATE** ____ **ZIP** _____

E-MAIL ADDRESS _____ P7GNC1

☐ **MY CHECK IS ENCLOSED** (PAYABLE TO SHONEN JUMP)   ☐ **BILL ME LATER**

CREDIT CARD: ☐ **VISA**   ☐ **MASTERCARD**

ACCOUNT # _____   **EXP. DATE** _____

SIGNATURE _____

 **CLIP AND MAIL TO**

SHONEN JUMP
Subscriptions Service Dept.
P.O. Box 515
Mount Morris, IL 61054-0515

Make checks payable to: **SHONEN JUMP**. Canada price for 12 issues: $41.95 USD, including GST, HST and QST. US/CAN orders only. Allow 6-8 weeks for delivery.

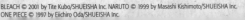